The Great
Missouri Raid

ALSO BY MICHAEL J. FORSYTH

*The Camden Expedition of 1864 and the Opportunity
Lost by the Confederacy to Change the Civil War*
(McFarland 2003; paperback 2008)

*The Red River Campaign of 1864 and the Loss
by the Confederacy of the Civil War*
(McFarland 2002; paperback 2010)

The Great Missouri Raid

Sterling Price and the Last Major Confederate Campaign in Northern Territory

MICHAEL J. FORSYTH

McFarland & Company, Inc., Publishers
Jefferson, North Carolina

LIBRARY OF CONGRESS CATALOGUING-IN-PUBLICATION DATA

Forsyth, Michael J., 1966–
The great Missouri raid : Sterling Price and the last major Confederate campaign in northern territory / Michael J. Forsyth.
    p.   cm.
Includes bibliographical references and index.

ISBN 978-0-7864-7695-4 (softcover : acid free paper) ∞
ISBN 978-1-4766-1923-1 (ebook)

1. Price's Missouri Expedition, 1864. 2. Price, Sterling, 1809–1867. 3. United States—History—Civil War, 1861–1865—Cavalry operations. 4. Missouri—History—Civil War, 1861–1865. 5. Kansas—History—Civil War, 1861–1865. I. Title.

E477.16.F67 2015   977.8'03—dc23   2015003453

BRITISH LIBRARY CATALOGUING DATA ARE AVAILABLE

© 2015 Michael J. Forsyth. All rights reserved

No part of this book may be reproduced or transmitted in any form or by any means, electronic or mechanical, including photocopying or recording, or by any information storage and retrieval system, without permission in writing from the publisher.

On the cover: Sterling Price, C.S.A. between 1860 and 1870 (Library of Congress); *background* Battle of Westport as depicted in mural in Missouri State Capitol (Wikipedia)

Printed in the United States of America

*McFarland & Company, Inc., Publishers
Box 611, Jefferson, North Carolina 28640
www.mcfarlandpub.com*

For Maryellen

Table of Contents

Preface	1
Introduction	5
1. "It looks very much like war..."	11
2. A Passion for Missouri: The Rebel Invaders	27
3. A Team of Outcasts: The Yankees	58
4. "A blow that had destiny in it"	93
5. Crossing the River	106
6. "Thermopylae"	118
7. Lost Opportunities	141
8. The "Picnic Period"	158
9. Westport	171
10. "This has been a disastrous day!"	200
11. "This unfortunate campaign"	216
12. Epilogue	229
Appendix A—Chronology	237
Appendix B—Order of Battle	242
Chapter Notes	253
Bibliography	271
Index	277

Preface

The historiography of the Civil War in the Trans-Mississippi theater is noticeably thin when compared to the volumes recording the epic events that occurred east of the Mississippi. Yet the history of the war in the far west is just as rich as that of the East, with stories of great leaders, incompetence, courage, tragedy, irony, and twists of fate. This book is an attempt to fill one of the significant gaps in the history of the war beyond the Mississippi River.

In my previous account of the Red River Campaign—embodied in two books[1]—I theorized that the Confederacy fumbled a tremendous opportunity to affect the outcome of the war. Discord among the leading commanders of the Confederate Trans-Mississippi Department led to indecisive results in the Red River Valley. The chance to capture the entire Army of the Gulf and accompanying Mississippi River Squadron was lost when the incessant arguing between General Edmund Kirby Smith and Lieutenant General Richard Taylor led to a schism. Smith, out of spite as much as any military purpose, detached two of Taylor's three divisions from the Louisiana front to chase Major General Frederick Steele's already stalled VII Corps in Arkansas. The decision allowed Major General Nathaniel P. Banks—commanding the Union Army of the Gulf—to escape with the navy's Mississippi River Squadron from central Louisiana. While the Confederates had successfully defended their territory, they had also passed on a chance to bag 30,000 troops and 19 gunboats. Had the Rebels captured the Army of the Gulf and naval squadron, they might have blunted Union momentum in other theaters. Potentially it might have cost Lincoln the election. However, as we know, the president won by a landslide because the armies east of the Mississippi were able to keep up inexorable pressure on the principal Confederate armies. It is easy to believe that the story of the war in the Trans-Mississippi ended here, but it did not. What happened?

The Rebels west of the Mississippi held the initiative following the twin defeats of Banks and Steele in the summer of 1864. Even though the Confederates had missed an opportunity for spectacular results at the operational level—and possibly the strategic—they had achieved a great tactical victory nonetheless. The question then arose of what would be next. This book is about what happened after the Red River Campaign and the Camden Expedition.

The Confederate Trans-Mississippi Department was the strongest of the South's three major theaters in 1864 in terms of momentum and force ratios, in spite of its being a backwater. The authorities in Richmond recognized this and through General Braxton Bragg—functioning as a sort of chief of staff for the Confederate army—sent orders directly to Taylor telling him to take his force across the Mississippi to reinforce desperate Rebel armies in the east. This was an utter impossibility with Union gunboats in control of and prowling the river.[2] However, could the Trans-Mississippi Department do something else to relieve their comrades to the east? The answer was yes, and the course Smith decided to pursue was an invasion of Missouri.

The ultimate purpose of the incursion into Missouri in 1864 was to cleave the state from the Union's grip, a grip many southern leaders erroneously believed was intolerable for the people of the state. The thinking was that breaking that grip could have the effect of hurting Lincoln at the polls in the northwest as the election approached. At this late date in the war, was such a possibility realistic? I say it was not. Once the Confederates dropped the ball in the spring along the Red River the chances for real results affecting the outcome of the war were gone. At best, the Great Missouri Raid led by Major General Sterling Price in the fall of 1864 merely diverted some troops away from the major theaters to the east. This may have delayed the inevitable end of the war by one or two months, but beyond this the invasion had few other tangible effects. Among the reasons for this is a failure of strategic and operational planning along with poor leadership at the upper echelons of the Confederate army.

That said, the campaign is still an intriguing story. It holds all the charm and tragedy that the more well-known campaigns in Virginia, Georgia, and Tennessee do. The raid encompassed a march of over 1,400 miles and involved a total of over 60,000 participants. In terms of scope, it dwarfs the more famous raids of J.E.B Stuart, John Hunt Morgan, Nathan Bedford Forrest, and even Sherman's march to the sea. Yet it is a story that remains largely untold and unknown. In telling the story, I will chronicle the planning, preparation, and execution of Price's raid. My hope in writing is to do justice to the story etched by the men who participated in the raid and in repulsing it.

In undertaking this research I became indebted to several individuals who assisted my effort in many tangible and intangible ways. Among these is my wife, Maryellen, who assisted me in finding sources, as well as copy editing and moral support. My deputy commanding officer, Lieutenant Colonel Russ Meyer, was a great help to me as I worked on this project. An author in his own right, he gave me suggestions in editing the drafts; also, as a military leader, he provided a sounding board for my ideas. My executive officer, Major Andrew Visser, a doctoral candidate in history at Stanford University, also reviewed the manuscript and gave me cogent suggestions to ensure the clarity of the text and adherence to the thesis. The staff at the Kansas State Historical Society were very helpful during my visit, finding sources and assisting me in the use of their treasure trove of resources. My travel buddy to several of the battlefields was Mr. Roger Watts, who worked for me while I was a brigade commander. He took personal time to accompany me to remote locations in Missouri and Kansas and I had some wonderful conversations with him about the events that occurred in these war-torn states. I would also like to thank Dr. Christian Keller, a noted Civil War historian and professor at the U.S. Army War College, for his reading of the drafts and incisive suggestions to make the final product more cohesive and accurate. Captain Robin Glebes is a fine U.S. Army engineer and he took the time to assist me with the cartography for the book. Mapmaking is one of the major failings of my previous books, but with Robin's assistance I hope that this shortcoming is remedied in the current volume. I wholeheartedly thank him for his help in making this a better book with sound graphic representations of the campaign and battles. Mr. Brick Autry, an interpretive guide at Fort Davidson State Historic Site, assisted me with maps and sources to better understand the trajectory of events and I thank him for his assistance.

Introduction

With the coming of autumn in 1864 the people of Missouri could expect that as the leaves fell a Rebel raid would come in their wake. It had become a routine during the course of the war for marauding Confederates to enter the Show-Me state and wreak havoc. These repeated incursions had actually spawned a running joke that Missouri had not four but five seasons: spring, summer, fall, raid, and winter. Thus, the populace was again bracing for the annual march of the ragtag raiders through the war-ravaged state. However, this year was to be different.

The year 1864 was a pivotal one in the Civil War. Armies were on the move throughout the breadth of the battlefront and, moreover, this was an election year. What happened in the theater of war would determine who won. In the East, by autumn Lieutenant General Ulysses S. Grant had pinned General Robert E. Lee's battle weary army into the trenches around Richmond and Petersburg. In Georgia, Major General William T. Sherman had likewise forced the Army of Tennessee, under General Joseph E. Johnston and, later, John Bell Hood, into fortifications in a desperate defense of Atlanta. The situation, while stalemated, did not augur success for southern arms. But in the backwater Trans-Mississippi something different was happening.

Rebel armies west of the Mississippi were on the move following a successful defense and counter stroke that drove twin thrusts back in Louisiana and Arkansas. By early April, Union forces under Major General Nathaniel P. Banks had driven his Army of the Gulf deep into Louisiana along the line of the Red River in conjunction with Rear Admiral David D. Porter's Mississippi River Squadron. Yet, with supplies running short and the river lifeline dropping in an unseasonable dry spell, Banks had come to grief at the hands of the aggressive Lieutenant General Richard Taylor at Mansfield. Following the defeat Banks tumbled back to Alexandria where, if not for the heroic efforts of a brilliant engineer and discord among the senior Rebel leaders, the former Speaker of the House might have lost the entire fleet and his army.

The disagreement in the Confederate high command resulted in a diversion of two-thirds of Taylor's army to that of Major General Sterling Price's forces in Arkansas. Here Price's forces were attempting to delay another Federal thrust toward Louisiana. Major General Frederick Steele's VII Corps was moving south from Little Rock in a poorly coordinated expedition meant to cooperate with Banks. Just as logistics proved an Achilles' heel for Banks, so too would it for Steele. Steele's advance bogged down when supplies ran low at Camden, Arkansas, well short of his objective and a linkup with Banks. At just this time Price's reinforced army, now collectively commanded by General E. Kirby Smith, began to present an intractable problem for Steele. Elements of Price's far-ranging cavalry began picking off Steele's foragers and supply columns. In late April, two such parties met with met with disaster at Poison Springs and Marks Mills, forcing Steele to beat a hasty retreat to Little Rock and lose his trains in the process. Thus, Steele's attempt to move south to link up with Banks ended in ignominious defeat and would become known as the Camden Expedition. Combined with Banks' embarrassing performance along the Red River, the situation seemed to indicate that Union arms would lose complete control of their gains in the Trans-Mississippi. The Union disaster presented an opportunity for the Rebels in this arena.

As mentioned, among the three theaters of war across the Confederacy the Trans-Mississippi Department ironically stood as the South's strongest. This was not due to the relative strength of the Trans-Mississippi, which was much smaller in terms of manpower than the Confederate armies east of the Mississippi. Rather, the Rebels west of the river were stronger in terms of the all important factor of initiative. The Army of Northern Virginia and the Army of Tennessee were both being strangled to death by larger Union armies that had the advantage of position and the ability to dictate what would happen. This was not the case in the far west. But what would the Confederates do with the momentum won in the wake of their successful defense of Louisiana and Arkansas?

This question came into sharp focus in the summer of 1864. The authorities in Richmond had always viewed the area west of the Mississippi as simply a source of manpower. In line with this, the initial thought in the wake of the Red River Campaign was to transfer troops across the river in order to reinforce the struggling armies to the east. In July 1864 General Braxton Bragg, now military advisor to President Jefferson Davis, issued an order to the department to effect a transfer of troops.[1] This amounted to a quixotic order because the Union navy controlled the Mississippi River and there was no way a sizeable Rebel force could redeploy to the east. In lieu of this, General E. Kirby Smith suggested that perhaps his department could do something else and still achieve a similar effect.

There were three possibilities open to Smith as late summer approached. First, he could attempt to retake New Orleans, a move that the irascible Richard Taylor clamored for. This move could cut the port off from Union access to trade from the northwest, thus strangling commerce. Such a move would prove difficult since the Federals controlled the river and the city was defended by a sizeable force. The second possibility was to seize a key point on the Mississippi—such as a bend—contesting control, which would force the Union to marshal forces to expel the recalcitrant Confederates. The issue with this course of action was that it would be difficult to select the best point to occupy, and even more prohibitive to use this location to contest boat movement on the river. It was already an established fact—based on Vicksburg and other experiences—that fortified points along the river could not halt river traffic. Thus, it appeared that this course was likewise not feasible. The final possibility was a full-scale invasion of Missouri. This alternative might produce multiple strategic results. By taking the capital at Jefferson City or the industrial center at St. Louis, or both, the Confederates could liberate the state from the hard hand of Union occupation; add the state to the Confederacy; provide moral and material aid to the northern peace movements; divert manpower away from Sherman and Grant's armies in the East; and potentially sway voters in the old northwest from voting for President Lincoln. After considering the possibilities, Smith decided upon an invasion of Missouri and placed Major General Sterling Price in command.[2]

The chance to liberate Missouri always filled Sterling Price with tremendous energy. In 1864 the opportunity seemed especially promising, as everywhere in the Trans-Mississippi Union forces were reeling. Furthermore, Price believed that the oppressed citizens of the state had endured enough of Union rule and desired a change. All that was needed was a credible Confederate force to enter the state and wrest Missouri from Union control. To do so, Sterling Price set forth three objectives for the campaign. First, he intended to take St. Louis and eject the Federals from the capital at Jefferson City. This would liberate the major cities while causing panic in places like Illinois where there was a great deal of "Copperhead"[3] activity. Thus, an invasion could materially aid their efforts to achieve a peace that favored the Confederacy. Also, Price intended to recruit heavily to build the strength of his army. Second, Price wanted to install a Confederate government at Jefferson City and add Missouri as the 12th state of the Confederacy. Third, as a result of wresting the state from the Union, he thought he just

Map 1. Route of Price's Army of Missouri during the invasion of Missouri (map by Captain Robin Glebes).

might sway the outcome of the election toward a candidate favorable to Southern interests.[4]

The problem with Price's plan was that it was completely unrealistic by this stage of the war. While Price might have actually succeeded in taking St. Louis or Jefferson City, he could not have held either very long due to assured Union efforts to take them back. Second, the peace movement in which Southerners of all social strata placed their faith was in many ways overblown with a more imagined influence than real.[5] Further, the Federal armies in the East were on the verge of major victories, particularly in Georgia. Finally, noting the previous observations, the incursion would simply not change the minds of the Northern electorate. Thus, the opportunity for the Trans-Mississippi Department to have any real effect on the outcome of the war had passed. When the Confederate army allowed Nathaniel Banks to escape from the Red River Valley in May, the last real chance for the Rebels in the far west to change the outcome of the war left with the Army of the Gulf.

Nevertheless, the Great Missouri Raid was a seminal event in the Civil War. The invasion, which during its course devolved into a raid, was the last major Confederate campaign in Northern territory. It covered a distance of over 1,400 miles in march and maneuver. This far exceeded other and more famous expeditions and raids such as Stuart's Ride around the Army of the Potomac in 1862, Morgan's raid through Indiana and Ohio in 1863, and even Sherman's march to the sea, which occurred almost simultaneously with Price's Raid in 1864. The troops involved numbered over 60,000 and a total of forty-three engagements occurred, including the largest one ever fought on Missouri soil.[6] While these statistics are astounding, they pale in comparison to the unprecedented brutality of the raid. Price's undisciplined troops, combined with uncontrollable guerrilla elements, inflicted unspeakable depredations on the people of Missouri and on the South's adversaries.

Aside from the fact that Price's Raid was too late to have an appreciable effect on the outcome of the war, it was also a tactical failure for several reasons. Chief among these is poor leadership, starting at the top. Price was incapable of commanding such a force because he did not possess the tactical acumen required and was physically incapacitated by obesity. Weighing in at close to 300 pounds, he could not mount a horse and thus could not provide the expected command presence required to control and inspire his troops on the march or in battle.[7] Poor discipline led to incredible breaches of acceptable conduct by the troops in war. Price's men stole from the very people they were supposed to liberate and pillaged without restraint. In addition, they and out-riding guerrilla elements murdered Union prisoners on several occasions. Shifting objectives over the course of the raid led to a total lack of coherence and purpose. The final reason for tactical failure was the unexpectedly stiff resistance of the Union army. In spite of their own appalling leadership failures, the Federals managed to pull together between 40,000 and 60,000 troops to expel Price and defeat him decisively at Westport, pursuing him relentlessly all the way back to Arkansas.

The failure of the raid doomed Price's dream of liberating his beloved Missouri and provided a reflection reminiscent of the final defeat of the Confederacy. Rather than diminishing control by the Union, the raid actually had the opposite effect of solidifying it. The national election, which Lincoln won by a landslide, was wholly unaffected by Price's invasion. Instead, the raid hurt the very people Price professed to be helping. The only objective he appears to have achieved was to prevent A.J. Smith's XVI Army Corps from joining Sherman's army in Georgia.[8] Thus, at most Price may have contributed to prolonging the war by a month or two, but even this possibility is doubtful. Therefore, the Price Raid served only to increase the already significant misery in Missouri while simultaneously producing a long casualty list that destroyed Price's force.

The road that led up to Price's Raid was long indeed. It starts with the story of Missouri. Of all the states ravaged by the Civil War, none was more negatively affected than the Show-Me state. Its people suffered immeasurably from the continuous tramp of armies across her territory and from the unmitigated violence perpetrated by guerrillas of both sides. Therefore, we begin with Missouri's inexorable path to war, which started with the state's admittance to the union.

1

"It looks very much like war..."

Missouri suffered horribly from the cataclysm of the Civil War. Although other states, like Virginia, Tennessee, and Georgia, experienced the devastating hand of war, Missouri arguably had an exponentially tougher time. The reason for this is the combination of conventional military campaigns that raged across the state and an intractable guerrilla war that started before the Civil War and lasted until the very end of it. These factors tore away at the very fabric of the society and destroyed the land as well. Some areas of western Missouri required decades to recover from the devastation. The method of war practiced in the state was particularly nasty, as roving bands of guerrillas mercilessly murdered, burned, and pillaged widely, while conventional armies freely foraged to sustain their operations.[1] Starting in 1861 Missouri became a frequent battleground for conventional forces, and guerrillas operated continuously throughout the war. Thus, the combination of regular and irregular warfare simply devastated the state. Further, the raw emotions and animosities found in Missouri represented a microcosm of the Civil War, with families literally fighting each other to the death.

Among the many causes of the Civil War was the series of compromises enacted by Congress in the years before the war. Each of these either centered on Missouri or directly affected events in that state. When the Kansas-Nebraska Act was passed in 1854 it sparked a nasty border war that proved a precursor to the conflagration of 1861. The concept of popular sovereignty effectively nullified the Missouri Compromise of 1820 and set a fuse on a powder keg that exploded when slave and abolition factions began jockeying for advantage over the question of whether Kansas would enter the union as a slave or a free state. The competition erupted in violence a full six years before the attack on Fort Sumter.

The Missouri Compromise was supposed to establish a protocol by which future states would come into the Union as free or slave based on geography. The intent was to maintain the delicate balance of political power between north and south peaceably. Soon after acquisition of Louisiana in 1803, the question of the expansion of slavery came to the fore in national conversation. The American people were migrating inexorably westward shortly after the purchase to lay claim to the abundant land. With that movement arose the issue of slaves in the territories. Southerners worried that without the enactment of legislation the more populous and free northern states would soon dominate the rural, slave South. Debate about how to maintain a balance began in 1819 as Congress developed a plan that would allow Missouri to enter the union as a slave state.[2]

Many of the settlers arriving in Missouri were transplants from Virginia and other southern states. They came west and found the fertile alluvial plain along the Missouri River suitable for growing tobacco, cotton, hemp, and other cash crops. Such crops were necessarily labor intensive, and as migrants from the South, the settlers brought along their labor pool: slaves. Among these transplants was the family of Sterling Price, who would become the Confederate commander of the Great Missouri Raid. Before long, a tidewater aristocracy had risen on the banks of the Missouri.[3] As the population grew, the people of Missouri began to organize for statehood. Thus, the slavery question became a central component to the issue.

The Missouri Compromise stated that slavery was prohibited north of the 36°, 30' parallel:

> Section 8. And be it further enacted, that in all that territory ceded by France to the United States, under the name Louisiana, which lies north of thirty-six degrees and 30 minutes north latitude, not included within the limits of the state [i.e., Missouri], contemplated by this act, slavery and involuntary servitude, otherwise than in the punishment of crimes, whereof the parties shall have been duly convicted, shall be, and is hereby, forever prohibited....[4]

However, one exception was made and that was to allow Missouri, with its high density of southerners and slaves, to enter the union as a slave state. The purpose of this exception was to balance the number of slave and free states, as Maine—which splintered from Massachusetts—was entering the union as a free state. This ensured that the Senate had equal representation from both free and slave states.[5] This arrangement worked for a short while, but one look at a map demonstrated to all that the North had far more geographic territory for free-state growth above the 36, 30' line. Indeed, by the mid–1850s free states outstripped slave by a sixteen to fifteen margin, with three more free states poised to enter the union by 1860. Thus, by the mid–1850s many southerners began to fear that their political power would fade before an onslaught of free states and an abolition movement in the North that demanded an end to the "peculiar institution."

The Democratic Party in particular worried about a loss of its power. Already the party was splitting between moderate northerners, led by Illinois senator Stephen Douglas, and fire-eating conservative southerners. To prevent a schism and better maintain a balance of power between the regions, Douglas hatched a plan to remedy the situation. Since pioneers from the North and South were moving west to populate the new territories, it made sense in Douglas' mind to send the issue to the people. Therefore, what he proposed—and what was later enacted as the Kansas-Nebraska Act—was that the citizens in the territories should decide the issue of whether they wanted to enter the union as a free or a slave state. The legislation proposed that "the act preparatory to the admission of Missouri into the Union, approved March sixth, eighteen hundred and twenty, which, being inconsistent with the principle of non-intervention by Congress with slavery in the States and Territories ... is hereby declared inoperative and void; it being the true intent and meaning of this act not to legislate slavery into any Territory or State, nor exclude it therefrom, but to leave the people thereof perfectly free to form and regulate their domestic institution."[6] Specifically, this appealed to the American ideal of allowing popular opinion to solve the problems of the day. The idea was dubbed "popular sovereignty." This seemed an excellent solution to a host of problems, plus it would reunite the Democrat Party under Douglas' leadership, making him the front runner in the next election for president.[7]

The Kansas-Nebraska Act, which President Franklin Pierce signed into law 30 May 1854, effectively nullified the Missouri Compromise, but its greatest impact was wholly unanticipated. Rather than putting to rest a nagging problem, Douglas helped to ignite an ugly border war between Kansas and Missouri. Shortly after passage of the act in May 1854, slavery and abolition factions began to mobilize, with both flooding Kansas with land claims. The opposing sides believed that if they could form the majority of the growing population in Kansas, when it came time to petition for statehood their preference would prevail. Pro-slavery Missourians, who were right across the border from Kansas, moved quickly, not even waiting for the bill to pass.[8]

Senator David Rice Atchison from Missouri was a driving force behind the migration of Missourians to Kansas in the attempt to influence the statehood decision. Anticipating the challenge posed by abolition forces, Atchison actively encouraged not only Missourians but also people from across the South to move to Kansas, lay claims, and vote for a pro-slavery state. Thus, with the help of allies in the South, the population of Kansas began to swell with supporters of slavery.[9] The supporters of abolition were not to be outdone by the slaveocracy and they just as quickly put their own organization in motion to gain political sway in Kansas.

As the Kansas-Nebraska Act was under consideration in the Senate, abolitionists such as Eli Thayer began to organize the Massachusetts Emigrant Aid Society. The idea behind this organization was to move entire New England villages to Kansas and, in effect, transplant northern society to the Great Plains. Thus, with such Yankee icons as steam power, schools, churches, and free thought, there would be no room for slavery. The venture, along with others, opened a floodgate of northerners to Kansas. Before long, border towns such as Kansas City and Westport began to swell with migrants moving west. Businesses in Kansas City catering to the transients boomed as they supplied the needs of settlers. Senator Atchison fumed as he observed the mass movement. Rather than saturating Kansas with pro-slavery Missourians, he had sent a challenge to the abolition forces of the North and they met it in spades. Later, southern histories would vilify the role of the aid society and embitter Missourians for decades.[10] For now, Atchison's strategy to add another slave state was backfiring. How could they reverse the tide in favor of slavery? Atchison's answer was to control the political discourse.

The key to controlling the conversation was winning at the ballot box, through legal and extra-legal means. By 1855, the population of Kansas had reached 8894 persons that included some 242 slaves. The territorial governor, appointed by President Pierce, was a conscientious man named Andrew Reeder. He had received several reports that certain factions intended fraud when time for an election drew near. To prevent this, Reeder commissioned a census in January 1855 to establish the baseline of expected voters. Upon learning the numbers, he set a date for the election. If the votes cast did not correlate with the population, he would then know cheating had occurred and where.[11] It was a good plan.

When the election took place on 30 March 1855 irregularities abounded. It seems that a Missourian named Ben Franklin Stringfellow hatched a plan for a migration of his fellow Show-Me staters on election day to cast their ballots and then return home.

He and other prominent Missourians such as Claiborne F. Jackson and Senator Atchison established the Blue Lodge to organize and execute the ballot-stuffing campaign. The lodge achieved astounding results. "[T]he Border Ruffians came in by the thousands," said one Free-Stater "and of course carried every precinct." When the votes were counted the pro-slavery forces had a huge victory and would dominate the Kansas territorial legislature. However, the total votes cast dwarfed the population numbers, revealing that ballot stuffing was rampant. In Lawrence, a place well known for its abolition fervor, the pro-slavery ballots outpolled free ballots by a three to one margin.[12] Clearly something was amiss.

Governor Reeder wanted to act decisively to throw out the fraudulent votes, but threats to his person gave him pause. The decision he made to certify the election was astounding for the manner by which it solved nothing. Reeder decided to certify the returns except for those that were clearly spurious. This resulted in a pro-slavery legislature being seated and outrage among the free-soilers. One abolitionist stated that the situation appeared so bad that "it looks very much like war."[13] Indeed, in a short period of time a full-up shooting war would break out pitting Kansans and Missourians against each other in a dress rehearsal for the coming national conflagration.

Soon after the disputed election the abolition faction redoubled their efforts to establish their control of the territory. In one of the steps taken to gain political ascendancy, the free-soilers first accelerated the migration to Kansas. Second, they flat-out rejected the soon to convene pro-slavery legislature. One prominent Lawrence citizen declared that the free citizens "must repudiate all laws enacted by foreign legislative bodies." Acting upon this declaration they assembled their own legislative body in Topeka. Third, they began raising militia companies to defend their rights. Finally, they ordered weapons to arm the units with the most modern rifles available. A shipment of specially ordered Sharps carbines arrived in time for the new companies to march with them through downtown Lawrence for the Independence Day parade.[14]

None of this sat well with pro-slave Kansans or Missourians. Fearing domination by a northern political movement, they took their own steps to enforce their will on the political process. Shortly after establishing the legislature at their capital in Lecompton the pro-slavery faction demanded the removal of the vacillating governor. Next, the Missourians made a declaration of their own commitment to fight and die rather than allow a "foreign majority" to rule their neighbor. In addition, the pro-slavery faction made their own appeal to bring in supporters from the southern states to counter the exploding free-state population. Finally, they began forming their own military organizations, setting the stage for a clash.[15] It would not take long before the opponents came to blows.

In December 1855 the so-called Wakarusa War began heralding the long-running conflict, which engulfed Missouri and Kansas. The trouble arose when a free-state Kansan ejected a Missouri pro-slave squatter from his property along Wakarusa Creek near Lawrence. When the pro-slavery sheriff attempted to arrest the free-stater a mob prevented him from doing so. Word of the incident spread quickly and the embarrassed—and outnumbered—slaveholders appealed for help from Missouri to put the arrogant free-soilers in their place. Soon Missouri militia companies were assembling on the border ready to march on Lawrence. These ragtag Missourians—dubbed "Border Ruffians" by a reporter from Horace Greeley's *New York Tribune*—began moving west under leaders like Jo Shelby, who would by 1864 become a household name in the region. The free-staters assembled their own "army" under such men as the vain and self-motivated politician James Lane.[16] The ensuing clash set a pattern of attacks and retaliatory strikes that intensified over the years.

The factions faced off in the spring of 1856 at Lawrence, just west of the Wakarusa. The pro-slavery forces, with the jilted sheriff present, surrounded the town demanding that the offending free-soiler surrender or the city would suffer the consequences. After some negotiation it was agreed that the sheriff and U.S. marshal would serve the warrants of arrest. However, when the demand to disarm the community was rejected the Missourians acted with a heavy hand. They sacked the offices of the abolition newspapers and then surrounded the Free State Hotel—also known as the Eldridge House— thought to be the arsenal of the free-soilers. When further demands to surrender the arms went unmet, Senator Atchison, leading a company of Missourians, ordered cannon to fire on the hotel. The "army" later blew two large kegs of powder in the building but failed to destroy it. The Missourians then looted the town and began returning to Missouri.[17] This event called for vengeance, and abolitionists, like the soon to become notorious John Brown, entered the fray.

The events that took place in Lawrence enraged the free-state citizens of Kansas and, since they actually outnumbered the Missourians, the ruffians would have a tough time retreating back to their state. John Brown and five of his sons would not let the injustice pass without striking a blow. Soon after the leaders in Lawrence called for assistance, the Browns assembled the local militia companies "to strike terror into the pro-slavery miscreants."[18] Among those reporting for duty was a German immigrant named August Bondi. This Austrian Jew was fairly typical of the recent immigrants from the German states at mid-century. He arrived at New Orleans in November 1848 after the failed revolutions that had attempted to overthrow the ruling monarchs in Europe. From New Orleans, he migrated to St. Louis with thousands of other new arrivals. By 1854, Bondi, who had fought for freedom in his native Austria, felt the need to move to Kansas "to help save the state from the curse of slavery." Within a year he had staked a claim in the territory, settling near the Brown homesteads. He soon became an intimate friend of the Browns, joining the "Kansas Regulars" militia, and would take part in the border war with these fanatical abolitionists.[19]

By late May 1856 Brown's men were tracking a group of Border Ruffians who had been raiding near the area of Bondi's claim. This group had actually burned down Bondi's cabin, scattered his stock, and stolen his provisions, but their luck would not hold for long. On the 24th of May, Brown had cornered his prey on the Pottawatomie Creek. He divided his force and moved in for the kill. As the Ruffians camped, unsuspecting of any danger, at the creek, the abolitionists launched their attack. In the melee Brown's men killed a dozen of the Missourians, old John Brown reputed to have personally hacked up a couple of them with a broadsword. As a result, he became notorious among Missourians and feared by the Ruffians. Correspondingly, he became an icon among the abolitionists. On 2 June his followers, including Bondi, cornered another group of Ruffians at Black Jack Creek. In this fight Brown led a frontal assault that broke the resistance of the Missourians and convinced them to surrender or suffer the same fate as those on the Pottawatomie.[20] The back and forth of this ugly border war would continue for another four years as both sides launched escalating retaliatory strikes. Meanwhile, the Free-Staters gained the upper hand in the political battle.

The Free-State politicians were active during this time of chaos, setting a date to meet at Topeka in order to write a state constitution, which they did on 15 December 1855. The latest territorial governor, Wilson Shannon, was determined to prevent the Free-Staters from convening their body to adopt the document so as not to give tacit approval to a legislative body in competition with the recognized one at Lecompton. Regardless of this, the Free-Staters came together on 4 July 1856 to convene what they viewed as the legitimate body. The United States Army troops in Kansas commanded by Colonel Edwin V. Sumner marched to Topeka to prevent the convention at the behest of President Pierce. The Free-Soilers decided not to allow a quorum so that they would not be "dispersed" by the army. Rather, they would bide their time until the next territorial election.[21] The rapidly rising Free-Soil population—protected by their own militia under Jim Lane—would assure a favorable outcome and force the federal government in Washington to recognize their claim to power.

The population of Kansas had been rising exponentially over a compressed time period. For example, a little over a year after Governor Reeder took the initial census of the territorial population the number of citizens jumped to over 15,000 by June 1856, representing a near doubling of the population in that time. The troubling aspect of this number to Missourians was the fact that most of the increase was represented by Free-Soil citizens. Further, this floodtide would continue until Kansas was admitted as a state in 1861 and beyond. By 1860 the populace stood at over 107,206 souls, or seven times the number in 1856.[22] Thus, regardless of their best-laid plans, men like Atchison could not stop Kansas' relentless march toward statehood as free ground. This population explosion would help the party of the Free-Soilers finally achieve their ultimate goal in 1860 when they petitioned for admittance to the union as a free state.

The rapidly expanding pool of Free-Staters, backed by their militia organization, were able to gain the upper hand in the polls by 1857. Shortly after President James Buchanan was inaugurated on 4 March 1857, he appointed a new territorial governor to clean up the mess left by President Pierce and the preceding governors. Governor Robert J. Walker was not cut from the same cloth as the previous occupiers of the office. He came to Kansas determined to ensure a fair and free election and to seat a legislature based on the will of the people. If this meant throwing out stuffed ballots, Walker would do that too. When the election was held 5–6 October 1857, the Border Ruffians again attempted to tilt the election as they had in 1855, though the fraud was not quite so widespread this time around. When the votes were counted there were precincts where the count did not jibe with the population. Thus Walker threw out the questionable ballots and the Free-Staters swept to power. As a result, they were able to seat a legislature and pass a constitution espousing free principles when they petitioned for statehood. In March 1858 the Free-Staters again assembled in Topeka, this time free from interference from the territorial governor or army. The representatives passed the constitution and established a pathway to statehood. By May the new legislature was petitioning Washington for admission to the union, which process would take a couple more years.[23] But in the meantime the Free-Staters had their victory and the border war would continue.

For pro-slavery Missourians the developments of 1857–58 were certainly a blow. In spite of their effort to prevent it, abolition forces prevailed in Kansas. The border war dragged on up until the beginning of the Civil War, as border incursions by both sides were regular occurrences. Incidents such as the Marais de Cygnes Massacre, where Border Ruffians killed four and wounded six Kansans in retaliation for raids by newly named Jayhawkers, were staples of increasingly brutal strikes. However, something had changed. The Missourians were not making the deep penetrations into Kansas they had previously.[24] The reason for this was the hostile populace that now far outnumbered them. Thus, while the raids continued, the daring strikes of the past became rare events. While the Ruffians did not shirk from a fight, they also understood that their survival was contingent on limiting risk and that meant raids closer to home. Although they were still fighting, the Missourians had in effect conceded Kansas to the Free State adherents.

So, what had the border war gained Missouri? While they lost Kansas, Missouri's Southern sympathizers gained invaluable fighting experience that produced a hard core of leaders and foot soldiers. These would provide Missouri a solid base from which to form Confederate units when the Civil War began. Men like Jo Shelby, William Quantrill, and David R. Atchison picked up lessons in the '50s and carried them forward into the coming conflict to supply a few competent leaders to a fledgling force for the South. These leaders would play important roles in the war and would fight with a vengeance when the Civil War did come. Further, they figured prominently in the Great Missouri Raid in 1864 in varying roles.

As 1861 approached, and with it the question of whether or not to secede from the union, the opinion of Missourians fell into three distinct camps. There were those who were against secession in all circumstances, while there were others who demanded immediate secession to join the Confederacy. Finally, there were those who were ambivalent to the prospect of secession, preferring instead to remain in the union unless provoked by some act of aggression against the state. At that point this group of "conditional" Unionists might consider a separation from the other states. Where one stood on the issue depended in large part on demographics and geography, with the majority firmly against leaving the Union. The counties bordering the Mississippi and Missouri rivers were the primary slaveholding counties. The northern Missouri counties tended to contain the small slaveholder populace. By contrast, St. Louis was a haven of recent German immigrants who were vociferous in their opposition to slavery. These demographics led to certain attitudes toward the question of secession when it became a hotly debated topic in 1860–61. The Germans, many of whom emigrated from Europe following the 1848 revolutions, had staunch Union sentiments and looked upon slavery as a moral evil. The small slaveholders north of the Missouri were Unionist in sentiment in large part because they were more connected to the states of the old northwest like Illinois and Iowa rather than to the South. The large slaveholders, who had migrated from southern states, were conditional Unionists. As long as Missouri maintained a non-hostile posture toward the South and the federal government respected Missouri's neutrality, these people were in favor of maintaining membership in the Union. Thus, when the southern states began to secede, the Missourians supported staying in the Union.[25]

When the question of secession was called into consideration at a session convened by the new governor, Claiborne F. Jackson, both the new Confederacy and the Union looked on with interest. Missouri called the convention in order to consider the state's status, on 28 February 1861 at Jefferson City. Former governor Sterling Price presided over the convention as a conditional Unionist and his position was reflected by most of the delegates. After debating the issue, it soon became clear that Missouri would not leave the Union, much to the chagrin of Governor Jackson, who desired such an outcome. When the votes were tallied the delegates overwhelmingly voted for the status quo and that Missouri remain neutral in the event of war.[26] For advocates of secession this last part would make handling Missouri a prickly proposition.

Missouri was a critically important state from a strategic standpoint and both sides had great interest in securing it. For one thing, Missouri was geographically situated to confer certain advantages or disadvantages on the respective antagonists. First, controlling the Mississippi River was critical to both sides, and if the Union maintained it they would have an easier time clearing the valley to the Gulf of Mexico. If the Confederacy gained control their forces could disrupt commerce deep into the old northwest. Second, the Missouri River sliced through the state, and controlling this tributary meant access to the west plus the resources found along the route. Finally, militarily, Missouri was like a knife jutting north into the heart of the west. Demographically, the state was a huge source of manpower. The 1860 census demonstrated that Missouri had 1.182 million people, of which 232,781 were military-age males between 18 and 45. Only six states had more potential military manpower and they were all in the North. If Missouri joined the Confederacy it would be the largest pool of military manpower in the South. When the war ended, over 149,000 men had served, on both sides, and of these 40,000 wore Confederate gray. Further, surrounding states, particularly Illinois, would be vulnerable to raids that could hurt morale in the northwest while lifting Confederate hopes for success. Finally, whichever entity controlled the state would have the industrial capacity centered in St. Louis and other river cities.[27] Therefore, Missouri offered each side a host of things beneficial. Thus, competition for control began in spite of the convention's declaration of neutrality, and it started soon after the delegates convened.

Soon after President Lincoln's inauguration in March 1861, the newly minted Confederate States Army fired on Fort Sumter, culminating a long-running crisis and precipitating yet another as the Civil War got underway. In order to subdue the Confederate states, Lincoln issued a call for 75,000 volunteers to put down the rebellion. Each state was issued a quota to fill out the army of volunteers and Missouri was asked to provide 4,000. Governor Jackson quickly refused the request, stating in reply that "your requisition is illegal ... and cannot be complied with."[28] But even before this Jackson had begun to position the state for secession. For example, shortly after his own inauguration in January 1861, he began to maneuver politically to deliver Missouri to the South by actively conspiring to seize the arsenal in St. Louis. With its enormous cache of arms and munitions, the arsenal would make a tremendous coup for the state and the South. As one author said, Jackson's "power for mischief was very great," as proven by later events.[29]

The union was not at ease during the time before Sumter either. A young firebrand officer named Nathaniel Lyon was working feverishly to thwart Governor Jackson's grab for the arsenal. The red-headed Lyon was a Connecticut Yankee and staunchly anti-slavery. During the border war in Kansas, Lyon served at Fort Riley, where his distaste for the Border Ruffians turned into outright hatred. As a federal officer before the Civil War, he had to enforce government policies that protected the Ruffians. But now he had authorization to put his considerable talents to stopping the Rebels and he started by thwarting Jackson's plans to take the arsenal at St. Louis. In a neat plan of political and military maneuvering, Lyon was able to organize the local militias with the help of community leaders, such as Francis P. Blair, for defense of the arsenal. Simultaneously, Lyon put the regular army troops on a war footing by strengthening the physical perimeter of the site with artillery.[30]

Soon after Sumter, Lyon assembled enough force to eliminate the threat to the arsenal. On 10 May he marched out of St. Louis with 8,000 men toward the makeshift camp of the Missouri state forces of Governor Jackson. The camp, named for the governor, was commanded by Brigadier General Daniel Frost. Surprising the Rebels, Lyon quickly surrounded the camp and sent in a message saying, "It is my duty to demand ... an immediate surrender of your command." Frost, after surveying the host of Federal troops outnumbering him ten to one, bitterly surrendered.[31] With this event, the threat was removed from the city, but Lyon would not rest here. Now that outright hostilities were on, Lyon, a newly minted brigadier, sought to clear the entire state.

By May Jackson began to move overtly to secure Missouri for the Confederacy. The surrender of Frost brought with it a wave of outrage among those conditional Unionists who were reluctant to consider secession. Previously, the constituency centered on the river valleys sought to maintain the status quo in the relationship of the state to the federal government. With Lyon's actions in St. Louis, Governor Jackson had the lightning rod event he needed to demand counteraction. Thus, on 14 May, at the behest of Jackson, the Missouri legislature passed a bill that provided for what would become the Missouri State Guard military organization. The organization divided Missouri into nine military districts aligned along the state congressional districts, from which the local commanders would recruit regiments. These would form divisions consolidated under command of Sterling Price, the former governor and veteran of the Mexican War.[32] The purpose of the organization was to deter the Federal troops from any further actions that infringed on Missouri's sovereignty. Initially, the intent worked as planned.

Brigadier General William S. Harney was the commander in Missouri at this time and he viewed the unfolding events with alarm because he preferred a more conservative approach to maintaining Federal authority. Lyon—known to all as a firebrand—had carried out his action at the arsenal with the support of Francis Blair, whose political pull subsumed Harney's authority as military commander. Harney sought to regain his rightful position and diffuse the crisis in some manner. Soon he struck upon the idea of meeting personally with Price as the new commander of the Missouri State Guard. Price consented to meet with Harney and on 21 May 1861 both commanders sat down at the table. They agreed to work toward "restoring peace and good order" within the state.[33] This agreement—dubbed the Harney-Price Agreement—for a time allayed the fears of some, but the fragile pact would soon fall apart as others pressed for bolder action to either deliver the state to the South or save the Union.

Francis Blair was outraged by Harney's timidity and he soon put his considerable influence to work in finding a stronger military leader. In a letter to the secretary of war, Simon Cameron, Blair stated that "the agreement between Harney and General Price gives me great disgust, and dissatisfaction to the Union men."[34] He also began leveraging the personage of his father, the elder Francis P. Blair, to ask President Lincoln to replace Harney with the energetic Nathaniel Lyon. The new president was sympathetic to Blair's assertion because he believed Missouri's neutrality was a farce that hid something sinister. The policy of neutrality "recognizes no fidelity to the Constitution," said Lincoln and further it was "treason in effect."[35] Lincoln acceded to Blair's request, and in early June Lyon replaced a shocked Harney. Governor Jackson hoped to continue the month-old Price-Harney arrangement and sought to meet with Lyon to determine if the younger man was amenable. The meeting took place on 11 June 1861 in St. Louis. A laborious meeting ensued during which the governor, Price, and their aides asked for assurance from Lyon that he would not attempt to assert Federal authority. In the end, Lyon emphatically refused and concluded that "rather than concede to the State of Missouri for one single instant the right to dictate to my Government in any matter however unimportant I would see you, and you, and you, and you, and every man, woman, and child in the State, dead and buried.... This means war."[36]

Indeed, it did mean war and in earnest in Missouri. Governor Jackson and Price immediately returned to Jefferson City and began to put the new state guard on a war footing, while in the political arena Jackson attempted to bring Missouri into the Confederacy. He was thwarted in this effort by the red-headed Lyon. Just as quickly as his Rebel antagonists had, Lyon organized his forces in Missouri for a campaign to first secure the capital at Jefferson City and second to drive the Missouri State Guard from the state.

The campaign began on 13 June 1861, when Lyon began moving on the Missouri capital. Within two days Lyon's forces had captured Jefferson City, which Governor Jackson and Price abandoned at the Federal advance. The Confederates would never again occupy the Missouri capital and it would remain firmly under Union control for the duration of the war. Lyon took little time to consolidate his gains at Jefferson City as he pressed ahead toward Springfield in southwest Missouri on 16 June. The burgeoning Confederate army had not idled the time away as Lyon moved across the state. As Price moved into the southwest corner of Missouri with the state guard, a Confederate army was moving up from Arkansas commanded by the famous Texas Ranger Ben McCulloch. Now a Confederate brigadier, McCulloch had received orders to move into either Kansas or Missouri as circumstances dictated to prevent extension of Federal authority. Price seized on the opportunity to cooperate with McCulloch in order to regain lost ground. McCulloch was not keen to join forces with Price for a couple of reasons. First, he thought that Price and the Missouri State Guard were little more than a rabble and that associating his army with Price could bring disaster. Second, since Missouri was not a Confederate state, McCulloch did not feel justified in crossing Arkansas' northern border. In spite of his misgivings, McCulloch agreed to join Price in Missouri, as Price convinced him that by entering Missouri McCulloch could better defend Arkansas. Further, they would be able to gather large numbers of recruits. Finally, pushing the Federals out of central Missouri could bring the state into the Confederacy, moving its northern border to the Iowa line.[37] The two forces united in July at Cassville in southwest Missouri, bringing the Confederate forces to a strength of about 12,000.

Lyon proceeded to Springfield and arrived there shortly before the Confederates began consolidating in the southwest corner of Missouri. Based on information he was able to gather from scouts and the intermittent contact his detachments made with the Rebels, Lyon knew that a large force was gathering to oppose him and his 5,500 men. If he pulled back from his advanced position in Springfield, Lyon would cede the initiative to Price and McCulloch. However, if he boldly advanced, catching the enemy by surprise, it was possible that the smaller Union army could disperse the half-trained Rebels, clearing the state. Lyon decided on the latter course of action, reasoning that a bold movement could "rout him [the Confederate army] before he recovers from his surprise," thus mitigating the risk of being outnumbered over two to one by his foe.[38]

By the first of August, both armies began to move toward each other. McCulloch, now commanding the combined Rebel forces, moved forward with about 10,000 men. The Missouri State Guard that had gathered at Cowskin Prairie and Cassville was much larger, approaching 18,000. But many of these men were either unarmed or untrained and the decision was made to leave these troops at the prairie encampment. Lyon, by contrast, moved from Springfield that summer day with a well appointed, compact army of 5,400 men consisting of regular and volunteer troops.[39] Within nine days the armies would clash at Wilson's Creek to decide who would control Missouri.

The Confederate army arrived at Wilson's Creek on 9 August 1861 and went into camp along the Wire Road. They did not know that a mere two miles away Lyon was preparing to drop a hammer blow on the unsuspecting Confederates. The plan of attack involved dividing the small Union army into two strike forces, one under the German brigadier general Franz Sigel and the other under Lyon's direction. Lyon would assault straight down the Wire Road while Sigel with a mounted force swung wide to the left to come in on the Confederate rear.[40] The problem with this plan was twofold. First, it divided Lyon's already small force into two in the face of a larger enemy. Second, once Sigel's force separated from Lyon there was no way to coordinate the separate attacks with the primitive communication methods of the day. As it turned out, these shortfalls proved the undoing of Lyon.

Lyon attacked the Rebel army just after dawn on 10 August, and because he was able to surprise the Confederates the Federals had initial success. Sigel did manage to attack Price and McCulloch in the rear, causing a great deal of confusion in the Rebel ranks, but his undisciplined assault failed once McCulloch was able to rally forces in that sector. Then, with the combined strength of over 10,000 men, the Confederates launched a counterattack on Lyon's remaining 2,500 troops. The death of Lyon on the field, combined with the overwhelming power of Confederate numbers, told the outcome by the afternoon. The tough little Union army had fought well but had lost over 25 percent of its strength. Thus, Major Samuel D. Sturgis, who succeeded to command, decided to retreat and did so in good order.[41]

McCulloch and Price had won a great victory and seemed poised to sweep Missouri clear of Federal forces, but their rocky relationship prevented greater results from flowing from the battle of Wilson's Creek. McCulloch decided to pull his forces from cooperation with Price at this juncture. His reasoning was that, in accordance with the instructions that the Confederate government had provided, the danger to the northern border of the Confederacy was now removed. Since this was now the case, he could return to Arkansas, which was inside the Confederacy. Aside from this logic, McCulloch was very uncomfortable working with Price. He came into the fight at Wilson's Creek considering the Missouri State Guard little better than a mob, and based on what he had seen in the fight he had confirmed his suspicions.[42] Therefore, McCulloch moved back to Arkansas immediately after the fight.

This turn of events demonstrates one of the frustrating aspects of the war in Missouri and for the entire Trans-Mississippi Department. Throughout the war the Confederate leaders in the department squabbled pettily with each other on a continuous basis, thus failing to cooperate for a cause bigger than the individuals involved. Also, Confederate strategy was never coherently articulated for the region or for Missouri, and there was little planning to link what happened in the west to the rest of the Confederacy. Finally, at the operational and tactical levels, Confederate forces within the theater—both regular and guerrilla—could never work together to achieve effects that could decisively defeat Union designs. The results of these factors was that Missouri never truly figured into Confederate national policy and therefore no clear articulation of strategy ever flowed from Richmond or Trans-Mississippi headquarters to provide direction to the forces.[43] Ultimately, every military effort by Rebel forces in Missouri was disjointed, haphazard, and disconnected from any discernible objective. Failure to bring the state into the Confederacy was a direct result of lack of coherent policy at the upper echelon of Confederate national leadership.

With McCulloch moving south, Price now had to decide what to do following Wilson's Creek. He could move on the capital at Jefferson City to establish a Confederate government. Or he could attempt to move on the jewel of the state, St. Louis with its resources. Finally, he could clear the Missouri Valley of Federals and recruit his army. The Union forces—now fully alarmed after Wilson's Creek—were mobilizing fast with overwhelming force to hold their recent gains. With this in mind, Price knew that retaking the capital or St. Louis was a pipe dream. Therefore, he began to swing northwesterly along the Missouri to clear the valley of Federal authority and recruit to fill his ranks.[44]

Union forces had begun to spread out along the Missouri Valley in the summer of 1861 garrisoning key towns. While in possession of these places, like Warrensburg and Lexington, they had seized bank deposits to prevent the funds from making it into the hands of the Missouri State Guard. Price decided to drive out these garrisons and retake the deposits in order to provide financial resources for his army. To do so, he issued orders to move northwest along the Missouri aimed toward Lexington. Here the Federal army had seized the town with over 2,000 troops and appropriated the bank.[45] Price determined to stop this activity and drive the Unionists out of Lexington.

On 13 September 1861 Price moved his army along the Missouri at Warrensburg to Lexington. Union forces at Lexington were commanded by an Irish immigrant named James Mulligan. His 23rd Illinois, consisting of mostly Irishmen, formed the core of the forces in the town. Mulligan had dug in his force on a hill at the Masonic College overlooking Lexington and the wharf on the river. The position was a good one, but it had a fatal flaw. There was not enough water to quench the thirst of his force and its animals.⁴⁶ Therefore, when Price invested the position on 18 September 1861 it was only a matter of time before the Federal force would have to capitulate.

The Battle of Lexington occurred 19–20 September and became famous for the manner in which the Confederates conducted the assault. Unable to approach over the open ground leading to Mulligan's entrenchments without heavy loss, the ingenious Rebels came up with a novel solution to the tactical problem. On the morning of the 19th, as the Union soldiers peered over the parapets, they viewed a moving line of hemp bales. The Confederates had appropriated several hundred of the heavy bales to use as a moving breastwork. Thick enough to stop bullets, the hemp bales proved surprisingly well-suited to assisting the Rebels in getting in close to the Union works. Faced with thirst and an overwhelming assault, Colonel Mulligan decided to surrender. Price accepted the surrender on 20 September.⁴⁷

With the capitulation, recruits began to swell Price's ranks to near 20,000. His campaign had proven overwhelmingly successful, as it had cleared the valley, provided needed manpower, and brought in financial and material resources. While Price did not yet know it, 20 September 1861 represented the apex of Confederate success in Missouri for the rest of the war. Never again—with the lone exception of the Great Raid in 1864—would Confederate forces in Missouri take such a preeminent position in the state.⁴⁸ What might have been accomplished had McCulloch not so fecklessly abandoned Price after Wilson's Creek? Price, even with his success, was forced to retreat shortly after Mulligan's surrender. Overwhelming forces were converging on Lexington and Price knew he would have to beat a quick retreat to southwest Missouri to keep from becoming entrapped. Further, the new recruits swelling Price's ranks were stretching his ability to sustain the army and they had to keep moving to do so. By October he was back in the southwest corner of the state, and with the retreat a new pattern of conflict in Missouri was ushered in for the intervening years until 1864.

For the next two and a half years Missouri was plagued by an incessant guerrilla war in which the popular image of brother against brother became a reality. This form of war was periodically punctuated by cavalry raids by regular Confederate forces, resulting in a steady devastation of the state. Major General John C. Frémont, who for a time in 1861 commanded Federal forces in Missouri, complained that "all operations had to be initiated in the midst of upturned and revolutionary conditions and a rebellious people."⁴⁹ The advent of open warfare exacerbated the border war that began in 1854 with the Kansas-Nebraska Act. By 1861 the old wounds were laid bare and both sides became increasingly brutal in settling old scores. An example of this retaliatory environment occurred in 1863 when Brigadier General Thomas Ewing, Jr.—Major General William T. Sherman's brother-in-law—arrested the mothers, daughters, sisters, and wives of guerrillas in western Missouri. The hotel in which they were lodged collapsed, killing several of the ladies, including "Bloody" Bill Anderson's sister and a cousin of Cole Younger. To exact revenge, the notorious William C. Quantrill launched a raid on Lawrence, Kansas, resulting in the razing of the town and the murder of hundreds of men and boys. In turn, Ewing retaliated by issuing an infamous directive known as General Order #11. This document effectively depopulated several western Missouri counties to prevent the guerrillas from gaining sanctuary and sustenance.⁵⁰ This pattern continued unabated until the end of the war and it devastated the state.

While this low-level war continued, the regular Confederate forces began launching their periodic raids into the state. The reason the Rebels' regular forces resorted to raiding was the twin losses of Pea Ridge and Island No. 10 in March and April 1862. These Federal victories at the east and west extremities of Missouri represented significant turning points in the war for control of the state. At Pea Ridge, Major General Samuel R. Curtis—Price's opponent during the Great Raid—decisively defeated the combined forces of Price and McCulloch commanded by Major General Earl Van Dorn. The heavy loss by the Rebels drove them south of Fort Smith in the central part of Arkansas.[51] A month later, Major General John Pope took Island No. 10 in the Mississippi River between Missouri and Tennessee, sending the Confederates tumbling south all the way past Memphis.[52] As a result, the Union consolidated control over Missouri and the locus of Confederate operations shifted to the line of the Arkansas River. This meant that the Rebels were based too far away from Missouri to sustain their forces and the only feasible way to maintain a presence was through cavalry raids. While these had some local successes and proved a nuisance to Federal forces, overall the raids achieved little beyond some tactical advantages and demonstrated the true failure of Confederate policy in the Trans-Mississippi West.

Confederate strategy for prosecuting the war west of the Mississippi had little coherence and in fact was an afterthought, as the entire focus of the government was first Virginia and then west of the Appalachians to the Mississippi. The commander of the Trans-Mississippi Department in 1864, General Edmund Kirby Smith, had the authority—in writing from the president and the Confederate congress—to formulate his own strategy for the region due to the disinterest in Richmond combined with the geographic isolation. Therefore, the policy decided upon by Smith had little relation to the rest of the country. Smith instituted a Fabian defensive policy whereby the Rebels in the department would always trade space for time to parry the blows of Federal forces. Smith was somewhat forced into this policy because the government continually stripped his department of men and resources for use east of the Mississippi River. By contrast, in the East Confederate armies routinely sought ways to take offensive action to achieve the national goal of independence.[53]

At the operational and tactical levels of war there was even less coherence. The raids of Missouri that occurred in 1862 and 1863 tended to have very short-sighted goals and lacked coordination. Typical of the objectives of these raids are those established by Brigadier General John S. Marmaduke for his April 1863 incursion. During this raid Confederate forces moved into the state to subsist. Further, these raids were not coordinated with guerrillas who were a continuous presence in the state. Had the Confederate forces thought more boldly and combined their effort between regular and irregular forces in 1862 and 1863, they may have been able to seriously contest Federal control of Missouri.[54] The Great Raid conducted by Price represented that bold effort, yet it came too late to affect the status quo in the state and the outcome of the war. It also continued to demonstrate the complete lack of focus on common operational objectives between regular and irregular forces.

The opportunity to execute the Great Raid arose from the Confederate success in the Red River Campaign and the supporting Camden Expedition. The Union Army of the Gulf, commanded by Major General Nathaniel P. Banks, launched the Red River

Campaign in March of 1864, in spite of the fact that it diverted from Lieutenant General Ulysses S. Grant's grand strategy for winning the war. Despite his misgivings, Grant allowed Banks to move forward so that he would not embarrass Henry W. Halleck, his predecessor. This decision set the conditions for a needless defeat that very nearly became a disaster. The Confederacy had within its grasp the opportunity to inflict one of the most devastating losses on Union arms in the entire war. Had the Confederates captured the Army of the Gulf and the nineteen gunboats of the Mississippi River Squadron they trapped at Alexandria, it is possible that the war's outcome could have been different. While this did not happen due to internal squabbling in the Confederate high command, the Rebels nevertheless won a significant victory.[55] They had not only driven Banks out of the Red River Valley they had also forced the supporting effort under Major General Frederick Steele back from Camden. This gave General Smith almost total control of the Trans-Mississippi and freed his forces to move in many different directions. Most important, the Rebels held the initiative. The question for the Trans-Mississippi Rebels following the successes was how to follow up the victory.

Lieutenant General Edmund Kirby Smith, Commander of the Confederate Trans-Mississippi Department (Library of Congress).

As spring turned to summer, the Confederacy began to seriously debate this question and the dialogue took place in Richmond, as well as west of the Mississippi. The situation for the Confederacy in the summer of '64 was becoming increasingly desperate. Around Richmond General Robert E. Lee's army was now pinned into the defenses running from Petersburg to the capital. To the west Sherman's Union armies were inexorably pushing General Joseph E. Johnston's Army of Tennessee into the fortifications ringing Atlanta. At Mobile, Major General E.R.S. Canby was moving to take that city in conjunction with the Union fleet in the Gulf of Mexico. Compounding the South's problem was the fact that Federal forces who had escaped capture in the Red River Valley were on their way east to tighten the vise at Richmond, Atlanta, and Mobile. Only in the Trans-Mississippi was there any flexibility. Therefore, General Braxton Bragg proposed to transfer forces from the Trans-Mississippi Department east to relieve the South's beleaguered cities. By 16 July 1864 Bragg issued the order on behalf of the president to "promptly aid by sending troops to defeat the plans of the enemy."[56]

A contending option was proffered by Major General Sterling Price, the victor in the Camden Expedition. He began to loudly clamor for an all-out invasion of Missouri, arguing that crossing the Mississippi was not feasible and the area of operations that would produce the greatest benefit for the Confederacy was in Missouri. The debate over what to do to capitalize on the victory in the Red River Valley would rage for the next five weeks, until Bragg suspended his order because of the inability to safely ferry troops from the Trans-Mississippi over the river.[57] This set the stage for Price's Great Raid, as Price's proposal became the only realistic alternative to take advantage of the initiative seized following the Red River Campaign.

Ten years of conflict along America's western border had led to this moment. Missouri was pivotal to the establishment of the state of Kansas and later, when the Civil War began, Missouri was critical to both sides. The vociferous irregular warfare that raged throughout the war illustrated the emotion elicited as former neighbors fought each other remorselessly. But this invasion would represent the decisive statement of the war that finally gave control of the state to the Union. The men who led both sides during the Great Raid understood what was at stake and made dispositions to counter each other. Ultimately, the personalities involved and their various levels of competence would dictate the outcome of Price's 1864 invasion of Missouri.

2

A Passion for Missouri: The Rebel Invaders

There is a tendency in military units for the command to take on the personality of the commander. This held true for outfits that fought in the Civil War. Perhaps no other army assembled during the war was more a reflection of the men who commanded it than the Confederate Army of Missouri. Similarly, the Union elements that opposed Sterling Price's army were a mirror image of their leaders. As a result, the outcome of the Confederate invasion of Missouri in 1864 had much to do with the character of the men who led the armies. Each army had internal strife, because of the conflicting personalities and varying levels of competence and experience, which had a direct impact on the decisions made during the campaign. It is the human element and the interactions among the leaders that make the story of the Great Missouri Raid such a richly textured history. Thus, an examination of the key leaders involved on both sides will provide an indication of how the raid unfolded in the manner it did.

The Confederate commanders were a colorful mix of former Border Ruffians, politicians, and professionals, and three of the four senior commanders were Missourians. The Confederate Army of Missouri had a distinct advantage over its opponents in that the army was a unified command, while the Union army was fragmented across different departments. In other words, the Army of Missouri had a clear chain of command and hierarchy of authority that facilitated the execution of orders, whereas their opponents in blue were split in separate commands, a situation that caused unnecessary issues for the pursuers. This was as much a factor in the outcome of the campaign as the personalities of the commanders themselves and on the Federal side exacerbated some of the frictions that existed between the commanders. Unity of command tended to enable the Confederate leaders to operate more seamlessly in spite of their personal idiosyncrasies. For the Rebels, arguably the most interesting figure involved in the raid is the man who served as the overall commander, Major General Sterling Price. No man in the Rebel army epitomized Southern hopes for Missouri more than Price, and his army came to embody his spirit. The indomitable Price was a reluctant Rebel, as he held conditional Unionist sentiments when the sectional crisis began to boil over in 1860. As such, he was fairly representative of the slaveholding Missourians who lived along the Missouri Valley and had migrated from other Southern states before the war.

Sterling Price was born in Prince Edward County, Virginia, in 1809 to a well-to-do planter. His father, while not fully accepted into the aristocratic antebellum society, nevertheless spent a lifetime attempting to achieve that status. He was descended from an old Virginia family of Welsh origin. While his father, Pugh, was not particularly wealthy, he was comfortable nonetheless and well situated in terms of his land holdings along the Buffalo River. Pugh's modest estate provided a good life for his family and labor was supplied by the slaves he held.[1]

Pugh Price was a member of the local militia company, as were most men of his status at that time, and he served as a first sergeant. When Sterling was three years old, Pugh left home to fight in the War of 1812. Since Sterling was so young, he would have had little recollection of this event. He would, however, recall with fondness the time he spent exploring the family farm. The farm focused on the production of tobacco, and during the 1820s the family prospered as the price of the leaf skyrocketed. In spite of this success, the Prices did not achieve full acceptance among the moneyed planter society of Virginia. This knowledge weighed heavily on Sterling, and he would spend the rest of his life struggling to attain the respectability denied to his father, respectability he thought was deserved.[2] In large measure he did succeed in gaining the prominence he desired, but it only came after the family moved to Missouri.

In the mid–1820s Sterling entered college at Hampden-Sidney in Richmond. Pugh felt that a young gentleman must have an education befitting his social status—or the one he hoped to achieve. As a result, his early schooling was focused on placing him in an appropriate institution of higher learning. After passing the entrance exams, Price started school in 1826. Sterling Price proved an indifferent student, as he found himself in trouble by breaking the school code of conduct. Further, he neglected his studies, achieving poor grades. He soon determined that college did not suit him and dropped out of school after one year. The elder Price, believing that Sterling would return home, had successfully groomed his son to assume the mantle of gentleman planter. Therefore, when Sterling returned home, he was quite ready to take on the responsibility of running the family estate. Instead, he decided to pursue a law career and accepted an apprenticeship with a prominent Richmond lawyer, Creed Taylor. It was during this time, under the influence of his mentor, that he began to develop his political opinions. This, combined with his Virginia planter upbringing, confirmed Price as a Jacksonian Democrat.[3]

Major General Sterling Price, Commander of the Army of Missouri (Library of Congress).

Just as Price was embarking on his professional career, the tobacco market collapsed, causing a crisis in the Price family, as their financial future was jeopardized by the fall. The only way to defray the lost revenue was to expand the estate. In antebellum society, planters were "land poor." In other words, wealth was determined by the extent of land owned by the planters and not by on-hand cash. To grow that wealth, the planter had to continually purchase more land through bank loans.

But since Pugh Price and his family were on a lower social wrung than the gentleman planters, Pugh found access to more land—and bank loans—closed to him. It is this fact that encouraged Pugh to look elsewhere to regain his prosperity. In the late 1820s, opportunity existed in the west, in Kentucky and other new states and territories beyond the Mississippi, to acquire new land at a cheap rate. Thus, in 1830 the elder Price, with his 21-year-old son, struck out for Missouri to start a new life and gain the respectability closed to him in Virginia.[4]

The Prices arrived in Chariton County, Missouri, and promptly purchased 4,886 acres of land in the fertile Missouri River Valley. The alluvial plain along the Missouri was perfect for growing cash crops such as tobacco. This area of Missouri was in the early stages of developing a thriving economy based on tobacco, cotton, and hemp. Sterling found Missouri an exciting land of opportunity and seized upon it to reach the coveted social status his father never found in Virginia. By 1840 the Price estate at Keytesville was prospering, making Sterling one of the wealthiest men in the state. He had also grown into an imposing figure physically. At over six feet and 200 pounds, he looked the part of the respected gentleman planter.[5] In addition to working hard to build a viable plantation, Price did a number of other things to build his resume as a first-rate citizen.

The first thing he did was enlist in the local militia company, much as his father did before him. Price's popular personality combined with his imposing stature facilitated his election to captain in the unit. This fact did much to accord him the respectability he sought, as officership and service in the 19th century brought societal acceptance on the frontier. The second path to elevating one's social status was entry into politics. For a southerner the Democrat Party was the means to solidify status as a respected gentleman. Already a confirmed Jacksonian, Price's foray into politics was logical and simple, and he seemed to excel in winning elections. In 1840 he ran for and secured a seat in the Missouri state house.[6] Within two years of that, the legislature elected him speaker, in spite of his noted lack of oratory skills. A mere two years after reaching the speakership, Price was elected to the Unites States House of Representatives. While his rise up the social ladder was rapid, it was the advent of the Mexican War that cemented his popularity in Missouri and assured him iconic status in the hearts of his fellow Show-Me citizens.

In 1846 Price was in his first term in Congress when President James K. Polk manufactured a war with Mexico based on long-standing territorial disputes and frictions caused by America's westward migration across the continent. With the war's outbreak, Price resigned his seat in August and accepted the commission of colonel in a Missouri volunteer infantry regiment. At this point, he held a fairly thin claim to military expertise. The totality of his experience amounted to militia drill and an ugly episode in which Missouri, using its state militia forces, drove the Mormons from the northwest corner of the state. Nevertheless, Price energetically recruited a full regiment in less than thirty days. Soon after organizing the unit, he received orders to report to Brigadier General Stephen W. Kearney at Fort Leavenworth.[7]

Upon arrival at Leavenworth, Price learned that his regiment—designated the 2nd Missouri Volunteers—would be brigaded with other frontier units and fitted out for an expedition to New Mexico, with Kearney in command of the whole. It is at this point that Price first exhibited one of his many flaws as a military leader. The reason for the summons of Price's regiment to Leavenworth was to provide needed infantry to form the core of maneuver firepower. But, upon learning that the regiment would have to march overland over 1,000 miles to reach New Mexico, Price unilaterally converted his unit to cavalry. This decision infuriated his superiors, yet they did nothing about it. The failure of Price's senior commanders to reprimand him for changing the composition of the entire force vindicated Price's decision in his own mind and reinforced his independent streak.[8] Price would continue to do as he pleased in all future campaigns regardless of any higher purpose. His action also endeared him to the troops, who fairly worshipped him for this decision, thus setting another pattern for his career. Missouri troops loved Price, giving him the nickname "Old Pap." The affection he garnered for looking after his men—even if his misguided decisions harmed the cause—probably rivaled that which Robert E. Lee achieved in the East. This love from the troops would never wane over the course of his career.[9]

The expedition to New Mexico made Sterling Price a household name in Missouri. After the long march, Kearney's little army arrived at Santa Fe. During that epic march, Price contracted cholera, being confined to his bed when the army reached Santa Fe. The illness's effects would dog him for the rest of his life, including during the raid in 1864. Due to his strong constitution, Price was able to recover from the debilitating effects and resume his duties in New Mexico, which seemed mundane at best. For some time it appeared that Price and his men would have little more than occupation duty to perform. It was during this sojourn that a second weakness in Price's military character was on full display. Because he was ever conscious of his reputation, he had a troubling tendency to allow lax discipline within the ranks. Low standards of discipline would plague him later in the Civil War, sometimes with detrimental effect on his plans and the cause. Further, his independence led him into several disputes with peers and superiors alike. Recalcitrance would recur throughout his military career, and, again, lead to trouble in carrying out his intent in future campaigns in the Civil War.[10] As time passed on the southwest frontier it seemed the only fighting Price would do was spar with other officers. However, as circumstances often allow, a great opportunity presented itself, and Price made the most of it.

The vast territory given to Kearney—upon which he had to assert American authority—forced him to spread his army out to maintain order, providing the opportunity for rebellion among native Indian tribes and Mexicans who were not pleased by their new government. Price was placed in command of the New Mexico Territory when General Kearney departed to take command in California. Two incidents then occurred that thrust Price into the limelight. First, the Pueblo Indians—having thrown off the Mexican yoke of power—sought to likewise prevent the Americans from asserting any. Second, during the revolt, the Pueblos killed the territorial governor, Charles Bent. Price acted quickly, displaying a positive trait the marked his career: decisiveness. In January 1847, he moved his cantonment and crushed the rebelling Indians in a series of small engagements, but he did not stop there. He took the initiative and marched straight into Mexico proper. Once in Mexico, Price defeated a scratch Mexican force and occupied the provincial city of Chihuahua. Then, in the closing days of the war, he moved out again to defeat a force of Mexicans, outnumbering his own three to one, at the Battle of Santa Cruz de Rosales. Because peace negotiations were underway—the Treaty of Guadalupe Hidalgo was signed before the battle—Price had violated orders by engaging the Mexicans. But, just as he had earlier escaped reprimand in mounting his regiment, he was simply scolded for his disregard of orders in this incident.[11] Thus, his insubordinate behavior was again vindicated in his own view. News of Price's exploits was trumpeted back home in Missouri and his reputation in the state reached iconic status.

Among the unfortunate side effects of this campaign was the fact that the success inflated Sterling Price's opinion of his own military ability, in addition to the fact that his recalcitrance seemed acceptable to higher authority. From this point forward, Price believed that, above all things, he was the model of the American military leader. This self-assessment grew out of the old model, idealized in history by the 19th century, in which the best military leaders were community leaders in their civilian pursuits. When time of war came about, these respected citizens would leave their stations in the community to serve in defense of hearth and home, just as the minutemen had in the Revolution. Americans, always suspicious of standing armies and career military men, had great reverence for this model citizen-soldier. Further, these men, because of the democratic values they espoused, were sure to succeed in the defense of the republic. Sterling Price now seemed the very personification of this image. While this was a vanishing pillar of American military readiness, few knew it at the time, and besides, a living hero such as Price was what the people at home really wanted. Thus, Price was the incarnation of legend and he knew it, much to the detriment of the future Confederacy.

Price returned home in 1848 and initially remained a private citizen, focusing on expanding his holdings and other business interests, but the politics of the day soon drew him back to public office. As a major slaveholder in Missouri, Price quite naturally joined that wing of the Democrat Party when it began to split over the issue. He rode his enormous popularity to the governorship in 1853. His administration witnessed the Kansas-Nebraska Act and the outbreak of the border war between Missouri and Kansas. Overall, Price's term as governor was not as momentous as the events unfolding around him. He administered the office in a competent manner, but few could positively nail him down on the issues of the day. While not a deeply thoughtful man nor blessed as an orator, he did have skill as a politician by his ability to pick a winning policy based on popular sentiment and avoid controversy.[12] This skill allowed him to maintain his huge popularity.

While making few public statements about the controversies on the border, as a slaveholder Price was clearly sympathetic to efforts to bring Kansas into the union as a slave state. Evidence of this is found in two instances. First, Price signed onto a resolution calling for Kansas's admission as a slave state. Second, and most important, Price did nothing as governor to rein in the Border Ruffians, which as chief executive he had a duty to do.[13] Thus, he indirectly poured fuel on the fire of the border war by not enforcing law and order to prevent the ever-escalating depredations in Kansas. In effect, Price's administration was a party to the events that brought on the Civil War.

Price left office in 1857 and returned to private life on his plantation after showing some interest in an open U.S. Senate seat. During this time, he became a backer of Stephen A. Douglas, author of the failed Kansas-Nebraska Act. When Douglas ran for president in 1860, it was on a platform of conciliation between North and South. Unlike some of his southern brethren, Price was not a firebrand for secession. In fact, he was a Unionist who believed that the slave states were better off within the union.[14] Even when the slave states began leaving the union, Price stood firm in his stance. Only some overt act of coercion in the state of Missouri by federal authorities could bring him around to support of secession.

Missouri was torn by the rapid succession of southern states leaving the union. As we have already seen, most Missourians favored the union, with a small minority calling for secession. Governor Claiborne Fox Jackson was among the latter, and he called a convention of delegates on 28 February 1861 at the capital. Price, representing Chariton County, was the presiding officer. As a "conditional" Unionist, he was in full agreement when the convention almost unanimously struck down the ordinance of secession. Price, however, was hedging his bets. He, along with twenty-two other conditional Unionists, signed onto a resolution at the convention declaring that "if the General Government will not wait till the country can, by conciliation and compromise, save the Union, Missouri should and will take the stand with her Southern sisters."[15] The "General Government" did not wait, and the incident that pushed Sterling Price into the secessionist camp occurred when Nathaniel Lyon broke up Camp Jackson and then abrogated the Harney-Price agreement.

Price's service to the South was both wide-ranging and comprehensive. He fought in almost every major campaign of the Trans-Mississippi theater. He also fought on the other side of the river in critical battles. Through it all, Price never lost sight of his primary goal, the liberation of Missouri from what he saw as the hard hand of the Lincoln administration. He would focus so intently on this objective that, regardless of policy, strategy, or plans on the part of the Confederacy, he would do whatever it took to achieve his goal. In many cases, this ran counter to the government and his superiors.

Price's first action was at Wilson's Creek. In this battle, he displayed all of his military character, both positive and negative. Before the engagement, he took issue with his superior Ben McCulloch on matters of strategy and tactical dispositions. In addition, the laxity of discipline displayed in Mexico came to the fore as he allowed his troops at one point to pilfer equipment from the units McCulloch brought north from other Southern states. Finally, Price demonstrated decisiveness and tenacity under fire. When it appeared that Lyon's little army would overrun the surprised—and much larger—Rebel army, Price personally intervened to stabilize the line and then lead the counter-attack that won the day.[16] However, the dissension sown before the battle would dog him after it concluded.

Ben McCulloch had been reluctant to enter Missouri before Wilson's Creek, as he viewed his mission as one to protect the Confederacy's northern border, which was the Arkansas-Missouri line. He had moved north into Missouri only when Price convinced him that he could best protect that border by acting decisively in Missouri. Moreover, the movement might actually shift the border northward to the Iowa line. When their combined forces defeated Lyon, McCulloch felt that he had accomplished his mission. Further, he worried that Price's poorly disciplined Missouri State Guard would infect his troops and he desired to break free of Price, which he did immediately after the battle. In a letter to Price written by McCulloch's adjutant he states that "the undisciplined condition of his [McCulloch's] men, makes it his duty to select some place as a camp of instruction—not so far from his resources," which meant Arkansas.[17] This left Price to his own devices, and he seized the initiative to clear the Missouri Valley.

Price's effort to clear the valley culminated in his greatest victory at Lexington. Three points are significant to his character as a military commander arising from this battle. First, his effort in striking out on his own demonstrates his independent streak, and it also shows that he would move of his own volition without reference to any other strategy. Second, the success built upon Price's already massive popularity and, as a result, solidified the connection between him and his troops. Thus, Price would always attempt to take care of his men as long as he had the capability. Finally, this victory served to further inflate his gigantic ego as to his military ability. This last element was probably that which was most detrimental to the very cause he was fighting for. All of his future decisions flowed from his belief that his opinion should garner respect because of his demonstrated ability.

Lexington was a tactical victory barren of any strategic gains. Price realized soon after the surrender of Colonel Mulligan's command that his position was untenable. Federal forces were moving to cut him off from the south and his swelled ranks were depleting his subsistence and supply services. Therefore, he retreated into the southwest corner of Missouri. Eventually, even this position became precarious as a new Union army under Brigadier General Samuel R. Curtis moved into southwest Missouri. Thus, Price was forced to continue the retreat into Arkansas, where he was soon reunited with his nemesis, Ben McCulloch.[18]

In the winter of '61–'62, the Confederacy saw the need for a single overall commander west of the Mississippi, and Major General Earl Van Dorn was appointed to the command. Van Dorn had his work cut out for him in bringing harmony to his command with McCulloch and Price as his primary subordinates. Van Dorn could never get the two diverging personalities to see eye to eye, but he did succeed in organizing an army. In addition, he used a bottomless reservoir of energy to bring all together to achieve some level of cooperation. The newly minted Army of the West, as Van Dorn styled it, moved north from Fort Smith, Arkansas, in late February to meet Curtis' thrust southward head-on. Van Dorn's intent was to defeat it and then move into Missouri, driving straight for St. Louis.[19] This was somewhat quixotic based on the size of his army and the logistical challenges, but such ambition was just the elixir Price needed to fire his own desires.

The Pea Ridge Campaign was short lived and disastrous for the Southern cause, as well as for Price's dream to liberate Missouri. The Confederate army moved forward in some of the worst weather imaginable, as snow and cold pounded hard on the soldiers of the Army of the West. Compounding the misery of the march was the precarious logistical situation with which the Confederate army was forced to contend. Van Dorn's plan was unsustainable because his logistical base at Fort Smith could not support an advance through the Boston Mountains, and these very same hills were barren of any subsistence. Nevertheless, the trekkers made quick progress, and within the first few days of March Van Dorn began to get a clearer picture of Federal dispositions.

The Union army was moving down the Wire Road in northwest Arkansas and had chosen to dig in—oriented south—along Sugar Creek to absorb the Rebel advance. With this knowledge Van Dorn decided to swing wide to the west and then march south once beyond Curtis' flank. This would give the Rebels the advantage of catching the Federal army by surprise from a direction that they did not anticipate. However, the imposing terrain feature of Pea Ridge forced Van Dorn to divide his marching columns so that he could bring the whole army on line in the field for the final assault. This flaw in Van Dorn's plan manifested itself on 6–7 March 1862 when Curtis—who had detected the movement—quickly reoriented his own line to the north and hit the separated wings individually before they could come back together after moving around Pea Ridge. Though Curtis was outnumbered three to two, he was able to neutralize this disadvantage when he hit McCulloch's column first and then turned on Price near Elkhorn Tavern.

In the fighting around the tavern, Price was out front leading his men and received a flesh wound in the arm. In spite of this, he refused to leave the field for medical care and led his men for the remainder of the battle with his arm in a sling, adding to his reputation and luster among the Missouri troops.[20] Nevertheless, the result of the battle was humiliating to Price, who believed he had borne the brunt of the fight with little support from Van Dorn. He was vociferous in his criticism of Van Dorn. Price was not happy about the treatment of his soldiers either. Regardless of this venom, he had little time to dwell on his lost dream for Missouri, for now the Confederate government called for the transfer of the Army of the West to the east side of the Mississippi, setting a pattern for the duration of the war. From now on the government in Richmond primarily viewed the Trans-Mississippi region as a manpower resource pool.[21]

Sterling Price was none too happy about the transfer east, but he complied. The purpose of the move east of the river was to shore up the rapidly collapsing defensive line in Tennessee. Since February 1862, Union arms had won several victories, sweeping the Confederates completely out of west Tennessee and pushing the Army of the Mississippi into northern Mississippi. Following the defeat at Shiloh, that army—commanded by General Pierre G.T. Beauregard—had retreated to Corinth, depleted and demoralized. The arrival of Price and his men from Missouri ignited a burst of new confidence, as "we were safe now," one resident of Corinth noted.[22] This confidence proved overblown, for on the night of 29–30 May, the Confederates abandoned Corinth, retreating to Tupelo. With the army safely in Tupelo, Price decided to make an independent trip to Richmond to advocate the Missouri cause directly with President Jefferson Davis.

The journey to the Rebel capital could probably be described as a triumphal procession, as Price was feted at every stop. This served to bloat his ego even larger than its already engorged state. In Richmond, he lobbied hard for his home state, making a number of specific proposals to facilitate its liberation. First, he proposed that the current Trans-Mississippi District be elevated to a full-fledged department. This would make the region coequal with the Virginia and Tennessee theaters of operation, thus enabling the department commander to better retrain his resources. Second, Price advocated that the government place a single officer in command of the whole. One would not have to ponder too long to surmise who Price might suggest to fill this position. Finally, he called for an immediate movement into Missouri to force "the withdrawal of Halleck's army" from north Mississippi.[23]

After a wait of several days, Price won an audience with the president and laid his proposal on the table, with an additional recommendation that Price receive command of the new Trans-Mississippi Department. President Davis, harried by the situation of Richmond under siege, was in a very irritable mood. Additionally, he was prejudiced against Price because Price was not a West Pointer and, in his opinion, no more than a military amateur. Davis heard Price out but politely refused to allow Price or his Missourians to return to the west. What was worse, Davis gave command of the new Trans-Mississippi Department to Major General John B. Magruder. Price, now livid, launched into a tirade against Davis. Thomas Snead of Price's staff recalled that Price said, "I will send you my resignation, and go back to Missouri and raise another army there without your assistance, and fight again under the flag of Missouri, and win new victories for the South." The combative Davis quickly retorted, "[Y]our resignation will be accepted General; and if you do go back to Missouri ... and win victories ... no one will be more *pleased* than myself, or—more *surprised*."[24] At this, Price stormed from the room and immediately penned his resignation.

Upon receipt of the resignation, Davis began to reconsider his position. Price was important politically to the president. If he allowed Price to leave the army, it could upset the governors and congressional delegations of the Trans-Mississippi states, with whom Price was immensely popular. This would, in turn, affect the morale and effectiveness of thousands of troops from those states. This fact, combined with the fact that Price did have some legitimate reasons for desiring a return west, softened Davis' stance. As a result, Davis, who believed that Price was the "vainest man he had ever met," wrote a calming letter to Price that placated Price's anger. Davis told him that as soon as the situation permitted, Price could return with his Missourians to the west side of the river. Once there, they could undertake a new campaign to free Missouri.[25] Price had once again acted independently and crossed the line of subordination. Yet, as with all previous instances, his acts were not reprimanded. Instead, he seemed vindicated and had secured all that he came to Richmond to gain. Thomas C. Reynolds, the new governor of Missouri, recorded that he had noticed a tendency Price had, "a disposition to plan and act for himself, not very subordinate towards official superiors."[26] Indeed, Price's belief in his own military judgment was magnified, but this time there were negative effects. The nasty affair served to alienate Price from Davis, guaranteeing that his future interactions with Richmond would provide little benefit.

From mid–1862 to the summer of 1864, Price would be denied the opportunity to move back into Missouri for a number of reasons. Chief among them was the situation in Mississippi. Beauregard, suffering from an acute medical condition, took a leave of absence. In his place, President Davis appointed Braxton Bragg as the commander of the renamed Army of Tennessee. Further, the Army of the West was placed under Price's command when Van Dorn was transferred south. Bragg sought to reverse the Confederate fortunes in Mississippi by going on the offensive. His plan was to move the Army of Tennessee by rail to Chattanooga in preparation for a drive into Kentucky. Price's Army of the West would remain in Mississippi to tie down Union forces there, giving Bragg more freedom of maneuver.[27]

Bragg made amazing initial progress in his Kentucky campaign. However, his army seemed paralyzed by mid–September 1862, as Bragg had lost his grasp of what the thrust was intended to accomplish. Union forces began converging on his stalled army from several directions near Lexington, Kentucky. Therefore, Bragg sought to create a diversion and he asked Price to take the offensive in Mississippi toward Corinth to relieve the pressure. To ensure that Price's attack was taken seriously by the Federals, Bragg told Price to unite with Van Dorn, who was now at Vicksburg. While this did not please Price, he need not have worried, because Van Dorn failed to reinforce Price immediately anyway. The result of this failure almost caused the destruction of the Army of the West at Iuka. Price dutifully moved forward to engage Union forces at Corinth, but unknown to him, Major General U.S. Grant had set an ambush along the way. On 19 September 1862, Price was nearly caught between two large Union contingents near Iuka; but he was able to escape because the phenomenon known as acoustic shadow had prevented the force closest to Iuka from hearing the battle noise to the south. Thus, the Union troops at Iuka failed to spring the trap.[28] Meanwhile, Price heavily engaged the other Federal force led by one of his future nemeses in the Great Raid, Major General William S. Rosecrans. As this action was taking place, Van Dorn did finally begin to move, arriving after the fight at Iuka. When he united with Price he immediately suggested a headlong assault on Corinth. The battle, occurring on 3–4 October, proved an utter failure and, worse, many of Price's precious Missourians fell in the battle.

Price would never forgive Van Dorn for expending his men so thoughtlessly in the fight at Corinth. He blamed Van Dorn for his imbecility and began clamoring for transfer back across the Mississippi. To secure this end, Price again traveled to Richmond to engage the War Department. He met with secretary of war James Seddon and the new governor of Missouri, Thomas C. Reynolds. Again Price advocated for a return west with his troops, and in this he was partially successful. While happy to receive orders to recross the river, Price would do so without his Missourians, who were to stay on the east side to shore up the crumbling line in Mississippi. This no doubt irritated Price, but he did get to move back west and he received a new command in Arkansas of combined Missouri and Arkansas troops.[29] Now Price believed that he would get another opportunity to enter Missouri. However, he would have to wait quite a while.

Price crossed the Mississippi on 18 March 1863, and, although happy he was back, his time in Arkansas throughout this year was extremely frustrating. The year 1863 was difficult across the entire Confederacy, and no less so in the Trans-Mississippi. As the new division commander in Theophilus Holmes District of Arkansas, Price suffered one defeat after another before the small army was nearly driven out of Arkansas. First, he took part in the failed assault on Helena, which was an abortive attempt to relieve the siege at Vicksburg. Close on the heels of the Helena affair, Vicksburg itself fell, slicing the Confederacy in two. Next, Brigadier General Frederick Steele took Little Rock, the capital of Arkansas, forcing Holmes, with Price in tow, into the southwest corner of the state. Price was disheartened at the thought that he would never return to Missouri, especially with the decrepit, frequently ill, and incompetent Holmes in command of the district. The Missouri congressional delegation agreed and began a full court press to have Holmes removed as commander in Arkansas. In the end, Holmes resigned his command in February 1864 due to the cacophony rising up against him.[30]

With Holmes' departure, Kirby Smith—in command of the Trans-Mississippi

Department since February 1863—had to fill the position in the district. This would not be an easy task in Smith's opinion. The logical choice for the command was Sterling Price, but Smith felt that Price was unqualified for the position. Yet who was available in the department that was equal to the task? Smith's answer was that there was no one. So, by default, Price was elevated to command of the District of Arkansas despite Smith's misgivings about Price's competence.[31] Price assumed command of the District of Arkansas at Camden on 16 March 1864 and his accession to this position opened the door of opportunity for his return to Missouri in 1864.

On the day Price took command, Major General Nathaniel P. Banks and the Union Army of the Gulf were already en route to Alexandria, Louisiana, having begun the Red River Campaign. Simultaneously, Major General Frederick Steele was making preparations to support the Red River Campaign with his own thrust south from Little Rock, with his objective point at Shreveport, Louisiana. Price, situated in Camden about halfway between Little Rock and Shreveport, was comfortably positioned to oppose Steele's movement. His command consisted of just over 10,000 troops, including cavalry and infantry, from throughout the Trans-Mississippi. Even before Steele stepped off from Little Rock, Price began to suggest that the best way to defeat Steele was to "send me into Missouri with a competent force."[32] While Price had not changed in his fervent desire to enter Missouri, the tactics he used with Smith to advocate his position marked a clear break from the past.

Heretofore, Price had a reputation for badgering and agitating his superiors to have his way. In 1864, his tactic and tone noticeably shifted. Rather than taking a direct and bold approach to obtain his ends, Price was now acting with deference to his commander. From this point forward, Price took an indirect approach in order to gain what he desired most. In his relations with Smith he was very cooperative and in correspondence complimentary. Evidence of this is demonstrated in the way he cheerfully complied with an order from Smith to give up all of his infantry to Richard Taylor in Louisiana. This order arrived as Steele's thrust was about to move south. In great contrast to what Price would have done previously, he immediately sent the troops south.[33] The change in tack by Price would have a salutary effect on Smith, who would incline toward supporting Price in future endeavors.

Price's performance in the Camden Expedition was, on the whole, competent. Kirby Smith himself provides more evidence of Price's transformation of character when he writes that Price's behavior was "prompt and unselfish" and that he demonstrated "skill and judgment" in the campaign to drive Steele back. This helped to bring Smith into Price's camp when it came time to determine the next step after Camden and Banks' defeat in the Red River Valley. One of the reasons Smith was leaning toward support for Price and his hints of a Missouri campaign was the irritating behavior of his other subordinate, Richard Taylor. In contrast to Price, Taylor was downright insulting to Smith because he disagreed with Smith over his decisions in the campaign against Banks. Thus, when Taylor began to clamor for action against New Orleans, Smith naturally turned toward the more respectful subordinate, Sterling Price.[34] In possession of Smith's ear, Price would now see his dream come to fruition.

Price would conduct the invasion of Missouri with an interesting cast of characters. Chief among his subordinates was the enormous personality of Joseph Orville Shelby, who commanded a division of the Army of Missouri. No other man had more of a passion for Missouri than Jo Shelby—with the possible exception of Sterling Price. Like Price, Shelby was not a native Missourian. Shelby was born in Lexington, Kentucky, to a distinguished family that gave that state its first governor, many courageous soldiers, and business magnates. The family migrated from Wales in the early 18th century and settled in Pennsylvania. The draw of the west soon pulled the first generation of Shelbys to the Appalachians and beyond. The vast wilderness held promise of adventure and cheap land, which Jo's great-grandfather, John, found irresistible.[35]

John settled in what is now Tennessee and during the Revolution fought at King's Mountain with at least two other Shelby men, including Jo's grandfather David. Following the war John Shelby became one of the largest landowners in Tennessee and represented Sumner County in the state constitutional convention. David Shelby married into a distinguished Virginia family and had eleven children with his wife. Among these was Orville Shelby, Jo's father. Orville was twice married, and his second wife, Anna Maria Boswell of Lexington, eventually drew her husband to Kentucky, where Joseph Orville was born on 12 December 1830. He was named after Anna Maria's father and Orville.[36]

Growing up in Kentucky, Jo Shelby was exposed to the best of everything and he had a wide array of friends who became influential on both sides of the sectional crisis. Orville Shelby was a man of great substance who made a fortune in the hemp business. During the 19th century hemp was nearly as profitable a cash crop as cotton. The reason for this was that hemp string and rope tied the bales of cotton. Therefore, producers had to have as much hemp to package the cotton as the crop proper. Thus, Orville had the means to ensure that his family, including Jo, had the best of everything.[37] This led to Jo's becoming a carefree youngster who was inattentive as a student—not unlike his future commander, Sterling Price.

Interestingly, Shelby's friends and playmates included none other than John Hunt Morgan, Francis P. Blair, Jr., and Howard Gratz. Morgan, like Shelby, would find renown as a cavalryman for the Confederacy, while Blair would serve the Union by securing Missouri for the North and as a corps commander in Sherman's army. Gratz facilitated Shelby's business interests before the war and Jo made his acquaintance following the death of his own father in 1835 when Jo was only five. At this point Benjamin Gratz— who was Jo's uncle—stepped in as the family benefactor. Eventually, in 1843, Ann Shelby married the elder Gratz, making Jo his stepfather.[38]

Jo Shelby and Benjamin Gratz developed a close relationship, giving young Jo the father figure he needed as a teenager. Jo Shelby would develop much of his worldview based on this relationship, and the aristocratic Gratz would introduce Jo to many of the most powerful Americans of the day, including Henry Clay, Francis Blair, Sr., and John J. Crittenden. With such influences in his developmental years, it is no wonder that Shelby became a Southern Democrat in outlook. As Jo approached his late teen years, Ben Gratz would see to it that his stepson received a proper education, one befitting a southern gentleman. Thus, in 1846 Jo Shelby went east to Pennsylvania to preparatory school so that he would be prepared for college.[39] It seems that much of Shelby's early life mirrored that of his future commander, Sterling Price.

Much like Price, Jo Shelby was an indifferent student and known as a prankster.

Nevertheless, he was a bright young man and qualified to enter Transylvania College, which he did in the fall of 1847. Even so, he carried his youthful exuberance with him into college and this was a factor in why he never graduated. Legend holds that Shelby and his friends took a cadaver from the medical department and replaced it with a live "corpse." Allegedly, the replacement was Shelby himself.[40] Such antics provide a window to view the man who would become a slashing, courageous cavalry leader. The same characteristics he demonstrated in jest on campus would manifest on the battlefield fifteen years later. Shelby was conniving, deceptive, and daring in his practical jokes and he would exhibit the same traits on a hundred battlefields.

The best years of Shelby's life were spent in Missouri. When gold was discovered in California in the late 1840s, a great migration took place carrying adventurers of all stripes westward. Jo Shelby, along with many Kentuckians, got caught up in the fever and went west to make his fortune, but he would find it in the Missouri Valley. The fertile valley was known for its ability to produce bumper crops, including hemp. So, in 1849, after dropping out of Transylvania, Shelby, with Howard Gratz and Frank Blair, Jr., moved to Missouri.[41] Much like Sterling Price, Shelby found everything there he needed to stimulate his active mind and to get rich.

Brigadier General Joseph O. Shelby, Commander, 3rd Division, Army of Missouri (The State Historical Society of Missouri, Art Collection).

Jo Shelby flourished when he moved to Waverly, Missouri, using his available financial resources to multiply his holdings many times. Much of his success is attributable to the use of slave labor. This naturally brought him into contact with like-minded planters living along the Missouri River. Their political outlook aligned with those of conservative Southern Democrats. By 1854, the migration to Kansas had begun pitting staunch antislavery northeasterners against the aristocratic planters. Shelby, along with his neighbors, felt threatened by this movement as an attempt to change their world. As a result, these men banded together to try to stem the flow of migration, igniting the Border War. Jo Shelby, with his status and charisma, became a natural leader among what would become the Border Ruffians.[42]

Shelby's participation in the Border War was in essence an apprenticeship for command when the Civil War began in 1861. Several of the key leaders in the future Confederate organization in Missouri were Shelby's close associates. These included Claiborne F. Jackson, who would as governor attempt to lead Missouri out of the Union, and Senator David R. Atchison, the firebrand Democrat who was determined to bring

Kansas into the Union as a slave state. Together with others, they formed the Blue Lodge Society to establish political dominance in Kansas, backing it with a quasi-military organization. As a member of this band Shelby would engage in both subterfuge and hard fighting. Initially, he participated in the political effort to stuff the ballot boxes during the initial Kansas territorial elections; but when this approach did not quell abolitionist designs, he turned to the martial approach.[43]

The most significant fight Shelby fought in was the 1856 sack of Lawrence. In this raid the Border Ruffians destroyed the presses of the free-state papers, looted stores, and tore up the Free State Hotel.[44] The raid gave Shelby experience in leading troops and gaining an understanding of the dynamics of cavalry operations. Among the lessons he took away was the need for speed, deception, and varying routes to infiltrate and exit the operational area. Shelby's ability to internalize these lessons would translate into the difference between success and failure, and he demonstrated that he learned well.

By 1860, Shelby and his associates had lost the Border War but were poised to join the South when the sectional crisis came to a head. Not all of Shelby's acquaintances were on board for the Southern cause. In particular, his own cousin Frank Blair had for some time agitated against slavery in the St. Louis newspapers. For a Kentuckian, such a stance on the issue was anathema. But as the election of 1860 drew closer, sides were chosen and the die was cast for the sectional conflict in Missouri. While his cousin was an unconditional Unionist, Shelby's loyalty—he having participated in the Border War—was as a conditional Unionist, though he sympathized with the secessionists in his views. Any slight spark would immediately push him into the secession camp. In fact, soon after the South fired upon Fort Sumter in April 1861, Shelby embarked on a mission to purchase musket caps for his childhood friend John Hunt Morgan in Kentucky for that state's defense of its neutrality. Shelby traveled to St. Louis to buy the caps and, ironically, was present at Camp Jackson on the day that Lyon, with Blair's blessing, forced Frost's Missouri militia to surrender. This made Shelby's choice for secession crystal clear and he threw his full support behind Governor Jackson.[45]

Events rapidly overcame political and military preparations of the Missouri secessionists; but under Jackson and Price's leadership, steps were taken to attempt to eject the Federals from the state. Jo Shelby became a captain in the Missouri State Guard, leading his old veterans of the Border War into Confederate service. Shelby's company, the Lafayette County Cavalry, assembled at Waverly in June and was ordered to join the rest of the Missouri State Guard in the southwest corner of the state. Here, at the Cowskin Prairie, the Missouri troops were organizing and the Lafayette Cavalry was assigned to the 2nd Division under Brigadier General James S. Rains. Shelby and his men were in action shortly after assembling because the Union army under Lyon was moving southwest from Jefferson City seeking a decisive battle that would drive the Rebels from the state. To determine Lyon's intent, Price threw his cavalry forward to feel them out.[46] Shelby was in the vanguard of this force.

Shelby's first engagement of the Civil War took place on 5 July 1861 at Carthage, Missouri, where he would play a key role in the Rebel victory. Franz Sigel was in command of Lyon's cavalry force, which was conducting reconnaissance forward to ascertain the Rebel dispositions. Sigel's force were significantly outnumbered when they made contact. Having gained the information he needed, Sigel decided to fall back on the main body. Rains' division would make this a difficult proposition. As Sigel's units were falling back, Shelby noted a gap in Sigel's line and rode right into it scattering them and nearly precipitating a rout, but Sigel was able to recover and make his getaway in good order. The first fight demonstrated some of the key characteristics of Shelby as a commander, including his aggressiveness, initiative, and out-front leadership. These traits would cement his reputation as the best cavalry commander in the west and make the Union army in Missouri fear the Confederate mounted arm in the Trans-Mississippi. Further, Shelby's leadership endeared him to his troops. One trooper described Shelby as a man who "looked like someone who had something to him."[47] It was these unique elements that would save Price's army from destruction in 1864.

Wilson's Creek occurred in August, and again Shelby would exhibit leadership that made him a rising star in the west. Lyon was now moving into southwest Missouri from Springfield hoping to defeat the Confederates before enlistments ran out and the Rebels mustered more strength. Simultaneously, Price and McCulloch were moving northeast to intercept Lyon with Rains' division in the vanguard. Captain Shelby was, with this force, actively seeking out the enemy. Price and McCulloch drew into camp on 9 August planning to move forward again in the morning. This did not happen, as Lyon's army struck before dawn on the 10th, surprising the Rebels along Wilson's Creek. Lyon's blow hit Rains' division especially hard, routing it and carrying Shelby's company along with it. Sterling Price's personal intervention stopped the stampede and Rains' division turned to deliver a blow of its own.[48]

Jo Shelby learned important lessons at Wilson's Creek that would stick with him throughout the war. For one thing, he learned that cavalry charging on horseback toward a formed infantry line was foolhardy. Soon after rallying, Brigadier General Rains assembled for a charge of Lyon's infantry on Oak, or "Bloody," Hill. With Shelby out front, musket fire from the Federal infantry decimated the horsemen. Shelby would never repeat such a maneuver the rest of the war, preferring instead to fight infantry dismounted, or when the enemy was running, on horseback in columns. Second, Rains' division went in with no fire support. With no ability to suppress the Federal infantry, they were able to concentrate their fire on the Rebels. Thus, the second lesson was to always bring artillery forward to support maneuver. Finally, Shelby learned to avoid being surprised by the enemy as the Confederates were at Wilson's Creek.[49] Shelby internalized all these lessons and applied them on many a field with tremendous success.

Shelby and his company rode north with Price's army to Lexington following Wilson's Creek. On the way, Shelby passed through his home in Waverly, which he would rarely see afterward. Since Lexington was primarily an infantry fight with a besieged force, Shelby saw little action. Soon after Lexington fell, Price retreated as converging Union forces were closing in on him. Shelby's unit was used to cover the retreat, to raid, and to recruit fellow Missourians in the fall of 1861. As fall turned to winter Shelby found himself in northwest Arkansas, the Federal army having maneuvered Price completely out of the state. From this point forward, Shelby would see his home only episodically as a part of a raiding force.

Shelby, still a captain, next fought at the decisive Battle of Pea Ridge. This fight was a disaster for the Missouri Rebels, although they fought well. Shelby's company was on the extreme left of the Confederate line at Pea Ridge just east of Elkhorn Tavern. As Price tried to flank Curtis' army, Shelby moved forward dismounted with his company, engaging Federal infantry. He so impressed General Rains that Rains mentioned Shelby in his report, saying, "Captain Shelby ... was much exposed and did efficient service.... [H]is men were dismounted and several under Lieutenant Colonel Bowman in the gallant charge across the field."[50] This was a disheartening loss for the South, and the Missourians in particular, because it solidified the Union's stranglehold on Missouri, a hold they would never relinquish.

Following Pea Ridge, Shelby took his company east with Price's army to Mississippi. Upon crossing the river, they were dismounted and the Lafayette County Cavalry was now infantry. Shelby would not long serve east of the Mississippi. His talent had come to the attention of the Richmond authorities and a colonel's commission was proffered in June 1862 with the condition that he could receive it only if he went back to Missouri to recruit his own regiment. This he readily agreed to do, and accompanied by John N. Edwards—who would become his adjutant and later his biographer—Shelby recrossed the Mississippi at Helena and made for Missouri to recruit his regiment.[51]

By late summer of 1862, Shelby was back in Missouri setting up a recruiting office in Waverly under the noses of Federal authorities. He sent out a published appeal to all Missourians: "By all you hold dear in life, by wife, by mother, by smiling babe, by your hopes of heaven, help us now drive back the invader!" In short order, Shelby had signed up one thousand men and organized them into companies. By October, he was back in Arkansas with his regiment to join the new army forming under the energetic Major General Thomas C. Hindman. At Pineville, Hindman was ecstatic to receive Shelby and his new regiment. He rewarded Shelby with his commission as colonel and elevated him to command of a brigade in Brigadier General John S. Marmaduke's new cavalry division.[52] This united Shelby with what would become a longtime friend and confidante and gave Shelby the opportunity to demonstrate his ability in higher command.

Shelby's chance to demonstrate his mettle would come quickly in the winter campaign that culminated in the Battle of Prairie Grove. It was during this engagement that Jo Shelby would show a skill for which he would become noted—the ability to cover a retreat. General Hindman had performed a near miracle in assembling an army of about 20,000 men in northwest Arkansas in November 1862 after the Army of the West had crossed the Mississippi following Pea Ridge. It was Hindman's intent that the army in the Trans-Mississippi would open up a third front in the war as a relevant theater for the Confederacy. He planned to again challenge Federal control of Missouri by moving his forces north. The Union commanders in Missouri caught wind of the plan and accordingly moved south to preempt Hindman's move. Union forces under Brigadier James G. Blunt—a future antagonist of Shelby in the Great Raid—reinforced by Francis J. Herron, moved into northwest Arkansas seeking a fight in late November.[53] The two armies clashed in the foothills of the Boston Mountains shortly thereafter.

Marmaduke's Division had moved forward on 3 December 1862 to discover the intent and dispositions of the Federal forces while hoping to deceive Blunt into moving into a disadvantageous position that Hindman could assault. At a place called Cane

Hill, Marmaduke stumbled upon Blunt's entire force. Blunt, having the advantage in numbers and infantry, pressed hard on Marmaduke, forcing him to fall back. Marmaduke called on Shelby to cover the retreat. Shelby knew that his cavalry was no match for Blunt in a head-to-head fight; so to delay Blunt's advance, Shelby devised a plan he would implement many times in the future. He decided to wear down Blunt's advance by having each company of his brigade form a battle line using the terrain to its advantage. The companies—all 30 in Shelby's brigade—were stacked in a column each about an eighth of a mile apart. The idea was to force Blunt to deploy multiple times while Shelby inflicted casualties upon Blunt's army the entire distance. Shelby would leapfrog the companies rearward when the fight became too hot. The stratagem worked perfectly and Shelby not only protected Marmaduke's division, he also wore down Blunt to the point that Blunt had to pull back and regroup.[54] Shelby would replicate this performance many times over the next three years, most notably in 1864 when he saved Price from destruction following the Battle of Westport during the Great Raid.

From the battles of Cane Hill and Prairie Grove, Shelby's brigade would receive the nickname of "Iron Brigade" because of its stout defense. But the outcome was as tragic as Pea Ridge had been nine months earlier and only a few miles to the north. While Hindman's solid little army had fought well, the timely arrival of Herron's reinforcements tipped the scales toward Blunt's Union Army of the Frontier at Prairie Grove in early December. Once again the Confederates retreated to the south toward Little Rock, with Marmaduke's division covering the retreat. Hindman's army was suffering from lack of food and had almost exhausted its ammunition during the campaign. It would take months for them to regroup, and by 1863 the Union army had control of all the state north of the Arkansas River.[55]

At this point Shelby's career took a turn, as his brigade became primarily a raiding force. Further, Shelby would cement a professional relationship and friendship with his superior John S. Marmaduke. This team made two raids into Missouri in 1863. While both commanders were excited to reenter their home state, neither event had any appreciable impact on the operational or strategic picture in the Trans-Mississippi. Yet the raids provided instruction to commanders and men alike in how to wreak havoc, preserve the force, and strike fear in the enemy at the tactical level. General Hindman needed some breathing space to recover from Prairie Grove, so he ordered Marmaduke to take his division north into Missouri to provide that relief. The first raid, in January, was meant to break the Union supply line between Rolla and Springfield so that the Federals could not move against Hindman and would possibly withdraw from the Arkansas Valley. The second raid in April aimed at St. Louis and was undertaken to retain Union troops in Missouri and to feed the cavalry that was struggling to subsist in Arkansas.[56] Both raids ultimately failed in their stated objectives, but they did provide the leaders and men with valuable experience.

In particular, Marmaduke and Shelby learned to work "together like forefinger and thumb." These two leaders developed a symbiotic relationship in which they seemed to understand what the other would do or how he would react in any given situation.[57] This would eventually prove fortuitous in 1864 when Price's force came under extreme pressure in the face of the enemy. The second element is that Shelby would learn how far he could push his men, and the troopers came to idolize their commander. Finally,

Shelby learned the art of destroying critical targets while extracting himself and his men from tight situations. In all of Shelby's future operations, his men demonstrated a keen aptitude for destruction and were never pinned down during the course of any operation. This fact, combined with the Iron Brigade's ability to cover a retreating army—learned at Cane Hill—caused Shelby to become known as the "Stuart of the West."[58]

What happened later in the year would nearly break Shelby's heart, almost killing him in the one engagement he participated in that was not a raid. Following the twin raids into Missouri, Theophilus Holmes, demoted from department commander to the command of the District of Arkansas, developed a plan to attempt relieving Vicksburg. The situation there was becoming desperate by late spring, as Major General U.S. Grant's army had pinned down Lieutenant General John C. Pemberton's Confederates in the defenses surrounding the town. The authorities in Richmond began clamoring for action to relieve the city and they were calling upon the army in the Trans-Mississippi to take the offensive. The department finally responded to the pressure by planning an assault on Helena, approximately 100 miles upriver from Vicksburg. The thought behind this operation was that if the Confederates could take Helena, situated on a strategic point overlooking the river, they could challenge control of the river and divert the Union army away from Vicksburg.[59] Thus, the Confederates would complicate the Union's plans for opening the river to the Gulf of Mexico.

The order issued by General Holmes for the assault was quite simple. Each division was to proceed to its designated attack position and execute a frontal assault against the Union army's entrenchments at dawn on the 4th of July. Marmaduke's division, including Shelby's Iron Brigade, was assigned Rightor Hill as its objective. Rightor Hill was strengthened by an earthwork called Fort Salomon, with open ground to the front making the attack on the hill a near impossible proposition. The Iron Brigade stepped off at dawn, moving into the teeth of the Federal defenses, and was promptly decimated. Supporting brigades failed to coordinate their assaults and Shelby's brigade took the brunt of the enemy fire. Seeing the hopelessness of the attack, Shelby gave the order to withdraw. In the process of trying to perform an orderly retreat, Shelby had two horses shot from under him and finally was struck in the elbow by a minié ball. In spite of a painful wound, Shelby stayed on the field until his surviving soldiers were out of danger. This wound would affect Shelby's ability to perform simple tasks for the rest of his life, as he suffered permanent nerve damage as a result.[60] The entire Confederate army suffered egregiously on this day, losing 1,636 men in the assault, the Iron Brigade taking its blows in proportion. The saddest part of the Helena debacle was the fact that before the assault even commenced Vicksburg had fallen. The entire sacrifice was for naught, and from this moment forward the Trans-Mississippi Department was cut off from the rest of the Confederacy.

After the unfortunate Helena affair, Shelby got his first chance for independent command. This expedition would become known as Shelby's Great Raid. Jo Shelby got permission to conduct the raid from the new commander of the Trans-Mississippi Department, Lieutenant General E. Kirby Smith, after hard lobbying by the recently installed new governor of Missouri, Thomas C. Reynolds. Shelby proposed such a move in a conversation with Reynolds, who responded simply with an affirmative: "Go."

Reynolds added that he would see to it that success would lead to the "buff sash of a brigadier."⁶¹ Shelby commenced his raid on 22 September 1863 from Arkadelphia, riding harder and further than any other Rebel cavalry expedition to this point in the war. The raid took forty-one days and wreaked enormous destruction through central Missouri, tearing up miles of railroad track and burning millions of dollars worth of supplies and equipment. In spite of the fact that every Union force in Missouri mobilized to capture Shelby, his 1,200 troopers thoroughly confounded their pursuers.⁶² The raid allowed Shelby to demonstrate what he was capable of and reinforced all of the lessons he had learned to that point in the war. Most important, Shelby gained a reputation as the best cavalry leader west of the Mississippi. He carried this reputation forward into 1864, and he became the rock upon which Price would lean every time a crisis arose and Price needed results.

As spring approached in 1864, the Union armies in the Trans-Mississippi were on the move. By April it appeared for a time that they might eliminate the Trans-Mississippi Department as a viable entity of the Confederacy. However, as already noted, the Confederates successfully parried the blows in Louisiana and Arkansas, and Shelby's Iron Brigade played an integral role. While Shelby is better known for his other exploits, like his 1863 raid, Camden may have been his finest hour. Finally confirmed as a brigadier by Congress in March, Shelby led his brigade forward to impede Steele in moving south. When Kirby Smith removed all of Price's infantry to fight in Louisiana, he left only horsemen to stop Steele. Shelby's brigade was in front, and to slow Steele, Shelby implemented a plan to destroy everything that could sustain Steele's army. Using skills learned throughout the war, Shelby removed food from the reach of Steele's foragers and struck at his supply trains. Further, the brigade harassed Steele so thoroughly that Steele's army could find no rest or food. As a result, Steele was forced to regroup at Camden. When the Confederates destroyed Steele's train at Marks' Mills—with Shelby playing the decisive role—Steele knew the campaign was over and he had to return to Little Rock.⁶³ This freed the Rebels to move into Missouri in the fall.

The stage was now set for Shelby's participation in the Great Raid. The previous three years had thoroughly prepared him for what would occur in Missouri in 1864. His responsibilities would multiply for the campaign as he rose to division command in Price's Army of Missouri. Shelby, with his division, would become the foundational unit of the army and the success or failure of the army would turn on the performance of Shelby. He would not let Price down.

One of the key partners in division command with Shelby during the raid was his old friend and commander John Sappington Marmaduke. Of all the senior leaders in Price's Army of Missouri, Marmaduke was the only native Missourian. He was born on 14 March 1833 in Arrow Rock, Missouri, to Governor Meredith Miles and his wife, Lavinia Sappington Marmaduke. Although John was a native of Missouri, his father had migrated from Kentucky, the home state of Shelby. Like Jo Shelby, Marmaduke was descended from a long line of prominent leaders. John's great-grandfather, John Breathitt, was the governor of Kentucky at the time of young Marmaduke's birth. Marmaduke never knew his great-grandfather, as Breathitt died in office when John was only a year old.

Much like his confidante, Shelby, and commander, Price, Marmaduke had a happy childhood growing up on a farm. These formative years produced what one might expect from a planter's son growing up along the Missouri River. Marmaduke's outlook was southern in orientation as a pro-slavery Democrat, even though his father leaned toward the unconditional Unionist camp. Meredith brought John up to take on martial airs as a soldier and saw to it that he was prepared for his future with a suitable education so that he could attend West Point. As a young boy, John attended Chapel Hill Academy in Lafayette County—the future home of Jo Shelby. In his son's middle teen years, Meredith Marmaduke sent him to the Masonic College in Lexington, the focal point of the battle in 1861. At age seventeen, Marmaduke went east to college at Yale, where he studied for two years starting in 1850. In 1852, he left Yale to attend Harvard for another year. Unlike Shelby and Price, Marmaduke was a much more accomplished scholar with an aptitude for learning. This talent won him the coveted appointment to West Point from Congressman John S. Phelps, a family friend, in 1853. He entered the academy later that year and attended the summer encampment on the plain. This would set him on a path to a career as a military officer and eventual command in the Confederate army.[64]

Marmaduke grew up with many luminaries in Missouri including his uncle, and later governor, Claiborne F. Jackson. Since Marmaduke's father was an unconditional Unionist, it is likely that the influences of friends and other family members were of greater importance. In particular, his uncle Claiborn had the most influence upon the young mind of Marmaduke when the secession crisis did come to Missouri. In 1861 Marmaduke did not hesitate to resign his commission to offer his services to Jackson as the war came to Missouri.[65]

Brigadier General John S. Marmaduke, Commander, 2nd Division, Army of Missouri (Library of Congress).

Marmaduke arrived at West Point much older than his classmates, at age twenty. At a time when it was not unusual to have sixteen-year-old cadets, Marmaduke must have seemed grandfatherly in contrast to his peers. While he was bright and had a thorough education before his arrival at the academy, John's final class standing reveals a young man who tended to enjoy a prank at the expense of his studies. In 1857 when he graduated, Marmaduke stood 30th out of a class of 38 students. This meant that he would not have the pick of branches within the army, as the higher performing cadets got the coveted slots in the Engineer Corps. In spite of this, the branch Marmaduke received suited him perfectly, as he got a lieutenancy in the cavalry.[66]

Marmaduke gained valuable experience as a leader in the 1850s before the crisis came to

Missouri. Upon being commissioned as a second lieutenant, Marmaduke found himself in the 1st United States Mounted Rifles. After a short stint there, he was transferred to the newly formed and elite 2nd Cavalry Regiment. This unit had many future Civil War senior commanders on both sides, including its commander, Albert Sidney Johnston. Additionally, Robert E. Lee, George Thomas, J.E.B. Stuart and John Bell Hood served in the ranks of the regiment. Serving with men of this stature certainly facilitated Marmaduke's development as a leader. Further, he gained leadership experience when the 2nd Cavalry was sent to Utah Territory to put down an uprising by the Mormons in late 1857.[67]

The Mormon War began in 1857 when President James Buchanan sent U.S. troops into Utah after declaring the citizens of the territory in rebellion against the government. The dispute revolved around the free practice of the Mormon religion, which they believed was guaranteed by distance from the central government at Washington. Buchanan sent the army in on 29 June 1857 when he issued the mobilization order to Lieutenant General Winfield Scott. The expedition assembled at Fort Leavenworth, and the 2,500 troops comprising the force began the march to Utah on 18 July. The army made its way west in packets, with the cavalry moving out last under Johnston's personal leadership. Marmaduke was in this group in September, and the westward trek proved a challenge to all the leaders. Starting the expedition so late in the season meant that a winter crossing of the Rockies would cause great suffering among the troops.[68] Motivating men to continue the mission under arduous conditions is probably the greatest lesson Marmaduke took from the campaign.

While the army was en route, several skirmishes occurred between the Mormon Navoo Legion and army wagon trains and non–Mormon settlers. The Mormon strategy was to deny sustenance to the army, preventing it from arriving in Utah or causing debilitating attrition among the force if they did make it to the territory. This, combined with winter conditions, halted movement of the army at Fort Bridger, Wyoming Territory, for the duration of 1857. Johnston did not recommence the expedition until spring 1858, finally arriving at Salt Lake City in April. The campaign ended here when territorial governor Brigham Young promptly surrendered with the understanding that a full pardon for all Utah citizens was forthcoming if they accepted the sovereignty of the U.S. government.[69] While Marmaduke was not involved in fighting, the journey taught the young lieutenant much about leadership that would be of value when his Confederate troops suffered during drawn out raids in Missouri. In addition to the critical lesson of maintaining morale, Marmaduke learned about sustaining the force and gleaned information from the outstanding leaders in the 2nd Cavalry. This would follow him into his career as a senior Confederate officer.

When the sectional crisis culminated in the firing on Fort Sumter, Marmaduke immediately resigned his commission in the U.S. Army and offered his services to Missouri under the erroneous belief that the state had seceded. He made his way back from New Mexico Territory, where he was posted in 1861, to present his credentials to the governor, his uncle, Claiborne F. Jackson. His father, while Southern in so many ways, objected to his son's actions as he was an unconditional Unionist. The young Marmaduke remained firm in his decision supporting secession and effectively split the family as well. Governor Jackson, desperate for experienced officers for the ragtag Missouri State Guard, quickly accepted the services of his nephew. Jackson commissioned Marmaduke as colonel of the 1st Regiment of Rifles in the Missouri State Guard.[70]

With commission in hand, Marmaduke got to work organizing his regiment at the encampment of the guard in Boonville, but this would prove an uphill climb. The Missouri State Guard lacked every necessity, which made efforts to train the raw troops difficult. Further, the Union army under Lyon was on the move toward the capital at Jefferson City, forcing the untrained troops to prepare for movement rather than focusing on their training. Lyon's little army took Jefferson City on 16 June 1861, with the government under Jackson fleeing shortly before the Unionists arrived. Wasting no time, Lyon pressed on the next day headed for Boonville to break up the Missouri State Guard training camp. Jackson arrived in Boonville and ordered the 1st Regiment of Rifles under Marmaduke to make a stand. Marmaduke favored withdrawal since he knew his troops could not fight effectively against Lyon's regulars. An argument ensued between the two before Marmaduke acquiesced to the wishes of his uncle. Predictably, the 1st Regiment fled the field before the well-trained Federal force. The Rebels ran so precipitously before the Union army that the Federals dubbed the engagement the "Boonville Races."[71]

Marmaduke was so angered by Jackson's failure to listen to his professional advice that he resigned his Missouri commission. Still interested in serving the Southern cause, Marmaduke traveled to Richmond to offer his services directly to the Confederate government. The fledgling Rebel government was desperate for trained, experienced officers and immediately proffered a commission as a first lieutenant in the regular Confederate Army. Marmaduke accepted the appointment as a cavalry lieutenant and left for the west to report to Brigadier General William Hardee for duty. By 1 January 1862, Marmaduke was elected lieutenant colonel of the 1st Arkansas Battalion.[72] Shortly thereafter, Marmaduke was selected to participate in an interesting program that the Confederate army attempted to implement.

In 1862 the Confederate army tried to form a hard core of regulars, establishing a national army based on the U.S. model. The legislation establishing the organization was passed by the Confederate congress on 6 March 1861. It authorized 15,015 men and 744 officers—almost exactly the strength of the regular U.S. Army at the start of the Civil War. In early 1862 the Confederate war department attempted to bring the organization to fruition by redesignating some state regiments with the moniker "Confederate." Among these was Marmaduke's Arkansas battalion, which was reflagged as the 3rd Confederate Regiment, with Marmaduke promoted to full colonel in the Confederate regular army.[73]

The 3rd Confederate Regiment was brigaded with Brigadier General Thomas C. Hindman's Arkansans in Hardee's corps of General Albert Sidney Johnston's Army of the Mississippi. In March 1862, the situation in Tennessee was deteriorating rapidly, as the Union army under U.S. Grant had cracked Johnston's far-flung defensive line in Kentucky. Nashville quickly fell after the capture of Forts Henry and Donelson, and the Confederate army had fallen back all the way into north Mississippi. It appeared at this point that the whole Confederate Department of the West might collapse. Johnston had different ideas. To recover the lost ground, he decided to conduct a surprise attack on the advancing Union army at their Pittsburg Landing bivouac. The 3rd Confederate would play a prominent role in what would become the important and decisive battle of Shiloh.

On 6 April 1862 Johnston spent the morning trooping the line of assembling soldiers, encouraging them before they went into battle. As he was moving along, he recognized one of his old lieutenants from the Utah expedition. Now a colonel, Marmaduke received his old commander and his words of encouragement. Placing his hand on Marmaduke's shoulder, Johnston told him that "we must this day conquer or perish."[74] For Johnston, these words would prove prophetic, as the Confederates would lose the battle and he would perish. Nevertheless, Marmaduke would do his part to win a victory for his commander.

Hardee's corps advanced toward Shiloh in the van of Johnston's army and made first contact with Grant's army at Shiloh. Marmaduke's regiment took some of the first prisoners of the day as they plowed through the Federal camp, causing chaos among the unprepared Union units. The 3rd Confederate continued to advance steadily throughout the morning, overrunning every position they encountered until they ran up against stiff resistance at a place called the Hornet's Nest. Braxton Bragg's corps had attempted to reduce this strongpoint for some time, but his brigades were unable to crack the defenders under Brigadier General Benjamin Prentiss. Elements of Hardee's corps—including the 3rd Confederate—reinforced Bragg in the early afternoon. As Marmaduke moved the regiment forward, a group of Union sharpshooters threatened the flank of a sister brigade. That unit requested assistance and Marmaduke responded by exclaiming, "Let's go for them!" The 3rd Regiment's charge, backed by artillery, proved sufficient in silencing the pesky marksmen. By 3:00 in the afternoon the Confederates were massing for the final assault on the Hornet's Nest. In spite of a heavy sheet of fire from the Union line, Marmaduke's regiment, with the rest of the charging Rebels, finally broke Prentiss' defenses.[75] With nightfall coming on, the Confederate army consolidated for a final attack in the morning to drive the Union army into the Tennessee River.

Unfortunately for the Army of the Mississippi, Grant's army was reinforced that night by over 17,000 soldiers from Major General Don Carlos Buell's Army of the Ohio. As the Confederates prepared for the morning attack, they were preempted by a surprise assault by Grant's reinforced army. In the melee to hold the ground taken the previous day, Marmaduke was severely wounded. He was evacuated from the field as the Rebels began their retreat on 7 April back to Corinth. Marmaduke was in the hospital for over a month and incapacitated for several more as he worked to recover from the wound. During that time, he was recognized for his leadership and valor at Shiloh by a promotion to brigadier general.[76] The next time Marmaduke took the field, at Prairie Grove, he did so as a general officer in command of a division, at 29 years of age.

In late September 1862 Marmaduke was transferred to Arkansas and reunited with his former commander at Shiloh, Thomas C. Hindman. Marmaduke was promptly given command of Hindman's cavalry division, with Jo Shelby serving as one of his brigade commanders. This began the association of Marmaduke and Shelby, which was both professional and personal and would prove beneficial to both men. By late fall, Hindman was planning for a campaign to clear northwest Arkansas of Union forces, followed by a movement into Missouri. His plans were upset when Brigadier General James Blunt moved first, challenging him for control of the region. To determine Blunt's intentions Hindman threw his cavalry forward into the Boston Mountains. Marmaduke encountered Blunt—who would crop up over and over as Marmaduke's antagonist—near Cane Hill on 28 November 1862. Blunt, having infantry and outnumbering Marmaduke, immediately attacked Marmaduke's division. Blunt's strength quickly came to bear, threatening to inflict a decisive defeat on Marmaduke in rough terrain. Having learned the information he needed, Marmaduke decided to withdraw to prevent becoming decisively engaged. He called upon Shelby to form the rear guard to facilitate the withdrawal, and as previously mentioned, Shelby performed splendidly, forever earning Marmaduke's admiration and gratitude.[77]

Marmaduke successfully extricated his division and reported the Federal dispositions to Hindman. Armed with the report, Hindman decided to attack Blunt before reinforcements could reach him, giving Hindman the best chance of defeating Blunt. On 7 December 1862, the two armies met at Prairie Grove, and Marmaduke played an important role, winning Hindman's praise in later reports of the fight. The division scouted forward of Hindman's army and made the first contact of the day. After developing the situation and reporting, Marmaduke's division received orders to protect the right flank while Hindman plunged ahead with the infantry attack interposing between Blunt and approaching reinforcements.[78] The combined force of Blunt and reinforcements from Brigadier General Herron prevented Hindman from sweeping the field. As a result, Hindman was checked and unable to continue his advance north into Missouri. One author would write that "it was largely because of Marmaduke's cavalry that the Confederates enjoyed what success they did" in the Prairie Grove campaign.[79]

Marmaduke covered Hindman's retreat to the south with a heavy heart. He, like every other Missourian, had high hopes of reentering Missouri to liberate the state. With the defeat at Prairie Grove, the Missourians were once again dejected, as they were after Pea Ridge. However, as a cavalryman, Marmaduke might have the opportunity to do something on his own. After arriving at Little Rock, Marmaduke and Hindman began discuss ways to disrupt Federal control in Missouri. The only feasible way to have any effect was through a raid focused on destruction of the depot at Springfield. Thus, Hindman authorized Marmaduke to launch the first of two raids he would conduct into Missouri in 1863.[80] These expeditions—conducted with his chief lieutenant, Jo Shelby—provided Marmaduke with critical experience as an independent commander that would help prevent Price's Great Raid from resulting in the complete destruction of the force.

The first raid stepped off on 31 December 1862 but it had only minimal operational effects on Federal control of the state, as already demonstrated. At best, both raids served only to give the Rebels and their commanders tactical experience. Marmaduke arrived at Springfield on 8 January 1863 and launched an unsuccessful attack on the Federal garrison, thus failing in the raid's expressed purpose. However, Marmaduke salvaged some good from the effort, as his men destroyed much of the rail link to St. Louis, as well as the garrisons along the route. Converging Federal forces pushed Marmaduke back to Arkansas by the end of the month.[81] While the Rebels had created a great deal of havoc, the Federals still had solid control of the state and Marmaduke was back in Arkansas. Therefore, the raid was not a success.

The second raid that Marmaduke led into Missouri took place in April and had a more dubious purpose and less effect on the operational picture in the state than had the January expedition. When Marmaduke returned to Arkansas in late January, there was little feed or forage for man or beast. With the land in the immediate vicinity of Little Rock stripped of sustenance, Marmaduke would not be able to sustain his cavalry. Further, without forage for the horses, the division would lose its striking power and effectiveness. As a result, Marmaduke concluded that the best way to prevent a decline in readiness was to keep his division on the move. He reasoned that if he was going to have to keep moving, he might as well conduct an operation in Missouri, and this is exactly what he did.[82]

The second raid commenced on 18 April 1863 and was spread out on a wide axis to provide the greatest ability to forage. The target of this expedition was Rolla, but the region surrounding the town was so stripped of provender that Marmaduke could not feed his force. He thus determined to divert further east toward Ironton and Cape Girardeau on the Mississippi. The entire raid was ill-fated, as a string of incidents of bad luck dogged Marmaduke, such as when a heavy storm foiled his plans to raid Bloomfield. The raid concluded with an abortive assault on the entrenchments at Cape Girardeau on 26 April. Assessing that the fortifications were impregnable, Marmaduke decided to withdraw to Arkansas. The net result of this raid was the destruction of some minor Federal outposts and the addition of about 200 recruits to the ranks.[83] Beyond this, Marmaduke's second raid was a failure, and further, it proved the strength of the hold the Union retained over Missouri. Yet none of the senior leaders from the state would acknowledge this fact. Finally, the raid demonstrated something about its commander. While Marmaduke was certainly a competent leader at the tactical level, he did not necessarily have the faculties for strategic thinking, nor did he have the flair of Jo Shelby. One trait he did have in ample quantity was an explosive temper, which he would soon exhibit at Helena.

The disaster at Helena was one of the saddest affairs to befall the Rebels west of the Mississippi during the entire war. With Vicksburg teetering on the brink of falling into Union hands, the government scrambled to do anything to relieve the city. The Trans-Mississippi contribution to the effort was an attack on Helena for the purpose of diverting Federal forces from Vicksburg and threatening the closing of the river further upstream. The attack took place on 4 July 1863, the day of the formal surrender at Vicksburg. Marmaduke was assigned Fort Rightor as his objective in the assault on Helena, supported on his left flank by the brigade commanded by Brigadier General Lucien M. Walker. Marmaduke was heavily repulsed by the Federals on Rightor Hill and he believed the reason was Walker's failure to support him as planned. Marmaduke's complaints found their way into his after action report, irritating Walker.[84] This began a series of barbs traded by Marmaduke and Walker that culminated in a contest of honor between the two.

Following the battle at Helena, Marmaduke accused Walker of cowardice for his actions at Rightor Hill, as well as perceived slights in rearguard actions as they retreated. Walker took offense, and in a note dated 2 September 1863 he requested clarification. Marmaduke responded with a thinly veiled insult noting that he was "determined no longer to serve under you." Later Marmaduke—though he never called Walker a coward—added that "General Walker avoided all positions of danger during the retreat," in effect accusing Walker of the cowardice he would not state explicitly. This was too much for Walker, who sent a request back to Marmaduke to "demand satisfaction" to defend his honor. Marmaduke agreed to Walker's demand to meet at 6:00 p.m. on 6 September outside Little Rock. That evening Marmaduke fatally wounded Walker, who died the next morning with a .44 caliber bullet lodged in his spine. After wounding Walker, Marmaduke's anger immediately subsided and a deep sense of remorse came over him. Though he was never punished for the incident, he always regretted what happened, and the incident may have tempered his behavior in the future.[85]

As the year 1864 approached, the Confederates in the west appeared to be on the ropes. But they would quickly turn the table of fortune to their advantage and Marmaduke would play a prominent—and infamous—role in this during the Camden Expedition. When the Union army launched the Red River Campaign and supporting Camden Expedition, the overmatched Rebels had a tough decision to make: where to make their main defense. Kirby Smith first decided to make the primary effort in Louisiana, leaving Sterling Price with the cavalry to delay and harass the thrust from Little Rock under Frederick Steele. Marmaduke and his division heavily contested Steele's southward march from the crossing of the Little Missouri River all the way to Camden, including a heavy engagement at Prairie D'Ane forcing Steele to Camden. However, it is at Poison Spring that Marmaduke won a lopsided victory and then entered the realm of controversy.

In mid–April 1864 Steele was desperate to supply his army with food and forage to enable them to continue south to Shreveport. To feed his army, Steele began to send out foraging parties from Camden to scour the countryside. One column consisting of 670 soldiers, including 438 from the 1st Kansas (Colored) was escorting 177 wagons filled with forage around Poison Spring on 17 April 1864. Sterling Price sent out a large cavalry detachment under Marmaduke to intercept the foraging party. Marmaduke made contact by springing a large L-shaped ambush that caught the train and its escort in a vise. After some hard fighting the Confederates overran the escort, forcing some of the soldiers to escape back to Camden while others surrendered, including the 1st Kansas. The controversy arose when Rebels from Samuel B. Maxey's division murdered the prisoners, even scalping some of their victims.[86] As the commander on the field, Marmaduke was responsible for this breach of the law of war and indiscipline of the troops. Yet he deflected the blame to some of the Choctaw soldiers in Maxey's unit. This incident points to something of a flaw in Marmaduke's character that first manifested itself in the Walker duel. While Marmaduke exhibited fine tactical acumen, he tended to be hotheaded, with an unwillingness to accept responsibility for his own actions or his troops when they crossed the line of decency. This was not helpful when discipline was of the essence in independent operations. Lax control would too often characterize the actions of the Rebels when they entered Missouri later in the year, thus pushing the very populace they claimed to be liberating away from their orbit.

The 3rd Division commander and key commander in the Great Missouri Raid was Brigadier General James Fleming Fagan. He, like his peers and Price, fought in all of the major battles that occurred in the west. However, unlike Fagan's fellow commanders, he was the only one who did not claim Missouri as his home state. Even so, his background is similar to the others, with familial ties to Kentucky and a later emigration to the west. James Fagan was born in Clark County near Louisville, Kentucky, in 1828 to a middle-class farm family. When James was ten years old, his father moved to the new state of Arkansas, settling in Little Rock. In addition to his farming occupation, James' father was a skilled craftsman and a contractor. When Arkansas sought to build its new state house, he was awarded one of the contracts and began working on the capitol soon thereafter. However, two years after arriving in Arkansas, Fagan's father died, leaving his mother, Catherine, to raise twelve-year-old James and his siblings as a widow.[87]

By 1842 Catherine Fagan had married Samuel Adams, a politician and state treasurer of Arkansas. As James's stepfather, Adams would have great influence on him and shape his world outlook. One of the reasons for this is that Samuel Adams would become governor of Arkansas in 1844 following the resignation of Archibald Yell. This occurrence introduced Fagan to the world of politics. Adams was a Democrat and a Unionist with southern leanings. Adams, a popular figure, was well-to-do and owned a plantation on the Saline River in southern Arkansas. This stabilized the financial situation for young Fagan, his mother and siblings, and gave him a planter's perspective. Yet, although Adams had brought a measure of prosperity to the family, he would pass away in Fagan's late teens, leaving Fagan's mother a widow once again. But this time Fagan would step forward to support the family, assuming the role of manager of the plantation to ensure it continued to produce.[88] As a result, he matured quickly and kept the family from falling into financial ruin.

In the late 1840s, the nation was restlessly pushing westward, inevitably causing a clash between the U.S. and its neighbor to the south, Mexico. By 1846 the U.S. was at war over the location of the southern boundary of Texas. Arkansas, a frontier state at that time, began to raise troops to fill the ranks of the army after the country declared war. Arkansas quickly raised several hundred men, and among these the 1st Arkansas Cavalry was formed under the command of former governor and sitting congressman Colonel Archibald Yell. James Fagan got swept up by war fever and immediately enlisted in the 1st Arkansas when the call for troops went out. By July 1846 the regiment received orders to march to San Antonio, Texas, to get arms and equipment for active service.[89]

Upon arrival the 1st Arkansas Cavalry was brigaded with other units assembling at the training camp at San Antonio, with all coming under command of an old War of 1812 veteran, Major General John E. Wool. Fagan would learn much about soldiering during his time with the army in Mexico, and among other things he would learn the value of discipline. At the training camp disease became rampant as men from around the country were pressed together into close quarters. Many of the men fell victim to various deadly diseases like cholera and measles. Dozens of Arkansans died before the regiment moved from San Antonio into the theater of war.[90]

In the fall, the new brigade was on the move to Chihuahua in Mexico to consolidate gains made by Major General Zachary Taylor's army in the wake of winning the battle of Monterrey. Initially, the 1st Arkansas engaged in picket duty to secure the area. This proved boring and uneventful except for the occasional ranchero raids[91] that would disrupt the boredom. Then, in February 1847, the Arkansans and Fagan fought their first battle, at Buena Vista.

General Antonio Lopez de Santa Anna, commanding all Mexican forces, decided to retrieve his losses by attacking the dispersed army of Zachary Taylor at Buena Vista. Santa Anna brought over 20,000 troops to the plateau near the town to oppose Taylor's 5,000 men. Over the course of the 22–23 February 1847 battle Taylor's army fought a desperate defense against repeated assaults by Mexican infantry and lancers. In all of these the 1st Regiment, with James Fagan, was in the thick of the fight. On the 23rd, when the American left flank collapsed, Colonel Yell led a countercharge that broke up the attackers and stabilized the defense. In the melee Colonel Yell lost his life, but the Americans won the battle and the Mexicans lost the initiative.[92] Fagan, as a young trooper, gained invaluable combat experience, but he also learned from Yell's example. Cavalry was best used for shock and could achieve this effect on the battlefield only if led from the front. Fagan would take these lessons forward with him into the Civil War when he would lead both infantry and cavalry.

Service in the Mexican War set Fagan on a path to success upon his return to Arkansas. After enlisting in the 1st Arkansas as a private in 1846, he returned home as a lieutenant, due to his bravery and leadership. This made him a respected citizen in his community along the Saline River. His newfound stature translated into his election to represent Saline County in the Arkansas state legislature in the 1850s. What makes this fact interesting is that Fagan won his election as a Whig in the overwhelmingly Democrat Saline County.[93] This demonstrates the popularity Fagan had achieved in the war, winning election by gaining crossover votes. As a Whig, he was a Unionist, but in the 1850s the party was dying and as a slaveholder he could not become a Republican and retain any self-respect. Thus, when secession swept the South, men like Fagan reluctantly fell in line when Arkansas finally left the Union and offered their services to the new Confederacy.

The new Confederate government was pleased to receive men of Fagan's experience and he was accepted into service in the Confederate States Army. After Arkansas made its decision to secede following Fort Sumter, Fagan raised a company of volunteers and became captain of the unit. Upon consolidation of several companies to form a regiment, he was elected colonel due to his experience and leadership ability. This unit became the 1st Arkansas Infantry when fully organized in the fall of 1861.[94] It is interesting to note that, unlike his peers in the Army of Missouri, Fagan would start his career in the Confederate army as an infantry commander instead of in cavalry. This would have no detrimental effects on his later performance as a mounted commander and may have even enhanced his ability through an understanding of the different major branches of the army. Not much happened in the first months of the war for Fagan, whose regiment was brigaded with a number of Louisiana regiments under the command of Colonel Randall K. Gibson. The brigade was sent east of the Mississippi and there continued to train and prepare to defend General Albert S. Johnston's long line in Kentucky.

In February 1862 Johnston's line cracked at Forts Henry and Donelson, and the Confederate remnants began consolidating at Corinth, Mississippi. The 1st Arkansas, now a part of General Braxton Bragg's corps, moved to Corinth forming the nucleus of the Army of Mississippi. Johnston, knowing the gravity of the situation, circulated among the various assembling units at Corinth. As he trooped the line he found Gibson's Brigade and told the brigade commander, "*We must win a victory.*"[95] This fledgling army began movement toward the encamped Union army at Pittsburg Landing on 5 April 1862. The next morning, Bragg's corps was third in the line of march, and by midafternoon the 1st Arkansas was involved in the struggle for the Hornet's Nest. After overrunning a series of Union encampments, the Rebels finally struck something solid near a sunken road bordering Duncan Field.

Following initial contact, Bragg began to spread his line out to the southeast of the field in an effort to flank the sunken road. In the meantime, he launched a series of frontal assaults on the Union held by Brigadier General Benjamin Prentiss's division. To reach their attack position, Fagan's 1st Arkansas and sister regiments had to pass behind other units already in line from Bragg's corps, including Marmaduke's 3rd Confederate. They had to push through a thick stand of undergrowth that broke apart regimental and brigade organization. In the midst of the thickets, nervous soldiers began firing into the underbrush, believing they were in contact with Union units. Unfortunately, it was Louisianans firing into Arkansans and vice versa. Colonel Fagan ran to the nearby 4th Louisiana and screamed to the nearest captain to "for God's sake cease firing."[96]

Once Fagan untangled the situation a new menace in the form of a Union ambush staggered the 1st Arkansas and Gibson's brigade. The foliage was so thick that the Confederates had marched to within 100 yards of the enemy line when the unseen Federal defense unleashed a sheet of flame, halting the Confederate advance. Fagan, leading from the front, had his horse shot from under him as he rallied the faltering advance. As he pulled back to re-form, Bragg came along and pressed Gibson's brigade forward once again to attack the hard-pressed Federals in the Hornet's Nest. Late in the afternoon the Rebels had successfully curled around Prentiss's division and forced the Federals to surrender.[97] Throughout the fight, Fagan was actively leading his regiment and encouraging the men to accomplish the mission through personal example. Just as Colonel Yell had led the 1st Arkansas Cavalry out front in the Mexican War, his young protégé applied that lesson starting at Shiloh. Fagan would throughout the war lead his units at the front and his men responded accordingly.

Shortly after Shiloh, the Confederacy recognized Fagan's bravery and leadership by promoting him to brigadier general and giving him command of a brigade. The promotion was effective 12 September 1862 and he assumed command of a brigade composed entirely of Arkansans in the Trans-Mississippi Department. Fagan joined the army that Major General Thomas C. Hindman was forming in northwest Arkansas. Fagan would soon see action alongside Marmaduke and Shelby at Cane Hill and Prairie Grove, starting an association that would last through the rest of the war. Fagan's new brigade joined Dandridge McRae's brigade as a part of Brigadier General Francis A. Shoup's division.[98] In late November, Hindman's men were on the move to drive the Federals from northwest Arkansas, and with luck, they would enter Missouri to challenge Union control of the state.

On 5 December, both sides were attempting to fix the position of the other near Prairie Grove. Brigadier General Blunt was marching toward reinforcements under Brigadier General Herron in an attempt to consolidate forces to prevent Hindman from defeating each column separately. Simultaneously, Hindman was pressing hard to bring Blunt to battle before he could unite with Herron. Blunt would win the race, much to the chagrin of Hindman. On 7 December, Hindman had his army on the road early, at 4:00 a.m. with Fagan leading Shoup's division as they advanced. Marmaduke's cavalry came into contact with Herron around mid-morning and Hindman passed his lead infantry division, Shoup's, to the front to initiate an all-out attack. Shortly after issuing the order, Hindman countermanded it and had Shoup set up a defensive position behind the Illinois River to receive Herron's attack. This effectively surrendered the initiative to the Federals, and Blunt did not fail to take advantage of it, moving to the sound of battle to concentrate with Herron. Fagan's brigade anchored this defense on the Confederate right flank. This made Fagan the key to the entire position, and he performed with skill and calmness, repulsing several attacks. At one point, he counterattacked, capturing a battery.[99] But, as we have already seen, the Confederates could not drive Blunt and Herron from the field and Hindman was forced to retreat.

Fagan had again exhibited competence and out-front leadership at Prairie Grove, as he had at Shiloh, with accolades again flowing his way. Governor Thomas C. Reynolds of Missouri wrote of Fagan, "[A]ll tell me Fagan is by far the best of the Arkansas brigadiers."[100] Yet, in spite of his effort, the Rebels had lost another battle, and the demoralized remnants of Hindman's army made their way to Little Rock to regroup. The next big battle for Fagan would occur at Helena, where once again the Rebels would have their hearts broken. As noted, Helena was an attempt to divert Union forces encircling Vicksburg to relieve that critical bastion. Theophilus Holmes marshaled his forces in Arkansas far too late to have any effect on the siege at Vicksburg. Nevertheless, the attempt to take Helena was made anyway on 4 July 1863, with James Fagan's infantry brigade taking on a critical role.

Holmes ordered Fagan to take Fort Hindman, which was one of several fortifications ringing Helena. With 1,770 men, Fagan was to launch a frontal assault at dawn on the 4th of July. Opposing him was a formidable earthwork defended by several hundred Union infantrymen. With only a slight advantage in numbers, Fagan launched his assault as ordered, with Sterling Price's division to his right and Marmaduke on the left. The assault was a disaster, serving only to produce a long casualty list for the attackers, including Fagan's infantry brigade. A combination of the stout Union defense, timing and coordination served to ensure that the Confederate army failed.[101] Fagan retreated with the rest of the Rebels, crestfallen at his losses and yet another defeat in battle and a misguided strategy. The Confederates again drew back to Little Rock to recuperate.

The sojourn in the Arkansas capital proved short lived, as the Confederates were soon driven from Little Rock by Frederick Steele's small army. Not only was a move into Missouri out of the question, but the Rebels also had now lost over half of Arkansas. The Confederate force now commanded by Sterling Price consolidated in southwest Arkansas around the town of Camden. It was during the upcoming Camden Expedition that Fagan would realize his greatest success as a commander, receive a promotion, and take command of a cavalry division. As the Red River Campaign got underway, Steele launched his prong of the operation from Little Rock on 23 March 1864. The advance was harassed by Price's sizeable cavalry forces he had marshaled at Camden. Key to arresting Steele's advance short of its objective at Shreveport was cutting off his lines of communication.[102] In this endeavor, the Confederates under Price were eminently successful, and Fagan wielded the blow that convinced Steele to give up the advance.

Steele had halted his army at Camden the first week of April because of the lack of sustenance available to his animals and men. By stopping in Camden—halfway to Shreveport—he hoped to gather the needed forage to continue the advance in conjunction with Banks in Louisiana. To counter this effort the Rebels launched an aggressive series of strokes to destroy Steele's trains and foraging operations. Marmaduke successfully destroyed a party of foragers at Poison Spring on 18 April 1864. However, the big blow came on 25 April when Fagan, with Shelby, all but destroyed Steele's train at the battle of Marks' Mill and severed his line of communication at Pine Bluff. In a well-planned and well-executed ambush, Fagan and Shelby fell on a train of 240 wagons guarded by about 1,600 men commanded by Lieutenant Colonel Francis M. Drake. In an admirable example of cooperation, Fagan and Shelby perfectly timed the attacks near the crossroads of Marks' Mill and captured the train and most of the guard force.[103] As a result of this brilliant attack, Steele abandoned Camden, making a hasty retreat that was dogged the whole way by Price's now reinforced army. Fagan traversed back through his home as the pursuit carried the Rebel army past the Saline River Valley. Thus, the table was set to follow up the successful defense along the Red and in Arkansas with a thrust into Missouri.

The men who commanded Price's Army of Missouri all had a passion for the state from which the army took its name—including Fagan, who desired an invasion into Missouri to relieve Arkansas. Each of the Confederate commanders had a vast amount of experience in all of the major battles fought in the Trans-Mississippi, as well as east of the river. They were all familiar with each other and they all had strengths and weaknesses that would come to the fore in the Great Raid. It is the Confederate army commander, with his division chiefs, that gave the army its collective personality and outlook. Price, Shelby, Marmaduke, and Fagan provided the direction, impetus, and energy to the Great Missouri Raid and would ultimately take responsibility for any successes and failures. The Army of Missouri, created for the Great Raid, was potent and ready to free Missouri, with a passion for their mission. Only one thing stood in the way, and that was a Federal force, its commanders just as determined as the Rebels to keep Missouri out of Confederate hands. The two sides would soon meet to decide the fate of the Show-Me state.

3

A Team of Outcasts: The Yankees

The commanders of the Federal forces—like their Rebel rivals—were an interesting mix of personalities with a myriad of strengths and weaknesses. Much as the Confederates were, the Federal commanders were very alike in their collective background and world outlook. The major difference between the opposing sides was the fragmented command structure of the Union army. The Confederate army, embodied as the Army of Missouri, was a compact, cohesive organization with a clear hierarchy of authority and unity of command under a single leader. By contrast, the Union army had no overall commander, as two departments had to cooperate to expel the Rebel invaders. In addition, all of the Union leaders were castoffs or marked men from other commands, with Missouri serving as a dumping ground for leaders deemed failures. These facts, combined with the idiosyncrasies of each individual, brought to fruition a host of frictions as well as a stunning victory. The Union men present a compelling story of courage, determination, and human frailty.

The first significant leader and commander of the Federal Department of Missouri was Major General William Starke Rosecrans. He had previously led one of the premier armies of the Union in the Army of the Cumberland. As Rosecrans' biographer said, he was a gifted man who "touched the edge of glory" but missed his shot at immortality because of the tragedy of Chickamauga. Rosecrans was born on 6 September 1819 in central Ohio, which at that time was a howling wilderness and the frontier of the United States. He was the eldest child of Crandall and Jemima Rosecrans. William was descended from an old Dutch family that had arrived in New Amsterdam—modern New York—in 1651. As some of the earliest settlers in America, the Rosecrans family became "militant patriots" at the time of the Revolution. The family even went so far as to change the spelling of their surname from Rosenkrantz to Rosecrans to avoid the accusation of being "Hessians." This started a tradition of soldiering, as Rosecrans' men fought in every conflict prior to the Civil War.[1]

Crandall Rosecrans fought in the War of 1812, serving under General William Henry Harrison in the Detroit campaign. In fact, Crandall served as Harrison's adjutant, giving the adjutant a high-level perspective of operations. After the war, Crandall settled in Ohio as a farmer. He also established a prosperous potash factory. Thus, when William was born, Crandall had established a comfortable standard of living. As William was growing up, his father imbued him with a strong work ethic and a tradition of military service. The frontier also provided William with a sense of adventure and resilience unique among midwesterners of that time.[2] Therefore, young Rosecrans' early life had all the elements that would develop a man of toughness. All that was needed was an education to prepare him for an appointment at West Point.

A formal education was hard to come by in frontier Ohio, so the task of teaching Rosecrans fell to his father and William's own initiative. Crandall Rosecrans taught William basics such as reading and addition, and the vast intellect of the son filled in the gaps. Reportedly Rosecrans was a voracious reader, indulging in the classics as well as history. In addition to his program of self-study, William worked in his father's business and clerked in a local store. Without the means to pay for college, Crandall suggested to William that he attend West Point, a prospect that excited William. He quickly sought the appropriate congressional appointment, which his representative, Alexander Harper, was inclined to bestow. A problem with giving the appointment was that William would have to pass the stringent entrance exams required by the academy for admittance. To prepare, he enrolled in Kenyon College for one year to hone his rough academic skills. This paid off, for in 1838 he received his appointment to West Point after passing the entrance exams.[3]

At the age of nineteen, Rosecrans entered the class of 1842, which included several generals from the Civil War like James Longstreet, Earl Van Dorn, and Don Carlos Buell. Rosecrans, in spite of his lack of formal education, was quickly identified as a young man possessing a superior mind. Throughout his time at the academy, he consistently ranked in the top ten of his class in all academic categories. He would eventually graduate fifth in the class of 1842, earning a commission in the prestigious Corps of Engineers. Peers and faculty alike used the term "brilliant" to describe the new lieutenant. In addition to his fine academic achievements, another aspect of his character became a subject of commentary. Rosecrans was a devout Catholic, and as a result, he became known as a "religious enthusiast." This identity would stick with him his entire life, as he would frequently engage acquaintances, subordinates, and superiors with questions of faith.[4]

Rosecrans entered the regular army in 1842 and his first duty station was Fort Monroe, where he worked on the seawall. After a year he earned a promotion and a professorship at West Point to teach engineering. Because of his great competence as an engineer he missed the Mexican War in 1846, as the War Department elected to keep him busy with projects up and down the eastern seaboard. While Rosecrans made significant contributions at various locations as an engineer, he did not enter the Civil War with any combat experience. This is a fact that bothered him, but he gave 100 percent to the jobs he performed during the Mexican War. Because of the slow

Major General William S. Rosecrans, Commander Federal Department of Missouri (Library of Congress).

pace of promotions and paltry salary of a first lieutenant, Rosecrans—who had married in 1845—decided to leave the army to pursue better financial opportunities in 1853.[5]

Rosecrans dabbled in a number of different career options between 1853 and 1861. Among the jobs he took were engineer for a coal company, president of a river transportation outfit, and partner in a fuel-oil refinery. It was in this last venture that he suffered a severe injury to his face while testing a newly invented lamp. This incident left facial distortions, giving his face the appearance of a "smirk" at all times.[6] Some observers during the Civil War considered the smirk a sign of an arrogant disposition. When combined with his sometimes sarcastic correspondence and a perception of recalcitrance on his part, he created many highly placed enemies during the war. During the inter-war period of the 1850s, Rosecrans also engaged in abolition activities and demonstrated support for the cause of liberty. Specifically, he served as the superintendent of a Negro Sunday school. His well-known religious zealotry and stance on abolition—in spite of being a Democrat—became a source of friction during the Civil War when he engaged in arguments with superiors about policy.[7] What this demonstrated was his determination to stand on his convictions regardless of potential consequences.

When the sectional crisis came to a head in 1860 Rosecrans was working in Cincinnati. He had successfully patented an odorless oil and his new factory was beginning to make money. But with the election of Lincoln and the Rebels' attack on Fort Sumter Rosecrans immediately offered his services to the governor of Ohio, arriving in Columbus on 19 April 1861, only five days after Fort Sumter was surrendered. Governor William Dennison quickly accepted and commissioned him a colonel, of Ohio volunteers, along with other notables such as George McClellan. The national government in Washington, also in need of West Point trained officers, upped the offer by sending him a brigadier general's commission in the regular army in May. In addition, Rosecrans received command of an Ohio brigade whose ranks included two future presidents, Rutherford B. Hayes and William McKinley, and a U.S. Supreme Court justice, Stanley Matthews. After some rudimentary training outside Cincinnati, Rosecrans marched with his brigade to Parkersburg, Virginia, to report to McClellan, a new major general in command of all troops in the Ohio Valley.[8] The formation of this little army began an association between Rosecrans and McClellan that would soon bring out on full display all of Rosecrans' brilliance as a commander and the character flaws as a subordinate that would eventually sink his career.

The army in western Virginia was assembling to take on a small Confederate force under Colonel John Pegram, sent there to protect the key economic region of the Kanawha Valley. This region was known to have many Union men all too eager to deliver the area to the North, and the Virginia Confederates aimed to prevent losing it. The Rebels were posted on Rich Mountain overlooking the town of Beverly. McClellan moved his force south to pinpoint the exact location of Pegram's small element. As McClellan probed forward, Rosecrans met a young man named Hart whose family owned large tracts of land around Rich Mountain. Hart offered to guide Rosecrans' brigade to the rear of the Rebel force in order to flank them. Rosecrans took Hart to McClellan and together they devised a plan to crush the Rebel force between Rosecrans' anvil and McClellan's hammer. McClellan would launch his blow once he heard Rosecrans engaged in the enemy's rear. The attack date was set for the early morning of 11 July 1861. This would be Rosecrans' first combat experience.[9]

As planned, Rosecrans began movement after dusk on 10 July so that he could be in position in time to begin the assault by dawn on the 11th. According to one participant it took some ten hours to complete the march, which included a hard climb up the mountain. Upon arrival at the attack position, Rosecrans made a shocking discovery. While they had successfully attained a position in the rear of the Rebels, Pegram had anticipated the move and detached a regiment to protect his rear. Thus, Rosecrans was confronted by a line of battle with two guns supporting the infantry. Nevertheless, he launched his attack in early afternoon versus morning and was met by stiff resistance. After about "two or three hours," during which time McClellan failed to launch his attack, Rosecrans finally broke the resistance to his front and forced Pegram from his position. In his first battle, Rosecrans, who was reportedly all over the field, won the fight and gained a reputation for courage and tenacity.[10] After the battle he also gained a reputation as a recalcitrant subordinate for his critical tongue and acid pen.

Rosecrans was incensed that McClellan had failed to support him. An eyewitness stated that McClellan heard the sounds of battle and should have launched his assault in accordance with the plan. Yet, for whatever reason, he failed to do so and, "in fact, left [Rosecrans] to win his own battle or to get out of his embarrassment as he could."[11] In his report after the battle, McClellan seemed to ride the coattails of Rosecrans to elevate his own role in the victory. While complimentary of Rosecrans, McClellan nevertheless amplified his own role, and this facilitated his eventual elevation to commander-in-chief of the Union armies in August following the disaster at Bull Run. Rosecrans, by contrast, bluntly stated that McClellan "did not attack" as planned, leaving him to his own devices.[12] Later, Rosecrans would come to believe that McClellan's promotion was due to Rosecrans' effort at his own expense. In this incident Rosecrans displayed his irritating tendency to criticize superiors openly and to take offense when credit due him was given to others. This would hurt him in the long run, as he made too many enemies in high places.

When McClellan was summoned to Washington later in July to receive command of all Union forces, Rosecrans assumed command of the Department of the Ohio.[13] Over the course of the next several months he would continue the campaign to clear the western counties of Virginia and in doing so win a promotion, an enhanced reputation for hard fighting, and command of an important army in the west.

Progress had been made in securing western Virginia, but there was still a great deal to do in order to permanently expel the Confederates. The Rebels were ready to up the ante by sending more troops and a new commander: Robert E. Lee. It did not matter who commanded, for Rosecrans would demonstrate clear competence in thoroughly defeating the Confederates and their greatest commander. In Lee's defense, he was hampered by incompetent and recalcitrant subordinates such as former U.S. secretary of war John Floyd and Virginia governor Henry Wise. Lee had taken positions on the upper Kanawha at Cheat Mountain to prevent any further penetration of the western counties. In mid–September, Rosecrans moved forward to drive Lee back by turning his defensive line. Rosecrans quickly forced back Floyd and proceeded to drive ahead to hit the remainder of Lee's force, However, mother nature and insubordination by Lee's lieutenants intervened to prevent Rosecrans from sealing a more complete victory. Incessant rains burst over the mountains in October, preventing all movement for the rest of the year.[14] Nevertheless, Rosecrans successfully drove the Confederates from western Virginia, enabling the Union to secure the area and set conditions for that part of Virginia to secede and join the Union as the new state of West Virginia in 1863.

In 1862, Rosecrans moved west to a new command in Major General Henry Halleck's department. He moved west as a new major general and with the mark of a winner, something of a rarity among Union generals—except for Grant—at that time. On 23 May 1862 Rosecrans stepped from a steamboat onto Pittsburg Landing and reported to Halleck, who immediately assigned Rosecrans command of two divisions in Major General John Pope's wing of the army facing Corinth and Beauregard's army in the wake of Shiloh. The Federal army was preparing to invest this important rail center in northern Mississippi. The Rebels under Beauregard prevented this by quietly slipping out of town on the night of 29 May. The Union army quickly occupied the town and began to spread out across west Tennessee, north Mississippi, and north Alabama to consolidate their hold on the region. Rosecrans was posted in the city, while other elements of the army fanned out.[15] This critical point would become a target for advancing Confederates in the fall, placing Rosecrans at center stage in its defense.

In September 1862, the Confederates were on the move across a thousand-mile front. Lee had invaded Maryland, Bragg was moving on Kentucky, and Van Dorn and Price would attempt to take Corinth to tie down Federal troops while retaking the vital rail center. Rosecrans was in command of what was designated the Army of the Mississippi, which was part of U.S. Grant's District of West Tennessee. Sterling Price made the initial move on 11 September in order to prevent any detachment of Union troops from moving into Kentucky to assist Buell against Bragg. Price moved north from Holly Springs in accordance with Bragg's wishes that he tie down Rosecrans. Price's intent was to interpose his force between Rosecrans and Buell in Kentucky. This would require a march north into Tennessee, bypassing Rosecrans at Iuka.[16] The coming engagements around Corinth would represent the first meeting as opponents between Rosecrans and Price, with the final encounter coming in 1864 in Missouri.

Rosecrans and Grant did not intend to make it easy for Price; instead they planned to ambush an unsuspecting Price near Iuka as he moved north. Rosecrans suggested to Grant a plan to trap Price between a stationary force—under Grant—with Rosecrans pushing Price onto the anvil. This necessarily required coordination between two converging forces to have success, a notoriously difficult maneuver even with modern communication systems. The signal to ensure Grant sprang the ambush was the sound of battle moving close to the stationary force at Iuka. This plan was eerily similar to the one devised at Rich Mountain between Rosecrans and McClellan. In actual execution, it had the same result, with Rosecrans doing all the fighting while Grant—who because of an acoustic shadow did not spring the ambush—sat idly by.[17]

It was in the aftermath of Iuka that a controversy developed between Grant and Rosecrans. Because Grant's men never heard Rosecrans initiate the battle, the anvil never closed the pincer that was to have crushed Price between the two forces. While this is no fault of Grant's, Rosecrans was irritated with him nevertheless, just as he had been with McClellan the previous year. The real issue was that Rosecrans committed his irritation to writing, a fact that Grant found intolerable, creating a permanent adversarial relationship between the two men.[18] With Grant as the senior commander, the antagonism would not turn out well for Rosecrans.

Following the inconclusive engagement at Iuka, Price withdrew south where he was reinforced by Van Dorn, who took overall command of the combined force of about 22,000 men. Simultaneously, Rosecrans consolidated his force at Corinth to protect the railway, his army consisting of about 20,000 well-entrenched men. The battle of Corinth in early October brought Rosecrans more accolades and command of an army. Price was returning south and there was no chance he could now slip past Rosecrans and Grant to aid Bragg against Buell in Kentucky. To have some positive effect in favor of Bragg, Van Dorn devised a plan to take Corinth, but he would approach it by making a wide sweep to the west and coming down from the north. He thought that by doing so the Confederates could avoid the earthworks ringing Corinth. This was a good plan, but Rosecrans anticipated it and prepared accordingly.[19]

During 3–4 October 1862 Van Dorn and Price's Rebels launched a series of desperate attacks on Rosecrans' defensive positions. The Confederates came very close to cracking the Federal lines and in a couple of instances actually entered the works, as in the fighting around Battery Robinett. Rosecrans was seemingly everywhere, plugging holes and encouraging the men. His leadership directly impacted the result, which was a resounding Union victory. The Confederates were decimated by the attack and Price withdrew from this second fight with Rosecrans smarting from the sting of defeat. They would meet again on another field. In the meantime, Rosecrans received attention from the president for his fine defense. He was a successful general—a commodity in short supply for the Union in late 1862—and there were critical commands that needed filling. Buell's dilatory actions in Kentucky got him fired from command of the Army of the Cumberland and President Lincoln filled the vacancy with the hero of Corinth.[20] The next year would see Rosecrans at his best and worst in command of this venerable army.

Rosecrans took command of the Army of the Cumberland at Louisville on 30 October 1862. In assuming this critical command, Rosecrans had a mandate, and that mandate was to lead the army into action. Buell, along with a host of other Federal commanders at that time, had gained a reputation for providing excuses for inaction. The president wanted this changed and placed Rosecrans in position to move immediately to clear middle Tennessee, reversing the previous dynamics. However, Lincoln would not get the action he sought for some time. When Rosecrans took over, he found an army in disarray and lacking in supplies for a campaign, the rail line cut to Louisville, and few horses for the cavalry. Therefore, he took several weeks to launch a campaign into middle Tennessee. As a result, the Lincoln administration became frustrated with him and lost a measure of confidence in his ability. Undeterred, Rosecrans held firm to his conviction that he had to prepare properly before moving forward. He even replied to one admonishment that "to threats of removal ... I am insensible."[21] In essence, Rosecrans was thumbing his nose at his superiors.

Finally, on 26 December—two months after assuming command, Rosecrans moved forward from Nashville to attack Braxton Bragg's Army of Tennessee around Murfreesboro on the Stones River. Rosecrans planned to initiate his assault on the morning of 30 December, but he did not count on his adversary beating him to the punch. Philip

Sheridan, a division commander, pointed out that "Bragg took the initiative, beginning his movement about an hour earlier ... than Rosecrans." Bragg's attack hit the Union left, rolling up Sheridan's division defending that flank. Rosecrans was at his best in a pinch, and at Stones River he demonstrated his best traits. As the army appeared to be collapsing under the assault, Rosecrans worked diligently to stabilize the defense. At one point, when riding along his front, his chief of staff, Colonel Garesche, was decapitated. Yet, as Sheridan pointed out in his memoirs, Rosecrans personally demonstrated the "importance of self-control ... with an appearance of indifference," allowing the army to recover from the shock of that morning.[22]

Rosecrans' staunch defense resulted in a victory and consolidation of the Federal hold on middle Tennessee. What is important about the victory is the morale boost it gave the Union and Lincoln. The Republicans had lost heavily to the Democrats in the 1862 mid-term elections, and the Army of the Potomac had suffered a devastating loss at Fredericksburg. Thus, Rosecrans provided a sorely needed reprieve from a stream of bad news. Congress voted Rosecrans its thanks and once again he was in the good graces of the administration.[23] The positive feeling would not last long. Lincoln soon wanted another forward movement, but Rosecrans would not deliver for several months and the administration would lose its patience in the process.

Rosecrans waited another seven months before he launched the Tullahoma Campaign in late July 1863. During this extended period, he exchanged a stream of correspondence with the War Department and administration officials. Washington "repeatedly pressed [Rosecrans] to undertake offensive operations." But, as Sheridan points out, "Rosecrans resisted with a great deal of spirit." Rosecrans refused to move until he could accumulate enough supplies to sustain his army in the barren region of the Cumberland Plateau, which he would have to cross to reach Chattanooga. In explaining this to General Halleck and the administration, Rosecrans used little tact, thus poisoning relations with Washington. While, as Sheridan points out, "feeding the army from the base at Louisville was attended with a great many difficulties," the government simply would not accept this as an excuse for inaction. Rather than try to assuage the War Department and the president, Rosecrans instead agitated them with his acidic pen. Thus, "out of this grew up an acrimonious correspondence and strained feeling."[24] When disaster befell Rosecrans later in the year, the ill feelings he had sown would bring forth bitter fruit for him.

Rosecrans initiated the Tullahoma Campaign on 26 July 1863. This nearly bloodless campaign effectively drove the Confederates from Tennessee and demonstrates the brilliance of Rosecrans as a strategist. The Confederate Army of Tennessee under Bragg occupied defensive positions between the Duck and Elk rivers, covering all the major routes to Chattanooga. It seemed that any forward movement on Bragg's positions would precipitate a battle disadvantageous to the Union army. To avoid this, Rosecrans devised a plan to either force Bragg out of his defenses or trap him there, giving the Federals a chance to defeat Bragg in detail. Rosecrans would move his army east, simultaneously feinting directly upon Bragg's position, then he would move south of Tullahoma, seizing the railroad bridge over the Elk. This maneuver was skillfully executed, forcing Bragg to stand in a position of disadvantage or fall back to protect his line of communication. Bragg chose the latter and in doing so abandoned Tennessee, including Chattanooga.[25]

The president was thrilled with Rosecrans' achievement, but a fatal blunder in September 1863 would ruin the brilliant and personally flawed Union commander. As the Army of the Cumberland continued south in pursuit of the fleeing Army of Tennessee, it became dangerously spread out across miles of mountainous terrain. Bragg, who was receiving reinforcements from across the Confederacy, sought to take advantage of the Union army's dispersion by attacking and destroying the pieces individually. Rosecrans realized his peril by mid–September and began rapidly concentrating the Army of the Cumberland just south of Chattanooga at a place called Chickamauga Creek.[26]

Bragg fumbled his opportunity because he had very poor information about the enemy and seemed more scared of the enemy than confident of his prospects. He told one subordinate, "The rat lies hidden at his hole ready to pop out when no one is watching. Who can tell what lies hidden behind that wall?" In other words, Bragg was more concerned about being surprised by Union forces debouching from the mountains than about attacking as the enemy poked his head over the wall.[27] Thus, he allowed Rosecrans just enough time to bring his army back together. When Bragg launched his attack on Rosecrans on 19 September, the Federals were reunited behind Chickamauga Creek.

Bragg's plan was to interpose the Army of Tennessee between Rosecrans and Chattanooga and turn him away from the Union's supply base. Bragg issued his orders to his commanders on the 18th for execution the next morning. D.H. Hill pointed out that "had this order been issued on any of the four preceding days, it would have found Rosecrans wholly unprepared." The Union army, however, was ready and badly bloodied the Confederates on that day. The following day the Rebels tried again and through a stroke of luck scored a tremendous victory. Early on the 20th Rosecrans was out inspecting his lines in the thick woods. As he trooped the line, he believed a gap existed and he ordered one of his divisions to shift to close it. The gap was imaginary, but in the process of closing the hole Rosecrans created a real one. It just happened that at almost the same moment Longstreet launched a heavy assault with his corps and found the hole and went right through it, dividing the Union army.[28] The entire line collapsed and elements of the Army of the Cumberland began streaming back to Chattanooga. Another element under the command of Major General George Thomas held firm and in the process saved Rosecrans' army from destruction.

It was Rosecrans' previous recalcitrance, combined with his behavior in the aftermath of Chickamauga, that landed him on the chopping block. Shortly after the collapse of the main line at Chickamauga, Rosecrans got carried away in the rout and did not stop before arriving in Chattanooga. Thus, he left over half the army to fend for itself as he found safety in the rear. Then his pessimistic dispatches to Washington about his ability to defend Chattanooga resulted in a complete loss of confidence in his leadership. Lincoln at one point commented that Rosecrans' lack of determination gave the appearance of someone who was "confused and stunned like a duck." Finally, Charles A. Dana, who was assistant secretary of war and traveling with the army, reported "the defects of his [Rosecrans'] character complicate the difficulty" of the situation at Chattanooga.[29] Given all of this evidence of Rosecrans' defeatism, Lincoln began to think of relieving him.

Lincoln chose an indirect method by which to effect a change in command. He created a new command called the Military Division of the Mississippi, which consolidated command of all the western armies under one man—U.S. Grant. There was no love lost between Rosecrans and Grant, as the two had sparred in the wake of Iuka and Corinth. As a result of the seeds Rosecrans had sown with his pen after these battles, Grant was not a fan of his generalship. As part of the creation of the new command, Grant was given the option of relieving any subordinate found wanting. In the wake of Chickamauga and his already low opinion of Rosecrans, Grant wasted no time in cashiering him. To retrieve the disaster, Grant chose George Thomas—the Rock of Chickamauga—to replace Rosecrans.[30]

In spite of Rosecrans' acid pen and his penchant for tardiness, he was a man of dignity. When the order relieving him came down on 18 October 1863—one month after Chickamauga—he took it with coolness and composure. He summoned Thomas and informed him of the change in command and provided an overview of the army's dispositions. The following morning at 5:00, Rosecrans departed without fanfare, as he was chagrined at leaving the army, which had a great affection of old "Rosey." Sheridan noted that "General Rosecrans quietly slipped away from the army. He submitted uncomplainingly to the removal, and modestly left us without fuss or demonstration.... When his departure became known deep and almost universal regret was expressed, for he was enthusiastically esteemed and loved."[31] Thus ended Rosecrans' career with the Army of the Cumberland. After remaining on the shelf without a command for about three months, he received appointment to command of the Department of Missouri on 28 January 1864, a critical command that was also far from Washington and represented a form of exile for disgraced leaders.[32] Nevertheless, Rosecrans took the command because he itched for action, thus setting up a clash between him and his old nemesis from Iuka and Corinth, Sterling Price.

William S. Rosecrans had two subordinates who would play key roles in turning back Price and the Great Raid. Each actor entered the scene at separate but critical points during the course of the raid, and both men turned in outstanding and pivotal performances. These men were Brigadier General Thomas Ewing, Jr., and Major General Alfred Pleasonton. Ewing, as commander of the District of St. Louis in 1864, had the first major encounter with Price's army at Pilot Knob. It was this fight that set Price on a course for disaster because it was here that he was forced to change objectives and, ultimately, the goal of the expedition. Thomas Ewing made a determined stand with a hodgepodge of defenders at Fort Davidson against a force outnumbering his by at least ten to one. If there is a true hero on the Union side from the Great Raid, it is Thomas Ewing. But who is this rather obscure figure?

Thomas Ewing, Jr., was the son of a well-known and respected Whig politician, Thomas Ewing, Sr. The younger Ewing was born in Lancaster, Ohio, on 7 August 1829. The Ewing family had deep roots in America dating back to the late 17th century when the family left Scotland for a better life across the Atlantic. They settled in New Jersey and Thomas's forebears fought in the American Revolution on the side of the colonies. His grandfather George was an artillery captain and earned some distinction at the battle of Brandywine. Following the war, George took his family west in search of good land, settling in Ohio, which in 1792 was the frontier and teeming with raiding Indians. Nevertheless, Ohio was a place to build a better life and enjoy the freedom for which the United States had so recently fought. George would have several children, and among them was Thomas Ewing, Sr., who would achieve great success as a lawyer and politician.[33]

The elder Ewing is a great example of the self-made man. He taught himself to read, was one of the first college graduates west of the original thirteen colonies, and, after admission to the bar, established a respected and profitable law practice specializing in real estate cases. These accomplishments and his determination to succeed were passed on to his son as he grew into a man. Thomas Sr. would eventually litigate before the Supreme Court of the United States, and his reputation as a lawyer enabled him to establish himself in politics. The older man would serve as a U.S. senator from Ohio and for two presidents as a cabinet member. Thomas Sr. married a young catholic girl named Maria Boyle and together they would have seven children, including his namesake. In addition, the charitable Ewings would adopt another, and this young man would have a lasting impact on American history. His name was William T. Sherman, who would become the most famous Union general after U.S. Grant.[34]

Thomas Jr. was truly a "chip off the old block," as he would follow very closely in his father's footsteps. The younger Ewing was groomed for a law career and as a politician. The senior Ewing sent Thomas Jr. to schools that set him up for entry into the profession, including the Lancaster Academy and Brown College. Additionally, Thomas Sr. introduced him to the national political scene. Though the Ewings hailed from central Ohio, on two occasions Thomas Sr. moved his family to Washington, D.C., upon his selection to serve in the cabinet. The first time was a stint when Thomas Sr. became the secretary of treasury for Presidents William Henry Harrison and John Tyler in the early 1840s. The second opportunity came in 1849 when Thomas Sr. took a position as the secretary of interior. On this return trip, Thomas Jr., now twenty years old, accepted a position as President Zachary Taylor's private secretary, giving the young man a true insider's view of the American political system.[35] The combined experience of his time in Washington imprinted Whig principles upon the young man. These included policies to encourage economic growth through infrastructure subsidies and free-soil stances as the sectional crisis approached. Altogether these budding views would make him susceptible to becoming a Republican and joining the migration to Kansas in the 1850s when such issues became central to the formation of that state.

After Zachary Taylor died in office, Thomas Ewing, Jr., attended Brown College to become a lawyer. It was here that his antislavery beliefs were stoked by the events of the day and his peers. The Fugitive Slave Law was passed during this time and students at the college railed against its passage. The events of the 1850s, occurring while Ewing was in college, drove him deeply into the arms of the free-soil movement and he honed his law skills accordingly. He did not finish school at Brown, ostensibly because he grew bored. Instead, Thomas returned to Ohio to begin law school in Cincinnati. Again, he did not finish, but this was not an obstacle to practicing law in the 19th century, for most lawyers did not even attend law school. Rather, they apprenticed under established lawyers before gaining recognition before the bar.[36]

Ewing took an apprenticeship in Cincinnati focusing on real estate litigation, just as his father practiced. Prospects for professional and political advancement, though, were not good, as Cincinnati was saturated with lawyers. However, opportunity lay elsewhere and young Thomas took full advantage of it. Kansas seemed to call his name, as its attributes lent themselves to Ewing's ambition. The first reason to move west was to accompany the great migration going that direction from the east, and Ewing's sense of adventure was piqued by this prospect. Second, the expansive land in Kansas had many claimants arriving daily to stake out their homesteads on the prairie. Inevitably, disputes would arise when claims overlapped and these cases would require lawyers specializing in real estate litigation. Third, since Ewing believed in expanding infrastructure, Kansas offered the opportunity to buy up cheap land and then sell it back to the government when the railroads began springing up. Finally, political prospects in Kansas were better for a young man than in Ohio. As the free-soilers moved to Kansas, Ewing saw an opportunity to build a constituency with grassroots legwork, since he shared many of the same beliefs with the migrants from northern states.[37] A young man as ambitious as Thomas Ewing could not pass up the chance to make a name for himself on the wild prairie of Kansas.

Hugh Boyle Ewing, Thomas' older brother and a future Union general, encouraged him to come west with him to establish their own roots in the sprawling territory of Kansas. Newly married and just making ends meet, Thomas decided to go to Leavenworth to determine if possibilities really abounded in Kansas. In 1855, he set out with his brother to the new town of Leavenworth across the Missouri River on the border of Kansas and Missouri. Thomas liked what he saw, and by the spring of 1856 he moved with his wife to Leavenworth to start a law practice and a land speculation business. Within months Ewing became heavily involved in the Kansas political scene, in addition to his business interests, and it seemed that all his ambitions would receive full satisfaction.[38]

Brigadier General Thomas Ewing, Jr., Commander, District of St. Louis and battlefield commander at Pilot Knob (Library of Congress).

In 1856 and 1857 Ewing, in partnership with his foster brother William T. Sherman and Daniel McCook, began litigating claims and purchasing land along proposed lines for the transcontinental railroad. The litigation fees allowed Ewing to live modestly, while the land purchases were pushing him deeply into debt until the company could resell it to the rail companies at a profit.[39] In the meantime, Ewing began building his political credentials, and it was here that he enjoyed his greatest success before the Civil War.

Thomas Ewing became a member of the Free State party in Kansas and, while he held abolitionist views, he was an outspoken moderate on the issue of slavery. The radicals in the party, led by John Brown and James Lane, agitated for aggressive action to ensure that Kansas would enter the Union as a free state. To them, this meant the use of violence to cleanse Kansas—and Missouri—of the scourge of slavery. Ewing, on the other hand, advocated a more deliberate and nonviolent approach to achieve the same goal. For him, this entailed organizing the population politically and using that organization to defeat the pro-slavery factions at the ballot box.[40] This is a very rule-of-law approach to solve a problem, one that would be expected from a lawyer and son of an eminent former senator and cabinet member.

Ewing proved the efficacy of his course of action in a courageous manner during the 1858 elections for the territorial legislature. As the chairman of the Free State Party's executive committee, Ewing took it upon himself to record voting irregularities in border counties to ensure the party would win control of the legislature. This would in turn provide the opportunity for the free-staters to overturn the pro-slavery Lecompton Constitution and replace it with a free constitution. Facing direct threat of bodily harm, Ewing personally monitored balloting in Kickapoo, Kansas. Many Missouri men crossed the border at Westport in January 1858 to vote in the election. Ewing meticulously catalogued how many men had voted during the day up to the closing of the polls. When the votes were tallied, far more votes had been cast then Ewing's count, producing a pro-slavery victory. Ewing boldly produced his evidence, which included the count and timing of ballots cast, demonstrating that the boxes were stuffed. Further, with the help of a friend, he found the fraudulent ballots after forming a posse to demand the corrupt official turn them over. With this additional evidence in hand, Ewing forced federal officials to overturn the initial pro-slavery result of the election, thus handing the victory to the Free State Party.[41] This act solidified his credentials for courage and as a party leader and Ewing's political career in Kansas took off from there. In addition, he had proven that a sound plan based on the rule of law could win Kansas without violence, and this made him popular among the people who desired peace.

Ewing's opposition to James Lane would have its consequences. In the late 1850s and early 1860s, the notorious Lane was arguably the most popular politician in Kansas. With a gift for fiery oration, he could whip a crowd into a frenzy and build his own political base as a result. Among Lane's supporters was James G. Blunt, who would ride Lane's coattails to high command later during the war. In spite of the rivalry between the two men, Ewing would actually defend Lane in court when he was accused of murder. Ewing deftly defended Lane, achieving an acquittal that for a short time halted the mud slinging between them. But, when the war broke out the antagonism between the two men would arise again to thwart Ewing's leadership in a key command. Nevertheless, he demonstrated his mettle by never backing down from Lane and executing his duty as he saw fit. Thus, moral courage honed in political battles would become his most important attribute as a military commander.

By 1860 the Free State Party was beginning to coalesce with the national Republican Party, and Thomas Ewing became a leading member in its formation in Kansas. The election of 1860 was a seminal event not only in Kansas, but also across the nation at large. The outcome would determine the fate of the union itself. Ewing threw himself into the campaign, actively working for Lincoln while self-promoting for statewide office. Ewing most desired a senator's seat, but the chair went to James Lane, much to Ewing's chagrin. Thomas would not fret for long because his recognized talent for the judiciary earned him the position of chief justice of the Kansas supreme court following admission to the union. On 29 January 1861, the Senate—now absent in objection to the southern senators—voted to admit Kansas to the union as a free state, to Ewing's supreme satisfaction. In short order on 9 February 1861 Ewing was sworn in as the first chief justice in Kansas at the age of 32.[42]

Two months later the Confederates fired on Fort Sumter, starting the Civil War. Lincoln quickly issued the call for volunteers to put down the rebellion, but Thomas Ewing was not among those who stepped forward. In contrast to all the other senior leaders who participated in the raid on both sides, he did not offer his services immediately, nor, for that matter, for a long time thereafter. Military service was not his first calling and he knew it, having had no training whatsoever. His profession was that of lawyer and judge. Based on this and a lack of confidence in his ability to serve as a military leader, Ewing elected to remain as the chief justice of the Kansas supreme court for seventeen months after the war began. This helped to stabilize his financial situation, which was troubled due to his large land debt. Also, he was able to establish a stable judiciary in Kansas by staying on board. Nevertheless, pressure to volunteer steadily rose to the point where he could no longer refuse.[43]

Among the motivations that convinced Ewing to volunteer was the altruistic desire to put himself on the line for the cause of the Union. Additionally, a less wholesome idea entered into his thinking. Ever ambitious, Ewing had his sights set on a continued and steadily rising career as a politician. If a man of 33 years of age, as Ewing was, failed to serve in the great conflict of his generation, it would taint him politically for the rest of his career. Only those with laurels earned in the war could write their ticket in postwar politics. Therefore, after mulling over these considerations, Ewing resolved to offer his services to the army in September 1862.[44]

In late summer of that year, Lincoln had issued yet another call for volunteers, this time for 300,000. Kansas was authorized to raise three regiments to meet the state quota set by the War Department. Knowing he could no longer sit on the sidelines, Ewing promptly tendered his services. The recruiting agent for Kansas was none other than Senator James Lane. In spite of animosities, Ewing received a colonel's commission, ostensibly as a slight toward the Kansas governor, whom Lane disliked even more than Ewing. Thomas Ewing began his military career as an officer by raising the 11th Kansas Infantry Regiment. Within six weeks he had the ranks filled and the governor mustered the 11th into Federal service on 24 September 1862.[45] Ewing's division commander was James G. Blunt and the department commander was Samuel R. Curtis, both of whom played prominent roles during the Great Raid.

One might have expected that the new regiment would spend time in camp receiving initial tactical instruction. This would not occur, for after just five days of rudimentary training Blunt pushed his division to the field on 29 September to move into northwest Arkansas to thwart Thomas Hindman's planned move on Missouri. The regiment did stop at Fort Scott for three weeks and Ewing maximized the time by insisting on drill training, but by 20 October they were in motion south destined for their first action. In what became known as the Prairie Grove Campaign, Thomas Ewing got his first taste of combat. Less than three months after entering Federal service, Colonel Ewing and the 11th would fight and win three battles, including the pitched battle of Prairie Grove. The 11th would play a large part and Ewing's performance put to rest any lack of confidence he had in his abilities. By all accounts, he demonstrated great ability as a regimental commander, making a positive addition to the command structure in the Union Department of Missouri.[46]

Along the road to Arkansas Blunt's division caught up with several Confederate Indian regiments near old Fort Wayne in the northeast corner of Indian Territory on 22 October 1862. The troops of the 2nd Kansas Cavalry under Captain Samuel Crawford—future governor of Kansas—made first contact by launching a headlong cavalry charge on the unsuspecting Indians. However, Crawford was greatly outnumbered and the Rebel Indians quickly turned the tables on the 2nd Kansas. Ewing—who was suffering from a recurrence of malaria—ordered his regiment to double-quick march forward to the sounds of the guns. With fixed bayonets the 11th, alongside their sister regiment the 10th Kansas, broke up the regrouped Confederates, driving them from the field.[47] In his first engagement Ewing proved aggressive and sound in judgment and he would continue to demonstrate those traits in all his military endeavors.

Blunt followed up on this small victory by driving straight ahead into Arkansas. Upon arrival in that state, Blunt plunged into the desolate Boston Mountains trying to locate Hindman's army. Marmaduke found Blunt first on 28 November at a place called Cane Hill, where Ewing and his regiment would have another crack at the Rebels. The fight at Cane Hill was an exhausting one for Ewing's infantrymen. The battle took place across several miles of the Cane Hill ridgeline as Marmaduke's cavalrymen steadily withdrew, forcing the Federal infantry to chase them. Though the 11th Kansas started out in reserve, by late afternoon they deployed forward to drive Marmaduke away from another of his successive defensive positions. The positions were protected by the terrain, forcing the Kansans to attack frontally. As the Federals drove home the attack, the Rebels melted away after inflicting losses on them. This continued until nightfall arrested the action, fortunately for the dog-tired 11th Kansas.[48] Ewing had once again performed well and under adverse conditions of winter and difficult terrain. This inexperienced colonel was proving an excellent find for the Federals west of the Mississippi.

Blunt and his division had expected to continue driving south, but Thomas Hindman outfoxed the Federal commander by quietly sweeping around Blunt's flank to interpose himself between him and Brigadier General Herron near Fayetteville. When Blunt learned of Hindman's move, he realized that he had to unite with Herron immediately to prevent the separate Union columns from individual defeat in detail. Blunt pressed his division hard and they began to arrive on the field at Prairie Grove by late morning of 7 December 1862. Colonel Ewing's regiment, along with others from Kansas, went straight from march column into battle. First they halted the Rebels who were advancing on Herron's position, and then launched their own assault up a hill overlooking the Illinois River. The Rebels stopped this attack, which then degenerated into an ugly inferno of fire in the valley, neither side giving ground. Darkness ended the fight, during which the 11th lost six dead and 76 wounded out of 291 men engaged. Following the battle, Ewing went to great lengths to care for his men, to the point that he ran afoul of his superiors. But the men of the 11th Kansas appreciated this and they developed a great affection for their commander.[49] Within thirty days Ewing had fought in three battles and was now an experienced commander in conventional operations. However, a coming promotion would thrust him into a difficult situation in which he would have to muster all his intellect and moral courage to deal with the festering guerrilla conflict along the border.

On 13 March 1863 Ewing received a well-earned promotion to brigadier general for his fine services in the Prairie Grove Campaign. However, the coveted promotion came with an unenviable position that would give the new general enormous frustration. Ewing might have anticipated receiving a brigade to command in the field. Instead, John M. Schofield, the department commander, appointed him as the commander of the new District of the Border. This district consisted of a swath of counties in western Missouri straddling the Missouri River and several counties on the Kansas border north of the 38th parallel.[50] This region on the Kansas-Missouri border just happened to be the area with the most intense guerrilla activity of any region across the country.

As already noted, the border war had started before the Civil War and continued unabated when the sectional conflict spread to the rest of the country. Unfortunately for the people who lived along the Kansas-Missouri border, the border war intensified and became a cauldron of brutality. The year 1863 would witness the greatest atrocities of the entire war. The perpetrators of these events were men like William Quantrill and "Bloody Bill" Anderson on the Confederate side, and Charles Jennison and Dan Anthony, known as the Redlegs, on the Union side. Both entities committed unspeakable acts against the innocent populace of Kansas and Missouri.[51] Just as Ewing took over in June, the most heinous incident was already in the planning stage.

In August of 1863, Quantrill led a band of guerrillas on a raid to Lawrence, Kansas, that would utterly destroy the town and leave 150 boys and men dead in the streets. The ostensible reason for the raid was in retaliation for the incarceration of several female relatives of key leaders in Quantrill's loose band. The women were placed in Federal custody in order to encourage the Rebel bands to tone down their depredations. While the women were incarcerated at the dilapidated Union Hotel in Westport, the building collapsed, killing four of the females and injuring several of the rest. This tragedy enraged Quantrill and, in the words of one of his followers, "[W]e were determined to have revenge, and so, Colonel Q and Captain Anderson planned a raid on Lawrence, Kansas...."[52] Thus, the wheels were set in motion for the most tragic event to occur in the Trans-Mississippi during the Civil War.

By 10 August 1863, Quantrill had solidified his plans for the attack on Lawrence by briefing his leaders and giving orders to assemble the guerrillas. The group came together in Johnson County, Missouri, and Quantrill issued final orders for execution of the raid. On 19 August, a horde of over 400 men began moving west toward Kansas bent on destruction. By the evening of 20 August, Quantrill and his men had crossed the Kansas border and, with luck on their side, had eluded Federal pickets strung along the border. As Quantrill's band closed in on Lawrence in the early morning hours of 21 August, the raiders forced locals to guide them quietly to the town. Once they got what they needed, the raiders killed the guides.[53]

At 5:00 a.m. Quantrill halted the column on a hill southeast of Lawrence and formed for the attack. A few minutes later, the raiders moved out at a gallop and thundered into the streets, achieving complete surprise, as no one offered any resistance. The atrocities began almost immediately, perpetrated by "Bloody Bill" Anderson and George Todd, who were not as interested in the Rebel cause as they were in murder and plunder. Quantrill was more interested in key targets such as James Lane, Mayor Collamore, and Redleg Charles Jennison. He was successful in killing only the mayor. Nevertheless, Quantrill had achieved a spectacular success, as well as having exacted a horrific cost on the citizens. The entire business district along Massachusetts Street was in ashes, over 100 dwellings were destroyed, and over 150 boys and men were dead. One of Quantrill's men later wrote that "a few innocent men may have been killed, but this was not intentional." This was a complete fabrication, as the opposite is actually true. The only people spared from the killing spree were women, and Quantrill gave strict orders to shield them. The raiders turned about by mid-morning headed to Missouri and successfully eluded their pursuers.[54] The whole incident caused a furor, with Kansans demanding retribution. Ewing was thrust into the center of this whirlwind and he provided a controversial solution.

Senator James Lane whipped up Kansans to a fever pitch in demanding revenge. He would also direct his wrath at Thomas Ewing, Jr. Lane accused Ewing of negligence in allowing Quantrill to penetrate so deep into Kansas. Further, Lane demanded the right to pillage select Missouri towns and to know how Ewing intended to respond to the Lawrence raid. Ewing was in a tight spot. Not only was he responsible for fighting Rebel guerrilla bands in his district, but he was also responsible for preventing vigilantism such as the action Lane was suggesting. Thus, Ewing was charged with maintaining peace and preventing violence, whatever the source. His solution to this intractable problem was both unique and controversial. Ewing decided to remove the population that supported the Rebel guerrillas.[55]

On 25 August 1863, only four days after the Lawrence raid, Thomas Ewing issued General Order #11, which would make him infamous in Missouri. The order stated:

Headquarters District of the Border
Kansas City, Mo., August 25, 1863.

First: All persons living in Cass, Jackson, and Bates Counties, Missouri, and in that part of Vernon County, included in this district, except those living within one mile of the city limits of Independence, Hickman's Mills, Pleasant Hill and Harrisonville, and except those in that part of Kaw Township, Jackson County north of Brush Creek and west of the Big Blue, embracing Kansas City and Westport, are hereby ordered to move from their present place of residence within 15 days from the date thereof. Those who within that time establish their loyalty to the satisfaction of the commanding officer of the military station nearest their present place of residence, will receive from him certificates stating the facts of their loyalty and the names by whom it can be shown. All who receive such certificates will be permitted to remove to any military station in this district or to any part of the State of Kansas, except all the counties on the eastern border of the state. All others shall remain out of the district.

Officers commanding companies and detachments, serving in the counties named will see that this paragraph is promptly obeyed.

Second: all grain or hay in the fields or under shelter of the district from which the inhabitants are required to move within reach of military stations, after the ninth day of September will be taken to such stations and turned over to the proper officers there; and report of the amount so turned over made to the district headquarters specifying the names of all loyal owners and the amount of such produce taken from them. All grain and hay found in such district after the ninth day of September next, not removed to such stations will be destroyed.

(Signed) H. Hannahs, Adjutant, by order
Brigadier-General Ewing.[56]

Thus, the order forced the people of the Missouri border counties of Cass, Jackson, Bates and part of Vernon out of their homes within fifteen days of issuance, or 9 September 1863. The only exception was for residents living within one mile of the towns specified in the order. Those who had sworn allegiance to the United States and held a certificate to that effect could move to a Federal military installation or anywhere in Kansas except the eastern border counties. Further, loyal residents had to move all grain and forage to military stations by 9 September. If by that date any foodstuffs were found in the named counties, held by loyal citizens or otherwise, the Union forces would destroy the remainder. This was sober medicine and yet the order satisfied no one.

Lane and his supporters railed against G.O. #11 as an ineffective remedy to festering rebellion. On the other hand, Missourians, both Rebel and Unionist, sent up a howl protesting to anyone that would listen against the barbaric order. The attorney general of the state of Missouri, George Bingham, vociferously opposed the order and when he failed to overturn it, took up a paint brush and rendered a lasting impression of what he deemed intolerable. That painting is titled simply *Order No. 11*. In spite of the cacophony rising against him, Ewing refused to budge, forging ahead in determination to implement the order. General Schofield and the Lincoln administration then backed Ewing, allowing him to move forward. It would take time, and Ewing would take a heap of abuse from several directions, but ultimately G.O. #11 worked since there was never again a raid on any Kansas town.[57] Ewing had once again demonstrated a high degree of moral courage. His days challenging Border Ruffians during the elections in Kansas had developed in him a vast reservoir of intestinal fortitude, and during the crisis days following the Lawrence raid he needed every bit of it he could muster.

Nevertheless, Ewing's days as commander of the District of the Border were num-

Order No. 11 **painted by George Caleb Bingham (State Historical Society of Missouri, Art Collection).**

bered. Senator Lane's disgust with Ewing had reached a point where he had to see him removed. Lane's motivations probably had more to do with protecting his political base and business prerogatives than with any real concern for the protection of Kansas. Therefore, he pressed the administration hard for a change of command. By January 1864 pressure on Lincoln from here and other directions reached a point where the president finally acceded. Schofield had angered Missouri politicians to the point he had to go, so he was reassigned to command of the Department of the Ohio. Ewing found himself exiled to Colorado to fight hostile Indians, but not for long. When William S. Rosecrans was moved to the Department of Missouri, he asked for a staff experienced in the region. He asked Samuel R. Curtis, in command in Kansas, for Ewing and got him. Ewing was placed in command of the District of St. Louis in February 1864.[58] This put Ewing on a collision course with destiny. Only months later he would come face to face with the Rebel Army of Missouri, full of leaders that would like nothing better than to capture the infamous issuer of G.O. #11. Yet, at Pilot Knob Ewing would again exhibit steel determination and turn in the best tactical performance of his military career. The decision he made at Pilot Knob changed the course of Price's Great Raid.

Following the successful defense of Pilot Knob and a harrowing retreat from the field, Thomas Ewing would fade from the scene as a major actor during the raid. Once Price decided to turn west away from St. Louis, another major actor under the command of Rosecrans entered the stage, and that man was the dapper Major General Alfred Pleasonton. Like his boss, Rosecrans, Pleasonton was a cast-off from the major theater of war to the east. This man was once the commander of the Army of the Potomac Cavalry Corps and had participated in every major campaign of that army through Gettysburg. He was moderately competent and had a talent for picking the solid young commanders who would make the cavalry in the East a formidable force. However, Pleasonton had a major character flaw that caused him to run afoul of his commander in the Army of the Potomac, George G. Meade. Pleasonton was a schemer with an ambition for high command, and his methods to obtain this goal led to his exile to Missouri.

Alfred Pleasonton was born on 7 July 1824 in Washington, D.C., to Stephen and Mary Pleasonton. Unlike the rest of his Union peers, he was the only senior commander who had no association with the state of Ohio. Stephen was a mid-level bureaucrat in the Treasury Department who had become a folk hero when he rescued several founding documents as the British burned Washington during the War of 1812. Among the papers he saved was the Declaration of Independence. Growing up in the nation's capital distinguished Pleasonton from his peers and antagonists who had rural upbringings. By all accounts he was very bright and could make his future one of great promise. Living in Washington provided access to a quality education, one that could bring admission to West Point. The young man, ambitious already at a young age, applied for an appointment to the academy as a fifteen-year-old. He passed the entrance exams at age sixteen and was admitted to the class of 1844 as one of the youngest members of the corps of cadets.[59]

The promise of Pleasonton's childhood years continued through his time at West Point. The small class of 1844 contained several notables who would serve at high levels in the Civil War such as Winfield Scott Hancock and Simon Bolivar Buckner. The class shrank over the course of four years to 25 cadets and Pleasonton consistently ranked in the top third. His academic performance resulted in a class ranking of seventh, earning him a choice of branch in the army. Pleasonton chose the prestigious cavalry—which ranked right behind the engineers in respectability—and his first assignment found him posted with the famous 2nd Dragoons. The regiment was stationed at Fort Atkinson, Iowa, on the frontier to police the Great Plains, which were populated by hostile Indians.[60] His regiment stayed on the move during his tenure, and Pleasonton accompanied his unit in extended operations from Minnesota to Texas. Within two years, he found himself in Mexico, where the army would recognize him for distinguished service and bravery under fire.

Upon the United States' declaration of war on Mexico, the 2nd Dragoons moved south, becoming part of Zachary Taylor's Army of Observation near the Rio Grande. When hostilities opened, Pleasonton was at the center of the action. When the Mexican army moved to engage Taylor's army to bolster Mexico's claim that the border was further north, the 2nd Dragoons made the first contact, allowing Taylor to respond. Recognition came quickly for Pleasonton as a result. For bravery under fire at Palo Alto and Resaca de la Palma, he received a promotion by brevet to first lieutenant. Unfortunately for the ambitious Pleasonton, the war moved further south into Mexico while his unit was left in northern Mexico to perform minor constabulary duties. However, immediately following the war he was recognized for outstanding service with a full promotion to first lieutenant.[61]

In the interwar years Pleasonton found himself performing administrative duties as an adjutant for his regiment, as well as other senior commanders. By all accounts, he proved to be a superb staff officer, and this was both a blessing and a curse. His skill as an administrator created quite a demand for his services. For example, Brigadier General William S. Harney made Pleasonton his adjutant for a campaign against the Sioux Indians in the Dakota Territory in the late 1850s. Pleasonton's fine performance kept him in such duties throughout the interwar years. Therefore, this kept him out of the line and field duty—where promotion came much faster. As his hopes for an appointment were of almost limitless ambition, this fact must have grated on Pleasonton. Thus, by the outbreak of the Civil War, he was only a captain with seventeen years service.[62] Even the outbreak of the Civil War did not bring immediate relief to his desire for advancement.

Major General Alfred Pleasonton, Commander, Provisional Cavalry Division, Department of Missouri (Library of Congress).

3. A Team of Outcasts

When the Civil War broke out Pleasonton was in Utah with his regiment, and as the senior captain he was in command. Even though the Federal government was in desperate need of trained soldiers, no call was sent to the 2nd Dragoons. Instead, the regiment continued to serve on the frontier, much to the frustration of Alfred Pleasonton. Finally, in the fall of 1861 the 2nd received orders recalling the unit to the capital in the wake of the disaster at Bull Run. Pleasonton took charge and marched the regiment east in an arduous 2,000 mile journey.[63] Yet even this move brought little action, as the Army of the Potomac under George McClellan was still building strength.

During his time at the capital, Pleasonton did his part to build the cavalry corps of the Army of the Potomac. While in Washington, a long overdue promotion to major came through on 15 February 1862, starting a meteoric rise in rank and responsibility during the war for Pleasonton. The process of organizing the army brought Pleasonton to the attention of McClellan. The commanding general brought the ambitious major up to his staff, where Pleasonton worked hard to gain McClellan's favor. In this, he was remarkably successful. His first action in the war came during the Peninsula Campaign in the spring of 1862. In his capacity on McClellan's staff, Pleasonton performed reconnaissance duties to gather information about the enemy. McClellan was apparently impressed by Pleasonton's performance and earmarked him for advancement. On 16 July 1862—only four months after his elevation to major—Pleasonton received a promotion to brigadier general in the cavalry and command of a brigade.[64] Thus, within a matter of months Pleasonton had advanced more ranks in one stroke of a pen than in his previous eighteen years of service. However, this was not as much attributable to his competence in the field as it was a demonstration of his ability for self-promotion. Pleasonton would soon gain an unsavory reputation as "the *bête noir* of cavalry officers ... a newspaper humbug."[65] In other words, his peers saw him as a man fixated on his own ambitions rather than the good of the army or his soldiers, a situation eventually leading to his exile to the west in 1864.

Pleasonton's first action as a large unit commander came at the battle of Antietam. His performance is characterized by one author as one that "failed to add luster to his reputation." The primary reason for this is the fact that Pleasonton did not provide what an army commander most needs from his cavalry—good intelligence. As the Maryland campaign got underway, Pleasonton's brigade was in the lead and he would make first contact at South Mountain. After the infantry drove the defending Rebels from key gaps in the mountains, Pleasonton set out in pursuit, but he did so with too small a force to have any effect beside annoyance. At Sharpsburg, he was unable to penetrate Major General Jeb Stuart's protective screen and thus could not determine the plight of Lee's divided army. Since Pleasonton could not divine the true state of the Army of Northern Virginia, he now resorted to providing McClellan speculation and wild rumors in lieu of real information. Young Charles Russell Lowell, colonel of the 2nd Massachusetts Cavalry, would later write, "I can't call any cavalry officer good who can't see the truth and tell the truth.... [I]t is the universal opinion that P[leasonton]'s own reputation and P's late promotions are bolstered up by systematic lying." Such poor reporting by Pleasonton would lead some to give him the sarcastic sobriquet of the "Knight of Romance."[66] In spite of this reputation, he was elevated again to command of a division following Antietam.

In the fall of 1862 Pleasonton began to work on the reorganization of the cavalry of the Army of the Potomac, which was his greatest contribution to the war effort. Heretofore, the Rebel cavalry led by Stuart had ridden rings around that of their Federal antagonists in the East. Much of the reason for this is that the Union cavalry was poorly organized. In a thoughtful memorandum written to his commanding general, Pleasonton recommended that the Army of the Potomac consolidate units into a corps, appoint a single commander answering only to the army commander, and organize the new corps with its own organic firepower so that it could conduct autonomous operations.[67] Joseph Hooker would follow these recommendations almost to the letter to establish what would eventually become the formidable instrument Sheridan would wield later in the war. For all his flaws, this contribution by Pleasonton made possible a significant leap toward the Army of the Potomac's eventual victory over the Rebels in the East.

Pleasonton rose to national prominence at Hazel Grove in the battle of Chancellorsville, thanks to a matter-of-fact comment to President Lincoln after the fight. Pleasonton's division was left with the main army when Hooker launched a large raid with the rest of the corps to divert Lee from the main attack. This left Pleasonton to picket the flanks of the advancing Union army. On 2 May 1863, Pleasonton's men discovered Lieutenant General Stonewall Jackson's flanking attack on the army arrayed around Chancellorsville. Jackson had already precipitated a rout on the hapless XI Corps, but Pleasonton notified headquarters in time to allow Sickles' III Corps to change front and arrest the panic. Pleasonton's role in the incident became inflated when Hooker introduced Pleasonton to the president, who was visiting the army after the defeat, as the man "who saved the Army of the Potomac the other night."[68] Three weeks later, Pleasonton was promoted to major general and command of the entire cavalry corps, thus succeeding in his ambitions for high command.

Pleasonton's second greatest act as a commander in the Army of the Potomac Cavalry Corps was in choosing the dynamic young leaders who took the organization to its zenith of glory, but he did this at the expense of a group of other men he disliked. During the short period of time between Chancellorsville and Gettysburg, Pleasonton began a systematic program of removing foreign-born officers in favor of young and flamboyant men such as George Custer. It was no secret that Pleasonton disliked immigrant officers, opining to a friend, "I have no faith in foreigners." As a result, Pleasonton wielded his new power to get rid of undesirables.[69] While his motivations are suspect, Pleasonton's program resulted in a substantially improved cavalry corps from a command perspective. Thus, while Pleasonton's days with the Army of the Potomac cavalry were numbered, he left a lasting legacy on the organization.

Lee sought to take advantage of his victory at Chancellorsville by invading Pennsylvania in June 1863. The clash at Gettysburg was the coming of age of the Union cavalry in the East. However, Pleasonton's role was diminished, much to the chagrin of this ever-ambitious man. Hooker was relieved of command of the Army of the Potomac on 29 June 1863 and replaced by Major General George G. Meade. Unlike Hooker, Meade did not view the position of commander of the cavalry corps the same as his predecessor had. Meade saw the job as a staff position rather than one vested with command authority such as his infantry corps commanders wielded. Further, Meade had little confidence in Pleasonton and wanted to keep him close at hand rather than allowing him a free hand in operations.[70] As a result, Pleasonton played a minor role in the action at Gettysburg, and such undertakings that he did supervise were failures. If he had left matters alone following Gettysburg, he probably would have remained in command, but ever the schemer, his conniving for further advancement produced the opposite result.

Pleasonton's problems in the aftermath of the great battle of Gettysburg began almost immediately. Meade was not very aggressive in his pursuit of Lee's defeated army. Pleasonton, however, was very forceful in his conviction that Meade should conduct a more aggressive pursuit. He agitated that Meade should seek to bring Lee to bay before Lee could return to Virginia. When Lee did make good his escape south, Pleasonton publicly denounced the failure to pin Lee down in Maryland.[71] This was just what certain political factions in Washington wanted to hear, as the Radical Republicans were looking for an excuse to dismiss the irritable and ill-tempered Meade.

On 7 March 1864 the Joint Congressional Committee on the Conduct of the War called Pleasonton as a witness to testify about the actions at Gettysburg, specifically decisions made by Meade. The powerful Joint Committee was an organ of the Radical wing of the Republican Party, which believed the conduct of the war by the Lincoln administration lacked the proper leadership, aggressiveness, and direction. Their remedy for this lack of fervor was political pressure from the legislative branch to press for greater action from the executive as they saw fit. The committee frequently called investigations and inquiries to attempt to force Lincoln to modify his policy for conducting the war. Pleasonton's testimony in 1864 led directly to Pleasonton's removal from command by an angry and indignant George Meade. Pleasonton—apparently undermining Meade in order to gain command of the army—publicly accused his commander of incompetence in the wake of Gettysburg. Further, he testified that Meade had thrown away the fruits of Gettysburg and thus, as far as "my own corps is concerned, I do not think General Meade has their confidence."[72]

Within a day, Meade got wind of Pleasonton's incredible testimony before the committee and wrote a puzzled missive to his wife stating that Pleasonton's disloyalty was "the meanest and blackest ingratitude." Meade then used his pen to demand to secretary of war Edwin Stanton that he receive permission to relieve Pleasonton. Stanton granted Meade's request and on 23 March 1864, a mere two weeks after Pleasonton's appearance before the Joint Committee, he received orders relieving him of command and transferring him to the Department of Missouri. Pleasonton's fortunes had now plummeted to rock bottom, for all officers knew that the West was where leaders were sent to wither away, far from the limelight in Virginia.[73]

Pleasonton packed up and dutifully moved west, reporting to Major General William Rosecrans. The commander of the Department of Missouri—an exile himself—assigned Pleasonton as commander of the cavalry in the department. It was in this capacity that Pleasonton served for the remainder of the war in total obscurity. Yet Pleasonton's best field service took place in the last year of the war. He would relentlessly pursue the fleeing army of Sterling Price in 1864, and the Department of Missouri cavalry would deal Price a death blow at Westport and Mine Creek in conjunction with the forces from the Department of Kansas under the command of a solid soldier named Samuel R. Curtis.

The venerable Samuel R. Curtis had performed great and competent service for the Union in the far west throughout the war. His greatest triumph came at Pea Ridge in March 1862, but he was soon shelved because of frictions he encountered with the Missouri governor and administration while managing his department. His actions during the Great Raid gave Curtis a measure of redemption, but he never fully retrieved his reputation. Samuel Ryan Curtis was born on 3 February 1807 at Champlain, New York, to Zarah and Phalley Yale Curtis. His parents were originally from Connecticut, but like many families at that time, they sought a better life and joined the great westward migration taking place. In 1809, the Curtises settled in Licking County, Ohio.[74] Thus, Curtis, like most of his Union peers, was an Ohioan raised in rough-hewn frontier fashion.

As mentioned, Ohio was the frontier of the United States in 1809 when the Curtis family moved to the state. It was a difficult place to live, as the earliest settlers had to scratch out a living from the surrounding wilderness. Further, hostile Indians still roamed the state and danger came from this quarter as well. Nevertheless, for a young boy this environment provided the right elements to produce a hardy and resourceful young man. By all accounts, Curtis became just this sort of man and his upbringing proved a happy and adventurous one.[75]

Samuel Curtis was able to secure a satisfactory education on the frontier. He attended public schools with his siblings, supplemented by home schooling from his parents. Curtis' two older brothers probably stimulated his intellect, because these young men became respected lawyers. While their attainments may have stimulated him, Curtis decided on a more varied career path. Striking out on his own, he decided to pursue an appointment to West Point. The entrance exams were quite difficult at that time, especially for a young man who had a public education. Thus, it took Curtis a greater amount of time to attain the coveted appointment than it did most of his fellow cadets. He finally gained an appointment to West Point at the age of twenty in 1827, making him among the older cadets.[76]

Major General Samuel R. Curtis, Commander, Federal Department of Kansas and the Army of the Border (Library of Congress).

In spite of his frontier education, Curtis managed to perform well enough to claim a commission in the U.S. Army. Further, the education he received introduced him to a lifelong passion, engineering. The U.S. Military Academy of the 19th century was known as one of the best engineering schools in the world. It is here that Curtis developed a love for the profession for which he would demonstrate a great aptitude. While he enjoyed his course work, he consistently ranked in the lower half of his graduating class.

When he graduated from the academy in July 1831 he stood ranked 27th out of a class of 33 cadets. His mediocre marks earned him a commission in the infantry branch. Curtis thus found himself posted on the frontier with the 7th Infantry Regiment in the Indian Territory.[77]

His first and only assignment with the 7th posted Curtis at Fort Gibson on the Great Plains. This area of modern-day Oklahoma is a barren grassland and, at that time, was in the midst of hostile, migratory Indian tribes. Young Lieutenant Curtis did not find life on a frontier army post stimulating to his interests. Therefore, in 1832, only one year after receiving his commission, Curtis resigned from the army to pursue his interests as a civil engineer. He returned to Ohio, where he took employment as an engineer working on road construction. He also found time to marry Belinda Buckingham and start a family, having several children with Belinda. Among his children was Henry Curtis, who would die at Baxter Springs during the Civil War.[78] Throughout the 1830s, Samuel Curtis engaged in a number of engineering projects, all with a common denominator. They consisted of efforts to bind the country together with an efficient transportation network to promote commerce and unity. Curtis would work on the National Road and various canals and champion the construction of a transcontinental railroad. In 1839, he developed a plan for just such a project and found an audience in Congress with John Q. Adams.[79] The lasting impact of engineering upon the character of Curtis was a passion for methodical processes underpinned by logic. He would carry this propensity for orderly endeavor with him to the battlefields of the Civil War and it would frustrate him when others did not share his demand for logic.

By the 1840s, the fertile mind of Samuel Curtis led him down a different path for a time. In 1841 he was admitted to the bar at Wooster, Ohio. He established a moderately successful private practice and settled into this profession until the start of the Mexican War in 1846. While practicing law, Curtis also engaged in military duties. He raised a company of militia known as the "Mansfield Blues" and he personally oversaw their training. He applied his methodical fashion to this training and the unit was reportedly quite proficient in drill. This, combined with his status as an attorney, made Curtis very well respected in Ohio. As a result, when the Mexican War broke out Curtis was appointed adjutant general of Ohio. Preferring instead to serve actively in the field, he received a commission as colonel of the 3rd Ohio Volunteer Infantry.[80] Thus, he gained practical experience as a field commander that would make him a valuable asset to the Union in 1861.

In June of 1846 Curtis received his commission and soon thereafter began the trek to Mexico with his regiment. Unfortunately, the 3rd Ohio did not see as much field service as Curtis might have desired. Rather, the regiment was used for garrison duty to consolidate gains made by Zachary Taylor's field army. In conjunction with this duty, Curtis served as the military governor of several of these points. In particular, he administered the occupation of Matamoras, Monterrey, and Saltillo. Immediately following the battle of Buena Vista, he assembled a large force to pursue the retreating Mexican army. This endeavor came up empty and a frustrated Curtis returned to his duties as military governor. As the war wound to a close, he was appointed to the staff of Major General John E. Wool, one of Winfield Scott's primary subordinates.[81] This array of positions, while frustrating at times, did prepare Curtis for command in the Civil War.

In particular, his time as military governor mirrored his duties as a departmental commander in Kansas. Further, his desire for order guided him through his myriad responsibilities. Thus, Curtis would provide the Federal Trans-Mississippi west with a competent leader—which were in short supply—when the time came in 1864.

Following the war with Mexico, Curtis returned to his passion—civil engineering. He accepted a post in the new state of Iowa designing and supervising watershed management projects on the Des Moines River. As the chief engineer he threw himself into the project. However, when the recalcitrant Des Moines River failed to cooperate in the most important aspect—making it navigable—the state legislature of Iowa terminated his employment.[82] An engineer of Curtis' talent, however, would not remain unemployed for long.

In 1850, the city of St. Louis needed a chief civil engineer to solve the significant engineering problems facing the city. It was in this job that Curtis made a lasting and gratifying contribution to the future of the city while satisfying his itch to develop and build. St. Louis in the 1850s had serious sewage, flooding, and drainage issues. Curtis attacked each with a vengeance and by 1853 he had instituted projects that rectified every problem and more. His multifaceted plan called for draining outlying swamps, establishing a viable sewage system, emplacing a levee, and dredging the Mississippi. Together, these projects markedly improved the infrastructure of the city and contributed to a sustained economic boom since the city could increase river commerce. Curtis might have stayed on in St. Louis beyond 1853 had it not been for the vagaries of politics. In that year the St. Louis mayor—Curtis' patron—did not win reelection and, as a result, Curtis lost his appointment as chief engineer.[83] Yet this development only opened up new opportunities for him.

In 1853 Curtis moved to Iowa permanently, taking a job in Keokuk as chief engineer for a railroad. In this position he surveyed line and advocated for a transcontinental railroad that would become "the highway of nations." In addition to this, Curtis also established a law practice at Keokuk and began to develop an interest in public service. He having developed a solid reputation in Keokuk, the citizens elected him mayor in 1856. By this time Curtis had coalesced a personal political philosophy. His proclivities to abolitionism carried him naturally into the arms of the new Republican Party. He quickly became a member of the party, and in the fall of 1856—less than a year after his election as mayor—he ran for, and won, a seat in the U.S. House of Representatives from Iowa's 1st District.[84] Thus, Curtis became one of the first Republicans elected to serve in public office in the United States.

Curtis' political career took off following this election. He was quickly reelected in 1858 and 1860 by large majorities. The people of Iowa seemed to appreciate the manner in which he represented them. One author states that "few men ever rendered more honest and successful service."[85] Multiple accounts of Curtis identify him in such terms. This enabled him to win elections, but it was his moral courage that endeared him to the people he represented and would later make him a competent, if not brilliant, combat leader. His vast reservoir of moral courage would build trust in his subordinates and prove indispensible to his service in the Civil War.

When the sectional crisis began to boil over, Curtis was serving in the U.S. House and never backed down from advocating for abolition policies, though dissolution of the Union troubled him. After several of the southern states seceded, Curtis participated in the so-called Peace Convention of February 1861 in Washington. He represented Iowa in the futile effort to find a compromise to the secession crisis. The attempt failed and within a month the Rebels sank any hope of averting war when they fired on Fort Sumter. Upon Lincoln's first call for 75,000 volunteers on 15 April 1861, Curtis promptly traveled back to Washington to offer his services. He joined the 7th New York as it arrived in Washington, D.C., to defend the capital, acting as a volunteer aide to the regimental commander until he could obtain a commission. Desperate for trained, experienced officers, Lieutenant General Winfield Scott and the War Department immediately authorized Curtis to raise Iowa volunteers and he returned to Iowa to begin the process.[86]

By 1 June 1861, Curtis had raised the 2nd Iowa Infantry and was mustered in as its colonel into Federal service. At age 54 and suffering from inflammatory rheumatism, he began an arduous and successful career as a commander in the Civil War. The ever-meticulous Curtis immediately instituted a program of drill and instruction to whip the new regiment into shape. However, the necessities of war intervened to cut the training short less than two weeks after commencement. Desperate for troops, on 13 June Brigadier General Nathaniel Lyon called on Curtis for assistance to guard the railroad between St. Louis and St. Joseph, Missouri. Curtis promptly moved forward to Hannibal, saving this vital supply line for Federal use. After two weeks on duty, Curtis—who had not yet resigned his House seat—went to Washington when the legislature convened for a special session on the organization of the rapidly expanding army. As one of the few members who had graduated from West Point and served in combat, his experience proved invaluable in drafting the legislation. While in session on 21 July 1861, Congress had to adjourn suddenly when panic struck the capital in the aftermath of the disaster at 1st Bull Run. Curtis reportedly moved to the front after the body adjourned to assist in stemming the tide of the leaderless mob streaming back from the battlefield.[87]

At the conclusion of the session, Curtis finally resigned from the House on 6 August and simultaneously received a promotion to brigadier general backdated to 17 May 1861. As Curtis was now armed with the new commission, Winfield Scott ordered him back to the west to report for duty in Missouri under Major General John C. Frémont. He arrived at St. Louis by mid–August and Frémont gave him command of the camp of instruction for new recruits and units at Jefferson Barracks. Curtis' talent and reputation for methodical processes and organization probably contributed to his superiors placing him in this job, which proved critical in building the Union army in the Trans-Mississippi.[88]

By fall, the command situation in Missouri was in shambles following the death of Nathaniel Lyon at Wilson's Creek. Frémont was widely considered incompetent, with Curtis providing his own criticism that "Frémont was unequal to the command of an army." President Lincoln agreed with the assessment and on 6 November 1861 Frémont was cashiered and replaced with David Hunter, while Curtis was elevated to command of the field army in southwest Missouri. Only days after taking command, Curtis made preparations for a winter campaign—a rarity in the Civil War, and in 19th century warfare, for that matter. The intent of the movement was to clear Missouri once and for all of Rebels and to move into northwest Arkansas to push the Confederates deeply into that state to keep them from coming back.[89] Campaigning in the winter was an inherently dangerous proposition from a logistical standpoint. The army had to stockpile a great deal of supplies and arrange appropriate transportation to support a moving army. Without a rail line or river, sustaining an army in hostile country made that army vulnerable to destruction. Luckily for Curtis, he had a logistic officer of incredible talent and drive, Philip H. Sheridan, who was appointed as chief commissary on 26 December 1861. The combination of Curtis' methodical problem-solving and Sheridan's energy ensured that the army would survive and win.[90]

The Union Army of the Southwest, as Curtis styled it, moved from Rolla to Lebanon, Missouri, on 29 December 1861 "for the purpose of initiation of a concentration of forces." It took a month at Lebanon to concentrate the scattered Union forces in southwest Missouri and for Sheridan to accumulate enough supplies of flour and corn meal to commence the campaign in earnest. The army first moved to secure Springfield on 10 February 62, which Price abandoned, slipping back into northwest Arkansas. This was the last time Price would set foot in Missouri until 1864, when he would again meet Samuel R. Curtis during the culminating phase of the Great Raid. Even at this early stage of the unfolding campaign, Sheridan began to form a positive opinion of Curtis. He states in his *Memoirs* that Curtis "impressed him deeply" with his "conviction" and determination. Curtis did not dally at Springfield after Price left the place, setting his army of 10,500 men in pursuit toward Arkansas.[91]

By 18 February 1862, the Army of the Southwest had arrived at Cross Hollows, about ten miles south of the Missouri-Arkansas border and just north of Elkhorn Tavern. Curtis fanned out the army toward Fayetteville and Bentonville to try to establish contact with the Confederates, but this would not happen. Price had retreated deep into Arkansas through the Boston Mountains. At Van Buren, Major General Earl Van Dorn combined Price's Missourians with Ben McCulloch's men to form an army of 16,000 men. On 3 March 1862, Van Dorn reversed Price's course and began an advance on Curtis' army to brush him aside and advance into Missouri to take "St. Louis and carry the war into Illinois."[92]

Meanwhile, Curtis had begun to make defensive preparations along a stream known as Little Sugar Creek. In his calculating manner, he laid out a strong line of resistance and had the army dig in. This line of works was facing south to receive an enemy Curtis thought would come up from that direction. However, the wily Van Dorn made Curtis' preparations irrelevant when he settled on a plan to sweep around Curtis' right flank. He did this discreetly through a series of forced marches, moving rapidly down from the north to surprise Curtis in his rear.[93]

During the night of 6 March, Brigadier General Franz Sigel sent out scouting parties that "heard the noise of wagons or artillery." Sigel believed that this represented an attempt to attack Curtis from the rear. He notified Curtis in the early morning hours of 7 March. The alarmed Curtis immediately faced the army about to meet the threat coming now from the north rather than the south. Curtis made the redeployment of the army without panicking and instead, in a determined manner, passed the orders that enabled his divisions to meet the enemy. By 8:00 a.m. on 7 March, Van Dorn ran into Curtis' army head-on rather than coming upon his rear area.[94]

Even though he had successfully repositioned the army, Curtis was in a tight spot.

His army was outnumbered three to two and had no fortifications to compensate for the inferiority. The action that commenced was a brutal two-day fistfight that sapped the strength of both armies. The battle of the 7th was in essence two separate engagements, with Van Dorn's army separated by the Pea Ridge promontory. The Union commanders, with Curtis providing solid direction, stubbornly held their positions throughout the day. The deaths of several key Confederate commanders, including Ben McCulloch, aided the Union's defense. During the night of 7–8 March, Curtis decided to continue to defend the position. He shifted his divisions closer together that evening for better mutual support and had them prepare for a counteroffensive to drive the Rebels away from their loose positions around Elkhorn Tavern. Just after dawn on the 8th the Union army initiated the action with an artillery preparation followed by an assault by the infantry. After a hard fight on the right, the Federals swept the Rebels and Price from the field.[95]

The victory at Pea Ridge was not only spectacular, it was decisive. Pea Ridge forced the reeling Confederates deep into Arkansas and unable to threaten Missouri for a long time. The Federals had struggled for a year to secure Missouri, but it was the Pea Ridge Campaign that secured the state for the Union for the rest of the war. Other than episodic raids, the Rebels would never again seriously threaten to wrest the state into the orbit of the Confederacy. Curtis deservedly received the lion's share of credit for the victory, which represented the zenith of his military career. He was promoted to major general on 21 March 1862 as a reward, and accolades came from all quarters. In a great testament to Curtis' services, Sheridan wrote that he "was deserving of the highest commendation, not only for the skill displayed on the field, but for the zeal and daring in the campaign."[96] Curtis seemed on his way to greater responsibilities, advancement, and fame; however, he would soon run afoul of civilian authorities due to his abolitionist convictions and inflexible way he would run a department. But, for now, he intended to take advantage of the benefit accrued from the victory at Pea Ridge.

In the aftermath of Pea Ridge, the state of Arkansas seemed open to the Union plan to wrest it permanently away from the Confederacy. Accordingly, Curtis laid plans to move on the Arkansas capital at Little Rock and drive out the Rebel state government. In the meantime, he had to take several weeks to restore the combat power of the army. The Army of the Southwest had lost 1,384 men out of 10,500 engaged. Additionally, the army was well over 100 miles from the nearest supply depot. In the 19th century an army had difficulty operating at such distances without a water or rail line of communication. The wilderness of northwest Arkansas had no such means of transportation, meaning that horse flesh had to haul supplies down from Missouri. Therefore, it would take time to stockpile supplies for another forward thrust. Finally, other commands in the East were considered more important, so Curtis was ordered to send regiments to those armies to reinforce operations east of the Mississippi. Thus, it was questionable if Curtis could hold Little Rock even if the army could get there.[97] Regardless of the uncertainty, Curtis intended to try.

The reduced Army of the Southwest commenced moving southeast toward Little Rock in the first week of April 1862. The army advanced along the axis of the White River Valley slowly and deliberately. However, the inability to maintain a secure line of communication and paucity of supplies forced Curtis from his objective at Little Rock.

Instead, he diverted to Helena on the Mississippi River, arriving there on 14 July 1862. While holding Helena would not secure the state for the Union, it would ensure a solid supply line down the Mississippi.[98] Further, Helena was a strategic point on the west side of the river about a hundred miles north of Vicksburg. Control of this place would secure the flank of any Union force moving downriver to take Vicksburg. Thus, Curtis used his own initiative to facilitate future operations of the war effort in the west.

In spite of Curtis' battlefield success, he was removed from field command to the challenging Department of Missouri in September 1862. This job lacked opportunities for battlefield laurels, but it was fraught with many other intractable challenges. Among these was managing the internecine guerrilla warfare in western Missouri, placating Unionist politicians, and dealing with an array of touchy subordinates.[99] This position would cause Curtis' reputation to go into eclipse due to his uncompromising stances on some sensitive issues.

Early in Curtis' tenure as department commander, he began to receive blame for a failure to suppress the guerrillas. Then Marmaduke entered Missouri on successive raids in late 1862 and early 1863. Although Curtis turned back Marmaduke in both his raids, criticism continued to flow. Then Curtis ran afoul of the Union governor of Missouri, Hamilton Gamble. The governor favored a conciliatory policy toward Southern sympathizers. Curtis followed a different course, severely punishing disloyal citizens with arrests and banishments. Further, he instituted a policy of emancipating slaves of those citizens, contrary to administration guidance on the issue. Therefore, Gamble petitioned President Lincoln for removal of Curtis. On 22 May 1863 Lincoln did just this because Curtis was unable to "reconcile the difficulty" between Gamble and abolitionist factions. Since Lincoln could not remove the civilian governor of a state, he had to relieve Curtis.[100] From May 1863 until January 1864, Curtis was a general without a command and tragedy in his personal life struck during his exile.

Major Henry Curtis became Major General James G. Blunt's adjutant following his father's relief from command in Missouri, where he had served his father in the same capacity. On 6 October 1863, the younger Curtis was accompanying Blunt from Fort Scott en route to Fort Smith, Arkansas. The party planned to stop at Baxter Springs along the way to Fort Smith in order to visit the small Union garrison posted there. It just so happened that on the morning of the 6th William Quantrill's Confederate guerrillas had planned a visit of their own to attack the fort that very morning. Quantrill's men had failed to penetrate the defenses and were regrouping outside the perimeter when a more lucrative target—Blunt's party, including the army band—was spotted moving south toward Baxter Springs. Quantrill broke off the attack on the fort and immediately fell in line to assault the moving column. The Federals panicked and Quantrill's men chased the fugitives, killing over seventy of the one hundred men in Blunt's escort. Among the dead was Major Curtis, who was shot through the head.[101] Obviously, the loss devastated Samuel Curtis, compounding the sting of his fall from grace.

Yet Curtis would not remain on the shelf forever. On New Year's Day of 1864, he was appointed as commander of the Department of Kansas. Through the middle of 1864, the department remained quiet and Curtis spent most of his time organizing his forces to chase hostile Indians in western Kansas.[102] But by late summer rumors began to spread that Sterling Price was planning to invade Missouri and then turn on Kansas, intent on destruction. Curtis would have to scramble to pull together enough troops to fend off Price's invasion. Political difficulties and bureaucracy obstructed his ability to establish a coherent defense. In the end, Curtis would realize battlefield success as spectacular and decisive as his victory at Pea Ridge as the Rebels closed in on the Kansas border in October 1864. But his contributions would go unheralded even after he turned in another outstanding command performance.

An array of men of varying levels of competence served under Samuel R. Curtis in the Department of Kansas, but the man who made the greatest contribution was James Gilpatrick Blunt. He was a man of great talent and enormous character flaws in one package. In battle, Blunt was a relentless driver who could not, nor would he, accept defeat. He was respected by his men yet called "the fat boy" at the same time.[103] As a military administrator he was a disaster, his organizations rife with corruption. The stain of his administrative failures prevented Blunt from realizing lasting fame and respect.

James Blunt was born in Trenton, Maine, on 21 July 1826 to John and Sally Gilpatrick Blunt. John was a farmer in this cold and wild state in the early 19th century. Like that of many of his peers and future adversaries, James's farm upbringing did much to shape his character by teaching him resilience and self-reliance. He would demonstrate these traits on numerous occasions, before and during the Civil War. In 1840 Blunt, at the young age of fourteen, struck out on his own, taking a job with a shipping company and becoming a sailor. He worked on a seagoing merchant ship four years. Upon his return from sea, he enrolled in the Ellsworth Military Academy in Maine. It was reputed that among Blunt's classmates was Joshua Lawrence Chamberlain. After attending Ellsworth—without graduating—Blunt moved west to Ohio, the home of several other future Federal commanders in the Great Raid.[104]

Upon arriving in Ohio, Blunt quickly enrolled in the Starling Medical College in Columbus, Ohio, in 1845. He studied under the tutelage of his uncle Dr. Rufus Gilpatrick. Four years later, he graduated from Starling and began practicing medicine in western Ohio. Between 1849 and 1856, two significant things happened in his life. First, he married fourteen-year-old Nancy Putnam, starting a family and, second, he joined the fledgling Republican Party, signaling his entry into politics as an abolitionist. Blunt actively campaigned on behalf of presidential candidate John C. Frémont in 1856, a man he would later come to detest during the Civil War.[105]

Blunt's burgeoning activism soon convinced him that he had to do more to remove the scourge of slavery, and for him this meant moving to Kansas to directly battle the forces of bondage. He moved to the territory in late 1856, settling in northeastern Kansas' Anderson County. Here he quickly became active in local politics and took a direct hand in fighting the pro-slavery Border Ruffians. The Ruffians had made several incursions into border county settlements, raiding the citizenry. Free-Staters, led by John Brown and others like Blunt, retaliated in kind to assert their rights. In one incident, Blunt led a posse to Fort Scott to protect abolition settlers from a group of pro-slavery men who sought to eject Free-Staters in Bourbon County. Blunt's men successfully drove off the slavery men with help of their Sharps rifles, providing Blunt with his first "military" experience and giving him a reputation as a man who stood by his convictions. He would also ally with Brown in moving fugitive slaves through the state to the north and participate in the founding of the town of Mt. Gilead on Pottawatomie Creek.[106]

Blunt's first experience in the local political scene came when he worked to convince the populace to boycott the 1857 elections in order to undermine the effort of Missourians to skew the outcome. As an organizer of this effort, he gained notoriety and a senate seat in the territorial legislature representing the abolition settlers. In 1859 he was chosen by the citizens of Anderson County to represent them in a constitutional convention held at Wyandotte. Blunt played a leading role in drafting the document, serving as the chairman of the militia committee and on the banking and corporations committee. It appears he got the chairmanship of the militia committee because he was the only delegate at the convention with any military training. As such, he had great influence in organizing the militia that would fight for the Union in the Civil War. He would also offer cogent suggestions on commerce and banking that focused on promoting economic activity while preventing corruption. Blunt's role brought him notoriety that would propel him to a general's commission in the coming conflict. But he also revealed a less than savory aspect of his character. At one point during the convention a reporter erroneously attributed a statement to Blunt that was not correct. Blunt personally confronted the reporter, who instead of retracting the error stated in a future story that Blunt was backpedaling. An infuriated Blunt accosted the reporter, denouncing him on the convention floor in a matter that was admittedly minor.[107] During the Civil War Blunt would demonstrate a penchant for grudge holding, and this would stunt what could have been a stellar career.

Major General James G. Blunt, Commander, Provisional Cavalry Division, Army of the Border (Library of Congress).

When the war came in 1861 Blunt was among the first to offer services to the Union forces in Kansas. On 1 May 1861, he enlisted in the company forming in Anderson County under the command of future Kansas governor Captain Samuel J. Crawford. Shortly after the company assembled they marched to Lawrence to join other companies that would constitute the 2nd Kansas Infantry Regiment. As the 2nd Regiment gathered, Blunt took the opportunity to raise a regiment of his own, the 3rd, in Senator James H. Lane's new brigade, which the secretary of war authorized him to recruit. Blunt's move effectively attached him to the star of Lane—known as the Grim Chieftain—giving Blunt a powerful patron in state and national politics. He would ride on the coattails of Lane until the Senator's untimely death by suicide when the war drew to a close.[108]

The 3rd Regiment assembled at Mound City and then marched to Fort Scott in August, with Blunt serving as its lieutenant colonel. The men elected him to this position, thus launching his military career as the second in command of a regiment. Blunt saw his first action a month later when a band of raiders crossed the border from Missouri under the command of Captain John Mathews. In addition to plundering homesteads across southern Kansas, Mathews' men burned the town of Humboldt. Blunt, in command at Fort Scott while Lane was chasing Sterling Price, took the initiative to pursue Mathews with some 200 men. He relentlessly hunted the Rebel raiders for 72 hours before cornering them in Indian Territory at their campsite on the Neosho River. Attacking at daylight, Blunt's command scattered the Rebels and killed Mathews.[109] This little fight earned Blunt a reputation as a hard fighter and relentless driver, beginning the rise of his star as one of the premier Union leaders in the western border region.

While all this was occurring, the Rebel army under Sterling Price had marched unimpeded across Missouri. They had won the battle at Wilson's Creek and captured Lexington and 3,000 Union soldiers, while fattening the army with Missouri recruits. Nevertheless, Price could not hold his gains because of his precarious logistical situation and was forced to retreat to the southwest corner of Missouri. John C. Frémont took command of the Union troops in Missouri following Lyon's death at Wilson's Creek, and he had an excellent opportunity to destroy Price in late 1861. But, Frémont missed the chance because, as Blunt recounted, he had a poor "conception of the military situation in his department ... and made very poor use of the means of his command."[110] This is the first time we see Blunt's critical assessment of others coming into play. His irascibility and altogether insubordinate direct criticisms of superiors would lead to his relief from command just as his achievements on the battlefield reached their zenith.

In April 1862, Blunt was unexpectedly promoted to brigadier general by the War Department and assigned duty as commander of the Department of Kansas. It is unclear how he came by this command as he did not solicit such a promotion. However, we could surmise that his positive performance in minor actions, combined with the patronage of James Lane, delivered him the command. Whatever the reasons, Blunt assumed departmental command on 4 May 1862 and, by his own account, he was "inexperienced in the routine of military affairs ... with many misgivings as to my qualifications."[111] Many unscrupulous subordinates and contractors took advantage of this fact, tainting Blunt with the stain of corrupt administration for which multiple investigations would dog his tenure. Only his instinctive understanding of what he needed to do in the field and his unquestioned bravery saved him from humiliation.

In late fall 1862, Blunt took the field to clear Missouri and northwest Arkansas from any further threat of Rebel invasion. Major General Thomas C. Hindman was known to be assembling an army in the vicinity of Fort Smith, Arkansas, for the purpose of wresting away Union control of the northwest corner of Arkansas and then advancing on Missouri to contest Federal authority there. Blunt aimed to stop this by preempting

Hindman's planned offensive. Blunt notified his superior, John M. Schofield, that he would advance in mid–November. By the 25th of November, both forces were moving toward each other on a long ridge called Cane Hill. Hindman planned to draw Blunt southward and circle around to the east to hit Blunt's army in the rear.[112] The key was Marmaduke's cavalry finding and fixing Blunt.

The Union commander actually pinpointed the Confederates first and pushed a superior force onto Cane Hill to defeat Marmaduke, enabling the commander to turn the tables on Hindman. On 28 November, Blunt attacked Marmaduke and in a long running battle, defeated him. Further, Blunt had coordinated with Brigadier General Francis Herron to combine forces to trap Hindman as he moved north. With the defeat of Marmaduke at Cane Hill, Blunt had upset Hindman's plans by his aggressive moves, yet this did not deter the Rebel commander. Hindman simply shifted the direction of his advance in the hope of catching Blunt off guard.[113] However, Blunt did not oblige him.

As Hindman began his movement in a bitter winter cold, Blunt pulled his force back to the north, closer to Herron's men moving south to reinforce him. Hindman was unaware of Herron's presence and thus, rather than surprising Blunt with an attack on his flank, Hindman was about to receive a jolt of his own. On 7 December 1862, Hindman had finally learned of Herron's proximity to his army and launched a headlong assault on Herron, interposing between him and Blunt. At first, Hindman's tactical decision paid off, but he did not stick to his decision to attack. Instead, he pulled his army into a defensive position behind the Illinois River.[114] This effectively passed the initiative to Blunt, who took full advantage.

Blunt and Herron now launched their own assaults, pinning Hindman in his defensive position. The fighting raged from mid-afternoon until darkness when the lack of visibility arrested the battle. Neither side gained any advantage from the battle, and both armies suffered grievous casualties. It seemed that the result was a draw tactically, but operationally and strategically Blunt won the campaign. This is because Hindman could not support his forces logistically, "considering that my men were destitute of food [with a] small supply of ammunition," and therefore, had to withdraw. The net result was that Missouri was saved and northwest Arkansas was permanently wrested from Rebel control. The campaign was Blunt's first major operation and battle and he performed with competence and, at times, with brilliance. What is more, he had the moral courage to act on his assumptions and vigorously pursue his intent. Whatever Blunt's failings as an administrator, he had ability on the battlefield and some people were beginning to take notice.[115]

A flurry of praise came Blunt's way in the aftermath of Prairie Grove. In Kansas newspapers extolled the victory and politicians discussed promoting Blunt with the War Department. Indeed, Blunt's name was submitted to Congress along with Francis Herron's for promotion to major general of volunteers in March 1863. Upon approval in May, Blunt became Kansas' first and only major general during the war. The promotion, however, came with a controversy, as Blunt's superior, John M. Schofield, was passed over. A feud was bubbling between the two men before Prairie Grove. Schofield believed that Blunt was too lax in his administrative duties with the Department of Kansas and launched investigations to weed out corruption in that department. For his part, Blunt accused Schofield of being a desk general rather than a fighter—as Blunt fancied himself. Blunt even went so far as to accuse Schofield of cowardice, as he "had deserted his command in the face of the enemy." An irritated and frustrated Schofield would later write that Blunt and his patron James Lane were "much more formidable enemies than the hostile army in my front."[116]

Although the two men would continue to trade barbs, Blunt had other business and that was fighting Rebels. Immediately after Prairie Grove, he drove straight for Van Buren to clear the Rebels down to the Arkansas River. On 27 December 1862, Blunt's army arrived and he reported ecstatically that "the Stars and Stripes now wave in triumph over Van Buren." In the process of capturing the town the Federals took four steamers laden with food intended for the hungry Rebels. This forced the Confederates to retreat to Little Rock, thus completing the victory of Prairie Grove. At the same time these events were unfolding, Schofield showed up in Arkansas to assume command in the field. He recalled Blunt and Herron to Prairie Grove, where the units went into winter quarters.[117]

Blunt soon broke free of Schofield for another independent command, bent on clearing the Indian Territory—present-day Oklahoma—of Rebel influence. The Rebels had used the territory as a launching pad for raids into Kansas throughout the war, including the spring of 1863. Confederates under Douglas Cooper and Stand Watie were on the move in southern Kansas attacking supply trains and isolated outposts like Baxter Springs, and even moving on Fort Scott. Blunt aimed to stop this and concentrated the forces under his command for offensive operations. On 5 July 1863, he moved south from Fort Scott in pursuit of Cooper and Watie.[118]

Blunt set a blistering pace to prevent the Confederates from escaping. The army moved 175 miles in five days, arriving at Cabin Creek, site of a stiff fight on 2 July between Watie's men and a Federal supply train escort. The Confederates withdrew south and Blunt moved in that direction to bring them to bay. On the 16th of July his force found the Rebels encamped at a place called Honey Springs. Blunt pushed his men all night to cross Elk Creek and arrive in position to attack at daylight on the 17th. Even though Cooper and Watie outnumbered Blunt—whose command was now the first integrated formation in the Union army—he nevertheless attacked "and after two hours of severe fighting, the center of their line was broken." Blunt was aided by a rainstorm that fouled the Southerners powder, enabling the attack to succeed. The Confederates retreated south and Schofield recalled him because he "was too far advanced and must fall back."[119] This irritated Blunt and reignited their feud, which would eventually prove fatal to Blunt's further advancement.

Following the campaign, Blunt pulled back and became severely ill from what was believed by some doctors to have been a severe reaction to sunstroke. When he finally recovered in the fall, Blunt found himself dealing with pesky guerrillas who were terrorizing southern Kansas. The notorious William C. Quantrill crossed into Kansas in October 1863, and Blunt went to work to secure the population. However, one of the most heartbreaking incidents of the war occurred at this time. Major Henry Curtis, Samuel Curtis' son, was serving as Blunt's adjutant general at this time. As was his custom, Blunt moved his headquarters forward to get close to the action.[120] In this case, the action was along the Kansas-Missouri border at Baxter Springs.

As discussed earlier, on the day that Quantrill's men set to attack the post at Baxter Springs—6 October—Blunt decided to move with his escort from Fort Scott to Baxter Springs. Quantrill's band had attacked the small fort and foraging parties that morning, scattering the foragers but unsuccessfully attacking the fort. However, a lucrative target appeared to the north: Quantrill's men sighted Blunt's escort. The general and his security detachment thought that Quantrill's men were Union soldiers, as they were wearing Federal blue that allowed them to get within "about seventy-five yards." By the time Blunt realized the mistake, the guerrillas had commenced their attack, with one Rebel noting that they went "at them in our accustomed manner, yelling and shooting and they scattered across the prairie." Blunt and Curtis attempted to hold the escort in line of battle, but panic quickly set in and Curtis was killed minutes after the fight started. Many of the dead in Blunt's detachment were killed after capture and riddled with bullets. Somehow, Blunt successfully rallied a handful of survivors and made it safely to the fort. Though he showed little emotion, his postwar "Account" demonstrates that the incident still held a sting that he regretted.[121]

Baxter Springs somewhat tainted Blunt's battlefield reputation and Schofield took the opportunity to use it and the investigations to rid himself of Blunt. Schofield forwarded a damaging report to Major General Halleck at the War Department and Lincoln in the White House accusing Blunt of fraud and corruption, further stating, "I am compelled to relieve…. Blunt from his command." Schofield requested authority to court-martial officers who were "unworthy." On 19 September 1863, Schofield relieved Blunt and ordered him to report to Fort Leavenworth for further instructions. Blunt proceeded there and fired off more acid laced missives against Schofield. It seemed that Blunt would remain shelved for some time, but Schofield was soon transferred east. In his place, the Lincoln administration appointed William S. Rosecrans as commander of the Department of Missouri and Samuel R. Curtis as commander of the Department of Kansas in January 1864. Blunt lobbied his old patron, Senator Lane, and by February 1864, Blunt was appointed commander of the District of the Frontier.[122]

In mid–1864, Curtis had Blunt chasing hostile Indians in western Kansas and Colorado. While not Blunt's first choice for employment, at least he was active, even if it was in a minor corner of the war. He would not remain there for long, as Price had launched the raid into Missouri in the fall. Curtis became uneasy at the prospect of defending his department with the lackluster commanders he had on hand. It would not take long for him to recall Blunt, with his reputation for aggressive fighting, to pitch into the Rebels.[123] Blunt would prove to be the right man for the job, as Curtis had the fighter he needed to arrest the advance of Price before he reached Kansas.

4

"A blow that had destiny in it"

Following the success of the Trans-Mississippi army in Louisiana and Arkansas in the spring of 1864, tremendous pressure began to mount in Richmond and Shreveport to do something to aid the struggling Rebel armies east of the Mississippi. The effort to decide upon a course of action took several months. By the time the Trans-Mississippi Department actually launched Price's expedition into Missouri, it was too late to have any appreciable effect on the course of events in the East. The leadership of the Confederacy, in conjunction with the Trans-Mississippi departmental command, considered a number of courses before reality dictated a move on the west side of the river. The overly centralized command apparatus, combined with quixotic expectations in Richmond, made choosing what to do a painful process. The debate over how the Trans-Mississippi forces could aid the war effort centered on three components. First was how the Confederacy should employ the forces available in the Trans-Mississippi. Second was who should command Confederate forces to achieve the established objectives. Third was what the goals were and how the force should organize to secure them. After a drawn-out debate lasting over three months, the Rebel high command made the decisions, but the result was too late and inappropriate for the capabilities of the Trans-Mississippi army as this stage of the war.

The Red River Campaign and its supporting effort, known as the Camden Expedition, concluded on 22 May 1864. For the Trans-Mississippi army it was a spectacular victory—but ultimately a hollow one because of multiple missed opportunities. Nevertheless, Rebel forces west of the river were in the unprecedented position of having the initiative and had the strongest army of any in the Confederacy in terms of relative strength and freedom of maneuver. Thus, employing these forces for maximum effect was critical as enormous pressure began to mount on the main Rebel armies in Virginia and Georgia. But, what should be done?

The Confederates began to consider a number of courses of action, all for the dual purpose of relieving pressure on the eastern armies and influencing the northern elections in November. The first course proffered was for an invasion of Missouri. While Frederick Steele was still in flight from Camden, Kirby Smith was already proposing the move into Missouri as the logical follow-up to the successful defenses of Arkansas. On 19 May 1864, Smith sent an order to Sterling Price to begin logistical preparations for a campaign into Missouri. Price, quite naturally, was only too happy to get started with accumulating supplies and laying plans for the operation. Smith intended to launch the expedition by August. He estimated that it would take several months to compile the needed supplies due to the rickety transportation system available to his department.

Further, waiting until August would allow crops along the route to ripen, facilitating the army's ability to forage for sustenance for man and beast.[1] However, waiting this long gave rise to circumstances that would disrupt Price's preparations. In the meantime, planning and discussion continued in earnest among the leaders in the Trans-Mississippi.

Governor Thomas Reynolds was also anxious to have the army move into Missouri in order to restore him to the capital of the state. He played the role of sounding board for both Kirby Smith and Price. On 2 June 1864, he opened up a correspondence with Price to determine the feasibility and prospects for an operation in Missouri. Price responded a week later with his assessment of what was possible. Specifically, he stated that "a concentration in Missouri will relieve the whole Trans-Mississippi Department south of it." Further, he believed thousands of recruits were waiting to join the colors as soon as a Rebel army could return to Missouri.[2] It is interesting to note that Price was thinking only in terms of Missouri and west of the Mississippi; he was not considering what might be good for the Confederacy as a whole.

This greatly encouraged the exiled governor, who saw even greater benefits accruing from a campaign in Missouri. In answering Price he suggested that "an expedition ... may take off some of the pressure on us in Virginia and Georgia." In another letter to Kirby Smith, Reynolds reiterated that a "powerful diversion in Missouri may enable him [Johnston] to force back Sherman weakened by detachments to defend that state." Additionally, it could divert Federal efforts to take Mobile while adding much needed recruits to the army. Finally, politically the invasion would bring Missouri into the Confederacy and Reynolds to the seat of state government at Jefferson City.[3] In contrast to Price, Reynolds was looking out for the welfare of the Confederacy as a whole, which is very commendable since he was the governor of Missouri. So it seemed that the potential benefits of a movement far outweighed any negatives. Yet the authorities at Richmond—specifically the Confederate pseudo-chief of staff, Braxton Bragg—had other ideas about how to employ the Trans-Mississippi troops.

In early July, while the department was preparing for the Missouri expedition, Lieutenant General Stephen D. Lee, commanding the Department of Alabama, Mississippi, and east Louisiana, sent an inquiry to Kirby Smith on behalf of General Braxton Bragg. In the letter, Lee asked Kirby Smith about the possibility of making a troop transfer east of the Mississippi River. In the message dated 9 July 1864, Lee wrote: "There is little doubt that Canby is now moving on Mobile with 20,000 troops. It is of vital importance that a part of your troops are crossed over the Mississippi, or you co-operate in such a manner as to divert their troops. General Bragg directed me to confer with you as to crossing troops." This correspondence effectively halted continued planning and preparations for Price's Missouri expedition. Instead, Smith directed that the department expend organizational energy in finding a way to satisfy Bragg's request. On 23 July, Bragg issued a directive to Smith telling him to make the crossing "with the least possible delay." This note changed the effort from a discussion of possibilities into a specified order from the military advisor to the commander-in-chief, President Davis. Therefore, Smith, through his chief of staff, William R. Boggs, dispatched his own order to Richard Taylor. He enclosed the order from Bragg and told Taylor to cross two divisions—Walker's and Polignac's—over the "Mississippi River with as little delay as possible."[4] For the next month the Trans-Mississippi Department and Taylor would feverishly—and in vain—search for a way to comply with Richmond's directive.

Richard Taylor had great incentive to make the effort to cross the Mississippi a reality. Taylor, the son of President Zachary Taylor, was locked in an acrimonious feud with Kirby Smith in the summer of 1864 that Governor Reynolds characterized as an "injurious quarrel." The reason for this was a disagreement between the men arising from decisions made by Smith during the Red River Campaign. Therefore, Taylor was willing to do anything in order to separate himself permanently from Smith. Taylor examined a number of different solutions to crossing the river, but in every case he found them impractical since the Federals controlled the river. Among the courses Taylor considered were the use of boats, a pontoon bridge, and swimming. To assist Taylor, Smith placed his chief engineer, Colonel H.T. Douglas, at Taylor's disposal.[5] Douglas got down to business soon after receiving his assignment.

Of the courses considered, only ferrying or bridging were remotely practical possibilities. As Colonel Douglas got to work assessing the feasibility of the two courses, he eliminated ferrying as a possibility. The reasons for that assessment were the scarcity of boats, the necessity to keep the divisions intact, and bringing the artillery and trains along in the transfer east. The boats available would require several trips to ferry the troops and equipment over the river. Plus, these were not adequate for carrying large equipment such as wagons and artillery. With Union gunboats patrolling the Mississippi, a drawn-out operation to ferry two divisions of over 4,000 troops with all their heavy equipment did not seem practicable. As a result of this analysis, Douglas wrote a letter of recommendation to Kirby Smith, sent through Taylor's headquarters, advising what he thought was the best course. Since "the main object [is] to cross the troops en masse in order that their organization may be retained and capable of entering at once upon an active field of usefulness ... it will be necessary to take with the troops subsistence, artillery, and trains. This can only be done by a pontoon."[6] In other words, Douglas was stating that if the expectation of the transfer was that Taylor's force would go straight into combat operations, then the only way to ensure it arrived intact for this purpose was to use a pontoon bridge. Therefore, he recommended this as the only feasible course of action, and Taylor "heartily approve[d] of Colonel Douglas' plan."[7]

Even to establish a bridge would require a herculean effort on the Rebels' part. Because of the unreliability of the Trans-Mississippi Department logistics and transportation networks, Douglas estimated that it would take him "thirty days to prepare everything." It was already 4 August 1864 when Douglas wrote this letter, and it would require a minimum of a month before the first soldier even set foot on the bridge to cross. The Confederacy simply did not have this luxury of time, as Douglas even noted that "the army in Georgia [is] now pressed almost to the wall."[8] In spite of the effort to marshal the resources to make the transfer, there were other factors the Confederates had to consider to bring the crossing to fruition.

Among the several challenges beyond resourcing was where to make the crossing. Site selection is critical to a pontoon bridging operation and it could not happen at any location. The entry and exit points had to have the proper topographical requirements from a stability and geographic standpoint, which the Federals were quite capable of guessing. Next, such an operation had to remain a secret until the last possible second—a difficult proposition in any war. A loss of cover would give the enemy the opportunity to get into a position to counter the bridging operation. Finally, there was the enemy. The entire operation seemed based on the outlandish assumption that the Union navy would remain inactive, thus enabling the Rebels to carry out their plan. This was pure fantasy, and yet the Rebels would advance their plans and prepare for several weeks before the realization of its impossibility finally set in. Nevertheless, Douglas proceeded in his mission to find a solution to fulfill the War Department's orders to the Trans-Mississippi Department.

Colonel Douglas realized that any attempt to bridge the river would require security from prowling Union gunboats. Therefore, he devised a plan for site protection involving the use of mines and artillery. He would obtain mines—called torpedoes by combatants of that time—from Alexandria, Louisiana, to place above and below the proposed bridging location to prevent gunboats from closing on the site. He would place the artillery to cover the minefields with fire in order to blast the halted ships on the perimeter: "I wish 100 torpedoes of 50 pounds each.... I would also recommend ... that the heavy guns ... [be] placed in battery opposite the proposed point of crossing."[9] The plan seemed logical, but could a line of submerged mines and a few siege guns really protect a bridge site across the wide Mississippi? As the Confederates continued to refine their plan and make preparations for the crossing, the answer would reveal itself as the reality of the situation became manifest.

There were several elements that made Douglas' plan unworkable and Kirby Smith had surmised this upon seeing the plan. First, how would Douglas get the mines emplaced across the Mississippi? At this point in the war, the Confederacy had no river navy and the Union had supremacy of the western waters. Thus, there was no feasible way to get the torpedoes to the middle of the channel and anchor them to stop the Federal gunboats. Second, could all this Rebel activity in making preparations to cross go undetected by the enemy? The answer to this was no. In fact, the Union navy caught wind of what the Confederates were planning and increased their patrols along the Mississippi at likely crossing sites. Union naval reports bear this out. In one report from Commander Robert Townsend to Acting Lt. J.S. Watson of the USS *Hastings*, the commander acknowledged that "the additional information you obtained during your last trip below, respecting the preparations made to cross over rebel troops to the eastern bank of the Mississippi, more thoroughly convinces me that it is necessary a gunboat should patrol the river between this point [Memphis] and Helena." Third, the rickety Rebel logistic system was unlikely to deliver the resources Taylor would need to sustain his force. As already discussed, Taylor would have to carry everything he needed with the two divisions. But the single ribbon of bridge would require hours to set up and then to cross the troops with all their supplies and equipage to sustain them. Bridging the Mississippi for any extended length of time would surely draw in prowling Union gunboats. Even if Douglas could get the mines in place and artillery to cover them, gunboats had already proven time and again that they could run past torpedoes and shore batteries. The best example of this was at Vicksburg. Therefore, it seemed impossible to move all the troops and resources in a reasonable amount of time without a Federal counter stroke to destroy the bridge. Finally, desertions began to pick up as the troops in the divisions of Walker and Polignac—from Texas and Louisiana—learned that they were designated to leave the Trans-Mississippi. This would drain the units of manpower, diminishing their strength and defeating the very purpose for making the crossing.[10] All of these factors became self-evident when the time came to execute the movement.

Richard Taylor knew this intuitively and when he moved forward to begin execution he quickly confirmed his suspicions of the impracticality of transferring any large mass of troops to the east side of the river. The plan called for making the crossing on the 18th of August at a place called Dolgin Wall. But that same day, Taylor wrote a dispatch to Kirby Smith informing him of the "impossibility of crossing any body of troops." Among the reasons Taylor enumerated for not making the crossing was the stepped-up patrols of the Union fleet. Additional reports by naval officers bear out Taylor's assertion. Commander Thomas O. Selfridge, commanding the 5th District, Mississippi Squadron, sent a message to Admiral David Dixon Porter stating, "The enemy threatened to cross in large force in the vicinity of Waterproof. I have accordingly concentrated the whole force of the district between Grand Gulf and Natchez." In a later and more extensive note to Smith, Taylor told him a crossing "would result only in injury to the whole command, [and] I assumed the responsibility of ordering a suspension of the movement." Smith in turn informed Richmond and sent orders through his chief of staff to "suspend the movement of troops across the Mississippi River."[11] Thus, the whole affair was a failed attempt to provide assistance to Confederate forces east of the Mississippi. It also struck up yet another controversy between Smith and Taylor.

During the course of the attempted operation to cross the river, Taylor at one point informed Smith that he intended to cross in advance of his troops in order to make preparation to receive them on the other side. It is very likely that Taylor's all too visible hatred for Smith motivated the attempt to cross ahead of the troops in order to permanently rid himself of his nemesis, Kirby Smith. The commander of the department did not agree with this decision and "positively forbid" Taylor from executing his crossing. This incensed Taylor, who in turn referred the matter to the War Department. Not to be outdone by Taylor, Smith appealed to President Davis to back him in his decision. The president claimed to know nothing about having ordered an attempt to cross the Mississippi. An embarrassed Smith was now seemingly on his own hook in dealing with his irascible subordinate. The whole matter was not cleared up until December, when Davis discovered documents that demonstrated that Bragg had taken it upon himself to order the crossing in the president's name.[12] In the meantime, Smith would have to continue dealing with his difficult subordinate, who had another idea in mind that might enable the Trans-Mississippi Department to succor the ailing armies to the east.

Richard Taylor offered that the best use of the Trans-Mississippi troops was a movement to either secure or isolate New Orleans. For Taylor, this seemed a logical extension of his victory over the combined force of Nathaniel P. Banks' Army of the Gulf and Admiral Porter's fleet in the Red River. As a Louisianan, Taylor greatly favored any move that would free his state from the hand of Federal occupying forces. All Taylor needed to carry out a campaign in the direction of Lafourche Parish and New Orleans was the infantry divisions that Smith had stripped him of to drive Steele back in Arkansas. Taylor began considering such a move before Banks evacuated the Red River

Valley. On 14 May 1864, he informed Smith of his intent to "throw myself into the Lafourche, [and] confine the enemy to New Orleans." Smith, however, never really gave Taylor's idea of a move on New Orleans any serious consideration. In Smith's correspondence he is almost scornful of Taylor's plans. Moving on New Orleans would have no effect on matters in the east and prove "barren of military results." Rather, Smith much preferred "to make the Arkansas Valley and Missouri the theater of operations." Smith invited Taylor to participate in a move into Missouri, but Taylor's acerbic reply to Smith's suggestion ensured that he would not join expedition.[13] Thus, Smith made the final decision to make Missouri the field of operations in the late summer and early fall of 1864.

With crossing the Mississippi and a move on New Orleans ruled out, preparations for a move into Missouri now became an urgent task for the Trans-Mississippi Department. In fact, Smith had never really stopped preparing for a Missouri expedition. On 1 August 1864, he convened a conference at Shreveport with Price, Governor Reynolds, and others to discuss the move, issuing orders on 4 August.[14] The authorities at Richmond acquiesced to the fact that they could no longer use the Trans-Mississippi as a source of manpower for the eastern armies. With this in mind, Bragg, Seddon, and Davis had to accept the fact that if they were to gain anything positive from the troops west of the Mississippi, then whatever the Trans-Mississippi army could do would have to occur on that side of the river. As a result, Richmond reluctantly endorsed the planned movement into Missouri. It was a logical expectation to conclude that Sterling Price would be the man to lead the expedition. However, there were some senior leaders in the Confederacy who began to question this premise and actively searched for an alternative to the egotistical Price.

Governor Reynolds and Kirby Smith carried on an extended discussion about who should command the invasion. Smith had long ago come to the conclusion that Sterling Price lacked the requisite capacity to lead a military operation and during those summer months actively sought out a replacement for Price. "He [Price] is absolutely good for *nothing,*" Smith confided in private to Thomas Reynolds.[15] Price's performance in the Camden Expedition had convinced him of this. During his dialogue with Reynolds, Smith shared one instance to confirm this assessment. During the late defense of southwest Arkansas, Smith had given Price the critical mission of guarding all the roads out of Camden. But when Smith arrived at Price's headquarters to take personal command, he noted that Price had failed to do so. The neglect of this key task allowed Steele to escape from Camden and the grip of the encircling Confederates, saving the Federal army to fight another day. From this and other incidences, Smith concluded that Price was "destitute of every military quality." One observer, an aide to Braxton Bragg, noted in a letter that Smith was considering sending Price east of the Mississippi to rid himself of this difficult and incompetent subordinate.[16] Thus, Smith sought Reynolds' counsel as to placing another man in command of the planned operation in Missouri.

Reynolds had his own misgivings about Price's qualification to command. Several Missouri generals had approached the governor to air grievances about Price's leadership and to request a change of command. Brigadier General John S. Marmaduke had served with Price for some time and had, in Reynolds' words, formed "a very low opinion of General Price's military capacity." Further, Price's staff protected him from criticism by blaming his subordinates for any failures while, conversely, claiming credit when they achieved success. Marmaduke was so pointed in his disdain that he claimed he would not serve under Price should he command a Missouri campaign—a position he later retreated from.[17]

This information seemed to confirm Reynolds' misgivings about Price's ability, and he began to consider who might command in his stead. There were a number of very competent officers Smith could choose from to appoint as commander of the expedition. First, there was Marmaduke, who had compiled an impressive record as cavalry commander. He was from Missouri and well respected among troops from the state. However, Marmaduke was only a brigadier general and Reynolds doubted that Marmaduke could galvanize the population of Missouri. Further, Price's staff would surely undermine Marmaduke's command should he receive the appointment to command over Price. Another man of ability was Brigadier General John Fagan, who, like Marmaduke, had a history of success as a cavalry commander. Yet appointing Fagan as the man to lead the campaign was more problematic than giving the job to Marmaduke. This was because Fagan was from Arkansas and had never set foot in Missouri. Should he receive the command, it "would excite jealousy of the Missouri officers." So clearly Fagan could not command the movement. Jo Shelby was certainly an attractive candidate. Following the war, Shelby would rank with the best cavalrymen the Confederacy produced and many people would speak of him in the same breath as J.E.B Stuart and Nathan Bedford Forrest. He was, by consensus, considered the best horse commander the Trans-Mississippi produced, with Sterling Price asserting, "I consider him [Shelby] the best cavalryman I ever saw."[18] Nevertheless, Shelby was junior to almost every other general officer in the department and, although he was a Missourian, elevating him to command of the Missouri campaign would not sit well with anyone. Richard Taylor and John B. Magruder were sound leaders, but Taylor's feud with Smith stood against his appointment and Magruder "was considered indispensible" as commander of the District of Texas.[19] Yet Reynolds was not discouraged, for he had taken a liking to a new man in the Trans-Mississippi Department, Simon Bolivar Buckner.

Major General Buckner was a fine officer from Kentucky whose competence, sense of honor, and propriety were beyond reproach. Reynolds petitioned the Richmond authorities in 1863 to bring Buckner to the Trans-Mississippi. A motivation behind this effort was to position Buckner to take Price's place if the opportunity should arise. Reynolds believed the popular Buckner would make a palatable replacement for Price among the Missouri troops, many of whom were transplanted Kentuckians. As he began to discuss the question of who could command the Missouri expedition, Reynolds began to present Buckner as a solution. "You know the very high opinion I have of General Buckner," Reynolds wrote to Smith. As he continued to discuss the command question, Reynolds offered a creative way to sideline Price: "He [Buckner] could maintain order, system & vigor in the administration of the Department." This would free Smith to take the field. Thus, Price could not complain about a junior officer taking charge of the expedition because Smith would be in charge. Then the campaign would have a competent commander, which would minimize the possibility of poor discipline within the force or diversion from the intent of the move due to Price's independent—and insubordinate—streak. Another idea was to make Buckner commander of the cavalry, while

Smith commanded the field army in a Missouri operation. But Buckner himself objected to this thought, stating that as an infantry officer, he did not have the requisite qualifications or experience to lead horse soldiers.[20] In the end, as Reynolds and Smith gave more thought to the matter, they concluded that Price was probably the only realistic choice to command the expedition.

On 1 August, when Kirby Smith convened the meeting at his headquarters in Shreveport, he took the opportunity to confer personally with Reynolds over the question of command and other matters. The purpose of the meeting was to discuss a Missouri expedition, even though the department was ostensibly still focused on crossing troops over the Mississippi to the east. Nevertheless, when the meeting got underway, Reynolds and Smith began to discuss whether or not Price was the right choice for command. Reynolds offered that there were two reasons why Price was probably the only man who could command the expedition. Both reasons were of purely political consideration. Price and his staff were skilled at building up a high military reputation for him. Thus, Price had a great following among Missouri's congressional delegation and the troops, and he still retained popularity among the citizens. Further, Richmond—including the president and secretary of war—believed that Price was the only acceptable commander for a move into Missouri. This fed the second reason why the only choice for the expedition was Price. The government was "dread [to create] political dissention" when it came to military matters. Therefore, Richmond would not support any other leader that might sow that dissention.[21] Interestingly, Reynolds proffered this weakness of the Confederate government as one of the reasons for the ultimate demise of the Confederate States of America. The inability to challenge recalcitrant and self-motivated leaders led to a lack of cohesive military command and strategy, in contrast to Union leadership that eventually weeded out most of that type of commander.[22]

Reynolds had one more suggestion to make to Smith with reference to Price's commanding the expedition. Since everyone was in agreement that Price was less than adequate as a military leader, the Rebels would have to take measures to mitigate his known shortcomings. Therefore, Reynolds suggested that Smith must surround Price with "the best division and brigade commanders and an unusually efficient staff." This, Reynolds believed, would cover Price's tendency toward allowing indiscipline in the ranks, his insubordination, and his poor administrative skills. As another means of keeping a tab on Price, Reynolds intended to accompany the expedition. This would allow Reynolds to keep Price's force focused on the political objective of capturing Jefferson City and installing a Confederate state government.[23] This seemed logical, but Price was still the commander regardless of brilliance of his subordinates. He would place his imprint on the command, and the men—and leaders—would tend to mimic his behavior. So, in spite of Reynolds' best effort to reduce the risk of Price at the helm with solid lieutenants as subordinates, the expedition would follow the course set by Sterling Price, much to Reynolds' chagrin.

With the matter of who would command decided, attention now shifted to the nature of the campaign and composition of the army. The 1 August conference continued with this line of discussion. As previously mentioned, the Confederate government in Richmond was becoming desperate to find some way to relieve the pressure on the Confederacy's eastern armies. Smith was sensitive to Richmond's concerns, so the discussion turned to the design of the Missouri operation to provide aid. First, the assembly had to decide upon operational and strategic objectives and, second, they had to determine what the force would look like to achieve the goals.

Reynolds, Smith, and Price came to fairly quick and simple agreement on the operational and strategic objectives. At the operational level, two key objectives were identified. First, the operation would force the Union to react to the invasion by diverting forces from east of the Mississippi to meet the threat in Missouri. Second, the operation would serve as a vast recruiting mission to feed the manpower-starved Confederate armies. One of the reasons the Confederates believed that Missouri was such a ripe recruiting ground was the continuing guerrilla activity within the state. For years, starting well before the war, Missouri had seen an unrelenting series of depredations. By 1864, it seemed that the level of violence had grown and this led to the assessment by Price and others that Missourians desired to throw off the yoke of Federal domination.[24] At the strategic level, the Confederates had three lofty goals to turn the tables of the war in their favor. First and foremost, the Rebels hoped that an invasion of Missouri would capitalize on disaffection toward the Lincoln administration by influencing the Federal election to the benefit of a peace candidate. Another goal was to foster unrest in the northwest in the hope that Copperhead organizations might rise up to break away from the Union. Finally, Governor Reynolds wanted to install a Confederate state government in the capital at Jefferson City, wresting the state from Federal control.[25] These operational and strategic objectives were well defined and could have a great effect on the course of the war if achieved.

One of the interesting operational objectives leading to a strategic end discussed at the conference was fostering unrest in Missouri and neighboring states, known in the 19th century as the northwest. It was no secret that there were several "copperhead" organizations in operation in the old northwest for the purpose of inciting rebellion against Federal authority. These clandestine organizations were known as copperheads because the members wore the head of a copper penny on their lapels to identify each other. One such organization was the Order of the American Knights, or the O.A.K., whose stated intent was to set up a northwest confederacy that would ally with the South. This society supposedly had a large membership in Missouri and neighboring states and Price's son Edwin was rumored to have been a member. A high proportion of its members were said to have infiltrated the Union state militia in Missouri. Price hoped to leverage this to generate a sort of fifth column in support of his expedition. While he confronted the conventional forces of Rosecrans' Department of Missouri, the O.A.K. would foster unrest behind the lines that would siphon away forces from the front line. Price also hoped that the unrest would spread to Illinois and other states in the northwest and ultimately disrupt the Federal election, throwing the vote to a peace candidate. The O.A.K. did issue orders on 1 October 1864 to mobilize in support of Price's expedition.[26] It was a bold plan and logical, but it was based upon faulty information and sheer fantasy. As we see from what actually happened during the raid, and later when the election took place, the belief that the O.A.K. and similar organizations could accomplish anything of consequence was overblown. One participant in the raid would later write that the O.A.K. members "were very much like the inhabitants of prairie dog villages.... When the coast is clear and nobody in sight, there is the most barking … but let a shadow darken the horizon, or a rifle crack in the distance, and, in a twinkling, every furious dog among them burrows deep" in the ground.[27] Nevertheless, Price would put stock in the O.A.K.'s capabilities and attempt to facilitate his operation by coordinating with them. The effort would fail.

While the leaders may have agreed on the goals and objectives, there was a disconnect between Smith and Price. Smith, the professional soldier, wrote his 4 August orders to Price and emphasized low-level tactical objectives. Smith's chief of staff, who penned the order, told Price:

> You will make immediate arrangements for a movement into Missouri.... [Y]our object should be, if you cannot maintain yourself in that country, to bring as large an accession as possible to our force.... Make Saint Louis your objective point of your movement, which if rapidly made will put you in possession of that place, its supplies, and military stores, and which will do more toward rallying Missouri to your standard than the possession of any other point. Should you be compelled to withdraw from the state, make your retreat through Kansas and the Indian Territory, sweeping that country of its mules, horses, cattle, and military supplies of all kinds.[28]

What is missing from the order is a discussion of the strategic ends and operational level goals, such as influencing the 1864 Federal election, establishment of a Confederate state government in Missouri, and diverting Federal forces from other theaters to deal with the Rebel campaign. The entire missive is oriented only on recruiting and raiding, which are lower level considerations lacking linkage to the higher strategic goals. As the commanding general of the department, Smith should have stayed at the strategic level, emphasizing what Price must achieve to facilitate achieving Confederate policy. Instead, he chose to focus on considerations more in the purview of a division commander.

Price, however, would decide to focus on the strategic ends, with emphasis on the political considerations. Price, as we have seen, was a politician at heart, even though he styled himself as a military man. The politician in him chose to zero in on the political aspects of executing the campaign and maintaining his popularity among Missourians. Additionally, Governor Reynolds, who would accompany the expedition, had a great influence on Price's thinking and reminded him by his presence that establishing a Confederate state government was central to the operation. Thus, a cognitive dissonance resulted, by which Price chose to focus on one set of goals to the detriment of the other when executing the Great Raid.[29] Price did this in spite of the fact that the force he took into Missouri was entirely unsuited for achieving the political objective of installing the Rebel government at Jefferson City. Therefore, before the movement even got started there was a division of effort between the leaders in spite of the seeming agreement at the conference.

Regardless of what they agreed to, could the Trans-Mississippi Department achieve such lofty goals and objectives at this point in the war? The answer to this question is "no" by late 1864. The main reason for this is that so much time was spent dithering on a decision to execute something. Nevertheless, a decision was made and in order to meet the stated ends the assembled leaders had to devise the means. However, the leaders would continue to waste time, as the decision making process now involved developing the composition of the force, and there were three possibilities. From the stated goals and objectives, the only way to bring them to fruition was to seize and hold Missouri. This required a full-scale invasion of an army of infantry, cavalry and artillery. It also required engineers to consolidate and hold the ground. The most critical branch composing the force for such an operation was the infantry. This branch is designed specifically to take and hold terrain, and when joined by cavalry and artillery, infantry forces are very formidable. Thus, to achieve the objectives at the operational and strategic level, as articulated by Smith and Reynolds on 1 August, an army with all branches was required in mounting a full-scale invasion.[30] With Smith's long years of service in the United States Army and, later, in the Confederate army, he had to know this. Yet he gave serious consideration to another possibility.

The other force composition considered was one made up of only cavalry. The mounted arm was designed for gathering and developing intelligence about the enemy. It also had the great capability of striking hard and destroying enemy vital points behind the lines or guarding critical points for the army to move unimpeded. Since the men were mounted, speed was the most important element of their combat power. However, cavalry cannot hold ground for any length of time. In the 19th century, cavalry lacked the firepower of infantry and the force had to keep moving to acquire vital forage for the horses. Therefore, cavalry could not achieve all the goals and objectives laid out by Smith and Reynolds. The best cavalry could do was to conduct a large-scale raid that might for a short time divert Union forces. Also, cavalry could not facilitate achieving Price's political objectives, such as installing a Confederate government in Jefferson City, because cavalry simply could not hold the capital for any length of time to allow the Rebels to reasonably claim possession.[31]

The final course—which received little real consideration—was a compromise solution. This meant that rather than concentrating the full strength of the Trans-Mississippi Department's resources with Price, Smith would provide some infantry to conduct an operation against Frederick Steele's Union VII Corps at Little Rock, Arkansas. The purpose of this operation was to protect Price's rear as he swept northward.[32] Smith would retain the remainder of the infantry for the defense of the department south of Missouri. The problem here was that the lack of a full concentration of forces in Price's command would not allow him to hold ground or conduct a proper cavalry raid. For Price to accomplish the strategic and operational goals, he would need the full infantry combat power the department had to offer in the divisions of Walker (now commanded by John A. Forney), Polignac, Churchill, and Parsons. This would give Price the ability to hold any ground he could seize. Tying the infantry column to an operation in Arkansas would deprive Price of the combat power needed to accomplish the mission as discussed in the August conference. In the end, a compromise solution was not workable.

As the conference concluded, it was decided that Price's force would concentrate the District of Arkansas' entire cavalry force, but it would contain no infantry. Smith specified in his 4 August order that Price's operation would move with a force composed exclusively of cavalry. He would report to Richmond that the reason for this composition was that there was no infantry available to task organize with Price's army. As already noted, there were four infantry divisions immediately available for operations in the Trans-Mississippi Department. Yet Smith told the authorities at Richmond that "the withdrawal of this force [making the Mississippi crossing] deprives the Trans-Mississippi

Department, upon which my dependence is placed for either offensive or defensive operations." Therefore, he said, "I shall push a cavalry force into Missouri."[33] This whole explanation for the use of cavalry only was a fabrication that Smith purposely pushed forward.

Smith wrote this dispatch to the president on 30 July, when it was true that the department was still searching for a way to effect a crossing of the river. But even at this point, as already noted, Smith harbored doubts as to the feasibility of crossing a large body of troops, which he stated days later to Richard Taylor. The final decision to call off the crossing was made on 18 August, and Price did not launch the Great Raid until 28 August.[34] It took Price another three weeks to marshal all his forces before entering Missouri. Thus, Smith had several weeks' time that he could have used to redeploy the infantry and task organize them to Price's army. Such an accession to what would become the Army of Missouri would have made it a formidable enemy for the scattered Union forces in that state. Yet Smith, who should have known better, retained the infantry, which would remain idle throughout the Great Raid. As a result, Price would carry only cavalry forward into Missouri.

All of these factors would lead to incongruence between stated goals and objectives and available capability. There were high expectations for this operation at all levels of the Confederate government and military. One observer of the events leading up to the expedition characterized it in somewhat grandiose terms, stating that the move was "a blow that had destiny in it."[35] While this statement was true, the result would have the opposite outcome from Confederate expectations.

There are five major reasons why the Great Raid was likely to fail before it ever crossed the line of departure. The first reason was the confused and ponderous decision making process that caused a four-month delay between conception of the idea and launch into Missouri. The idea for a campaign originated at the conclusion of the Camden Expedition in mid–May. Yet Price did not enter Missouri until mid–September. This dallying while trying to decide what to do gave the Federals in Missouri time to prepare, in spite of their own myriad of issues. Second, the Confederate logistic system was so unreliable that it took months to accumulate the supplies and transportation assets required to sustain the effort. Even this intense effort would fall short of the needs, causing the Rebels to wait until late summer when crops were ripe to supplement the provisions they would carry. Third, there was Price's incompetence, exacerbated by his lack of experience leading cavalry. As events demonstrated, he was not the man to lead an operation of such high expectations for the Confederacy. There were several other leaders who might have performed better, but political considerations prevented Rebel civilian leadership from giving men like Shelby, Fagan, or even Taylor serious thought. Fourth, the goals and objectives were not well articulated. In spite of the fact that the leaders agreed to several important ends, Smith would focus on pure military considerations in his orders, while Price honed in on the political aspects discussed in the conference. Further, the ends the leaders developed were probably far beyond the military capability of the department in September of 1864. Finally, the force structure for the operation, composed entirely of cavalry, was inappropriate for anything beyond a raid. A cavalry force is best suited for rapid movement and hard hitting to destroy specific targets. The goals and objectives identified demanded a force that had the offensive power to take and hold ground, and that meant infantry in the task organization. Thus, there was a disconnect among ends identified, the way to approach execution of the campaign, and the means provided to accomplish the ends.

The Rebel leaders had wasted precious time in pulling the operation together and then failed to link expectations with resources to achieve them. This would undo the operation. Ultimately, this failure rested with the leaders at all levels. The Confederate War Department, particularly Bragg, was asking too much from the isolated Trans-Mississippi Department. Kirby Smith, a long-serving professional, failed to establish the linkage in his orders between the strategic ends, operational objectives, and tactical execution. Nor did he adequately articulate to his higher authority what the department was capable of or clearly communicate to Price in his written orders. Price, the independent thinking politician, would do what he wanted to do, regardless of what Smith told him, and that was focus on the political considerations. This was fully anticipated by both Smith and Reynolds, as their discussion about who should command bears out. Price would follow his previous pattern of behavior in everything he did in Missouri. All of these factors made the possibility of success a remote prospect. The only real chance the Confederates had would reside in whether or not the Federals could respond to the invasion competently. As it turned out, it was a close run thing.

The Confederate Army of Missouri would begin assembling in Camden, Arkansas, after Price received his orders from Smith on 4 August 1864. Two of the three divisions would finally move from southwest Arkansas on 28 August, cross the Arkansas River on 6 September, and unite with Shelby's division in northern Arkansas at Pocahontas by 14 September 1864. The Army of Missouri would finally enter Missouri on the 19th, setting in motion a fateful chain of events that would seal the fate of the state and the Confederate Trans-Mississippi Department. The Federal Department of Missouri under William S. Rosecrans and the Department of Kansas commanded by Samuel R. Curtis would scramble to meet the threat. The ability of Rosecrans to coordinate the defense of his department with his adjacent commander in Kansas would mean the difference in who would control the state ahead of the critical 1864 Federal election. In spite of Confederate issues, as events would demonstrate, the Union defense was totally unprepared and had to cobble together enough force to turn Price back. Thus, the Great Raid was a nail biter instead of a walk over for the Federals.

5

Crossing the River

Once the decision for an invasion of Missouri was finally made, the Rebels began frenetic preparations to launch the operation. Price's army had to gather transportation and supplies, organize, and assemble before final departure into Missouri. Just to make it to the state line of Missouri would require a small operation in its own right. The bulk of the Confederate army under Price was located at Camden in the southwest corner of Arkansas. Between Price and the border was the U.S. Army VII Corps commanded by Major General Frederick Steele. Therefore, in order to conduct the offensive, Price would have to either dispose of Steele or fix him in place at Little Rock. All of this activity could not go unnoticed by the Federals in Missouri, and Major General William S. Rosecrans learned of a storm coming in his direction and began to frantically prepare his widely scattered forces to meet Price. This would prove a difficult task because of a host of issues that included a lack of trustworthy soldiers, poor and spotty intelligence about the enemy, and a fragmented command structure. In spite of all this, the Federals in Missouri would pull it together in time to fend off Price's grim horsemen. The reasons the Federals were able to do so was the continued dithering on the part of the Rebels in preparing for the operation and the ponderous manner by which Price moved a cavalry column. This chronic plodding would prove one important factor of the many that would undo the Great Raid.

When Price returned to Camden from the Shreveport conference he had orders in hand for the one thing he wanted more than anything else—an operation to retake his home state. Needless to say, he was anxious to get things moving and upon his arrival back at Camden, he reported, "I made immediate arrangements for a movement into Missouri."[1] Several challenges awaited him, though, the first of which was the supply situation. Food and forage were issues mainly because of a problem with transportation. The Confederacy never really had a problem producing enough food to feed the armies. Rather, the Southern quartermasters could never move foodstuffs to the point of need because of the South's rickety transportation network, and this problem would plague Price's invasion of Missouri. However, the task of feeding the army was mitigated somewhat because there was forage available early on due to the harvest season, which began as the army moved north. Other problems would, nevertheless, continue to persist.

Just as important as feeding the troops, the army had to carry adequate ammunition for an extended campaign through Missouri. The Confederates could not minimize this need through foraging. The only way to keep the army supplied with powder and bullets was to carry it. A sizeable wagon train was available for Price's army, thanks to the Federal army. The Confederates had captured several hundred wagons during the

Camden Expedition. The problem was that the Rebels needed to fill those wagons to kick off the campaign. Plus, the wagons needed serviceable animals to pull them. A report on 10 August by the Trans-Mississippi inspector of field transportation chronicled his difficulty in obtaining animals. "About 70 percent of the animals [are] received in an unserviceable condition," he stated. Governor Reynolds took note of the failures of the quartermaster when he wrote letters to the Missouri state logistician at Marshal, Texas, on 17 August 1864 exhorting him to greater efforts to supply good horses and mules. Price had planned to cross the Arkansas River on 20 August, yet he was still stuck in Camden waiting for ordnance supplies on that date. He would wait another eight days before he had accumulated adequate ammunition stores to step off from Camden.[2] This delay in moving would bode ill for Price and set the tone for the entire operation. It also gave the Federals more precious time to prepare to meet the Rebels.

Another challenge to starting on time and developing speed and momentum was the scattered disposition of Price's forces. Though his headquarters was at Camden, his command was literally spread across the entire state of Arkansas. The staff was in Camden and had to fit out for field operations. Sixteen miles away, Fagan and Marmaduke's commands were centered at Princeton and Tulip. The units under Fagan and Marmaduke were not physically concentrated at these places though. In order to sustain the men and animals, the units had to disperse across the surrounding countryside for food and forage. For example, Cabell's brigade of Fagan's division was located at Monticello, several miles from Princeton. Cabell's command was spread from along the Arkansas River from Pine Bluff all the way to the Mississippi. Thus, before moving, Fagan and Marmaduke would have to call in their regiments and brigades to establish the march order before heading north. While this task sounds simple, assembling a number of disparate units for a movement is always an operation fraught with friction, consuming time. Finally, Jo Shelby was hundreds of miles away in northeast Arkansas with his command. Like Fagan and Marmaduke, Shelby's men were scattered at many locations, including Sulphur Rock and Batesville along the White River Valley.[3] Price would have to bring these widely dispersed units together and then organize them for action with a coherent command structure. All of these tasks would take time, while to the east ailing Confederate armies daily became more desperate for relief.

Before Price could even bring his army together he would have to deal with the enemy, under Frederick Steele, which still controlled wide swaths of Arkansas. The Federal army in Arkansas consisted of the VII Corps at Little Rock and other points along the Arkansas River from Fort Smith to Pine Bluff. It contained 34,753 troops of all arms present for duty according to strength returns for September 1864.[4] But of these, less than 20,000 were available at Little Rock for defense. The rest were scattered about north of the Arkansas River guarding places like supply depots, hay stations, and rail switches. These points were vulnerable to a large raiding force, which could pick them off one by one. In spite of its scattered disposition, the Federal army in Arkansas was a formidable force that could upset plans for the invasion of Missouri. If these attempted to contest Price's movement north, he could become bogged down and never reach the Missouri state line. The Confederate army, as previously mentioned, was headquartered in southwest Arkansas and would have to elude Steele and fix his forces in place to make it into Missouri. Also, after Price made it into the state he had to find a way to ensure Steele did not turn north to combine with Rosecrans. Part of this responsibility was Kirby Smith's as the department commander, but Price needed to address it for the success of his operation.

As Price planned for the assembly of his army, he also devised a deception to facilitate a successful movement north in order to fix Steele's corps in place. Price's intent was to make Steele believe that his movement north was actually an operation directed against Little Rock instead of a campaign into Missouri. To do this, Price turned to Jo Shelby, his most active and capable commander. Price ordered Shelby "to make an attack, when in his judgment he should deem it advisable, upon Devall's Bluff and the railroad between Little Rock and the White River in possession of the enemy, and by diverting their attention from my own movements enable me to cross the Lower Arkansas—the route then proposed—and unite our forces without danger of failure." Shelby was already raiding in northeast Arkansas to disrupt Federal supply lines and destroy as many exposed outposts as possible. Price's intent in his new instructions to Shelby was to turn Steele's attention away from Price's column moving north toward Missouri. A disruption of Steele's supply chain at Devall's Bluff meant he could not organize a pursuit of Price moving into Missouri, giving the Confederate Army of Missouri freedom of maneuver. Further, Price planned a number of feints along his march route to make it appear that he was aiming to strike at Little Rock.[5] The feints, combined with Shelby's raiding, would make it appear that Price planned mischief within Arkansas rather than Missouri. The plan was sound, and more important, Price had selected the right man for the job.

Shelby started his raid on 24 August with an attack by 2,500 men from his division on a small Federal outpost guarding a hay station near Brownsville on the railroad Price identified in his instructions. The Union unit manning the outpost was a detachment from the 54th Illinois Infantry Regiment, and when they saw the Confederate column approaching the Federal soldiers mistook it for a routine Union patrol. Shelby's men managed to get in close, mitigating the advantage of infantry rifle fire. "The surprise was complete," noted Shelby in his report. Shelby captured 150 men, 200 small arms, and a mountain of supplies. Emboldened, he began to roll up a series of small Federal outposts that day. By the time he reached the last outpost, the Union forces had spread the alarm and the men in this one were ready. Shelby had learned that a large relief column was headed toward the outpost threatening to reverse his successes thus far. With time against him, he dismounted some of Colonel David Shanks' brigade to break the Federal defenders. After a sharp fight, Shanks overran the outpost, capturing the defenders. Shelby "immediately countermarched and 'double-quicked' to the rear, the bullets of their friends [the relief column] all the while ringing fierce."[6] The raid had already netted over 500 prisoners and a mass of assorted supplies, while spreading panic all along the White River Valley.

In a fortuitous twist of luck and good timing, Confederate forces from the Indian Territory under Colonel Stand Watie had conducted a series of raids near Fort Smith in western Arkansas. In one of these actions, Watie had actually captured a steamboat loaded down with foodstuffs for the garrison at Fort Smith. Small garrisons up and down the Arkansas and White rivers were isolated and this series of setbacks in late summer played on Steele's mind, just as Price had hoped. To the east, Shelby had successfully cut off Little Rock from the main supply route on the Mississippi. Near simultaneously, Rebels to the west had isolated Fort Smith from Little Rock. Further, Price began moving on the 28th of August headed for Little Rock. Frederick Steele now began to hunker down to defend the Arkansas capital, believing, as he stated in his 26 August report, that he must "hold the line of the Arkansas." Steele's tone convinced superiors of the danger to Little Rock and diverted a division of Major General A.J. Smith's XVI Corps in his direction. This division was commanded by the capable Brigadier General Joseph A. Mower, a rising star in the Union army who would play a frustrating role attempting to run down Price.[7] Thus, Price had successfully fixed Steele in place by exploiting his fear of isolation and a direct attack. Steele would do nothing for the next two months to challenge Price, aid Rosecrans, or disrupt Price's retreat from Missouri.

Price began moving north on Sunday, 28 August 1864, from Camden scooping up detachments of Rebel cavalry as he moved forward. At Princeton, sixteen miles north of Camden, the commands of Fagan and Marmaduke joined Price and his staff. On the 30th, Price continued on and picked up a couple more regiments at Tulip, nine miles further down the road. The next day Price was forced to send a couple of pieces of artillery back to Camden for lack of draft horses. For the next six days he made his way uneventfully to Dardenelle on the Arkansas River. He did direct Fagan and Marmaduke to make a series of feints toward Little Rock, and these further convinced Steele that he was vulnerable to attack. Dardenelle was the place chosen to cross the river free of interference from Steele. This town is about sixty miles west of Little Rock and well-suited to facilitate the Rebel's crossing of the river. Upon reaching the village, Price placed Cabell in charge of securing the crossing site and facilitating the movement over the river. Price had planned to bridge the river and had accordingly brought along a pontoon for that purpose. However, the low level of the stream allowed Price to ford the river in lieu of setting up the bridge. Arriving at Dardenelle on the 6th, the Confederates had made only 165 miles in ten days. A factor that may have slowed the column was that the pontoon bridge Price brought along was necessarily cumbersome. Yet, as one writer points out, this is an average march of sixteen miles a day, which good infantry can achieve. But Price was commanding an army composed entirely of cavalry.[8] Thus, one might have expected a mounted force to make twenty or more miles a day. This did not happen, and two reasons for it were Price's lack of experience leading cavalry and the fact that he was riding in an ambulance.

At the time of the expedition Price's health had deteriorated to such a point that he weighed close to 300 pounds and could not mount a horse. Further, in July he asked two physicians to travel with him to Shreveport for the planning conference because he was reportedly sick.[9] His poor physical condition, combined with his deficit of experience leading cavalry, did not bode well for positive results from the operation. Speed was of the essence for the Confederacy, and it did not seem that Price had the drive to press forward with the vigor the situation required. Indeed, as he was slowly making his way toward the Arkansas River, Atlanta fell on 2 September 1864 to Sherman, negating one of the strategic objectives of the campaign. Already it seemed that the expedition would produce little in the way of relieving the pressure on the Confederacy's eastern armies or sway the Federal election.

The army forded the Arkansas on 7 September, "with the water coming up to the bed of the wagon," one witness noted. The army then changed direction to the northeast in order to rendezvous with Shelby's rampaging brigade. For the next eight days, Price plodded along by fits and starts, at times making 32 miles a day and on others only thirteen. On 15 September, Price, with Fagan and Marmaduke, linked up with the lead elements of Shelby's command at Powhatan. The following day the rest of Shelby's men arrived, finally concentrating the army at a single location: Pocahontas, Arkansas. The record is contradictory as to the time line for Shelby's linkup, as Price's written report states it occurred on the 13th and 14th of September, and the attached itinerary prepared by Price's assistant adjutant general, Lieutenant Colonel Lauchlan MacLean, states it happened on the 15th and 16th. Regardless of the disagreement, both Price's report and the itinerary agree that General Order #8 was issued on the 18th, and this document established the formal organization of the Army of Missouri on 18 September 1864.[10]

General Order #8 formally activated the Confederate Army of Missouri for the purpose of conducting the campaign in Missouri. Not only did the order state the task organization, it also provided the initial march orders to the divisions, as well as discussing matters of discipline and disposition of captured property and prisoners. When Price finally united the army at Pocahontas, it contained approximately 12,000 men, although this is only an estimate. The reason for this is that only Shelby's division submitted an accurate strength return when the army began to organize. Of the total number of troops, it is believed that the army had some 4,000 unarmed men and another four to five hundred men were dismounted. One participant stated that the unarmed men "were almost worthless as soldiers" and a burden to the army. Even Shelby's division, arguably the best in the army, had 181 men dismounted.[11] From these statistics we can deduce that Price's army had less than 10,000 effective men. The army would have to achieve success in recruiting in Missouri to have the strength to defeat the Federal army, and, more important, obtain arms for the new recruits and unarmed men. This was a tall order by any measure.

The Army of Missouri was composed of three divisions (see Appendix B), with one each commanded by Fagan, Marmaduke, and Shelby. Fagan's division—officially the 1st Arkansas Division—of four brigades, one battery of artillery, and three separate battalions, contained almost 5,000 men, all from Arkansas. This was a strong division of battle-hardened men commanded by tested brigade commanders such as dependable Brigadier General William L. Cabell, who is credited with designing the well-known Confederate battle flag.[12] Marmaduke's division was officially the 1st Missouri Division, and was composed entirely of Missourians. This division had less than 3,000 troops in two brigades, two artillery batteries, and an engineer company. It also had sound brigade commanders, including Brigadier General John B. Clark, who would assume command of the division when Marmaduke was captured at Mine Creek. Finally, Jo Shelby commanded a newly formed division for this campaign. Although he was the junior of the three division commanders, Shelby commanded a large division at just over 4,000 men, nearly as strong as Fagan's division. Shelby had three brigades, one battery and one section of artillery, and the bulk of the unarmed recruits.[13] Price would entrust Shelby with keeping the recruits in hand and would come to rely on Shelby as his "fireman." Wherever the fight was hottest, Price would push Shelby into the breach. Overall, the army was very well organized into a compact unified command that contrasted markedly with their fragmented Union opponents. Nevertheless, as a cavalry organization it was only suitable for raiding, which was diametrically opposed to Price's intent.

The time Price took to organize the army was inordinately long, as was his leisurely pace in reaching the rendezvous point. Dr. William M. McPheeters, Price's chief surgeon, recorded that the army "rested again today at Pocahontas, although I am sorry to say that it was not because it was the Sabbath but because the command was not fully organized." Setting the task organization, a job that should have taken no more than a day, consumed over three. This gave time to the enemy to prepare for meeting the Rebels, although Price's men did get a short rest before crossing the state line into Missouri. Finally, on the 19th of September, Price started moving north with his entire force of 12,000 men. General Order #8 prescribed the order of march and initial objectives for each division. Each division would march on parallel routes into Missouri and consolidate in the vicinity of Fredericktown. Price specified that Marmaduke would march on the right, Fagan in the center advancing on Greenville, and Shelby on the left moving toward Doniphan. The flanking columns would keep ten to thirty miles between themselves and the center in order to take advantage of available forage along the route. Price would move with Fagan in the center, and he required each commander to render a daily report. Interestingly, he also specified "the center column will march as nearly as practicable eighteen miles per day." As already noted, anything less than twenty miles a day is a plodding pace for cavalry. The lack of speed played into the hands of the Federal army in Missouri and Kansas, allowing them to prepare defenses to meet the Rebels. The last part of the order addressed discipline. Price expected the division commanders to control "straggling and plundering."[14] Unfortunately, the division commanders would fail to carry out this last instruction, and the indiscipline displayed by the Rebels would drive the populace away from their cause, much to the detriment of the Confederacy and Price.

The Army of Missouri stepped off from Pocahontas on Monday, 19 September 1864, bound for the namesake of the army. That day, Price finally returned to his home state after a two and a half year absence. "Today we have entered the State of Missouri with our forces in fine health and spirits," he jubilantly reported. The going was apparently difficult since, in the same message, he chronicled the "very rough" roads. Yet the Rebels were clearly in high spirits, as the column still made twenty-two miles on the first day, making camp at Indian Ford on the Current River, just inside Missouri. Dr. McPhetters happily wrote in his diary that he *"entered the State of Missouri ... with an army which God grant may be a victorious one and relieve this down trodden state."* As the army lightly strode along, it also reported encountering Federal scouting parties after crossing the state line.[15] The alerted Federals would now accelerate their preparations to meet Price, as they had proof positive that the Rebels were on their way.

William S. Rosecrans had received a great deal of intelligence and rumors—though these came in haphazardly and not from an organized network—that a Rebel campaign into Missouri was in the offing. Such a move was his greatest fear. The first piece of hard intelligence intimating that something was afoot arrived in Rosecrans' headquarters on 30 August 1864. Brigadier General John B. Sanborn, commanding the District of Southwest Missouri, sent Rosecrans two letters found on the body of a dead Rebel captain. In the first one, dated 23 July 1864, the Rebel officer told his reader they "are hoping to receive orders soon to move northward." The second, written the next day, again states the anticipation of orders to enter Missouri, and the author also discusses in much detail the disposition of Confederate forces in Arkansas. While these letters did not give details about the direction of a movement or objectives, the correspondence did warn Rosecrans that he might need to ensure that his forces were prepared to defend the department. A few days later, Federal scouts captured a Rebel quartermaster who had a letter on him that stated, "I will be on the march for the state [Missouri] by Monday [19 September] [and] we will be at Jefferson City no less than ten days from the time we start."[16] As more information came into headquarters, Rosecrans was able to make a prediction as to where a blow might land.

Another flurry of messages began streaming in during the first few days of September indicating that there was a great deal of truth to the rumors. On 2 September, Lieutenant Commander Thomas O. Selfridge of the Mississippi River Squadron reported that three deserters reported that the Rebels intended to invade Missouri with a large cavalry force. Also, that same day, Major General C.C. Washburn, commanding the District of West Tennessee, sent twin notes to Rosecrans and Major General E.R.S. Canby, commanding all Union forces west of the Mississippi:

> I have just received advices from two different sources, both of which I deem reliable, that a big raid is on foot for Missouri, led by Price and Shelby. An escaped citizen from near Batesville, who left five days ago, says that they were preparing ten days rations there for 12,000 men when he left, and it was understood that Price, with Marmaduke and other forces, had crossed the Arkansas River and were moving toward Missouri, and would be joined at Batesville by Shelby's forces, about 4,000 strong.[17]

This was amazingly accurate intelligence from a common citizen. The next day, Washburn received another report, from Lieutenant Commander S.L. Phelps of the Mississippi River Squadron, which he forwarded to Rosecrans and Canby. Washburn's note discusses Phelps's latest intelligence and concludes, "I am pretty well satisfied that a raid of large proportions is being made on Missouri."[18] Rosecrans was already nervous about such an eventuality, and he immediately began making dispositions to meet the enemy.

The biggest issue facing Rosecrans was the paucity and dispersion of his available forces. On paper, it appeared that Rosecrans had a significant host available to him. But, on closer examination it's clear he had serious disadvantages that if not rectified in short order would lead to disaster in Missouri and possibly Kansas. The strength returns of 30 August 1864, right before Price invaded Missouri, show that Rosecrans had 14,016 soldiers in the form of state volunteer regiments mustered into Federal service and the Missouri State Militia. The state volunteer units were qualitatively the same as U.S. regulars in terms of training and experience and came from both Missouri and several of the surrounding states. The Missouri State Militia—known as the MSM—was formed in late 1861 as a federally funded organization for use in the exclusive defense of Missouri. These units proved very effective, but they were spread around many Missouri towns and villages. Rosecrans also had 3,950 active soldiers from a peculiar organization known as the Enrolled Missouri Militia. The EMM, as it was called, was an organization of part-time soldiers, and although containing some dedicated troops, the units were of uneven ability and performance in combat. All of the units were dispersed across the entire state of Missouri in five districts and thirty-three towns to protect them from Confederate guerrillas.[19]

Rosecrans actually had more than enough soldiers to defend Missouri, but the dispersed condition made the state vulnerable to a Rebel invasion by a large, concentrated force such as the one Price was commanding. The state volunteer regiments in Federal service alone amounted to more than enough troops to deal with Price's entire command and they were seasoned veterans. However, Rosecrans had to bring them together to defend vital points, like St. Louis and Jefferson City. Likewise, the EMM would have to muster as well, but, as already discussed, their quality was a question mark. The Enrolled Missouri Militia began as a sort of home guard commanded by Federal officers in January 1862. Missouri had a military organization when the Civil War started, but the Missouri State Guard was dominated by secessionists. Thus, the Missouri State Guard became a Rebel force, leaving the state with no defense. The provisional Union government needed to remedy this situation because the level of guerrilla violence was rising. Therefore, the original purpose of the EMM was counterinsurgency operations. All able-bodied Missourians who had taken the oath of allegiance to the Union were required to serve in the organization. The soldiers served periodically on active duty based on need. By some estimates, there were a total of 50,000 men in the EMM, although in August 1864 there were only 3,950 soldiers in uniform. To defend Missouri, Rosecrans would have to call these men out and assemble them rapidly.[20] The returns of October 1864, during the main period of Price's raid, show that Rosecrans was only partially successful with the call out of the militia. On 31 October, 14,833 men were in the ranks of the EMM. While not an overwhelming number, these, combined with Rosecrans active forces, were more than Price could handle.[21]

Rosecrans had already recognized that the EMM required streamlining to ensure that they could react in an emergency. Previously, the EMM had demonstrated a lack of efficiency in assembling and reliability in combat. In June 1864, Rosecrans issued General Order #107 to remedy the problems. In the order, he specified that each county in Missouri should recruit two companies of 100 men each to protect the area from guerrillas. These new companies were called the Provisional Enrolled Missouri Militia, or PEMM. The order prescribed certain employment and assembly requirements to streamline rapid concentration of the state's defenses. As it turns out, G.O. #107 did little to improve the state militia's efficiency in any facet of readiness. In fact, it may have made matters worse because the order added yet another layer of bureaucracy on an already complicated labyrinth of state defensive measures.[22] Ultimately, this would cause additional friction when it came time to concentrate to defend Missouri, and time was the critical element in that defense as Price began moving north.

Rosecrans began frantically pulling his forces together on 12 September 1864 with orders to his commanders. He also sent out orders to mobilize the militia to reinforce the soldiers in Federal service on the same day and even appealed for men to join the ranks via newspaper announcements. While he sorely needed these men in the ranks, he was concerned about their reliability. Rosecrans, as was Price, was privy to the rumors that the EMM was infiltrated by O.A.K. members. As early as July, Rosecrans took steps to mitigate clandestine activities by arresting lodge leaders. He then took action to ensure that his commanders had full control of the remaining men by breaking up EMM units if they exhibited a tendency toward rebellion.[23] Thus, he had taken the initial measures with his own resources to meet the threat, but he did not think this was enough.

Rosecrans needed more reliable troops and preferably hardened combat veterans. It just so happened that at this time there was a source to satisfy his need in the form of the XVI Army Corps. The soldiers of this corps were veterans of Vicksburg, the Red River Campaign, and, most recently, fighting Nathan Bedford Forrest at Tupelo to protect Sherman's supply line. The corps had just received orders to join Sherman by moving north up the Mississippi and then back south via the Tennessee. Rosecrans learned of Smith's orders on 2 September from General Washburn, commanding at Memphis. Washburn told Rosecrans that Major General A.J. Smith would arrive at Cairo, Illinois, with 6,000 men from one of his divisions within three days for a stopover before moving on. Smith's other division was already diverted to assist Steele at Little Rock should Price attack at that point. Washburn suggested that in the event of an "emergency" Smith and his men could be diverted to meet a contingency.[24] Armed with this information, Rosecrans took immediate steps to have the XVI Corps sent to Missouri to reinforce his threatened department.

On 5 September, with intelligence piling up intimating that Price was heading north, Rosecrans wrote directly to the secretary of war, Edwin M. Stanton, apprising him of the situation and requesting that the XVI Corps come to his department to operate against Price. The accession of these infantry troops would instantly give Rosecrans a stout and credible force to contest Price's expedition. The secretary referred the dispatch to Halleck, who in turn consulted Grant for guidance. Grant told Halleck to check with Sherman in Georgia, and if the threat to Missouri was credible then Rosecrans was authorized to divert Smith.[25] On the 7th of September, Grant wrote to Halleck with positive orders to "stop General A.J. Smith at Cairo." Halleck immediately telegraphed Cairo to stop Smith at that location. On the 8th, Smith reported that he had arrived at Cairo and he would await further orders at that point. Rosecrans requested that Smith move further north up the Mississippi to Cape Girardeau, Missouri, on the 9th in order to get into position to monitor Price's movements and cover St. Louis. Finally, on 10 September, Grant directed that Smith was temporarily attached to the

Major General Andrew J. Smith, Commander, Union XVI Army Corps (Library of Congress).

Department of Missouri to "operate against Price & Co."[26] With Smith's Corps, his own forces, and the Enrolled Missouri Militia, Rosecrans would have about 34,000 troops to confront the 12,000 of Price's Army of Missouri.

This exchange of correspondence over the disposition of the XVI Corps caused a controversy among the War Department, Grant, and Rosecrans. As already mentioned, Rosecrans had a very poor working relationship with both Stanton and Grant. During this period, Rosecrans had corresponded directly with the War Department since receiving the initial intelligence of Price's impending operation. In doing so, he had bypassed two echelons of command between his department and Stanton. The secretary of war was quite irritated in dealing with Rosecrans because he correctly deemed it within the purview of Rosecrans' theater commander, Major General E.R.S. Canby. Thus, on 12 September Stanton referred the matter to Grant. This perturbed the general-in-chief, who took care of the matter at hand. Stanton then instructed his inspector general to send a terse order to Rosecrans that read:

> The Secretary of War directs me to say that your dispatch of yesterday has been referred to Lieutenant-General Grant, who will give the necessary instructions thereupon. The Secretary of War further directs that your attention be again called to paragraph 451 of the Army Regulation, which indicates the office of the Adjutant-General as the proper channel of your official correspondence with this Department. Should you not be able to communicate with General Canby, in the event of needing instructions on military operations, you will address yourself to Lieutenant-General Grant through the Chief of Staff of the Army.
> By order of the Secretary of War:
> Jas. A Hardie
> Colonel and Inspector General, U.S. Army[27]

This flap over correspondence would prove the first in a string of missteps—which included a timid response to Price and lack of coordination with Curtis during the Great Raid—that would lead to Rosecrans' permanent relief from command.

Once Rosecrans had successfully lobbied for the acquisition of Smith's Corps, he turned his attention to identifying the points that he needed to defend. He surmised that there were several possibilities for objective points that Price could choose to direct his forces against. First and foremost was the biggest prize in Missouri, St. Louis. Second, the Confederates might attempt to take the important railhead and supply depot at Rolla. Third, taking the political center at the Missouri capital of Jefferson City could deliver the Rebels an enormous coup, denying the state to Federal authority during the election. Finally, Springfield was an inviting target representing the seat of Federal authority in southwest Missouri. From here, Price could launch follow-up assaults toward Kansas City, Jefferson City, or Rolla. To react to Price's operation, Rosecrans sent out a series of orders on 13 September 1864 to all his district commanders to "concentrate outposts."[28] Beyond this, Rosecrans seemed irresolute and indecisive. Although he had sent orders to his subordinates to consolidate forces, it would take him another eleven days before he took positive steps to establish a coherent defense at St. Louis and other points. Rosecrans was content to allow Price retain the initiative and let him call the shots, and then he reacted once he had concrete information on Price's intent. Rosecrans could have taken the initiative by challenging Price's advance, but instead, he took a more passive approach. Such vacillating would provide Price with an opportunity to wreak havoc. Had Rosecrans sought to deny Price the initiative by implementing a forward defense, which he had the capability to do, Price could have been expelled from Missouri with little damage to the state.

As the district commanders concentrated their forces at the key points, additional intelligence piled up at Rosecrans' headquarters. Between the 13th and 24th of September, a number of reports came in that allowed Rosecrans to make a better guess as to Price's objectives. On 13 September, Rosecrans wrote a note to his adjacent department commander, Samuel R. Curtis, to warn him that Price "may go up to Pilot Knob, join [Brigadier General Douglas H.] Cooper, and go into Kansas." Then, on 16 September, a series of messages streamed between St. Louis and outlying districts identifying Pilot Knob, Cape Girardeau, and Bloomfield as initial targets of Price's army. The next day, Brigadier General Sanborn reported that the Rebels "have not come through the Boston Mountains, but is reliably reported to have gone to Batesville."[29] Since this was in eastern Arkansas, Rosecrans could reliably surmise that Price was focused on St. Louis, Rolla, or Jefferson City.

On 20 September, the day after Price crossed the state line, another bevy of messages from forward outposts flowed into department headquarters. These demonstrated that the Army of Missouri was spread across a fifty to sixty mile swath of southeast Missouri, which was within the area of responsibility of Brigadier General Thomas Ewing, Jr. Over the next four days, more and more evidence inundated Rosecrans confirming that Price was targeting a major city in eastern Missouri. Rosecrans believed that the objective was either St. Louis, with its mountain of supplies and communication center, or Rolla, the great transportation hub and supply depot. The defenses of these two places were at this point imperfect. To reach either location, the Rebel army would have to move through a narrow pass on the Iron Mountain Railroad at the small village of Pilot Knob. Once through the pass, Price could move east on St. Louis or west toward Rolla. Guarding the pass at Pilot Knob was the earthen Fort Davidson, commanded by Major James Wilson, with a few hundred men from the 3rd Missouri State Militia Cavalry and several pieces of artillery. To provide the time to improve the defenses at St. Louis and Rolla, Rosecrans had to delay Price's forward progress at Pilot Knob for as long as he could. Therefore, Rosecrans ordered Thomas Ewing to Pilot Knob with a brigade of A.J. Smith's Corps "to patrol and garrison the Iron Mountain Railroad, reporting to Major General A.J. Smith."[30] This would stiffen the resistance at Pilot Knob and buy precious time for Rosecrans to improve the defensive posture at both places. Pilot Knob would earn the moniker the "Thermopylae of the West" because of the similarities historians would draw between this battle and the ancient Spartan defense of the pass by that name in Greece.

This compilation of evidence finally energized Rosecrans to establish a coherent defense of St. Louis and Rolla. Had he used the previous two weeks to properly array his forces and improve the defenses of the vital centers, defending Pilot Knob would not have taken on as much importance. But now, with his back against the wall, Rosecrans flew into action. He called out the home guards in the city of St. Louis, as well as all able-bodied civilians, to improve the fortifications. He also declared martial law and ordered A.J. Smith, with his corps, up to St. Louis to add backbone to the resistance. Finally, he wrote to Admiral David Porter to request two gunboats to patrol the river in the vicinity of Cape Girardeau.[31] Simultaneously, Rosecrans began to warn Major General Curtis in Kansas that, while eastern Missouri was currently in the path of Price's army, Curtis' Department of Kansas could be next on the agenda of the Army of Missouri.

The first note from Rosecrans to Curtis came on 13 September 1864, when he warned Curtis that Price might "go into Kansas" after crossing the Arkansas River. However, at this point, intelligence was still spotty as to Price's intent. Nevertheless, Curtis did not want to take chances, and in order to prepare his department he warned Governor Thomas Carney of Kansas: "I may again have to ask the militia of Southern Kansas to aid in checking the Rebels." The network through which Curtis got his information was spotty at best. On 20 September, he had reports that Price was at Cane Hill in western Arkansas near the old Prairie Grove battlefield. In a note that hinted of extreme anxiety, Curtis told Governor Carney on that day to "please notify your militia to be ready." This was not true, but unlike Rosecrans, who ceded the initiative to Price, Curtis wanted immediate preparations made to meet the foe. As the preponderance of evidence finally demonstrated that Price would hit eastern Missouri, Rosecrans penned two notes to Curtis. In the first one, he told Curtis that the Army of Missouri was near Fredericktown in southeast Missouri, and in the second he told him that there was no information that Price had any significant force at Cane Hill. Therefore, Rosecrans no longer had any doubt that Price intended mischief directed toward St. Louis or Rolla. But, Rosecrans cautioned Curtis that "a raid into Kansas is no doubt desired and watched with anxiety."[32]

As Price's Rebels moved further into Missouri, fear spread across the countryside and in St. Louis. The *Daily Missouri Republican* newspaper in St. Louis was publishing articles each day apprising the citizens of the city about Price's progress as he moved north.[33] Yet Rosecrans' vacillating had cost the Federal Department of Missouri precious time it could have used to prepare for the defense of the state and its vital points. However, the Federals had several advantages, including manpower, provisions, and fighting from a fixed defense. By contrast, Price was short-handed, foraging for sustenance, and possessed homogenous mounted forces who were no match for prepared defenses. If Rosecrans could set his defense in time, not only would he defeat Price, he also would have the opportunity to deal a death blow. Therefore, both commanders had to move quickly in order to achieve their objectives. For Price, speed was critical, because if he could strike while the Union army was unprepared, he could still realize some of his political objectives, such as taking Jefferson City. Yet as the expedition unfolded, Price would make a series of decisions that would fumble the initiative and transform the nature of the operation into a large raid ensuring that Price would have little success.

6

"Thermopylae"

Within days of entering Missouri, the Rebel army that bore the state's name would have its first significant clash with Federal forces at a place called Pilot Knob. This nondescript village some eighty-six miles south of St. Louis was the gateway to the picturesque Arcadia Valley, and in happier times it was the center of economic activity in the region. Mining was the engine of the economy, for there were vast, high quality iron ore deposits in the rugged ridges. However, in late September 1864, Pilot Knob was the center of a rising storm in Missouri. The ferocious little battle of Pilot Knob was a fight that did not have to happen. In fact, if Price had adhered to his objectives, the battle should never have happened. Price could have bypassed the small garrison at Fort Davidson, outside Pilot Knob, and maintained the momentum of his advance. But by deciding to attack this isolated and insignificant outpost, Price squandered the chance he may have had to capture St. Louis. Thus, the entire character of the campaign would transform from one of seeking to achieve important strategic and operational objectives to a giant raid. As a result, Price would achieve almost nothing and nearly have his army destroyed, and it all came about because of the decision to attack a small earthen fort in a beautiful valley.

The Arcadia is a lovely valley with high ridgelines, few roads, and a source of abundant natural resources. In 1864, the valley was of vital importance to the Union cause. The main reason for this was the ironworks at the north end of the valley. Iron, of course, is the critical material needed for the manufacture of weapons, and control of Missouri gave the Union a steady source of metal. In 1861 the Union leaders of the state realized that they had to secure the valley to ensure a steady flow of iron to the foundries and machine shops in the North. The valley runs north to south and was a natural avenue for an invading army to move through in order to reach St. Louis. With its rich farms, Arcadia could sustain an army along the route, and the north-south orientation was like a dagger pointing at the prize city on the Mississippi River. The iron works were connected to St. Louis and the river by the St. Louis & Iron Mountain Railroad. The railroad terminated at Pilot Knob and the iron works at the village. The main terrain features at the north end of the valley were the twin mountains of Shepherd and Pilot Knob, separated by a narrow gap. The village of Pilot Knob was north of the gap, nestled into the mountain of the same name. The town of Ironton was south of the gap, and about 1,000 yards south of that village was the town of Arcadia and old Fort Curtis, which was constructed to protect the iron works by preventing access through the gap from the south. Fort Davidson was about 400 yards west of Pilot Knob and north of the gap. It was constructed in 1863 because Fort Curtis was ineffective at that location

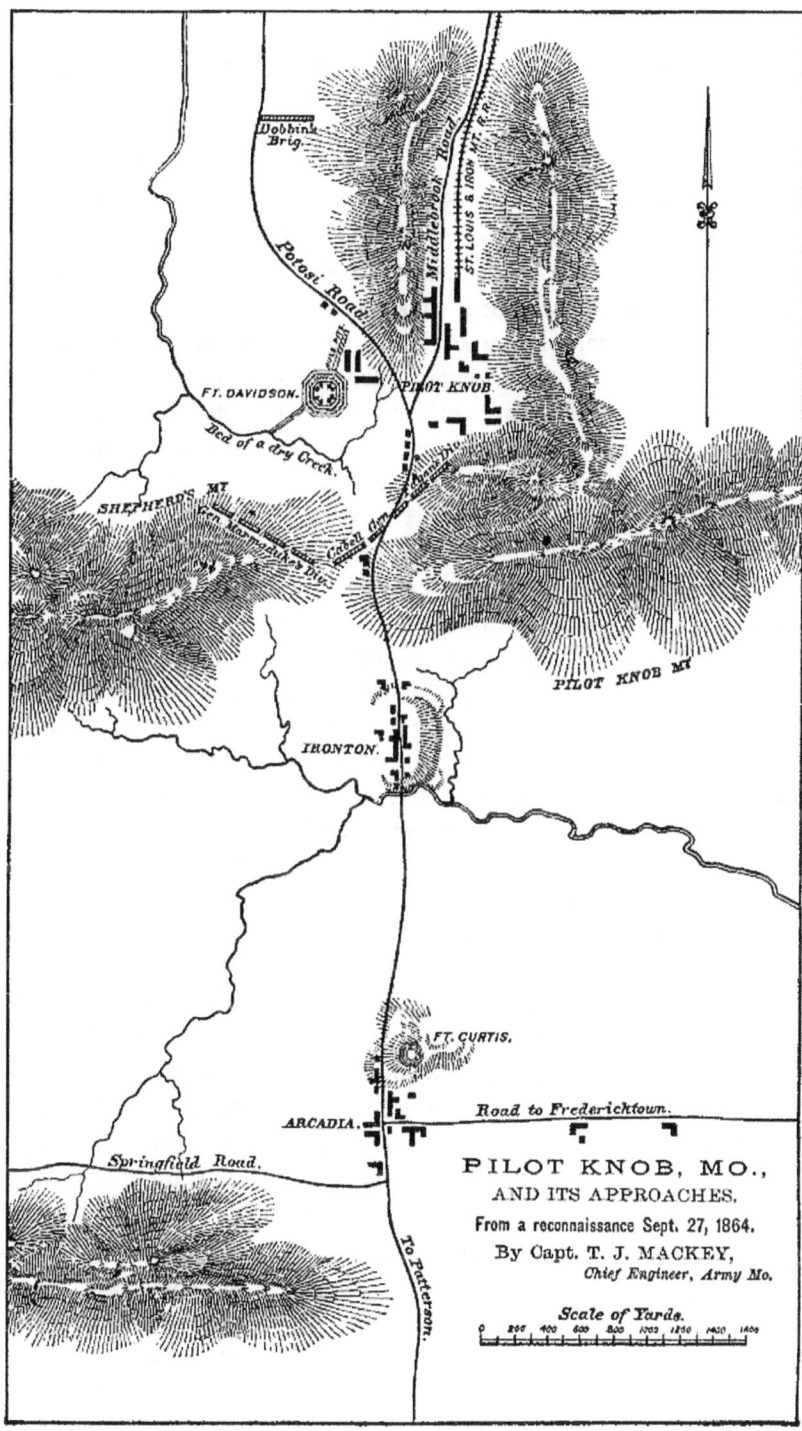

Map 2. Original map of the Battle of Pilot Knob drawn by General Price's chief engineer, Captain Thomas J. Mackey (*OR*, Series 1, Vol. 41, Part 1, p. 708).

in its purpose to protect the works from guerrillas, who could approach the mines and railroad undetected.[1]

Fort Davidson was constructed by Federal forces to better secure from raiding guerrillas the ironworks, mines, and railhead at the north end of the Arcadia Valley. As already noted, this was not the first fortification built by Union forces in the valley. In 1861, the 33rd Illinois Infantry erected a fort, named Fort Hovey for the commander of the regiment. The 33rd was the first of many Federal units that would serve here, including the 21st Illinois commanded by an unimpressive looking colonel named Ulysses S. Grant. Located at the south end of the valley on a hillside overlooking the Fredericktown Road, this fort—renamed Fort Curtis in 1862—was recognized as useless because it did not protect the critical nodes in the valley from the primary threat, guerrillas. As a result, the local commander in January 1863 recommended the construction of a new outpost closer to the all-important iron deposits. To protect the mines and railroad at Ironton Gap, the new fort would have to be built at the north end of the valley near Pilot Knob, known locally as the Knob.[2] The exact point to build the fort was a matter of debate.

Tactically, the best place to site a fort is on high ground, and there were many such points like Shepherd's and Pilot Knob Mountain. However, there were a couple of problems with these choices. First, there was no immediate source of water on the high ridges overlooking the Arcadia Valley and Ironton Gap. Second, placing a fort on top of the ridges put the troops out of position for providing adequate protection for the mining facilities and railroad—the very issue with Fort Curtis. Therefore, the Federals would have to construct the fort on the plain south of Pilot Knob where there was a reliable source of water and terrain that aided the ability to secure the vital points. Building the fort on the plain below the ridgeline meant that the post was vulnerable to plunging fire if the Rebels could emplace artillery on the surrounding hills. Local commanders calculated that this would never happen. The fort was more than adequate to deal with guerrilla activity and, at most, the Confederates might bring up some regular cavalry and infantry. But the Rebels could never bring up heavy guns to threaten a fort on the plain. Thus, the decision was made by Brigadier General John W. Davidson to build the fort that would bear his name in the field south of Pilot Knob.[3]

Construction on Fort Davidson began in the spring of 1863 with several units, civilians, prisoners, and contrabands—runaway slaves—supplying the labor. To speed the work along, the regimental quartermaster of the 1st Nebraska Infantry issued a half cup of whiskey per day to each man working on the fort. By September 1863, the Union army completed the new post and garrisoned it with several hundred men. One of the men who served in the fort described it as "hexagonal and each side 40 yards long, or 240 yards around and 80 yards across.... Fort Davidson then mounted 32-pound siege pieces or pivot guns, some 12 or 14 feet long, and if we remember rightly, they weighed 9000 pounds. Then there were three 24-pound howitzers, with limbers so they could be hauled on the field."[4] The fort was on slightly higher ground than Ironton Gap, allowing the guns to dominate this critical point. The parapet was four to six feet high fronted by a moat dug to a depth of six feet and ten to twelve feet in width. The parapet also had shallow trenches to accommodate riflemen, and, at intervals, platforms were built to emplace artillery around the perimeter.[5] The fort was a formidable work as long as the assumption that the Rebels could throw only cavalry and infantry at it held true.

Fort Davidson had a revolving door of units garrisoning it. In September 1864, it contained elements of four Missouri regiments in its confines, along with several pieces of heavy and field artillery, plus two Coehorn mortars. These consisted of one company each of the 1st Missouri State Militia Infantry and 50th Missouri Infantry, three companies of the 2nd Missouri State Militia Cavalry, three companies of the 3rd Missouri State Militia Cavalry, and a section (two guns) of the 2nd Missouri Light Artillery. When General Ewing arrived on 25 September to take personal command of Fort Davidson, he brought along elements of the veteran 14th Iowa Infantry, with the new 47th Missouri Infantry and four guns from the 2nd Missouri Light Artillery following them a short time later. In addition to the 866 uniformed soldiers, an unknown number of civilians and free blacks shouldered a musket or manned the guns in the fort. All told, approximately one thousand men were assembled at Pilot Knob to defend the vulnerable Fort Davidson. The artillery was an odd assortment of calibers and guns. First, the fort mounted four 32-pound siege guns, which were usually found in the defense of the seacoast. In addition, there were three 24-pound howitzers reinforcing the heavy guns, backed by the two mortars. The mortars were 24-pounders that could fire at high angles to deliver plunging fire into protected areas like a ditch or creek bed. The heavy guns and mortars were manned by volunteers from the 47th Missouri and freedmen who offered their services. The four additional pieces of field artillery from Battery H, 2nd Missouri Light Artillery, brought the total number of light guns to six. Unlike the heavy guns in the fort, these were mobile and available for maneuver on the field. Finally, Captain William Montgomery, commanding Battery H, designated two guns of the six for use in skirmishing outside the fort to delay and disrupt Rebel deployment of their forces.[6] The combination of the fortification and the firepower made it appear that Fort Davidson was impregnable, but this was an illusion, for the earthwork had significant vulnerabilities.

Fort Davidson, as previously noted, sat on low ground in the Arcadia Valley. In normal times, the fortification was adequate for defending the mines and northern valley from marauders. But, as General Ewing noted, "The fort was always conceded to be indefensible against any large army having serviceable artillery."[7] Ewing was quite right in stating this because the surrounding hills—Pilot Knob and Shepherd mountains—dominated the plain. If an army ever rolled through Arcadia Valley and had effective artillery, they could emplace the guns on the hills compromising Fort Davidson. Since the hills were only a few hundred yards from the fort, it was within easy range of any pieces the enemy could push to the top. The plunging fire would render the trenches and gun emplacements untenable and weaken the magazine at the center of the earthwork. Thus, deciding to defend Fort Davidson against an invading army would prove a difficult prospect. Indeed, the narrow gap at the north end of the Arcadia Valley looked very much like Thermopylae, and the few defenders believed they were there on a mission of forlorn hope.[8]

Sterling Price's Army of Missouri was moving north at a deliberate and glacial pace for cavalry. It is 104 miles from Pocahontas, Arkansas, to Fredericktown, Missouri, the rendezvous point for the three divisions of Price's army.[9] This means that the Army of

Fort Davidson with Shepherd Mountain in the background. Note that the mountain dominates the fort (photograph by the author).

Missouri, which was composed entirely of cavalry, was traveling slightly more that seventeen miles a day. Such a rate of movement gave the Union forces in Missouri time to get ready to meet the Rebels. Then, Price would make a fateful decision that further retarded forward momentum upon arrival at Fredericktown.

The Federals did have something to do with the Confederates' slow advance. Major James Wilson, commanding the garrison at Pilot Knob, sent out several scouting parties south from Fort Davidson to find the Confederate army. A series of contacts and skirmishes occurred that necessarily forced Price's divisions to deploy to disperse the pesky Federal scouts. One of these skirmishes happened near Doniphan, Missouri, just north of the border, and it was typical of the initial firefights that happened early in the campaign. Elements of Company K, 3rd MSM Cavalry, encountered Shelby's wing of the Army of Missouri in the streets of Doniphan on the 19th of September. "[I]t was broad daylight," recounted Sergeant J.C. Steakley, "when we charged through the streets, the Confederates going helter-skelter in every direction."[10] Such aggressiveness by the heavily outnumbered Union cavalrymen would dog the Rebels as they moved north toward Fredericktown.

The scouts would continue their mission until they had enough information to accurately pinpoint the Rebel location and direction of movement. This was difficult and dangerous work. In one instance, Steakley and his band were surrounded by several hundred Confederates. Boldly, the Federals charged their attackers to escape the noose. With the exception of a few men captured, they successfully eluded the trap. The men the Confederates bagged were later brutally murdered, the first of many atrocities that occurred during the course of the campaign.[11]

By the 22nd the Federal scouting parties had the intelligence they needed and rapidly retreated to the north to report their findings. At Patterson, north of Doniphan, the scouts again skirmished with Shelby's troopers. From this engagement Sergeant Steakley noted the strength and identity of the invaders. His small detachment was cornered in a thicket and "took to the fields" to escape capture. Yet they still had two men who were picked up by the enemy. These unfortunates, Corporal W.W. Proffet and Private A.M. Youngblood, when captured by a squad of the enemy were "shot then and there." The survivors returned to Pilot Knob and reported to Major Wilson. The intrepid major sent out parties toward Patterson, Centerville, Fredericktown, and Farmington.[12] From these widely scattered outposts, Wilson was able to determine that the Rebels were in great force, fully mounted, and heading north to Fredericktown. Further, he could guess that from there the route of march would funnel the Confederates through the Arcadia Valley.

It took some time for the scouts to return to Pilot Knob to render their reports. Yet Major Wilson, like any good commander, was skeptical of some of the information. But the number of reports coming in was too much to deny. On 24 September 1864, Rosecrans wrote to Halleck stating that "a very formidable invasion by southeast Missouri" was afoot. Due to the gravity of the situation, Rosecrans felt he needed a strong commander forward to organize a defense and delay the Rebels. This would give him time to prepare St. Louis and Rolla to meet Price. Therefore, on 25 September Rosecrans sent Brigadier General Ewing to stem the rising tide.[13] Ewing was the perfect choice for the mission Rosecrans had in mind.

As Ewing boarded the train for Pilot Knob, the scattered Rebels were beginning to reassemble at the predetermined Fredericktown in southeast Missouri. Shelby was the first to arrive at Fredericktown, on 23 September, with his advance capturing the town and a supply of goods. The divisions of Fagan and Marmaduke arrived over the next 48 hours, having more circuitous routes to Fredericktown. At this point, Price had to decide upon the next objective pursuant to reaching the ultimate prize of St. Louis. He called a council of war on the evening of the 25th to confer with his generals. From scouts and locals, he learned that the garrison at Pilot Knob stood ripe for the picking with approximately 1,000 men. If he moved forward to St. Louis without disposing of them, they could threaten his rear. Further, intelligence indicated that none other than the infamous Thomas Ewing, author of the despised G.O. #11, was in personal command of Fort Davidson. Another troubling piece of information stated that Ewing had forced local Southern sympathizers from their homes and into the fort. Finally, Price learned of the arrival of A.J. Smith and elements of the XVI Corps in the vicinity of St. Louis. Price may have concluded from this intelligence that he could no longer take the city. Therefore, taking Fort Davidson seemed an attractive alternative. It would boost the morale of his army and Rebel sympathizers. In addition, capturing the place would provide a treasure trove of arms for his unarmed recruits.[14] While he was leaning toward an attack on Fort Davidson, Price wanted to hear from his division commanders before making the final decision.

Generals Fagan and Marmaduke arrived at the council first and gave their opinions before Shelby got there. Both of these seasoned veterans favored Price's plan as the logical next step of the campaign. Then Shelby walked into the room, completing the council. Price then solicited the opinion of his junior division commander by stating, "Shelby, let us hear from you." Shelby recalled, "I favored moving rapidly on St. Louis." He believed that St. Louis was the real prize and would "give the Southern element [in Missouri] a chance to aid the South." He then went on to express his objections to an attack on Pilot Knob. "It would only cripple and retard our movements," he said. "I knew too well that good infantry, well intrenched, would give us h—l."[15] Thus, Shelby concluded that taking St. Louis was feasible, but only if they moved quickly and, besides, this was one of the stated objectives of the campaign. Why deviate from it now, Shelby offered. Events would demonstrate the wisdom of his opinion.

The more senior leaders disagreed with Shelby. To reach St. Louis, the army would have to clear the route so as to leave nothing in the rear to disrupt the offensive. Since his senior commanders seemed to agree, it solidified Price's own belief that he was correct. As a result, he issued orders for an early morning march on the 26th to take the garrison at Pilot Knob. While Shelby disagreed, he nevertheless saluted and carried out his assigned duties. The next day, Price assigned Fagan and Marmaduke the task of actually taking Fort Davidson. Thus, they would move northwest from Fredericktown to the Arcadia Valley. Shelby would swing around to the north of Pilot Knob to isolate the garrison, destroy the railroad bridge over Big River, and block any reinforcements from reaching Pilot Knob. There was a real danger of this. Price knew A.J. Smith's forward units were at Desoto and Mineral Point, about halfway between St. Louis and Pilot Knob on the Iron Mountain Railroad.[16] With the orders issued, the conference broke.

Thomas Ewing arrived at Pilot Knob on 25 September with reinforcements from the 14th Iowa Infantry, from Smith's Corps, and found the environs at Pilot Knob aflutter with activity. Major Wilson had pushed more scouts down the main roads that led to Pilot Knob, while other soldiers were improving the defenses. Ewing redoubled this effort when he observed the area. He knew the fort was vulnerable to artillery, so Ewing "had the roads leading up the hills obstructed." Further, he ordered fields of fire around the fort cleared of timber and vegetation that could give the Rebels cover and concealment. More forces arrived in the form of six companies of the 47th Missouri Infantry and four guns from Battery H, 2nd Missouri Light Artillery, under Colonel Thomas C. Fletcher. The colonel was actually on the ballot in November running for governor of Missouri as a Republican, yet he accepted the call to duty and rushed to Pilot Knob with his men. This brought the fort up to 886 men, the effective strength it would have for the battle along with something over 100 citizens and freedmen who volunteered to fight.[17]

With this accession of forces, Ewing decided to reinforce the forward outposts, paying particular attention to watching Shut-in Gap. This pass is about four miles southeast of Pilot Knob and the road that runs through it connects Pilot Knob to Fredericktown. The purpose of the outposts was not just to detect the enemy, but also to fight a delaying action. This would buy time for the fort to perfect its defenses. Ewing also took time to organize his command structure to fight as efficiently as possible. To accomplish this he assigned command of all the infantry to Colonel Fletcher. The thirteen guns and two mortars at Pilot Knob were assigned to the command of First Lieutenant David Murphy, adjutant of the 47th Missouri. Finally, Ewing gave command of the cavalry to the "gallant" Major James Wilson, who commanded the garrison before Ewing's arrival on the scene.[18] This provided Ewing with a responsive structure for command and control, which as events would prove, facilitated the survival of the defenders.

The Union outposts near Shut-in Gap made their first contact with the Rebels on Monday, 26 September. A short time after noon, pickets from the 47th Missouri had just sat down to eat lunch when "a close column of cavalry advancing by platoons on the Fredericktown road" came into view. This was the advance of Fagan's division, a brigade commanded by Colonel W.F. Slemons with his Arkansans. The sergeant of the guard sent a runner back to headquarters to inform Ewing and warn the rest of the outposts. Meanwhile, the outposts became sharply engaged with the advancing Rebels of Fagan's division. Sergeant Azariah Martin of the 47th Missouri reported that the firing sounded "like pop-corn in a hot skillet."[19] This small company of infantry was no match for the two divisions that Price had moving west down the Fredericktown Road toward Pilot Knob. So the infantry slowly withdrew, firing as they fell back. They eventually fell in with Major Wilson's 3rd Missouri State Militia Cavalry and a section of artillery near Arcadia. Here Wilson intended to offer stiffer resistance.

The reports of contact near Shut-in Gap reached Ewing in the early afternoon of the 26th. While he knew that a large force confronted him, he was not certain if this was Price's whole army. He thought it was possible that only a portion of Price's army was headed through the Arcadia Valley and the rest may have swung around to the north to cut the railroad near Mineral Point.[20] All of this Ewing reported to Rosecrans in a 3:30 p.m. dispatch that day. He added that there was little doubt Price had his whole army in Missouri, but Ewing was still unsure of the direction the main body of the enemy would take. Therefore, he intended to stay put at Pilot Knob to further develop the intelligence as to Price's strength and intent. Ewing closed the dispatch, stating, "I think I can hold the fort against 5,000 cavalry, and shall stand fast until I learn more as to Price."[21] Rosecrans had certainly picked the right man to command his forward outpost at Pilot Knob.

The Rebel advance now reached the town of Arcadia and began skirmishing with Major Wilson's command. It was mid-afternoon and the Confederates had made steady progress in their advance on Pilot Knob. Now, however, resistance stiffened. As the Rebels approached Arcadia, Wilson put his force into line and charged the enemy, pushing them back. He then withdrew to a new position near Ironton and invited the Rebels to attack. In line were two companies from the 14th Iowa, the 3rd MSM Cavalry, and the section of artillery Ewing had sent to reinforce Wilson. The field in front of the Union line was open, offering an excellent field of fire. It was after 3:00 p.m. when the Confederates launched an assault on the line. However, the Rebels ran into a buzzsaw, which halted them and forced them back some distance.[22] This did not last long though, for the Rebels were simply too numerous for Wilson's small battalion.

The Rebels recovered near Shut-in Gap and drove forward once more. Men were beginning to fall on both sides under the "terrific" fire. In the melee, Major Wilson was wounded "in the front part of the head and knocked from his horse." While this wound was not life threatening, it was quite painful and caused a "considerable hemorrhage." However, he quickly regained his horse and ordered a withdrawal. The entire Federal line lost its integrity and pockets of men made their way back to their starting point at Ironton. The Confederates kept up the pressure, cutting off knots of Federal soldiers attempting to retreat. The Rebels broke off the fight when darkness and rain set in that evening.[23]

While the Rebels flooded the valley preparing to overrun Fort Davidson, Ewing was busily readying to receive them. First, he sent word to Wilson's command to block the gap at Shepherd and Pilot Knob mountains. Second, he sent infantry detachments from the 14th Iowa up Shepherd Mountain to challenge the Rebels' ability to move up its slope to emplace artillery. Finally, he "forwarded up the railroad all quartermaster and commissary stores not needed in the fort, and all the rolling stock" north to keep it out of enemy hands. Plus, he sent all the quartermaster wagons rearward for the same purpose.[24] Ewing was determined to fight it out at Pilot Knob and summed up the events of the day in a message to Rosecrans: "I can hold the fort against 4,000 or 5,000 cavalry and four pieces of artillery. I think I am now informed to my satisfaction that the enemy has more than [that] at Fredericktown.... Evidently a considerable body of the enemy are upon me."[25] Rosecrans replied, "You can probably make it too expensive for the rebels to take the Knob." With this prophetic message, the die was cast for the first major battle of the Great Raid.

Tuesday, 27 September 1864, dawned with a chill rain in the air and both sides anticipating a heavy clash. Marmaduke's division had now closed behind Fagan with the intent of supporting the latter's forward movement that day. The Rebel plan called for Fagan's division to drive the Union forces out of Arcadia and Ironton and then to secure the Shepherd-Pilot Knob gap to allow a concentration of forces to assault Fort Davidson. Once Fagan secured the gap, Marmaduke was to come forward and move to the left of the pass, forming for attack on the slopes of Shepherd Mountain. Fagan, in possession of the gap, would spread out to the right at an angle to Marmaduke at the base of Pilot Knob Mountain. Further, Marmaduke was to run artillery up to the crest of Shepherd Mountain so that he could suppress the guns and infantry in the fort before and during the assault. Once all parties were set, Marmaduke and Fagan would make a coordinated, simultaneous attack to take the fort.[26]

Price had wanted simply to pound Fort Davidson into surrendering utilizing his artillery but changed his mind. As he had begun making preparations for the attack, some local citizens of Ironton and Arcadia came to see him. Upon his agreeing to see them, the citizens asked him not to shell Fort Davidson. The reason for this was that Ewing had forced several prominent Southern citizens into the work as a sort of human shield against bombardment. Further, these local people assured Price that the civilians in the fort were not Union men and therefore would not take up arms against the Confederate attackers.[27] Based on this, Price shifted to a more infantry-centric plan of attack, though he still intended to employ his field artillery. It is interesting that he made such a decision. As already noted, the citizens inside the fort were volunteers who fully intended to fight alongside the Federal soldiers. The citizens who came to Price obviously represented some sort of ruse devised by Ewing to convince Price to refrain from using his artillery. Ewing knew as well as anyone how vulnerable Fort Davidson was to plunging fire from artillery. Though we have no evidence that Ewing conjured this deception, it is reasonable to surmise that he did. At any rate, Price failed to verify the veracity of these citizens and used his artillery sparingly during the disastrous attack, much to the chagrin of many a young Missouri and Arkansas Rebel.

On Tuesday, 27 September 1864, Fagan again advanced to push the Federals out of Arcadia and Ironton to secure the Shepherd-Pilot Knob gap. "So the ball has opened," Dr. McPheeters noted as Fagan ran into the bluecoats that day. Over the next several hours Fagan encountered warm resistance before securing his objective. Cabell's brigade was leading Fagan's division this day, and while the going was tough, Cabell made steady progress. During the night, Price had managed to bring his whole army into the Arcadia Valley. When the Federal officers braced to receive the onslaught, one young captain noted, "[T]his is Price's whole army coming in here." Skirmishing began at daybreak as Cabell deployed his large 2,500-man brigade. As they spread out, the Rebels overlapped Major Wilson's battalion by several hundred yards. As the Rebels moved around his flank, Union Captain William J. Campbell went to confer with Major Wilson. The major told Campbell to move back to the Shepherd-Pilot Mountain gap at the "double-quick ... and I will close up the rear." Campbell "immediately obeyed the order" and retreated to the gap amid a scene of chaos. Campbell would recall that this meeting in the field was the last time he saw Major Wilson alive.[28]

The fight now shifted to the gap, just south of Fort Davidson. Ewing knew he could do little to stop the Rebels from pouring through the gap; at best he could only delay them. To do this, he ordered Wilson's battalion to place men on Shepherd's and Pilot Knob mountains to contest the ground. This, he hoped, would prevent the Rebels from placing artillery on the slopes to shell the fort and to report enemy dispositions. Soon after establishing their defense, the Federals "were fired up at long range and the enemy's cavalry in large numbers began to advance upon us." Artillery from Fort Davidson began to contest the Confederate advance, forcing them back for a time and terrifying the Union skirmishers as the rounds "whirred" overhead.[29] The Rebels, getting an initial taste of what an attack on the fort might mean, decided to try a new tactic.

At this point, Federal outposts observed a flag of truce moving toward their position and held their fire momentarily. According to one witness, it was about noon. A representative from the Federal commander met the bearer of the flag, Lieutenant Colonel Lauchlan A. Maclean, Price's adjutant, between the lines and inquired as to the nature of the truce. Maclean responded that General Price demanded the surrender of Fort Davidson. The forward skirmishers got the message back to the fort and Ewing. "I knew it was a trick," Ewing stated in his after action report. The Federal commander believed the ruse was intended to give the Rebels time to get through the gap and mass their forces unmolested. Therefore, he "ordered him [Wilson] to renew the fight at once." Ewing also believed that if he surrendered the post—which he never gave an iota of consideration—the Rebels would "play ... [a] Fort Pillow game on me." This last was in reference to the massacre perpetrated by Confederates in Tennessee on United States Colored Troop units.[30] Ewing probably believed that the Rebels would have special incentive to commit depredations upon the author of the hated G.O. #11. Thus, the fight for Fort Davidson would continue.

For the next two hours "a long and obstinate struggle followed in which the enemy lost considerably in an unsuccessful effort to pass the defile." One of the reasons for the difficulty the Rebels had in moving through the pass was the fact that the guns in the fort dominated the gap. Therefore, the Confederates had to move over the hills to get into position for an assault to avoid the firepower in the fort. But fighting over the hills was exhausting work because of the climb combined with the brush, timber, and rocks. Further, the Union soldiers made the Rebels perform this act under fire, contesting every inch of ground. Eventually, the overwhelming number of Confederates in two divisions drove back the two companies of Union defenders in the hills. Many of the Federal skirmishers had to make a run for it to escape capture. Not everyone made it back to the safety of the fort. As Fagan's division came rushing over Pilot Knob Mountain, Major Wilson and a squad of men became separated and cut off from their comrades on the main skirmish line. The group was soon captured. However, the Federals counterattacked, throwing Fagan's men into disarray. Wilson took the opportunity to evade his captors and started back to the fort. They had not gotten far when Lieutenant Colonel John P. Bull, with 200 Arkansans, noticed a Union major and some privates between the successive Rebel lines. He quickly went after Wilson and his men, capturing them a second time.[31] A few days after this, injustice would befall the unfortunate major and his soldiers.

Most of the other skirmishers from the 14th Iowa and 3rd MSM Cavalry made it back to the fort around two o'clock in the afternoon. A lull settled over the battlefield characterized by an eerie silence as the Confederates now formed for the assault. Between Marmaduke and Fagan, the Rebels brought some 7–8,000 soldiers to bear against the Federals in Fort Davidson, many more than the 5,000 Ewing felt comfortable defending against. Ewing had around 1,000 men in a fort that was poorly sited, as already noted. General Cabell sought to take advantage of this vulnerability by pushing two guns from Captain W.M. Hughey's Arkansas battery to the top of Shepherd's Mountain. The guns opened up soon after reaching the top and shells began exploding over the parapet of the fort. Private Azariah Martin remembered that "a fragment struck a man at my left. He fell diagonally in front of me, grasping the right breast of my jacket ... at the same instant I felt something ... strike my left hip. It was the fragment of a bursting shell. His weight and the shock of the piece of shell striking me caused me to fall with him down the steep embankment."[32] However, this was the extent of the effectiveness of Cabell's guns.

The Rebel gunners displayed a frightening level of incompetence in their use of artillery. Rather than emplacing the guns down on the forward slope of the mountain, they deployed them on the crest. As a result, the tubes could not be depressed adequately to place effective fire on the fort. Therefore, most of the shells impacted beyond the earthwork. Then, before Cabell could check the accuracy of the firing, he received orders to conduct the assault, ending the artillery preparation before it really got started. One Rebel would recall, "We poor privates in the ranks expected to see the enemy shelled out of the fort in double-quick time. It certainly could have been done, in a few minutes; but instead of this, Gens. Price and Fagan ordered a charge."[33] The assault against Ewing's dug-in infantry proved a disaster.

It was now late afternoon and there was only three hours of daylight left to make a full-scale attack on Fort Davidson. Marmaduke's division formed up on the Confederate left at the base of Shepherd's Mountain oriented to the northeast with Fort Davidson about 1,000–1,200 yards away, just out of effective musket range. Fagan's division formed on the right at the base of Pilot Knob Mountain and at the edge of the village of Pilot Knob. Fagan was oriented to the northwest, thus the two Confederate divisions formed a "V" at almost right angles to each other. The ground between the fort and the attackers was entirely open, with a few folds in the terrain that could offer momentary cover during the course of the assault. The most prominent terrain feature on the attack axis was a dry creek bed in front of Marmaduke about 200 yards from the walls of the fort.[34] Based on the nature of the ground, the prospect for a successful assault was slim.

Neither of the division commanders questioned Price's orders. In fact, Fagan claimed his division alone could take the fort. Marmaduke told Price that with artillery support "he could take the works in a few minutes." General Cabell, commanding a brigade in Fagan's division, vehemently disagreed with his commander. From the tone of his after action report, and according to other witnesses, Cabell was not enamored with the thought of making the attack. Nevertheless, as a good officer, he executed his orders to the best of his ability after he was told to execute. At around 3:00 p.m. "the attack commenced and for an hour and a half the [fire of] musketry and artillery were very rapid." The Federal soldiers inside the fort must have had a feeling of dread as the long lines of dismounted cavalry emerged onto the open plateau upon which Fort Davidson rested. "In due time the attacking column, having deployed into line just beyond point blank of our guns, began to advance," said Lieutenant Murphy, commanding the artillery. "The rebel yell arose upon the silent air," he continued. As the Confederates came into range, Murphy blasted them. Surprisingly, these men of Marmaduke's division made it to the dry moat around the fort. Then they wavered and retreated, with fire speeding their repulse along.[35]

Brigadier General William L. Cabell, Commander, Cabell's Brigade, 1st Division, Army of Missouri (Library of Congress).

Fagan's division fared no better in this first assault. Part of the problem with the attack of the divisions was their lack of coordination as one stepped off before the other. Marmaduke launched his attack before Fagan, and thus, both division attacks were piecemeal. By the time Fagan launched, Marmaduke was already running for cover in the dry creek bed. In spite of this, Cabell's brigade of Fagan's division made it to the ditch outside of the fort. Since scaling ladders were needed to get over the walls, the attack stalled in the moat and, like Marmaduke, Fagan had to beat a rapid retreat under fire.[36] In spite of the lack of success, the Rebels regrouped and made a second attempt to take it.

An interesting incident occurred as the first assault began that could have caused a disaster for the defenders of Fort Davidson. As the skirmishers who were contesting the Rebel advance came back to the fort, they were unable to raise the drawbridge over the ditch. Thus, the fort was open to entrance by the Confederates if they could bring sufficient force to bear at the sally port. Ewing himself noted the gap in his defense and immediately moved to remedy the deficiency. He called to Captain Campbell above the din and told him to "get twenty men—volunteers—to stand at the gate *till the death!*" Only five men responded to the plea, but with those men, Campbell blocked the passageway with barrels "and made it secure."[37] Even though the Rebels noted the opening and attempted to exploit it, fire from the fort prevented them from reaching the gap. Campbell left the small guard at the sally port and returned to the fight.

As Campbell returned to the parapet, the first assault had already begun to subside. Within minutes the second attack launched in another attempt to enter the earthwork. "We could count three long lines, each four ranks deep, coming from two directions," recounted Captain Campbell. As the Rebels came on, "artillery and musketry mowed down their ranks." Lieutenant Murphy displayed rare courage and leadership in directing the artillery in the fight. In spite of heavy fire picking off his gunners, Murphy was able to maintain a high volume of fire that stiffened the resolve of the infantry. In spite of this, the attack came dangerously close to breaching the defense. "Cabell's men rushed right up to the enemy's works," recalled Rebel John Darr, a member of Cabell's brigade. General Cabell was personally leading the charge and as he made it to the moat, his horse was shot from under him. Meanwhile, in the fort, the Federal soldiers redoubled their effort to repel the attackers. The artillerymen could not depress their guns adequately to engage the Rebels in the ditch, and they now began to throw hand grenades. These primitive bombs, known as Ketchum grenades, resembled a dart with an elongated ball like an egg at the end. These were a new invention that would become a staple of trench fighting in the First World War. Ketchum grenades and artillery shells with short fuses drove those from Cabell's brigade back with heavy casualties. Private Darr would later write, "[T]his charge was one of the most unreasonable blunders ever made."[38]

During the course of the second charge a curious incident occurred within the fort. It seems that some soldiers found a barrel of whiskey meant for medicinal purposes. In the middle of the fighting, Captain Campbell noticed men leaving the firing line on the parapet to partake of the libation. Some of the erstwhile soldiers were liberally imbibing, so the captain decided to see what the interest in the barrel was about. Upon discovering the reason, he reported it to Ewing, stating that the contents of the barrel "would whip us quicker than the enemy." In response, Ewing placed a guard on the whiskey, but not before a number of the men became staggering drunk, thus reducing the firepower in the rifle pits.[39]

The struggle for Fort Davidson was not yet over. The Rebels were not deterred by the previous failures and had a little time left before darkness would envelop the field. They had managed to find cover in the dry creek bed between Shepherd's Mountain and the fort. Under this cover, elements of Fagan's division, mainly from Cabell's brigade, re-formed for one last try to get into the work. Beside them in the creek bed was Clark's brigade from Marmaduke's division, which had done some hard fighting of its own that

Fort Davidson looking south from the direction of Shepherd Mountain. This is the ground over which Cabell's Brigade and adjacent units moved to conduct their assault on the fort (photograph by the author).

afternoon. As the Confederates readied for the attack, sharpshooters in the creek bed were wreaking havoc upon the artillerymen in the fort. One by one, the Rebels were dropping the gunners with well-aimed shots. While this would lessen the weight of heavy firepower, it did nothing to reduce the rate of fire from the infantry. Thus, when the hapless Confederates debouched one last time from the creek bed, they were met by a wall of musketry. The Confederates never got closer than 200 yards to the ditch in front of the fort. Fagan was much chagrined at the multiple failures of his division to breach the works after he had boasted so adamantly that he alone could take it. In order to redeem his reputation Fagan asked Price for one last opportunity to take the fort before darkness set in. Price refused and Cabell commented that this "was a damned wise decision."[40] The uncoordinated attack receded as dusk set in and a cool drizzle began to fall over the field.

After the firing had died down the Federals were in a state of euphoria and perplexity. The small Federal force, outnumbered eight to one by the Rebels, had successfully defended the fort. But could they hold it tomorrow against a new assault? Thus, the men and their leaders were pleased with their performance and apprehensive for the future at the same time. Ewing had to decide what to do based on the situation, and none of the alternatives seemed to have any promise of success. As he surveyed the situation, he had three courses of action. First, he could stay in place and continue to fight it out. Second, he could surrender his command to Price. Third, Ewing might attempt an escape to Federal lines to the north or west.[41] Following a council of war and his own analysis, he would choose the last option.

The first course of action was not feasible for a couple of important reasons. Not only was the Federal force still heavily outnumbered, they were also now low on ammunition and probably could not sustain a heavy engagement like they had fought that day. If they ran out of ammunition, the Confederates would overrun the fort and atrocities could occur. Ewing had reason to believe this could happen. The example of Fort Pillow was fresh in his mind, but another key piece of information convinced Ewing that the Rebels had murder in mind. Late on the evening of the 27th, Lieutenant Colonel Alonzo Slayback, commanding a Rebel Missouri cavalry battalion, sent a message into the fort by a local woman advising that Ewing not attempt to fight it out. Slayback claimed that if the fort was overrun, it might become difficult to control the frenzied Confederate troops. Instead, Slayback recommended that Ewing surrender to save lives.[42]

Surrender was not feasible either, for two reasons. First, giving up would place Ewing at the mercy of the Confederates. As the author of the hated G.O. #11 there is nothing Price, and his men, would have desired more than getting their hands on Ewing. The undisciplined Rebels would likely seek their own brand of revenge on the Federal commander if they captured him. Also, the Federals had many black troops and freedmen serving in the ranks at Fort Davidson. These men had performed outstanding and valorous service during the battle. Ewing feared that if he surrendered, the Rebels would single out these men for maltreatment or murder. Even if the white troops were well treated, Ewing knew that was no indication of how the black troops might fare, as the examples of Poison Spring and Fort Pillow demonstrated.[43] Therefore, surrender was not an option, leaving a breakout attempt as the only reasonable chance to save the force.

While Ewing had in his mind what he wanted to do, he decided to put it to a council of his officers before making the final decision. In attendance at the council of war were Colonel Thomas Fletcher of the 47th Missouri, several company officers of the 47th, 14th Iowa, and 3rd MSM Cavalry, and members of Ewing's personal staff. Ewing laid out the situation and the courses of action to the assembled officers. Then he conducted a vote by secret ballot. When he counted the votes, "the result was 'evacuate,' by a majority of one." So, while this confirmed Ewing in his decision, the split vote could have been cause for concern, as some officers clearly disagreed. However, Ewing issued orders for an evacuation after midnight. Even though there was a high degree of disagreement among the leaders, they all began preparations for the retreat with single-mindedness regardless of their personal opinions.[44]

The men in the fort began preparing to evacuate after 10:00 p.m. on the 27th. General Ewing was very concerned "that the preparations for the retreat might be observed," but a piece of good fortune intervened to protect the Federal garrison. During the fighting that day the Confederates had set fire to the ironworks. The flames eventually spread to the nearby charcoal pile that was used as fuel for the furnaces. This slow burning energy source "glowed and flamed all night" and "lit up the whole valley as bright as day."[45] This bright red fire actually masked Federal activity in the fort because the fire was so bright it blinded the Rebels to the south. Thus, the only concern of the Federals now was the Confederates of Dobbin's brigade, posted by Price north of Fort Davidson to complete the encirclement. However, another piece of good luck and incompetence combined to assist the desperate Union soldiers.

Sterling Price wanted to ensure that, regardless of the outcome of the battle, he could bag the Federal defenders. To do so, he posted Colonel Archibald S. Dobbin's brigade, consisting of about 1,500 men, a mile north of Fort Davidson on the Potosi Road. The purpose of placing Dobbin here was to observe the avenues north of the fort and block them should Ewing attempt to break out. Dobbin's single brigade was 50 percent larger than the entire Federal garrison, so it seemed logical that they could prevent any attempt to escape. However, in another shocking display of incompetence, Dobbin failed to picket the road, posting his units one to two hundred yards up a hillside overlooking the road.[46]

Ewing's plan for escape required several well-coordinated elements to come together. First, the Federals had to mask their movement and for this they placed muffling material consisting of straw and tents on all planked surfaces, like the drawbridge, and wrapped the wheels of cannons and wagons with rags. Second, Ewing ordered the destruction of all excess ammunition and equipment. To do this, the Federals spiked the heavy guns and made arrangements to blow the magazine by laying a long, slow fuse to the interior, in which they "made a pile of powder as large as a haystack." This would ignite and then spread in a sympathetic explosion to the remaining twenty tons of powder, preventing the Rebels from laying their hands on the supply. Finally, Ewing had to identify the order of march to facilitate rapid movement. The battalion of the 14th Iowa would lead the evacuation, with Captain William Campbell in command of this advance guard. They were followed by the 47th Missouri and Colonel Fletcher, who commanded all the infantry. Tucked in the center were the six field guns of H Battery, 2nd Missouri Light Artillery, commanded by Lieutenant Montgomery. His guns could move to the front or rear to support the entire column. Finally, Captain H.B. Milks of the 3rd MSM Cavalry would command all the cavalry and the rear guard. After about four hours of frantic preparations, the column formed up for movement as Sergeant W.H. Moore took charge of setting the fuse to the magazine.[47]

Sometime between two and three in the morning, Ewing gave the order to Colonel Fletcher to begin the movement. Price's army lay just outside the ramparts, oblivious to what was going on in Fort Davidson. The column moved directly north up the Potosi Road bound for Mineral Point, where Ewing believed the advanced units of A.J. Smith's corps were posted. Every man in the column was likely worried that their effort to evacuate would be discovered by vigilant Confederates. The hills on the right side of the road were dotted with the campfires of Dobbin's brigade. Yet there was an eerie quiet that spread over the field as the nervous men trudged north in silence. It is a tribute to the discipline of the Federal officers and men that they were able to leave the fort completely undetected. Dobbin's men were huddled around the campfires and no officer had thought to place pickets on the very road the Union men were using to make good their escape. None of the Rebels saw the Federals, even though they were less than two hundred yards away from them.[48] Another reason for the failure is that the light from the campfires affected the night vision of the Rebels, accentuating the darkness around them. Thus, several hundred dark forms of Union soldiers successfully eluded the surrounding Confederate army.

The Confederates were not all slumbering that night. Price had set details to work building scaling ladders to facilitate one final assault on the 28th. The Rebels would never use them, as the Federals were several miles up the road before the Rebels realized the enemy was gone. They should have known better after the magazine exploded with a thunderous crash sometime around 4:00 a.m. Ewing had left a small detail under Sergeant Moore to light the fuse and ensure the destruction of the magazine. They also had to make one final sweep of the perimeter to ensure no stragglers were left behind. The detail found five men sleeping inside the fort, and after waking them with great difficulty, Moore lit the fuse and hightailed it out of the fort. Ewing's main body was about a mile beyond Dobbin's brigade "when the explosion took place and the heavens were illuminated." The detail was only 75 yards from the sally port when the magazine blew, raining shells down all around them. Price's men heard the explosion, too, but inexplicably failed to investigate, believing that the conflagration was an accident. Dr. McPheeters remembered that "a tremendous explosion was heard, shaking the whole earth," and yet Price failed to verify what had just happened.[49] Thus, another act of incompetence ensured the Federal escape.

Before daylight on the 28th, Ewing sent a ten-man detail ahead to make contact with A.J. Smith to request relief, as the telegraph lines were cut by Shelby late on the 26th. The detachment never made it to Mineral Point. Shelby's brigade had forced Smith's advanced units back and taken Potosi. As the ten men with Captain Hills moved north, they encountered some of Shelby's men and "fell upon about twenty-five Rebels in the town of Caledonia and routed them," taking one prisoner. The detail returned with the Rebel captive and reported this information to Ewing. With this knowledge, Ewing knew that he could not reach Smith on the Potosi Road because the Rebels had blocked that route with Shelby's brigade, but an alternate route was available. "I therefore at once left the Potosi road and took that through Webster [now Palmer, Missouri] toward Rolla," reported Ewing.[50] Thus, instead of seeking to link up with A.J. Smith, Ewing now intended to make for Rolla, where Brigadier General John McNeil commanded the Union supply depot in central Missouri.

As daylight illuminated the Arcadia Valley, the Rebels were preparing to move once more upon the works of Fort Davidson. Price was still under the impression that the enormous explosion was an accident and that the Federals would surely surrender before the superior Confederates could make an assault. Sometime before 8:00 a.m. on the 28th of September, Rebel pickets discovered that Fort Davidson was deserted. Word quickly made it back to Price, who had made his headquarters in a house in the village of Arcadia. Upon hearing this news, Price issued orders for a pursuit with Marmaduke taking the lead. Simultaneously, he sent messengers to Shelby directing him to cut off Ewing's retreat, catching the Federals between the two columns.[51] While it was a good plan, Ewing had too much of a head start for Price to bag him so easily.

Even after Price issued orders to pursue, it took time to get the movement organized. Ewing had already been moving for at least five hours when the Confederates discovered the Federals were gone, and it would take a few more before the Rebels were on the road after them. By one account, Marmaduke did not get started until almost noon, and the messages to Shelby miscarried so that he was unable to block Ewing's retreat. Between 3:00 a.m. and sundown on the 28th, Ewing's column made 31 miles, stopping at the hamlet of Webster. The Union soldiers and accompanying civilians and freedmen moved this entire distance unmolested.[52] Thus, Price had incompetently managed yet another aspect of this young campaign.

At Webster, the Federal soldiers were still 55 miles from Rolla, but only 35 miles separated them from Harrison—modern-day Leasburg—on the main rail line. If the column could reach Harrison, then they could receive reinforcements from Rolla to contest their pursuers. To effect this, Ewing again called on Captain Hills and ten men to take the advance to Franklin and telegraph Generals McNeil and Rosecrans to apprise them of the situation and request assistance. He also issued orders for the column to rest until midnight and then hit the road west to continue the retreat. On this occasion, the route chosen by Ewing was a providential decision. The road "to Harrison led nearly all the way along a sharp spur of the Ozark range, separating the waters of the Huzza and Courtois [rivers], and through a gorge of the Huzza, walled in with untraversable cliffs."[53] In other words, the narrow road was on a constricted ridgeline with steep slopes and a river on either side. Therefore, the flanks of the column were protected from attack and the only way to attack the column was from the rear. The narrowness of the ridge meant the Rebels could get only a few men in line to assail the Federals, who could easily parry the blow with their rear guard. So, by the time the Rebels could catch up, they were unable to get adequate force in position to break up the retreat.

Marmaduke and Shelby combined forces on the Potosi Road late on the 28th. It was then that the two Confederate commanders realized that Ewing had slipped between them. They combined forces now and turned off the Potosi Road for the road to Harrison, which the Rebels called Leasburg, in pursuit. Ewing's men were back on the road to Harrison just after midnight on Thursday, 29 September. The Rebels under Shelby and Marmaduke would finally reestablish contact on this day, and their effort to bring the Federals to bay would prove frustrating. The Federal soldiers moved for several hours in "intense dark" through a storm. It rained all night, making the movement miserable for man and beast. "We groped our way with great effort and little progress," Ewing reported. The column had no contact with the enemy until 8:00 on the gray morning of the 29th.[54] This was Marmaduke's advance guard, and from this point until the Confederates turned back in front of Harrison the Federal soldiers were in almost continuous contact with the enemy. In spite of their exhausted state, the Union soldiers moved on and fought with grim determination. Nobody wanted to become a prisoner of the Rebels for fear of revenge following the one-sided battle at Fort Davidson.

To ensure that the Rebels could not break through the rear guard, Ewing reinforced it with four infantry companies from the 14th Iowa and 47th Missouri and added a section of artillery. He placed all of this and the cavalry under the command of Major H.H. Williams, 10th Kansas Infantry, Ewing's aide-de-camp. The terrain greatly aided the retreating Federals. The only direction from which Marmaduke and Shelby could attack Ewing was the rear on that very narrow ridgeline. The reinforced rear guard, therefore, was able to fend off every charge that the Rebels made. The attacks seemed to reinvigorate the Union soldiers, who "forgot that they had marched 40 miles and were tired." The civilians traveling with the column were a different story. Every time the Rebels hit the rear, the civilians caused a panic within the main body and "nearly sacrificed it" each time.⁵⁵ Nevertheless, the discipline of the soldiers restored order and enabled the retreat to proceed.

Eventually, the Federals debouched onto an open plain as the ridgeline flattened out a few miles from Harrison. This change in terrain, combined with a greater ability of the Rebels to bring more men into the fight, made it tougher for Ewing's tired soldiers to fend off the Confederates. At one point, on the Meramec River, the Rebels were able to overlap the line of the rear guard, forcing Ewing to put in all the troops to push the enemy back. Once he had done so, he put the militia back on the road as the rear guard slowly backed rearward under pressure. The Union soldiers were now only three miles from Harrison, and the column went to the double-quick march "and jogged on into Leasburg [Harrison] without further trouble."⁵⁶ It was now late afternoon and the Federals had marched and fought for the past eight hours, since first contact.

When the Federal soldiers arrived in Harrison they had completed a 66-mile march in a mere 39 hours. However, their ordeal was not yet over, for the Rebels under Marmaduke and Shelby were determined to capture Ewing and his small band. The combined force of Shelby and Marmaduke numbered well over 5,000 men, more than five times as many men as Ewing had available. The Federals had arrived just before dark, and as they filed into Harrison a steady drizzle came down to dampen their spirits as well as their bodies. But, shortly after dark, a stroke of luck occurred that elated every Union man. "The sound of an approaching train was heard," recalled Captain W.V. Lucas of the 14th Iowa. When it arrived, many men mounted cars thinking the train had arrived to evacuate them. Officers quickly gained control of the situation and made the men dismount, sinking their hopes.⁵⁷ However, once they realized what the train contained, all was well.

The train originated in St. Louis and was en route to Rolla when it arrived at Harrison. As if by providence, it was loaded with hardtack, bacon, ammunition, picks, shovels, and whiskey. Every item was desperately needed by the hungry Federals, "excepting the whiskey," Captain Lucas pointed out. Many of the men probably disagreed with the captain on this last point, but all agreed that the food, ammunition, and entrenching tools were a godsend. The men quickly unloaded the train and began entrenching, using the boxes that contained the tools, food, and ammunition as makeshift breastworks. After they filled their stomachs, the morale of the soldiers rose precipitously.⁵⁸ They all knew that the train full of supplies evened the odds, enabling them to put up a tough defense.

Ewing's men were oriented in a semicircle on the south side of town. The railroad tracks represented the northern boundary of Harrison with the town south of the rail line. Just three-quarters of a mile from town lay the Union lines and the Confederates were just beyond that in the wood line. As the men labored on the fieldworks, Ewing began to worry that the Rebels might attempt a night assault. To prevent this and provide early warning, he wanted to illuminate the area. A couple of barns surrounded by haystacks separated the Union works from the Confederate lines. Ewing asked Captain Campbell for a volunteer to set the barns and haystacks on fire. Campbell turned to Captain Lucas to see if anyone would perform the dangerous mission. Corporal Earl J. Lamson immediately stepped forward to volunteer. Lucas accepted the offer after warning him that the mission was very dangerous and that he might not live to see his wife and child again. Lamson acknowledged the risk but said he was going anyway. He stripped his clothes off, except his underwear, took off his shoes, and slipped out into the darkness. During what must have seemed like hours to them, the men intently looked out over the field for a sign of light in the barns. "After what seemed an age someone described a dim light" in one of the barns. "The tiny light developed into a big blaze and soon became a conflagration," remembered Lucas. Then shots rang out and Captain Lucas had momentary thoughts of what he might write to Lamson's wife. Minutes later, the underwear-clad Lamson bounded over the works—mission accomplished.[59]

The fire from the barns burned all night and the Rebels made no attempt to attack the fast improving Union lines. In the morning, everyone expected an attack on the outnumbered Union defenses, but it did not materialize. The Rebels were in no better condition than the ragged Unionists. "We bivouacked upon the field of Leasburg [Harrison] supperless and rationless," said Shelby. The rain added to the discomfort of the Rebels. As dawn of 30 September revealed another gray morning, the Confederates were not anxious to assault what appeared a formidable earthwork. Fresh in Marmaduke's memory was the failed charges on Fort Davidson, and the Confederates had little stomach for an assault. Members of Shelby and Marmaduke's staff rode forward to examine the Federal defenses around Harrison. Upon making their report to the generals, Shelby and Marmaduke conferred on the possibility of a successful attack. The two division commanders "decided after considerable discussion that they would probably lose more men in attempting to storm our position than an uncertain success would justify."[60] Thus, the Rebels decided to withdraw and rejoin Price.

Shortly after the Confederates began to withdraw, the exhausted Federals were startled by the approach of another force from the north. Around midnight of the 30th, Ewing had sent a citizen to Rolla with a message for General McNeil requesting relief for his exhausted troopers. Though he did not know it, the troops they saw approaching from the north were part of the relief force. "Troops approaching from the north!" the pickets called out. The defending soldiers now tensed up, thinking they were surrounded. However, in a few minutes their fears vanished when the pickets followed up their initial call with "they carry the stars and stripes!" Shortly, Colonel John L. Beveridge, soon to become the governor of Illinois and commanding a relief column from Rolla, rode into the works and presented himself to Ewing with his 17th Illinois Cavalry. The ordeal was over. The next day, Saturday, 1 October, the men marched out of Harrison toward Rolla. After a few miles, a train met them and the infantry climbed onto the cars, with the cavalry and artillery following with their draft animals. Ewing and his intrepid command arrived at Rolla that afternoon to "a haven of rest and safety."[61]

In the aftermath of the assaults on Fort Davidson, Sterling Price began to assess the effects of his disastrous decision to attack. What he found must have given him cause for concern. As a result of the engagement at Pilot Knob and the subsequent pursuit of Ewing's force, Price lost between 1,000 and 1,500 men. Exact casualty numbers are not available because Price never made a precise count of his losses, yet another example of his haphazard military administration. In his after action report he admits to losing "14 officers and 80 men killed and wounded [in Marmaduke's division] and the loss of Fagan's was doubtless greater." Price's count seems purposely evasive to cover up much heavier losses due to the tactical incompetence displayed on the field. Though he did not record a count of the casualties, Dr. McPheeters noted in his diary, "[O]ur wounded were quite numerous." Therefore, we must give credence to Union estimates, which are based upon statements by Ewing's surgeon, Thomas W. Johnson. He made a physical count of Confederate casualties left behind by Price in makeshift hospitals and the killed buried on the field. The number 1,500 is probably an overestimate, but based on the intensity of the battle and the meticulous nature of Johnson's accounting, the Rebels lost no less than 1,000.[62] This means Price lost over 15 percent of his effective force. For an army conducting offensive operations, a loss exceeding 10 percent is considered devastating and would force the army to regroup before continuing a campaign.

The losses would make it difficult for Price to achieve his strategic and operational objectives because he no longer possessed the combat power to accomplish them. However, more devastating is the loss of that precious resource in war—time. The diversion toward Pilot Knob to reduce Fort Davidson cost Price at least five days. Shelby pointed out in the council of war on the 25th that taking the fort was a difficult task, and he proposed instead that the Rebels bypass Pilot Knob, marching immediately on St. Louis. While it is not certain that the Confederates could have taken St. Louis, the loss of time ensured that they could not. During those five days, Rosecrans finally mobilized the city for defense. On the 27th a public notice was posted in the *St. Louis Daily Republican* calling discharged soldiers back to the colors to strengthen the city's militia units. Further, notices were published on subsequent days calling out the city guard and announcing that B. Gratz Brown—Shelby's cousin—commanded the city defenses.[63] Thus, Rosecrans took advantage of the time Price gave him and used it to prepare for defense.

The final effect of the battle at Pilot Knob was the loss of morale among the Rebel troops who made the assault, while simultaneously providing the Union cause a piece of positive news locally and nationally. The Fort Davidson assaults sapped the fighting spirit of Fagan and Marmaduke's divisions. Seeing so many of their comrades killed or maimed left those who remained unwilling to sacrifice their lives in upcoming battles. As a result, Shelby's division was the only one Price could count on to fight in a tight battle. He would call on Shelby repeatedly over the next month to bail out the other divisions when defeat threatened. Newspapers in the state described the assault and defeat of Price at Pilot Knob, while at the national level *Harper's Weekly* published a short article recounting Ewing's effort and how Rosecrans was "actively taking measures to meet the emergency."[64] All of these factors would lead Price toward changing his objectives in the campaign, as well as the character of the expedition. He would soon decide to change it from an operation to take and hold ground to one for which the force composition was more suited—a raid.

The Union gained much from Ewing's "Thermopylae-like" defense of Pilot Knob. First, they inflicted a crippling blow on the Rebels difficult to recover from. Second, the time gained facilitated the ability of the Federal Department of Missouri to establish coherent defenses. Finally, the successful defense demonstrated to those Missouri citizens who may have supported Price's incursion to reconsider their position, and on the national stage it allayed fears for the safety of St. Louis. One of the stated goals of Price's campaign was to recruit his army and bring them south to augment the Trans-Mississippi Department. This first disastrous engagement—as well as undisciplined

Confederate behavior—discouraged recruitment and caused a failure of this key purpose of invading Missouri. All of this was made possible because of the iron will and competent command exercised by Thomas Ewing, Jr. His defense of Pilot Knob was the crowning achievement of his military career and it would ensure that the Rebel campaign in Missouri failed. Ewing's inspired performance was in line with his character, and when Rosecrans ordered Ewing to Pilot Knob he had picked the right man for the challenge.

The Union army under Ewing did lose significantly during the battle and evacuation. But the advantages accrued for the defense of Missouri, and ultimate defeat of Price, far outweighed the losses. Nevertheless, the loss of comrades and friends was not mitigated for those who fought at Pilot Knob, in spite of their great service. Of the approximately 1,000 defenders of Fort Davidson, Ewing reported a loss of 200 killed, wounded, and missing. To this he added 150 more casualties resulting from the subsequent retreat to Rolla.[65] Thus, the small Union force at Pilot Knob lost 350 men, amounting to 35 percent of the total force, which a modern army would consider destruction. An interesting statistic is that the 1,000 defenders inflicted casualties at least equal to their total force while losing a high percentage of their own number. This is an amazing testament to the ferocity of the Union defense and it served as a cautionary note for the Rebels for the remainder of the Great Raid.

Among the Union missing was the intrepid Major James Wilson of the 3rd Missouri State Militia Cavalry and several of his soldiers. Major Wilson had commanded at Pilot Knob before Ewing's arrival and he had a reputation as an outstanding guerrilla fighter. Wilson had actively scouted the area south of Pilot Knob and provided Rosecrans and Ewing much of the intelligence of Price's movements early in the campaign. During the fighting in Arcadia Valley, it was Wilson and his command that so effectively contested the advance of the Rebels. His efforts enabled Ewing, and eventually Rosecrans, to fully develop situational understanding of Price's force composition and intent. When Wilson was captured, it represented a severe blow to Ewing, for he had lost his cavalry commander and a fine leader.

Wilson was captured with two of his men on the afternoon of 27 September. Following his capture, Wilson was taken to a "prison corral" the Rebels had established in the town of Arcadia. As already noted, he had received a painful wound to his head during the fighting on the 26th in the valley. Sometime on 28 September, Dr. Seymour D. Carpenter, a Union man working with the blessing of the Confederate medical directorate, went to the prisoner laager to see to the needs of the Federal prisoners. Dr. Carpenter dressed Wilson's wound and "this was probably the last surgical attention he received and from this time forward he did not receive a single act of courtesy or civility from his captors." When the Confederates moved north from Pilot Knob, they force marched the prisoners on foot along with them. Over the next five days, the Rebel cavalry moved 80 miles with their prisoners in tow. The miserable Union men were fully exposed to the elements, which had begun to turn cold with early fall.[66]

On Monday, 3 October, a guerrilla commander named Colonel Timothy Reeves lined up all the prisoners under heavy guard facing him. Reeves then instructed the prisoners to give their names and units. Those who reported their unit as the 3rd MSM Cavalry were told to move forward two paces from the line. Among the prisoners were six men from the Third: Major Wilson, Corporal William W. Gourley, Privates William C. Grotts, William Scaggs, John W. Shew, and John Holabaugh. Three other men from the Third had the wherewithal to discern what Reeves was doing and lied about which unit they belonged to. This saved their lives. Another prisoner—who remains unknown—stepped forward claiming that he belonged to the Third, believing these men were the first to receive paroles. Instead, Reeves marched Major Wilson and the six enlisted men into the woods, where the men learned of their fate. The condemned men were lined up before a firing squad and killed by a volley of musketry. The other prisoners clearly heard the fateful volley—as they received their paroles.[67] The men of the 3rd MSM Cavalry were singled out because they were considered traitors by the Confederates, and as a militia regiment that fought guerrillas, Price's men believed them criminals, especially Wilson.

With this heinous act, the first phase of Price's Great Raid came to an end. The first act of the drama shaped the rest of the campaign, much to the detriment of the Confederate cause. Price had entered Missouri in order to eject the Union state government, establish a Confederate one, recruit his army, and influence the Federal elections in a manner favorable to the Confederacy. At the operational level, he was ordered to take St. Louis, capture the enormous Federal depot there, and spread panic among the Unionists in Missouri and neighboring Illinois. But with his decision to reduce Pilot Knob Price jeopardized his ability to achieve any of these objectives. Thus, as Price and the Army of Missouri entered the next phase of the operation, they were at a major crossroad. Should Price continue on to St. Louis and attempt capturing it? Or should he divert to Jefferson City to pursue the political objective? Finally, should he change the entire nature of the campaign and convert it from an operation to take and hold ground into a large raid? Price's decision would affect the entire character of the expedition in the days that followed.

7

Lost Opportunities

In the aftermath of Pilot Knob, Price faced a series of tough decisions. The choices he would make would have far-reaching effects in the Trans-Mississippi Department and beyond. His original strategic objective was directly linked to the political situation, and that was to wrest Missouri away from the Federal Union. To do this operationally, he needed to take either St. Louis or Jefferson City or both. This challenge to Federal authority in the state just might affect the outcome of the national election in a manner favorable to the Confederates. The defeat at Pilot Knob seriously upset the strategic calculus. While Price had fumbled so far, there was still opportunity to recover and make some great gain for the South. Plus, Price had some additional capability in the form of roving guerrilla bands that he could use to achieve some critical objectives if he would avail himself of the resource. Ultimately, he would fail because he had a fundamental inability to match his capabilities with established objectives, to the detriment of the Missouri Rebels and the entire Southern cause.

In the days leading up to Pilot Knob, Price may have already decided to divert from St. Louis to other geographic objectives.[1] "I received at Fredericktown satisfactory information that ... the Federal General A.J. Smith was encamped about ten miles from St. Louis with his corps," Price reported. Up to this point, Price's army was oriented on an axis to arrive before St. Louis. This intelligence certainly gave Price reason for pause, as his after action report suggests.[2] Yet he probably still held out a measure of hope that he could take the city, because he did not make a definitive decision to divert the march until after the defeat at Pilot Knob. His advance to take Pilot Knob was likely a test to determine his ability to contend with a Federal force on the defense. Had Price successfully taken Fort Davidson on 27 September with minimal loss, he might have decided that he still had some chance to take St. Louis and issued orders to do so. However, the resounding defeat before Fort Davidson, combined with the troubling information of Smith's arrival, convinced Price that an attempt to take St. Louis would fail: "While at Ironton, receiving information that the Federal force in St. Louis far exceeded my own two to one, and knowing the city to be strongly fortified, I determined to move as fast as possible to Jefferson City, destroying the railroad as I went, with a hope to be able to capture that city with its troops and munitions of war."[3] Price had now come to the first decision point, and a combination of circumstances including his dawdling, poor tactical decisions and Federal efforts to prepare a proper defense forced him to change his operational objective from St. Louis to Jefferson City. Additional circumstances would force his hand in the coming days, which would change the entire character of the expedition.

Governor Reynolds, who had joined Price for the campaign into Missouri, was beside himself with anger. Reynolds gave vent to his emotion after the campaign in an open letter to the *Marshall (Texas) Republican* published on 23 December 1864. His pen drips with venom toward Price as he recounts the commander's incompetence. "He [Price] lost several hundred of his best soldiers in the repulsed attempt to storm the well ditched fort at Pilot Knob," Reynolds wrote. Then, "the garrison, unobserved, evacuated the place by night," he continued. With open contempt, Reynolds stated, "General Price refused to order an immediate pursuit."[4] This caused abandonment of the drive on St. Louis in favor of a move on Jefferson City. Since Reynolds was keenly interested in the installment of a Confederate government at the Missouri capital, his anger was assuaged somewhat. In a letter to Price written on 2 October, Reynolds reassuringly expressed his hope that the army "would restore him [Reynolds] to the executive chair."[5] But his irritation would remain concealed only if Price could deliver on securing the political objective of the campaign. Thus, Reynolds would not remain calm for long.

While the drama was unfolding at Pilot Knob, another theater featuring heinous acts of violence was happening to the north. As Price approached the Missouri border in late September guerrilla bands began to swing into action to aid his invasion. Earlier that month, he had sent a message north into Missouri as he approached from Arkansas. The note was intended for the leaders of the most prominent guerrilla bands in the state, including William C. Quantrill, George Todd, and William "Bloody Bill" Anderson. The letter reached George Todd in mid–September. The message informed the bushwhackers of Price's imminent invasion and requested that the partisan leaders aid his march. Specifically, Price wanted the guerrillas to disrupt the Federal lines of communication, attack isolated outposts, and cause a general disruption of Union command and control.[6] George Todd had no problem with this request, and he quickly put his men in readiness to oblige Price's desires.

Todd and Anderson began a reign of terror north of the Missouri River that exceeded anything yet seen in the border war. The men in Todd and Anderson's groups were young products of the long and ugly war that had sprung up along the Kansas-Missouri border in the 1850s. Many were drifters or men who had lost loved ones to the Union Redlegs and Jayhawkers. They had developed a deep hatred for Unionists and had no inhibitions in committing unspeakable depredations, and they would demonstrate their ability to perform such acts over the next few weeks.

Price's attempt to coordinate his conventional operation with guerrilla activities in the state was an astute move on his part. In modern parlance, the combination of conventional and unconventional operations is known as compound warfare. The idea behind compound warfare is that simultaneous regular and irregular operations will place insurmountable pressure on the enemy. The partisans hit high-value targets in the enemy's rear areas in order to cause disruption to his systems and divert frontline forces to secure critical nodes. The resultant paralysis facilitates the regular force's ability to accomplish its objectives.[7] Thus, Price's effort to cooperate with the guerrilla leaders had great potential to facilitate the success of his army. However, his initiative would have far less success than he hoped for two reasons. First, Price's notorious inattention to administrative and operational details would leave the guerrillas to choose what they thought were the best targets, but these did not necessarily help the army. Second, the guerrillas' undisciplined interest in loot made them inattentive in destroying the targets they did choose. So while the guerrillas would cause panic in the Union high command their effort would ultimately fail to assist Price in achieving any of his goals.[8]

On 23 September, Todd's band struck first. A company of the 3rd MSM Cavalry was escorting a small supply train from Sturgeon to Rocheport. As they moved along the road, the 3rd MSM Cavalry stopped at an apple orchard to take a short break and sample the fruit. Todd's men, as chance would have it, were moving in the opposite direction and stumbled upon the militiamen. Todd quickly put spurs to his horse and charged with his guerrillas into the surprised Union men. Most of the 3rd had not ventured far from their mounts and were able to make a getaway. Several, however, fled on foot and the bushwhackers ran them down, brutally murdering fourteen men and capturing the trains.[9] This threw the region north of the river into an uproar, but it was only the start of the period of violence.

Brigadier General Clinton B. Fisk, the young, 36-year-old commander of the District of North Missouri, jumped into action to try to stop Todd and Anderson, but he had little to work with. Aside from the 17th Illinois Cavalry and a detachment of the 1st Iowa Cavalry, Fisk's force comprised three Missouri militia regiments posted at critical points on the railroad north of the Missouri River. Some of these units were of unreliable quality. One outpost at Keytesville surrendered wholesale to Todd's men on 20 September. An incensed Fisk believed some of the Missouri militiamen were disloyal. "Cowardice and treason combined caused the loss of Keytesville," reported Fisk.[10] With such material available to defend his district, Fisk had his work cut out for him.

Shortly after the engagement near Rocheport, Todd combined his guerrilla band with "Bloody Bill" Anderson's. William Anderson was 25 years old and had a notorious reputation for brutality. Atrocities committed by the Unionists had contributed to transforming him into a killer. Three of Anderson's sisters were among the ladies who were killed or maimed when the building they were incarcerated in at Kansas City collapsed on them in 1863. The war in Missouri produced a monster as a result. Anderson was known for showing his opponents no mercy and mutilating the bodies of his victims. Today, Anderson would likely receive a diagnosis of psychopathic mental illness by medical professionals, but in the Civil War, his behavior—as reprehensible as it was—gained notoriety in the Confederacy for his success against the Federal enemy.[11]

After Anderson combined with Todd, they moved east along the railroad toward Centralia. They arrived at Centralia on the morning of 27 September—the same day as Price's failed assaults on Fort Davidson. About 80 guerrillas accompanied Anderson as he rode into town. The original intent of their raid on Centralia was to cut the railroad and telegraph lines running through town. As a matter of course, the bushwhackers began rummaging through the town to find items useful to them. By chance, they found a supply of new boots and a store of whiskey. The Rebels had begun to freely imbibe when at 11:30 a.m. they heard a whistle alerting them that a train was inbound. The bushwhackers, many of them now drunk, converged on the train. The cars contained 125 passengers, and once Anderson's men had stopped the train, they ordered all the passengers off to shake them down.[12] This was the start of a frenzy of violence.

As the passengers filed off the train, the guerrillas discovered twenty-five unarmed soldiers among the travelers on their way home on furlough. Anderson had the soldiers and civilians separated into groups and turned his complete attention to the bluecoats. The guerrilla leader then made a speech to the soldiers about the wrongs inflicted on southern Missourians and concluded by informing them that they all would die. In a moment twenty-four of the soldiers lay dead after Anderson took the remaining man, Sergeant Thomas Goodman, to use him for an exchange of one of his men the Federals held prisoner. Anderson and his men then turned on the civilians, robbing them and killing several. They continued their psychopathic frenzy by scalping and mutilating the bodies for hideous trophies. This phase of Centralia concluded when the bushwhackers set the depot and train afire and then set the burning cars in motion down the track.[13] The atrocities had only started.

Nearby, a Union patrol was approaching Centralia, and the commanding officer, Major A.V.E. Johnston, saw the smoke from the burning train. He decided to investigate and stepped into a vortex of violence. Johnston was leading a 155-man detachment from the new 39th Missouri Mounted Infantry. As the 39th entered town they found a scene of wanton destruction. "The sight of the mangled bodies of the soldiers almost maddened them, and they galloped on after the bushwhackers," stated the *St. Louis Daily Republican*. Major Johnston found the Rebels encamped at a place called Fullenwider's Pasture. The bushwhackers knew the Federals were approaching and mounted their horses in readiness. When Anderson realized that he—with Todd's band—outnumbered Johnston's detachment, he decided to fight. Then, to his surprise, the Federals dismounted to fight as infantry. Anderson then charged the Federals at a gallop. The inexperienced 39th fired high with their single shot rifles and before they could reload, Anderson's men were upon them. A killing melee ensued and the bushwhackers killed almost all of their assailants. They returned to Centralia and butchered the guards Johnston had left in town. Of Johnston's 155 men, 123 were killed and mutilated. "Most of them were shot through the head, then scalped, bayonets trust through their ears and noses cut off, privates torn off and thrust in the mouths of the dying," Fisk reported to Rosecrans. The *Daily Missouri Republican* decried the outrages and the Union high command resolved to hunt down and kill Anderson.[14] The young guerrilla leader's days were numbered.

While the bushwhackers were wreaking havoc north of the Missouri River, Price was redirecting his columns toward a new objective, Jefferson City. Marmaduke and Shelby pursued Ewing until 1 October, leaving Fagan to take the lead of the column. Price still probably harbored hopes that he might take St. Louis. After some hasty tidying up of the Pilot Knob battlefield, Price put Fagan on the road to the northeast. Yet he left several hundred severely wounded men in makeshift hospitals, stressing the ability of the local civilian populace in the valley to care for them. Nevertheless, on 29 September, Price was on the move making twenty-two miles on the Potosi Road toward St. Louis. As Fagan's division camped that evening, Brigadier General M. Jeff Thompson—the famous "Swamp Fox" of Missouri—arrived and offered his services to Price. Governor Reynolds sent a letter to Price in which he stated that "it would give me personally great pleasure" if he, Price, could find an appropriate command for Thompson. The army commander would establish one in order to leverage Thompson's outstanding leadership in the army.[15]

On the 30th Price was back on the road on an axis of advance leading toward St. Louis. Shelby and Marmaduke had decided to break off their pursuit of Ewing and were moving eastward to rejoin Price. This meant the whole army appeared to be advancing on St. Louis. As he continued forward, Price sent Cabell on a mission to destroy the railroad and telegraph station at Franklin. The purpose of this was to cut off the city from the western part of the state and instill panic among the Federals. The efficient Cabell and his brigade "completely accomplished [the mission] with small loss to us, as Cabell always did when in command." As Cabell's men fanned out around Franklin, they destroyed everything of value to the enemy and swapped their own worn-out mounts for fresh ones they found in abundance near Union. Cabell also found the enemy at Union and "fought A.J. Smith's infantry corps for nearly two hours." He successfully drove them back and camped at Union that night.[16] Cabell's advanced troopers were within 35 miles of St. Louis, but this was as close as any of Price's men would get to taking the ultimate prize in Missouri. Price's column had moved a mere ten miles on this day, with the rest of Fagan's division camping at Richwoods, which represented the point where he had to make a definitive decision on his objective.[17] The next day Shelby and Marmaduke reunited with the army, but Price knew his chance of taking St. Louis was almost zero.

Price had scouts and spies fanned out across his front and in St. Louis. The information he received from the environs of the city finally convinced him that any hope of taking St. Louis was a pipe dream. His spies had witnessed a flurry of activity as Rosecrans pressed the citizens into service to defend the city. All business was suspended, citizens were digging fortifications, and the city home guards under B. Gratz Brown were preparing to fight. The city papers trumpeted all the preparations in the city, providing an open source of intelligence for Price to consider. Plus, the skirmishing Cabell had engaged in with A.J. Smith's corps indicated that taking St. Louis was a difficult proposition. With the repulse at Pilot Knob fresh in his mind, Price now made the decision he had sought to avoid. The army would now move to Jefferson City. On the morning of 2 October, Price issued the orders and the Army of Missouri turned its back on St. Louis and headed for Jefferson City.[18] While he had changed the objective, Price's operation was still a mission to take and hold ground. He had not yet shifted the nature of the operation to a raid, but as he approached Jefferson City, he began to reconsider this as well.

Rosecrans could not relax with Price's turn to the west. Neither Jefferson City nor Rolla were prepared to receive an attack by the Army of Missouri, and another frenzied effort was required to put things in order for defense of both cities. Rolla and Jefferson City were in Brigadier General John McNeil's District of Rolla and Brigadier General Egbert Brown's District of Central Missouri. Like every other military district in the state, the available troops were thoroughly dispersed across a series of outposts. McNeil's path to service in the Union army is an interesting story. He was the oldest of Rosecrans' five district commanders at 51 years of age. He was born in Canada in 1813 when the United States was at war with Great Britain and actively attempting to wrest Canada from Britain's grip. McNeil was a hatter by trade and moved to Boston as a young man to ply his occupation. Finding little success, he moved to St. Louis because the city was a major hub for fur traders. St. Louis provided much greater opportunity, and McNeil quickly established himself as one of its leading citizens. Leveraging his good name, he was elected to the Missouri legislature in 1844. When the war started, he had climbed the ladder of success to become the president of an insurance company. He was a leader among radical Union factions in the city and commander of a German militia company. McNeil would spend the entire war in Missouri fighting guerrillas and running the critical supply base at Rolla until Price arrived in 1864.[19]

Brigadier General Egbert Brown took a different but no less interesting path to district command in Missouri. Brown was 48 years old in 1864 and another old hand in the struggle for Missouri. He was from Toledo, Ohio, and served as city clerk, councilman, and mayor of that city. He moved to Missouri in 1852 to seek opportunity in the railroad business. As with many other Union men in St. Louis, Brown was a member of the radical faction, and when the war broke out he was instrumental in holding the state in the Union. He received a commission in the 7th Missouri Infantry in 1861, and within a few months received a promotion to brigadier general. While he never participated in any large battles until 1864, Brown fought in numerous skirmishes and engagements, with the defense of Springfield serving as his most notable achievement. In that engagement, during Marmaduke's second raid into Missouri, Brown was severely wounded, losing the use of one arm. During the first three years of the war he had garnered a distinguished reputation as a staunch commander on the battlefield and solid administrator. He had recovered enough from his wound to resume command, and Rosecrans assigned him to the District of Central Missouri in 1864.[20] Thus, his district and Jefferson City were squarely in Price's sights when October rolled around.

Brigadier General John McNeil, Commander, District of Rolla and 2nd Brigade, Provisional Cavalry Division, Department of Missouri (Library of Congress).

Another man who would soon play a prominent role in the defense of Jefferson City and beyond was Brigadier General John B. Sanborn, commander of the District of Southwest Missouri. He was 38 years old in 1864 and had gained a great deal of battlefield experience during the war. Unlike his fellow district commanders, Sanborn was not a Missourian and had performed most of his service east of the Mississippi. Born in New Hampshire, he moved to Minnesota, in 1854, where he practiced law until the outbreak of the war. When the conflict began, Sanborn took the position of adjutant general of Minnesota, charged with raising regiments for the war effort. After performing in an outstanding manner, he accepted a commission as the colonel of the 4th Minnesota Infantry. Sanborn took his regiment to Tennessee, where he joined the Army of the Tennessee after the battle of Shiloh. From there, he fought in the battles of Iuka, Corinth, and Vicksburg. He was promoted for his competent battlefield performance to brigadier general on 4 August 1863 and later transferred to Missouri as a district commander.[21] He had his headquarters at Springfield when the call came to move his troops to aid the state capital at Jefferson City. Now, with the Rebels bearing down on Jefferson City from the east, Rosecrans began issuing orders to bring all of his district commanders and their troops together to defend the capital. Brown, McNeil, Sanborn, and Fisk would then work feverishly to consolidate their outposts at the city in order to place it in a state of readiness to receive Price.

Though Price may have settled on a new objective, Rosecrans had no idea if his adversary was aiming for Jefferson City or Rolla. Therefore, he had to fan his units from St. Louis out along Price's route of march in an attempt to determine just where he was headed. This would take time and would mean that any defense implemented would be hasty at best. Curiously, Rosecrans was thinking only in terms of defense at this point. When Price entered the state, Rosecrans ceded the initiative to the Confederates, opting to wait on the defensive. Even now, after Price had been thoroughly defeated at Pilot Knob and turned away from St. Louis, Rosecrans still did nothing in the way of making preparations for offensive action. Thus, he continued to allow Price to dictate the course of events. Rosecrans intended only to react to the enemy, placing the state at the mercy of the Rebels.

A.J. Smith's lead elements, along with a few militia regiments, were actively attempting to determine Price's intent after he turned to the west. On Monday evening, 3 October 1864, Rosecrans got the information he needed when Colonel Lewis Merrill's 2nd Missouri Cavalry captured a Confederate lieutenant of engineers as the Rebels were leaving Union. Merrill discovered that the young officer enjoyed imbibing and decided to ply the lieutenant with enough alcohol to loosen his tongue. Subsequently, Merrill learned a great deal from the indiscrete officer. Specifically, the man told Merrill that Price, with 12,000 men and conscripts, was headed for Jefferson City and had no intention of moving on Rolla. Smith's scouts gathered much the same information, leading him to conclude that "the enemy have undoubtedly gone to Jefferson City."[22] Merrill quickly forwarded this intelligence to Rosecrans, who in turn forwarded the information to Brown, still in command at Jefferson City.

Even before Rosecrans knew of Price's true intent, he had issued orders to his district commanders to prepare the center portion of the state for defense. From 28 to 30 September, Rosecrans sent orders to his district commanders in the western part of Missouri. Generals McNeil, Brown, Sanborn, and Fisk each received a message from the department commander telling them to "push every available man in your command to Jefferson City with all possible dispatch." This would consolidate the entire available force of the districts of North Missouri, Central Missouri, Southwest Missouri, and Rolla at the capital city. The purpose of concentrating here is twofold. First, Rosecrans suspected that if Price turned away from St. Louis then Jefferson City was the next feasible target since it was the political center of the state. Second, concentrating at Jefferson City was a central location from which Federal forces could move to confront Price if he went somewhere else. Of course, moving all volunteer and regular troops to

Jefferson City would leave other places open to raids by bushwhackers like "Bloody Bill" Anderson and his band. So, to provide for security in the absence of the volunteer troops, Rosecrans also issued orders "to call into service the enrolled militia."[23] While not as proficient as the volunteers, the enrolled militia would at least keep the guerrillas from running unchallenged across the state. It was a prescient decision on Rosecrans' part to concentrate at Jefferson City, but he should have taken this step weeks earlier when he knew Price was moving toward Missouri. His hesitation made the defense of the capital a close-run affair.

The turn of the Army of Missouri westward now raised the concern of the commander of the Federal Department of Kansas. "Where are you driving him [Price]?" Curtis inquired of Rosecrans. In truth, Rosecrans was following Price, not driving him, and every step to the west was cause for Curtis to worry about the safety of his department. If anything, his department was in worse shape for defense than that of Rosecrans. On paper, Curtis had some 4,000 troops, but these were scattered to the west of the state fighting hostile Indians. The Kansas State Militia numbered some 10,000 men; however, calling them out to defend the border was to prove difficult. On 6 October, Rosecrans sent a message informing Curtis of his turn to the west and that he was "on the old stage road to Jefferson City."[24] Obviously, Price now posed a threat to Kansas, and as the Army of Missouri moved closer, Curtis' fears rose in proportion to their proximity.

In the meantime, Rosecrans' district commanders were making belated preparations to receive Price at Jefferson City, marshaling all available regiments from throughout central and western Missouri. McNeil suggested to Rosecrans that an operation to delay the Confederates along their route of march would prove beneficial to their efforts to fortify the capital. The Rebels' axis of advance was along the tracks of the Pacific Railroad and the stage road from St. Louis to Jefferson City paralleling the Missouri River. Along this route were a couple of excellent spots the Federals could use to delay Price and provide more time for preparation to defend Jefferson City. These locations were the bridges and fords on the Gasconade and Osage rivers. Recent rains had raised the level of these streams, providing very few feasible crossing sites. Using an educated guess, Federals could determine the best places to fortify to prevent an easy crossing by the Rebels.[25] Rosecrans did issue orders to this effect, but a coherent effort to delay the Army of Missouri miscarried in the confusion of the moment. Thus, it was left to the local commanders to cobble together an attempt to slow the Confederates.

Two men who gave the advancing Rebels a stiff and heroic challenge on the Gasconade were Captains Charles Eitzen and Francis Onken. Each of these men commanded a company of the 34th Enrolled Missouri Militia, which was raised in the town of Hermann on the Gasconade. Aware of the advance of Price's army, they decided to mount a defense of the Pacific Railroad bridge over the river to delay their progress. In a pouring rain on the evening of 3 October, these captains moved their 150 men into position on the west side of the river to stop Price's entire army. Upon arriving at the bridge, they set their men to work by scouting the approaches and establishing obstacles to Rebel movement, such as removing planking from the bridge. Some fainthearted militiamen left the ranks, but those who remained with the intrepid captains provided excellent service in defending the bridge.[26]

Remarkably, the 150 men of Eitzen and Onken confounded Price's army for two full days. In spite of the lack of orders from higher headquarters, the captains exercised admirable initiative in establishing their defense. When the Confederates arrived, they discovered that their way was obstructed by the small band and the obstacles they emplaced. Therefore, Clark's brigade, in the lead of Marmaduke's division, had to search for an alternative crossing point. This took time, and when they finally did cross the river, Clark began to curl around the flanks of Eitzen and Onken. When it appeared they would soon be surrounded, the two captains conferred and decided to pull back. Onken would "never [have] left the Gasconade bridge," he later reported, if he had more men.[27] Nevertheless, the effort of these two men bought two days of precious time for the Federals to establish a coherent defense at Jefferson City.

Another opportunity to slow Price presented at the Osage River, and this time the effort received positive orders from the commanders at Jefferson City. Yet it appeared the departmental commander was looking for excuses not to mount a vigorous pursuit of Price. Rather than ordering Smith forward to press the rear of the Army of Missouri, Rosecrans issued G.O. #185, making the protection of manufacturing facilities the priority for his forces moving west from St. Louis. As a result, when Price arrived at the Osage River, "fording it easily" on 6 October, a mere eight miles from Jefferson City, A.J. Smith's corps was only four miles beyond Union—closer to St. Louis than Jefferson City.[28] The pressure of a pursuit would have made the defense of Jefferson City infinitely easier, but Rosecrans left the work to his district commanders, ceding all pretense of initiative to Price.

Brown, Fisk, Sanborn, and McNeil did a fairly thorough job pulling their collective forces together for the defense of Jefferson City, and as work on the fortifications progressed, their confidence in the handiwork rose in proportion. All of the districts' units arrived at Jefferson City by 5 October 1864. Forced marches brought them together as the Confederates were bearing down on them from the east. When this collection of generals came together, one of them would have to take command in order to bring order out of the chaos. Curiously, Clinton B. Fisk—the youngest of the assemblage—held the earliest date of rank, and therefore he assumed command.[29] In spite of his age, the generals gave Fisk their full cooperation, and Fisk provided sound direction in putting Jefferson City in a state of defense.

The defenses around the city, while hasty in nature, were very solid and would present a difficult problem for attacking Confederates. Fisk and his cast of generals had about 7,000 troops on hand at Jefferson City, along with eight pieces of artillery from batteries of the 2nd Missouri Light. Before all the troops arrived, Egbert Brown reported on 30 September that he had the citizens of the city out in the field constructing eight miles of fortifications in an arc around the city anchored on the river. Further, those who were capable of handling a rifle were pressed into duty as a home guard to back up the regular troops who would man the trenches. When Fisk arrived, the outlines of the defense began to take shape. He reported: "Preparations for the defense of Jefferson City are progressing finely. The capitol will be made a citadel and a line of brick buildings on High street will cover a large force of defenders. Long lines of rifle pits are being dug. I am confident that Jefferson City will not fall into the hands of the invaders."[30] In addition, the terrain around the capital provided many advantages for defense. The

Osage River, eight miles from Jefferson City, provided a fine advanced line of defense to slow the Rebels and inflict losses as they approached the city. Closer to the capital was Moreau Creek, which provided an inner line to the front. Finally, the main line of defense was based upon the trenches erected around the city. The Moreau provided the fortifications an obstacle to Rebel movement, while the flanks of the meandering line were anchored on bends on the Missouri River. Thus, the Federal lines were assailable only from the south. With only four places to cross the Moreau and the river, the Union defense was solid. With the Rebels still miles away crossing the Gasconade, the assembling Federals would have time to improve upon these natural and man-made defenses to the point where a successful assault by Price would come at great cost. When the Army of Missouri reached the capital, Price would have to decide if the prize was worth the cost. His decision would affect the entire nature of the campaign.

Meanwhile, the Rebels were approaching the Osage. Brown, and then Fisk, had deployed scouts to determine the direction of Price's approach and his strength. Using the Osage to strengthen their defense, Fisk's advance units sought to make the river crossing difficult. Initially, he had about 800 soldiers from the 4th and 7th Missouri State Militia cavalries guarding the fords. But, with the influx of reinforcements from the surrounding districts, Fisk forwarded another 2,400 men and 8 guns to the Osage to challenge the enemy.[31] Crossing the Osage would prove far more difficult than brushing aside the militia on the Gasconade. To ensure the crossing was successful at a low cost, Price turned to his most reliable commander, Jo Shelby.

Before attempting a crossing on 6 October, Shelby moved forward to the Osage to conduct a personal reconnaissance. He did not like what he found. The recent rains had swollen the stream, ensuring that an "advancing force would suffer not only the disadvantages of crossing a wide and deep stream under fire, but also from a perfect ignorance of the enemy's numbers." After examining the problem, Shelby settled on a course of action. First, he would send Colonel David Shanks north to take the Pacific Railroad blockhouse, which guarded the 1,000 foot bridge over the river. Shanks would then burn the structure to cut off Jefferson City from St. Louis, blocking any Union reinforcements coming from that direction. Second, Colonel Frank Gordon would "make a vigorous demonstration at Castle Rock" crossing to fix the Federals. Finally, with the balance of the division, Shelby would move six miles below to flank the Union soldiers with a "forced passage." Although resistance proved heavy, "a terrible fire of infantry and artillery swept the other bank" as his dismounted squadrons waded the river, securing the other side. Shelby then passed Shanks through the forward lines with the Iron Brigade—Shelby's old unit—to "press the retiring enemy hard." The losses on both sides were fairly light, each losing 50–60 men, including three to four Rebels drowned in crossing.[32] Price now had a foothold south of the capital, and he encamped the night of 4 October on Moreau Creek in preparation to move on the city the next morning.

While Price's army camped outside Jefferson City, the Union generals met for a council of war. Even though they had done an outstanding job putting the city in readiness to meet the enemy, they were still nervous about their chances of success. Fisk put his concerns in writing to both Curtis and Rosecrans, to whom he pleaded for reinforcements. "Can you send us a battery of artillery at once?" he asked Curtis on 5 October. That same day, Fisk warned Curtis "that if we do not make a successful defense he [Price] will be into Kansas City in a short time." The next day he exhorted Rosecrans: "I trust the troops from below [Smith's] are close upon the foe." Rosecrans response gave little hope for assistance, as all he did was assure Fisk that "all you need is coolness and determination to slaughter them." Thus, the evening's meeting took on an air of urgency. During the discussion the four generals agreed to their dispositions. From east to west were Brown's makeshift brigade, Sanborn's men, and then McNeil. Interspersed among the infantry were several guns from the 2nd Missouri Light Artillery's B, C, and L batteries. Forward of the main line were several hundred troops from the 6th and 8th MSM cavalries behind Moreau Creek with orders "to fall back slowly" when pressed by the Rebels.[33] Although the Union commanders did not know it, they were in better shape than they thought.

At around 7:00 a.m. on Friday, the 7th of October, Cabell's brigade moved to the front to force a crossing of the Moreau. The creek had steep sides, which were slick from the rain and morning dampness. This made the crossing a challenge, and, combined with "the enemy in large force" on the other side, would make the whole operation dangerous for the men in the ranks. As Cabell deployed for the attack, he met "a stubborn resistance." Using the Bolton Ferry road, the determined Confederates gained a foothold on the far side of the creek. Following instructions, Colonel Joseph J. Gravely, commanding the 8th MSM Cavalry, began slowly falling back toward Jefferson City. Once the Confederates pressed an attack, he would pull back to another defensive position. This forced the Rebels to deploy into line of battle again and again, causing attrition and slowing the advance. By afternoon, the Union advanced guard had fallen back to the Jefferson City fortifications, while Price's army spread out to invest the city.[34]

"The ball is opening earnestly," Fisk reported to Rosecrans. "We have fought them sharply from the Moreau bridge on the Bolton road, killing and wounding a large number.... Our men are now forming in the trenches." During the assault across the Moreau, the venerable Colonel David Shanks, commanding Shelby's old Iron Brigade, received a mortal wound. Shelby rode over to his brigade commander to inquire about his condition and found Shanks was already dying. Shelby reportedly wept at the loss of his friend, but after a few kind words left his side to direct the ongoing engagement. This loss might have been catastrophic, but another charismatic leader was waiting in the wings. Price immediately replaced the stricken Shanks with M. Jeff Thompson, who would more than fill the shoes of his predecessor in the coming days.[35]

As the Army of Missouri fanned out on the ridges overlooking the city to invest the defenders, many a Rebel soldier was impressed by the view below in the valley. "My brigade occupied the heights in full view of the city," reported Cabell. However, their senior leaders' attention was drawn to the fortifications and prospects for success in taking the city. Price had reached a critical decision point. Meanwhile, the Federals were also enamored of the display put on by the Rebel army before them. Taking positions in the hills, the Rebels were clearly visible to the Federals in the trenches. The sight of so many Rebels motivated the Union soldiers to redouble their efforts to improve the fortifications. As both sides made their dispositions, an artillery duel broke out. The Federals of the 2nd Missouri Light batteries of Captain Charles Thurber and Lieutenant John Sutter handled their guns with skill, "dismounting one of his [Price's] pieces at the first fire." The Rebels responded, but "all of their shot fell short or missed their aim." Once again, the incompetence of the Rebel gunners ensured that they would provide little of value to Price's army. As the firing echoed across the valley, the Rebel commanders "conducted an inspection of our [Federal] earthworks." Then, with dusk approaching, the Rebels "moved back about two miles and went into camp."[36] That evening, Price called his division commanders together to discuss the situation amid an air of apprehension.

At the council of war that night, Price asked the assembly what they thought the prospects were of making a successful assault. Unlike the conversation among the commanders on the eve of Pilot Knob, the men were more pessimistic this time. Based on the day's reconnaissance, each man agreed that any attempt to attack the works at Jefferson City would result in high losses and it was probable they could not take the city. Further, one of Price's spies had just returned to his lines and provided him an ominous report. "Upon overtaking me he informed me that I would be pursued by 24,000 men from St. Louis, [and] 15,000 from Jefferson City," stated Price. This convinced Price that any chance of capturing Jefferson City had passed, since he would likely—so he believed—have to fight almost 40,000 Federals with his force of less than 10,000 armed men. As a result, "it was determined not to attack the Yankee fortifications" and Price decided to abandon Jefferson City and continue the march westward on the morning of the 8th.[37] Therefore, while the Federals were making last-minute preparations to receive an assault on Saturday morning, their adversaries had decided to bypass their objective. Much to the Federals' surprise, the Rebels withdrew from the field, marking an anticlimactic outcome to this phase of the campaign.

On 8 October 1864, the Federals were up early and in the trenches. "The movements of the enemy during the night indicated his preparation to mass his force to assault our right [McNeil's brigade]," Fisk later reported. "The rebels were massing their whole force in my front," added McNeil. As a result, McNeil had his men working "industriously" to strengthen his part of the line. As dawn broke across the horizon, the Federals girded themselves for the assault they knew was coming. The Rebels did appear momentarily en masse on the Union front, but this was only a demonstration. In short order, by 8:00 a.m. the Confederates turned away from the Federal fortifications, taking the Springfield road to California, Missouri. McNeil articulated this event with a twist of irony, stating that "with the appearance of day came the disappearance of Price's army." Thus, the concerns the Federal generals had expressed in their council on the night of the 6th were unfounded. Newspapers such as *Harper's Weekly* extolled efforts of the defenders of Jefferson City, as Price was turned back yet again.[38] The district commanders would have little time to celebrate as they quickly transitioned from a defensive posture over to the offensive under a new commander, Major General Alfred Pleasonton.

Price's decision to turn away from Jefferson City was the real turning point in this campaign. The focus of the expedition had been to achieve strategic objectives that involved taking and holding ground, in particular the political centers like Jefferson City, a move designed to wrest the state from the Federal orbit, install a Confederate government, and sway the Federal election. The movement west from the capital transformed the campaign from one focused on strategic goals to a raid of limited tactical value.[39] Thus, Price was scaling back his own expectations for what he thought he could accomplish, and in the process the entire nature of the operation had changed. The Army of Missouri was never really capable of doing what Price wanted. As a cavalry-centric force, the army was far better suited to conducting a raid than holding ground. Therefore, at least now the army was properly configured for the remainder of the expedition. However, what, at this point, could Price accomplish that could benefit the Trans-Mississippi and Confederacy while hurting the Federals?

A raid carried very different connotations for a commander as opposed to an operation to take ground. A raid required speed and discipline, as well as a clear target set that was linked to a larger operational objective. Unfortunately, Price was not the right commander to accomplish any of the above. His pace throughout the campaign, described by Shelby's biographer as "slowness of movement," was plodding at best.[40] Further, Price's riding in an ambulance was bound to inhibit any incentive to pick up the pace. Price was also a poor disciplinarian. From start to finish, his men were barely controllable, committing depredations upon Union and Southern sympathizers alike, and their actions became especially pronounced after Pilot Knob. This drove those with a predilection to support the Rebels away and into the arms of Union leaders. This lack of discipline was squarely the responsibility of Price. Finally, he had a habit of failing to articulate his intent clearly. One contemporary noted that Price's "fickleness of purpose [was] totally incomprehensible," and as a result, his army often acted in an uncoordinated manner, as at Pilot Knob.[41] Nevertheless, if Price could rectify these shortfalls, there was much he could accomplish.

There were three things that Price could do to achieve something of substance for the Trans-Mississippi and the Confederacy after he converted the campaign into a raid. One of the original purposes of the expedition was to recruit for the Trans-Mississippi army. Price still believed—erroneously—that the ground in Missouri was fertile for recruiting. Therefore, as he moved into central and western Missouri, a prime objective was bringing men into the ranks. Next, there were several key Federal supply and command nodes, such as Forts Scott and Leavenworth, that if destroyed would seriously weaken the Union army west of the Mississippi. Finally, a rampaging Rebel army in Missouri and Kansas would demonstrate the weakness of the Federals and possibly influence Northern voters in the upcoming election.[42] Price's force was well organized to do all of these things—if he could articulate a plan, focus on the targets, and keep his force well in hand. He would fail on all counts because most of his assumptions were erroneous and he was incapable of providing clear orders and maintaining discipline. Instead, Price would see his army nearly destroyed in the weeks ahead.

The decision to abandon Jefferson City did not sit well with Governor Reynolds. He had accompanied the expedition into Missouri ostensibly to have the army place him in the executive chair in the capitol. Doing so would represent a serious blow to Unionism in the state and perhaps hurt Lincoln at the ballot box. So it was with great hopes of success that Reynolds rode with the army to Jefferson City. The exiled governor came within eyeshot of the prize on 7–8 October, only to see his fondest dream dashed. When this happened, Reynolds became livid with anger toward Price. He gave full vent to it in his open letter published by the *Marshall (Texas) Republican* in December. First, he criticized Price for "the dilatory march from Pilot Knob to Jefferson City." This plodding, combined with Price's failure to convince the bushwhackers to destroy the railroads in north Missouri, had allowed the Federals to reinforce Jefferson City and "diminished our chances of securing the capital." As Reynolds continued writing, his pen became shriller and his contempt for Price barely concealed. "The State House," he wrote, "with its lofty dome, lay that day in full view of a gallant army confident of victory." But then, the "next morning, whether wisely on correct information that large reinforcements had reached the enemy in the night, or unwisely from hesitating generalship or mistaken policy, Gen. Price suddenly ordered a retreat." The "disappointment" was simply too much for Reynolds.[43] Though it was probably not feasible for Price to have taken Jefferson City, this did not matter to Reynolds. He was emotionally invested in the endeavor to take the capital and his seat as governor. Any outcome other than securing Jefferson City was only going to disappoint Missouri's erstwhile Confederate governor.

The day the Rebels turned west on the Springfield road, a new Union commander arrived to take the reins at Jefferson City in the form of Alfred Pleasonton. With his arrival, the effort to counter the Great Raid took on a new energy and coherence it had heretofore lacked. Pleasonton had arrived from the east in March 1864 following his relief from command of the Army of the Potomac's Cavalry Corps. Rosecrans assigned him to command of the District of Central Missouri. In that capacity, Pleasonton had gained a familiarity with the lay of the land in central and western Missouri, which would serve him well in the coming pursuit of Price. Before Price launched his expedition, Pleasonton took a leave of absence to New York City for health reasons, and Egbert Brown succeeded him when he left.[44]

Only days after he left, Rosecrans realized that he needed a commander of unique talents to command his cavalry. He immediately decided to recall Pleasonton. In a short message dated 22 September 1864, Rosecrans wrote, "[C]ome back as soon as possible. There will be a heavy invasion. You will command the cavalry."[45] Pleasonton had well-known talent as a first-rate organizer and administrator as well as a sound field commander. Thus, Rosecrans' decision to recall Pleasonton was another prescient one. The entire Union campaign to this point had been lackluster—with the exception of Ewing's inspired defense of Pilot Knob—with Rosecrans forfeiting all pretense of initiative to Price. But with the appointment of Pleasonton to command the cavalry, this was about to change.

Pleasonton arrived in St. Louis on 30 September, and that same day Rosecrans published G.O. #184 appointing Pleasonton to command. On 1 October, Pleasonton signed an order assuming command and proceeded with caution toward Jefferson City to organize his forces for offensive action. He arrived one week later at Jefferson City, on 8 October, the same day Price decided to abandon the capital. Pleasonton wasted no time on arriving in Jefferson City, and he began organizing the command he found there to mount a pursuit. The total command amounted to between 6,000 and 7,000 men. Pleasonton could not use all of these for the pursuit because he still had to protect the city. In Special Order #1, he decided to leave a little over 2,000 men. With the remainder, he organized three provisional cavalry brigades under district commanders Sanborn, McNeil, and Brown. As evening approached on the 8th Pleasonton pushed one forward after Price under the command of Sanborn.[46] In less than 24 hours of his arrival at Jefferson City, Pleasonton had already fired the moribund Federal command with new life. Additionally, Rosecrans ordered Smith's XVI Corps forward to assist Pleasonton in the pursuit. Things had certainly changed for the better in the Federal camp.

The danger to the critical points in Missouri had passed, as Price's march was now taking him away from most of the valuable targets. While Rosecrans could relax with a sigh of relief, his counterpart in Kansas had reason to worry. Samuel Curtis had monitored the situation in Missouri ever since Price entered the state in September. Although apprehensive early on, his worry had turned to grave concern when Price turned westward from Jefferson City. With Price's every step, Curtis's worries deepened. The reason for this is that Curtis had a mere 6,956 men in Federal service in his department. A good portion of these soldiers were in the western part of his territory under Blunt fighting Indians, leaving only 4,000 readily available on the Missouri border. Therefore, Kansas was utterly defenseless in the first week of October. Curtis was in close contact with Generals Brown and Fisk as the Army of Missouri approached Jefferson City. Brown had written on 4 October that "the appearances are that the enemy are moving up the [Missouri] river." With this news, Curtis now swung into action to defend his department, as he believed Price was headed for Kansas.[47]

Curtis wrote Governor Thomas Carney of Kansas on 5 October to request that he call out the state militia to defend Kansas from invasion: "The Rebel forces under General Price have made a farther advance westward, crossing the Gasconade, and are now at the railroad bridge on the Osage, about fifteen miles. Large Federal forces about Saint Louis and below tend to drive him toward Kansas.... To prevent this and join in efforts to expel these invaders from the country I desire that you will call out the entire militia force."[48] The governor, however, was deeply suspicious of Curtis' motivation behind the appeal to call out the militia. Carney did not really believe that Price's army was headed toward Kansas. The reasons for this were complex and rooted in politics. The national election was only a month away at this point, and Kansas would hold its state election simultaneously. Senator Jim Lane's faction and his gubernatorial candidate opposed Carney in the coming election. In 1864, senators were elected by their state legislatures, not directly by the people as they are today. Therefore, if Lane's faction could retain the majority in the state election, Lane would win another term in the U.S. Senate, while shutting Carney's men out of important positions in the state.[49]

Carney believed Curtis was a puppet of Lane, based on his political leanings. He also believed that if he called out the militia, then they would not have the opportunity to vote in the state election in November. Carney suspected that the motivation behind the call-out request was an elaborate Lane plot to sabotage his chances for reelection. As a result, Carney was not prepared to issue the necessary orders.[50] This was additional cause for anxiety for Samuel R. Curtis, which he described later as "perplexing" in his after action report. The closer Price came to Kansas without the governor issuing the call for militia, the greater Curtis' concern for the security of his department.

Curtis did not wait for Carney to issue his call-out before taking steps to assemble his own meager resources. On October 8, Blunt arrived at Fort Leavenworth in response to an earlier order from Curtis, and he immediately began organizing the regular troops on hand into a division for action in the field. While Curtis was working to pull all resources together, Governor Carney was still unsure of the true circumstances in Missouri. He had written a proclamation on 8 October 1864 to call out the militia, but he must have thought about holding it as a hedge. On 9 October, Carney wrote Rosecrans by telegraph asking, "[A]re we in danger here from Price? Inform me." Within two hours Rosecrans replied, "I think no effort should be spared to secure yourselves from Price."[51] Though still not thoroughly convinced, Carney finally released the proclamation.

"The State is in peril," the proclamation began. "Price and his rebel hosts threaten it with invasion. Kansas must be ready to hurl them back at any cost." Curtis announced it on 9 October, and he set the wheels in motion to organize his department for defense. Orders were issued to assemble the militia at various locations to organize. Curtis created two divisions under his command that he styled the Army of the Border. Blunt was given command of a provisional cavalry division, consisting of mostly active Federal units, to assemble at Paola. The second division was commanded by Major General George W. Dietzler, the adjutant general of the state of Kansas. The militia was to assemble at various points and then consolidate at Shawnee to prepare for action.[52] Though doubts remained on the part of the governor, things were finally beginning to move in Kansas. Price had moved with impunity for the first few weeks of the Great Raid, but now the Federals were starting to get their act together. The Army of Missouri was about to have some difficult days ahead of it, but before that would happen the army would enjoy a respite before the hardship.

The turns away from St. Louis and Jefferson City represented turning points in the campaign, but they also represented something more ominous for the Confederates. Price's decision not to attempt to capture either city was a tacit acknowledgment that the Federal authority was stronger than anything the Rebels could offer as a challenge. Further, it also became a statement that the only operation the Confederates could mount was a raid and such a lower-level tactical operation was no more than an annoyance to the Federals at this point in the war. While a raid had the potential to achieve operational and strategic effects, it required detailed planning, discriminating target selection, and disciplined execution. Sterling Price, as a commander, had a history of sloppy planning, haphazard issuance of orders, and a tendency to underwrite indiscipline. As a result, when he decided to convert the campaign from an operation to hold ground to a raid, he turned a long shot into a forlorn hope.

Price missed multiple opportunities to achieve operational and strategic success due to his inattention to detail. For example, he failed to leverage the "fifth column" of guerrillas in Missouri to aid his expedition. Though he established communication with Missouri guerrilla leaders, he did not issue a clear plan to coordinate the movement of his army with the bushwhackers nor provide a list of targets. Without this, the guerrilla leaders were free to hit whatever targets they thought best, which usually consisted of those that benefited their own desire for loot. This may or may not have assisted Price's movements or impeded Federal counterstrokes. Also, Price's slow rate of march allowed the Federals precious time to prepare their defenses at Pilot Knob, St. Louis, and Jefferson City. Thus, Price's aimlessness rendered any chances to achieve real results almost nil.

The fact that Federal performance to date—with the exception of Ewing's—was so lackluster only magnifies the level of Price's incompetence. Rosecrans' forces had acted entirely on the defensive from the time the Army of Missouri entered the state until Pleasonton arrived at Jefferson City. Rosecrans seemed to spin his wheels early on trying to determine how to respond to the invasion. He sent Ewing to Pilot Knob at the last moment, and only Ewing's brilliant performance delivered up the victory over Price. Then Ewing waited until the last minute to ready St. Louis for defense and dawdled in assisting his district commanders as they worked feverishly to defend the capital. In spite of Rosecrans' dismal performance, Price was unable to take advantage of his antagonist's shortcomings. However, all this was about to change. Fired by the energetic Pleasonton and the meticulous Curtis, the Union performance would greatly improve.

As Price entered central and western Missouri, his slow pace would come to a complete stop as his army enjoyed the hospitality of Southern sympathizers. The Army of Missouri was entering the phase of the Great Raid known as the "picnic period." Price's decision to take a holiday in the midst of the raid gave the rapidly improving Federal command an opportunity to destroy the Army of Missouri. The stage was set for a tumultuous end to the Great Raid, as the Federals were preparing a huge trap for Price. The only question at this point was whether the various Union commands could cooperate adequately to bring the Army of Missouri to bay. If they could, another Pea Ridge, or worse, for the Rebels was in the offing.

8

The "Picnic Period"

With the latest decision to abandon a major objective of the campaign, the Great Raid entered a short phase known as the "picnic period." Because Price chose to take a respite in mid-stride of the expedition, he provided the Federal army with a golden opportunity to destroy the Army of Missouri. At a time when speed and precision were of the essence, Price decelerated his already slow pace. Further, his effort to recruit, foment an uprising among Southern sympathizers, and attack critical enemy nodes in an attempt to sway northern voters fell flat. The reason for this is that Price, and many other Confederate leaders, had a woefully flawed estimate of the favorability of the Southern cause in Missouri. These factors, combined with rapidly improving Union leadership, would place the Army of Missouri in a situation that could bring about its destruction. Ultimately, the difference between survival and destruction of the Confederate army would come down to whether or not the fragmented Federal command could cooperate adequately to close the trap.

The "picnic period" began on 8 October 1864, as Price turned west from Jefferson City, and lasted until 18 October, when the Army of Missouri left Waverly bound for Kansas. Price proceeded away from the Missouri capital on a Saturday morning down the Springfield road. Shelby's division had the advance while Fagan's division constituted the rear guard. Price reported that his rear guard was shadowed all day by McNeil—actually Sanborn's brigade—and at one point Fagan attacked. The column turned sharply off the Springfield road early in the afternoon toward California. It was here that Sanborn initiated a heavy attack on Fagan's flank as half his division was still moving through California. The result of this action was the near loss of the Army of Missouri's ammunition train. According to one witness, the crisis was the result of careless security measures on the part of the rear guard. Quick thinking by Brigadier General John B. Clark narrowly saved the train.[1] This incident is yet another demonstration of the lack of discipline that was rampant in the Rebel army.

By the first evening, the bulk of Price's army camped around Russellville some seventeen miles west of Jefferson City. Price intended to parallel the Missouri River, where the vast majority of the populace was of Southern sympathy. On 9 October, the army was back in the saddle moving west bound for Boonville. As the troops continued the trek, they were continuously badgered by Sanborn, forcing the rear guard to deploy several times. In fact, the assault was so aggressive at one point that Price had to send back units from both Marmaduke and Shelby's divisions to reinforce a hard-pressed Fagan. This infusion of force put an end to Sanborn's effort for the day, but not before they had worn down Price's men and inflicted some casualties. The Army of

Missouri spent the night on Montineau Creek, having marched twenty-six miles during the day.[2]

Sanborn inexplicably withdrew all the way back to California following the engagement of the 9th, claiming to need supplies. This unfortunate order released the pressure on Price, allowing him to move at a more leisurely pace and enjoy a pleasant welcome from the local population. Sanborn stated in his report, "My command had been out of rations for thirty-six hours, the men had become much exhausted, and I could not learn of any train on the way to me." Therefore, he decided to return to a point where he could obtain subsistence. He continued: "Four days' rations were procured and issued at California and the command moved back to its front of Boonville ... the 13th of October."[3] Two factors likely led to Sanborn's decision to break contact. First, the ad hoc nature of Pleasonton's provisional cavalry division organization did not have adequate arrangements for logistic support in a pursuit. Second, Pleasonton had not yet perfected the command and control system for the hastily formed command. In such a situation, a commander may err on the side of caution rather than aggressiveness, which is exactly what Sanborn did.

Sanborn's waiting until the 13th of October to reestablish contact with Price allowed the Rebels to put distance between the army and its pursuers, which Price did not take advantage of. Sanborn's decision did not please many in the Union camp. Leaders in the Department of Kansas felt that letting up on the pressure gave Price time to gather supplies and retain the initiative. Had Sanborn stayed in close contact with the enemy, Price's ability to maneuver would have been quite limited. Thus, forces to the west may have laid a tight trap for Price earlier in the campaign.[4] While the Federals failed in this respect, Price gave them a second chance because of his own inactivity and supply issues.

Price arrived in Boonville on 10 October and received a rousing welcome from the people of this decidedly Southern-leaning town. "My reception was enthusiastic in the extreme," Price reported. "Old and young, men, women, and children, vied in their salutations," he continued, "ministering to the wants and comforts of my wearied and war-torn soldiers." "The citizens were in great excitement and all the southern portion of them overjoyed at our arrival," Dr. McPheeters recorded. General Cabell, at the rear of the column, added that "the good citizens, especially the ladies, provided my command with an abundance of good and substantial things." Indeed, one of Cabell's men confirmed that "good Southern ladies ... supplied us with plenty of good things for our supper."[5] This respite would prove the high-water mark for Price and his men, but it masked a number of issues surrounding the expedition, including supply, recruiting and coordination with local guerrilla leaders.

As the expedition progressed, the Army of Missouri had accumulated an ever increasing number of loaded wagons in the train. By the time Price left Boonville the train had grown to the bloated number of 500 wagons full of loot. Seemingly, the army had no problems in terms of provisions, but this was an illusion. By the time the Army of Missouri reached Boonville, discipline, already poor, began to seriously break down. Without a regular supply line, the Army of Missouri was forced to forage. Much of the foraging and gathering of supplies was little more than looting, which the Rebels performed in an indiscriminate manner. It mattered little to Price's ragtag soldiers if the local populace supported the Southern cause or not. If the soldiers wanted something, they took it and most of the items were of little military value. Governor Reynolds wrote Price on 10 October to complain about the indiscipline of the army and the lack of needed supplies. "[S]tragglers and camp followers are enriching themselves by plundering the defenseless families of our own soldiers in Confederate service," he stated. Simultaneously, Reynolds noted that the horses in the army were suffering "for want of shoes."[6] What was Price going to do about the situation? The answer to this question was, "Nothing."

The wagons were loaded down with loot and Price was determined that he would not lose the train. While he was guarding the booty, the morale of the army was sinking due to indiscipline and the supply problems. Further, the army's rate of march, already at a snail's pace, slowed because of the impediment of the massive train. Also, the plundering was alienating the very Southern population the army was supposed to liberate. One participant characterized the army that arrived at Boonville as a "rabble of deadheads, [and] stragglers." M. Jeff Thompson, now commanding Shelby's old Iron Brigade, agreed with this assessment and added that "the plunder of Boonville nearly completed the demoralization for many officers and men ... [who] now wanted to turn southward and save what they had."[7] Thus, the Great Raid as a military operation was breaking down, and Price's inability to impose discipline and provide guidance would ensure that little of value would result.

One objective Price pursued vigorously at Boonville was the recruitment of new soldiers for the Trans-Mississippi army. Many did actually rally to the Confederate standard, as one witness noted that "recruits are coming in by the hundreds." According to Price, some 1,200 to 1,500 men—unarmed—were added to the ranks. This number is in addition to several hundred the army had picked up along the route of march since entering Missouri.[8] It appeared that here was a tangible manifestation of success for the operation, but even this proved illusory. Further examination shows that what Price described as recruiting was, in many cases, conscription. While there is no doubt that some of the recruits were volunteers, many became unwilling participants in the raid. A typical example of a conscripted Missouri Rebel is the case of William T. Dameron. When Shelby's division swept through Randolph County, Missouri, a "recruiter" forced the twenty-seven-year-old, married father of four into Rebel service.

William Dameron was a farmer and former member of the Enrolled Missouri Militia in his area. While he had a brother in the Confederate army, he had remained loyal to the Union. When the Army of Missouri arrived in Randolph County, recruiters fanned out to begin conscripting all available military-age males. Sometime early in October a Captain Hiram arrived at Dameron's house with a squad of men. The captain informed Dameron that he was now a soldier in the Confederate army. Further, he told Dameron that if he attempted to desert "they would kill me."[9] When informed of the possibility of dying as a deserter, Dameron agreed to accompany the squad for duty with Shelby's Division.

Dameron mounted his own horse and rode to Thomasville to report as instructed on October 15. As the army moved westward, it carried along a ragtag group of unarmed "recruits" who were under guard as the column traveled. Dameron was not long a soldier in the Rebel ranks. A detachment of the army was operating near Springfield and made contact with Union forces in the area. Dameron recounted, "I left at that time"—an apparent desertion. The Union forces captured him and turned him over to the provost marshal at Springfield, ending the erstwhile Rebel's service. However, Dameron's troubles were not yet over, for he would spend the next several months in prison in St. Louis. The provost was reluctant to release Dameron until his loyalty was properly established. Therefore, the young farmer had to endure a long drawn out process of interviews and have friends from his home county vouch for him before obtaining his release in the spring of 1865.[10]

Dameron's story is fairly typical of most of the recruits Price took into the army. It is true that Price did bring a few thousand new soldiers into the army during the course of the raid. In his report, he put the number at 5,000 that he picked up during the Great Raid, far below his grandiose estimate of 20–30,000 he claimed would join when he was advocating for the campaign. His relative lack of success in recruiting demonstrates that the claim of vast support for the South in Missouri was simply fantasy, yet most Confederate leaders were blind to this fact. Further, the rate of desertion among these recruits at the conclusion of the raid should have lifted the scales off the eyes of men like Price. Toward the end of the raid, after the army suffered grievous defeats at Westport and Mine Creek, the recruits left the army in droves. This left a pitiful few, who would suffer privations in the retreat south.[11] Even this did not convince Price of the failure of the cause in Missouri. He was so wedded to his own perceptions of Southern patriotism in the state that he would never consider any other ideas, to the detriment of the very cause he was in Missouri to promote. Other factors also tended to diminish support for the cause in Missouri, including the internecine guerrilla warfare afflicting the countryside.

On 11 October 1864 a group of bushwhacker leaders and men arrived at Boonville to confer with Price. "Bloody Bill" Anderson rode at the head of a band of between 100 and 200 men. The guerrillas presented quite a shocking sight to all who saw them that day. One thing in particular caused revulsion among the top leaders of the Army of Missouri. Attached to Anderson's and several of his men's saddles were shocks of human hair from scalps they had taken in previous engagements. When Price saw this hideous sight, he refused to meet with Anderson until the offensive decorations were removed. For Price, the epitome of Southern chivalric manhood, Anderson's behavior was an unacceptable display not worthy of his conception of honor. Since Anderson was eager to have an audience with Price, he agreed to remove the disgusting trophies. Price then received the notorious Anderson, who, though reviled for his atrocities, still commanded respect as a fighter within the Army of Missouri, including Sterling Price.[12]

On the afternoon of 11 October Price received his guest, who presented him with a gift of silver-plated pistols. Price happily accepted Anderson's generous present and declared that if he had an army of 50,000 men like Anderson's band he "could hold Missouri forever." Once the pleasantries were completed, the commander got down to business. Specifically, Price sought Anderson's help to facilitate the success of the raid. In order to prevent a coherent pursuit of the army by Union forces, Price wanted Anderson to destroy several key bridges on the North Missouri railroad.[13] Finally, it appeared that Price was attempting to leverage a readily available combat multiplier for use in conjunction with his regular forces.

Nothing positive would come of the meeting or the mission Price assigned to Anderson. Price's attempt to implement compound warfare was too little, too late. The operation was already nearly a month old by the time Price met with Anderson. Had he met with him earlier or sent positive orders at the beginning of the campaign to strike targets as he did now, Price might have achieved substantive effects enabling him to secure his strategic objectives. But, at this point, the burning of a few bridges would provide only temporary tactical advantage. Also, Anderson and his men were the wrong force to do anything of substance. Their undisciplined quality, primarily motivated by loot, would drive them away from the target and toward satisfying their immediate desires.[14] This is exactly what happened after they departed Boonville.

Anderson crossed back to the north side of the Missouri River and was quickly diverted from his mission by the promise of plunder. His men began raiding towns in Montgomery County, including Danville, where they looted stores, burned homes, and killed a few militiamen. As Anderson's band rode along, alarmed Union commanders marshaled their forces to pursue the bushwhackers. Therefore, Anderson was unable to focus on his mission to destroy the railroad bridges, because he had to elude his pursuers. After several days of running, Union militia finally caught up with Anderson near Albany, Missouri, on 26 October 1864. In a sharp skirmish, the Federal force, commanded by Lieutenant Colonel S.P. Cox and a Major Grimes, broke up Anderson's band after the notorious leader was killed. Vindictive Union soldiers were ecstatic at having successfully killed Anderson, and in a fit of rage they cut off his head and mounted it on a telegraph pole. The Union officers were allowed to keep his watches and arms, while money found on his body was given to families Anderson had wronged.[15] Though the mutilation of Anderson's body was a heinous act by the Federals, his death marked the beginning of the end of the bushwhackers' long reign of terror in Missouri. Not only was Anderson dead, he had also failed to accomplish his mission, allowing Federal forces to mass against Price as he moved westward.

As Price dallied at Boonville, another objective that the general had articulated for the campaign came to naught. Before Price launched the expedition, he had sought to foment an uprising in Missouri and some of the states in the old northwest through the secretive copperhead organization known as the Order of American Knights (O.A.K.). As noted earlier, Price had made contact with leaders of the O.A.K. before crossing the border into Missouri in an effort to foster unrest behind Union lines. Price had planned to turn this unrest into a full-fledged uprising after he had achieved success on the battlefield in Missouri. This would bring out members of the O.A.K. to challenge Federal authority in the state as the conventional operation pressured the Union forces in the field. The action by the O.A.K. behind enemy lines sabotaging the rear areas would facilitate additional victories by Price's Army of Missouri. Price optimistically believed that an uprising, combined with his invasion, might cause the secession of some of the northwestern states to form another confederacy that would ally with the Southern cause. General Cabell noted that Price placed "great faith" in the organization.[16] However, all of this thinking was yet another fantasy conjured up by Price and other Confederate leaders.

One of the reasons Price might have believed that the O.A.K. could provide material aid is that his son, Edwin, may have had an association with the group. Governor

Reynolds suspected that Edwin was a member and cautioned the elder Price against tainting his image by becoming involved with the organization. However, the intelligence Sterling Price received from his son and other sources probably led to his rosy assessment of the capabilities of the O.A.K. Thus, one of the strategic objectives Price had identified in preparation for the expedition was to leverage the O.A.K.'s capabilities to aid the operation while lowering the morale of the Union cause. This could possibly lead to a loss of Federal authority in the northwest, or at least the swaying of voters away from Lincoln and toward a peace candidate. Reynolds may have suspected that Price wanted to play a leading role in setting up a northwest confederacy, which was disloyal to both the North and the South. Price resented Reynolds' implications, but he was not deterred by the governor's suspicions in attempting to establish contact.[17] Price believed he had laid the groundwork for this and entered Missouri with high hopes for cooperation with the O.A.K.

Indeed, John H. Taylor, supreme commander of the O.A.K. in the state of Missouri, was prepared to collaborate with Price after the Rebels entered the state. On 1 October 1864, shortly after Pilot Knob, Taylor issued a call to arms for all members: "Morning dawneth. General Sterling Price with at least 20,000 veteran soldiers is now in your State. Through your supreme commander ... you invited him to come to your aid.... All able-bodied men of the O.A.K.s are hereby called upon and required to render military service in behalf of our cause. All true Knights will yield prompt obedience to the orders and commands of General Price." The proclamation then goes on to prescribe ways members could aid and abet Confederate forces. Some of the methods included directly joining the Army of Missouri, seizing munitions, taking Federal installations, infiltrating the Union militia, and conducting guerrilla operations. Taylor concluded by exhorting O.A.K. members to action with the organization motto: "Resistance to tyrants is obedience to God."[18] If the membership responded, they could make things interesting for the Federals and provide material aid to the Rebels.

To Price and the army's chagrin, the O.A.K. blustering was little more than a fizzle. When the Army of Missouri reached Boonville on 10 October, absolutely nothing had come of Taylor's call to arms. As in other areas of the northwest, planned conspiracies by copperheads failed to cause any unrest worth noting. Shelby's biographer described the O.A.K. as nothing more than "chattering prairie dogs," which was an apt depiction of the organization.[19] The membership was made up of men full of talk who had little real appetite for confrontation. As a result, one of the key objectives of Price's expedition had no effect whatsoever, and all the faith Price placed in leaders and members of the O.A.K. was overblown. Like so many other aspects of the campaign, Rebel leadership had made a poor estimate of the true situation in Missouri, and they were completely out of touch with the people.

While Price and his army wasted away the days at Boonville, the Union camp was busy plotting the demise of the Rebel army. To the east, Rosecrans and Pleasonton were making arrangements for a pursuit, while to the west Curtis was perfecting his organization for a defense. Based on the incident with Sanborn's withdrawal from contact with Price, it was clear to Pleasonton that he must refine his command and control architecture before proceeding with the pursuit. While Pleasonton was flattening his organization to make it more efficient, he received the welcome acquisition of another brigade under the command of Colonel Edwin Catherwood. This brigade was part of A.J. Smith's corps and Rosecrans detached it from Smith to give Pleasonton greater striking power. This addition gave Pleasonton a total strength of over 6,000 horsemen with which to pursue Price.[20] The arrival of Catherwood made Pleasonton's division a formidable command indeed. All of these men were well-mounted and armed. Further, they were experienced combat veterans of either conventional campaigns or counter-guerrilla operations. Price would have no rest once the picnic in central Missouri broke in mid–October.

Meanwhile, A.J. Smith's infantrymen were valiantly trying to catch up to Pleasonton. They might not have had such a hard march if Rosecrans had not held the XVI Corps so long in the vicinity of St. Louis. It will be recalled that Rosecrans had maintained a tight leash on Smith until Price was well on his way west to Jefferson City. Then, once Rosecrans confirmed this information, he put Smith to work on infrastructure repairs rather than pursuing Price, all to the frustration of Smith and his men. But now the situation had changed and Rosecrans pushed Smith forward once Price cleared Jefferson City and headed west to Kansas.[21] Further, the XVI Corps was about to receive its own heavy infusion of reinforcements in the form of its lost division.

Brigadier General Joseph Mower's 2nd Division, XVI Corps, had flailed away far from the action in Missouri for several weeks. In September, Frederick Steele had retained the division in defense of the Department of Arkansas if Price's intended target was Little Rock. When Price's true intent was confirmed, Steele released Mower for use in countering Price's move into Missouri; however, Mower would not immediately rejoin the corps. As Mower moved north, he was directed to cover the eastern flank of the state, meaning the key town of Cape Girardeau on the Mississippi. Once it was clear Price did not plan to move in that direction, Mower was ordered to rejoin Smith and his parent headquarters, the XVI Corps. To do this he would have to march several hundred miles across central Missouri. When Mower finally caught up with Smith, the corps would number about 9,000 hardened veterans.[22] Combined with Pleasonton's large cavalry division, the Department of Missouri was finally putting a credible force in the field. If they could coordinate their march west with Curtis in Kansas, Price would find himself in big trouble.

As the Department of Missouri was making final preparations to pursue Price from the east, Curtis was struggling to put his uneven army in the field to the west. Even though he had finally convinced Governor Carney to call out the Kansas militia, many restrictions on its use made it difficult for Curtis to plan the defense of the state. As Price was basking in the hospitality of Southern sympathies at Boonville the Union army in Kansas was rapidly assembling to defend her soil. James Blunt arrived at Fort Leavenworth on 8 October 1864 to take command of the regular volunteer troops in the department. Major General George Sykes, formerly commander of V Corps, Army of the Potomac, was the commander at Fort Leavenworth but was unable to take the field, so Curtis replaced him with Blunt on 10 October. These would form a division and "right wing" of the Army of the Border. When Blunt took charge he immediately began to organize his command for efficient use in the field. He divided the wing into three provisional brigades under the command of Colonel Charles Jennison, the famous Jayhawker, Colonel Thomas Moonlight, a skilled leader, and Colonel C.W. Blair. The first two brigades were all regular volunteer troops with a wealth of combat experience. The third brigade, under Blair, was made up of Kansas militia, and Blunt would have serious issues utilizing this brigade because of political considerations.[23]

The second division of Curtis' Army of the Border was made up entirely of Kansas state militia commanded by the state adjutant general, Major General George Deitzler. The militia began assembling in accordance with Deitzler's orders immediately following Governor Carney's proclamation calling out all able-bodied men. Carney issued the proclamation on 9 October, and it would take some time to consolidate the men at their assigned assembly areas. Once this occurred, Deitzler ordered the militia to concentrate in the vicinity of the border at Olathe and Shawneetown. Surprisingly, the Kansas militia assembled within a matter of days at their assigned points and began consolidating along the border south of Kansas City. A typical example of the effort to assemble is the story of the 2nd Kansas State Militia. Private Samuel J. Reader was a young farmer who served in the regiment and left a vivid account of his and the Second's experience in the campaign. He answered the governor's call within a matter of hours at Topeka. On the 12th of October the regiment marched for the border. The unit made it to Shawneetown—over 100 miles from Topeka—in two days. There "the greater part of our regiment received new Enfield rifles." By the 14th of October, Curtis was ready to organize his army and issue orders for the defense of Kansas.[24] However, political considerations would soon limit his ability to establish a coherent defense.

The capability of the Kansas state militia was questionable at best. Of the 10,000 men who answered the call to arms, practically none of them had any combat experience and very little training. Because the Kansas militia was not a federalized force, they were haphazardly equipped and organized. For example, almost none of the militiamen wore a uniform. Therefore, to identify themselves on the battlefield, the commanders ordered the men to pin a red badge of cloth or scarlet leaves in their hats. This gave rise to the derisive nickname for the Kansas militia, "the Sumach Milish," for the sumac leaves that identified them.[25] Since few had any training, there was little discipline imposed within the units. Men could, for all practical purposes, come and go as they wished. Arms were not standardized, presenting logistical problems, which would prove difficult to sustain in the field.

Another problem with the militia was in its organization. When the militia began arriving at Olathe and Shawneetown on 13 October, they came as individual units. This was unwieldy since the thirteen regiments and five independent batteries of the Kansas State Militia were not brigaded. In other words, all regiments were commanded by a single man, General Deitzler.[26] Such a large organization under the command of one leader far exceeded the generally accepted span of control for large units, which is three to five subordinate elements. This organizational flaw was not rectified, and here was yet another issue that would work against efficient employment of combat power in the field.

In spite of all the obvious issues in the Kansas militia, the organization had one positive element that could serve to overcome some of its drawbacks, and that was in the realm of motivation. Kansas had suffered mightily for ten years at the hands of Missourians who sought to impose their will on Kansas. Cross-border raids by the Ruffians, and later the bushwhackers, had become a staple of the ugly war that raged between

Missouri and Kansas. The nasty attack on Lawrence by Quantrill in June 1863 that resulted in 150 unarmed men and boys dying and the town being razed is the archetypal example of this internecine war.[27] Thus, the Kansans had great incentive to prevent this massive raiding force from crossing the border. If they could get organized and deployed in time, there was much the Kansans could do in spite of their significant disadvantages.

While the militia was arriving south of Kansas City, Curtis began conducting reconnaissance to determine the optimum area to defend Kansas from the Army of Missouri. Curtis moved forward toward Independence, Missouri, taking note of potential areas where the terrain would favor defense and provide an advantage to his green troops. The idea behind a move into Missouri was that Curtis believed the best way to defend Kansas was forward *in Missouri*. Thus, as he made his way into western Missouri, Curtis identified a few suitable points to establish a strong defense. These consisted of high ground overlooking rivers to present an obstacle to any attacking column, providing natural reinforcement to a defensive position. The Little and Big Blue rivers each had these important characteristics, but political considerations would dictate the choice of river that would anchor the defensive arrangements.[28]

Even though Governor Carney had finally called out the Kansas militia, he and many militia leaders still doubted that Price was headed toward Kansas. Further, these same leaders balked at moving across the Kansas border into Missouri. The governor objected because he believed moving into Missouri would take the soldiers—the voters—too far from the polling stations to return in time for the election. Many Kansans believed that they were obligated only to answer the call to arms to fight in Kansas. Private Reader reported that his "neighbors came to me and stated that we were likely to be marched across the line into Missouri. He was opposed to any such movement, believing it would give the radical Government the power to retain us in the field indefinitely. He asked my opinion, I replied that he had better follow [orders]...." Therefore, they resisted complying with orders to cross the border. Thus, Curtis once again had to engage the governor and militia leaders to encourage the men to cross the border to defend Kansas. Through a process of cajoling and pleading, Curtis was finally able to convince some of the leaders to allow a forward movement into Kansas. Although he wanted to push them out to Independence, he compromised and accepted a defensive line on the Big Blue River, only a couple of miles from the state line.[29] While it was not Curtis' preferred course of action, the Big Blue was a formidable position.

As Curtis finalized his plans and prepared to issue orders to occupy the defensive line, a couple of curious incidents occurred that would make it difficult to implement his plan. First, although Curtis had reached consensus with most of the militia, a small portion in Deitzler's left wing still refused to move into Missouri. Deitzler agreed to allow these units to stay in Kansas on the border to guard against incursions. With the remainder, Deitzler moved up to positions along the Big Blue to establish the main defense.[30] Blunt, commanding the right wing, had the same issue, but his method of dealing with the problem was diametrically opposed to Deitzler's solution.

Blunt was an energetic, near-fanatical abolitionist with a passion for defending his adopted state of Kansas. Blunt would do anything to stop the Rebels, even if it meant crossing the entire state of Missouri. He could not understand why other men from

Kansas did not share his drive. Therefore, when one of his units refused to cross the border, he viewed it as mutiny. On 14 October, Blunt reported to Curtis that he was having "considerable trouble in getting the militia into fighting trim." By the 16th, this "trouble" had exploded into a full-fledged confrontation between Blunt and his two militia commanders. Blunt was planning to move into Missouri that day to establish contact with Price's Army of Missouri so that Curtis had an idea of the direction and intent of the Rebels. On the 15th, Blunt had issued orders for the march into Missouri, but Brigadier General William H. Fishback and Colonel James D. Snoddy refused to obey them.[31]

Fishback was upset with command arrangements Blunt had made in forming his division. The 3rd Brigade was composed of Kansas militia, which Fishback, as a brigadier in the state militia, felt he should command in the field. Blunt, however, had other ideas. He placed the brigade under Colonel Blair, whom he trusted. But Blair was only a colonel and Fishback, as a brigadier, could not stomach taking orders from a man he outranked. Therefore, when Blunt issued orders to Blair for 3rd Brigade, Fishback, as the second-in-command of the unit, refused them for two reasons. First, he claimed he could receive orders only from Major General Deitzler, the state militia commander. Second, he did not believe the militia could serve outside of Kansas. As a result, Fishback issued his own orders, telling Colonel Snoddy to march his 6th Kansas State Militia regiment to the Kansas state line and remain there to defend the state. On the morning of the 16th, Snoddy moved his regiment west of the state line in compliance with Fishback's order.[32] When Blunt heard this, he lost his temper and took personal action to rectify the situation.

The 6th K.S.M. regiment was moving west toward Kansas when, in the distance, the men could see another regiment moving to intercept them. As soon as Blunt heard that Snoddy had turned the 6th regiment back to Kansas, he ordered the nearest unit, the 15th Kansas, to follow him. He then led the regiment in the direction of the wayward 6th to halt the unit in its tracks. When Blunt reached the 6th, he ordered the 15th into line of battle to halt them. He then moved toward Snoddy and ordered him to halt, placing him and Fishback under arrest. Blunt had every intention of conducting a court-martial to convict them both of mutiny, but this came to naught. Senator Samuel C. Pomeroy of Kansas intervened to obtain Fishback's release and the course of events overwhelmed Blunt in the coming days to prevent him from carrying out his plan to court-martial Snoddy. The significance of this event demonstrates Blunt's drive and determination, as well as his courage. He would not allow anyone to derail his plans and his bold action put an end to the mutinous behavior of the Kansas State Militia. They would go on to serve with "an enthusiastic desire to meet the enemy," Blunt himself later noted, in spite of the ill feeling drummed up by the K.S.M. leaders. The militia "cheerfully performed every duty required of them" after the malcontents were removed.[33] James Blunt was certainly an asset for the Union cause on the border.

As the "picnic period" came to a close, time was running out for Price and the Army of Missouri. The Union forces in Missouri and Kansas had, after much hand-wringing, finally managed to put a formidable army in the field to contest Price's march. To the east, Pleasonton was perfecting a cavalry force that would unrelentingly serve as a hammer in the closing days of October 1864. A.J. Smith's now intact infantry corps was moving rapidly west to cooperate with Pleasonton in setting a trap for Price. These men of Rosecrans' Department of Missouri would attempt to push Price onto Curtis' force from the Department of Kansas to crush the Army of Missouri in a vise. In the west, after a herculean effort Curtis had succeeded in convincing and cajoling politicians and militia leaders to put a credible defense of Kansas together in the nick of time. Blunt's right wing of the Army of the Border was headed east toward Pleasant Hill to establish contact with Price in order to determine his intent and direction. Meanwhile, Curtis was establishing a stout line of defense with a mix of volunteer units and K.S.M. These men formed an anvil to stop Price, while the Federals from Rosecrans' department under Pleasonton and Smith pushed the Confederates upon the blocking force to prevent its escape south. If the Federals could coordinate all the moving pieces, Price would be in serious trouble and could see his army destroyed.

As the events unfolded in Missouri, officials in Washington were quite displeased. Price had crossed the border into Missouri on 19 September and now, almost a month later, the Federal Department of Missouri had done little to stop him. From the distance between Washington, D.C., and Missouri, it appeared to the president and others that Rosecrans was sitting on his hands and allowing Price to run wild through a state that supposedly was under Federal control. When Price left Boonville heading west on 13 October, it seemed that Union forces would simply allow him to leave unmolested. An annoyed Lincoln sent a cipher message to his aide in St. Louis asking, "[W]hile Curtis is fighting Price have you any idea where the force under Rosecrans is? or what it is doing?[34] Lincoln never received a reply, but Rosecrans apparently had finally taken to the field, as correspondence from him the same day indicates that he was in "Camp near Davis' Creek" en route to Lexington, Missouri.[35]

The president already had a low estimation of Rosecrans' ability by this time in the war. As the commander of the Army of the Cumberland, Rosecrans seemingly always had an excuse for inaction, and the lack of a coherent response to Price's invasion was in line with his previous pattern of performance. Chief of staff Henry Halleck had also grown frustrated and sought some way to prod Rosecrans into action. His correspondence reflected his irritation at the lack of information from Missouri. On 14 October, Halleck told Grant that "Rosecrans' telegram [of the 13th] is all I have from Missouri." Secretary of war Stanton likewise wanted more done and wrote to Grant that same day to state that he was concerned about matters and was meeting with Phillip Sheridan to discuss them. Grant felt the pressure and vented his frustration to Halleck, inquiring, "[H]as Rosecrans yet come upon Price? If he has not he should be removed at once.... There is no reason why our forces should not move without delay." He concluded the message with a statement of disdain saying that "anybody ... would be better than Rosecrans." Months later, Grant's irritation with Rosecrans had still not abated, and he recorded it in his final report of operations in July 1865: "The impunity with which Price was enabled to roam over the State of Missouri for a long time, and the incalculable mischief done by him, shows to how little purpose a superior force may be used. There is no reason why General Rosecrans should not have concentrated his forces, and beaten and driven Price before the latter reached Pilot Knob."[36]

Rosecrans' inability to make a decision early on in the campaign had allowed Price to run amok across Missouri. He forfeited to Price the initiative and this gave Price the ability to dictate the unfolding of events. As Rosecrans' superiors observed this from afar, it seemed to confirm their already low opinion of him. Therefore, they began to search for an alternative to replace the commander of the Department of Missouri. Rosecrans' failure to adequately communicate the situation did not help him, and within a few weeks the president would again shelve the hapless Rosecrans.

For the Confederates, the "picnic period" was coming to a close, as they could dally no longer. Price left Boonville on the 13th bound for Waverly, another friendly town and home of Jo Shelby. As the army moved west, Price had concluded that his new target was Fort Leavenworth in Kansas. This rich storehouse, if captured, could arm the entire Army of Missouri and cause panic in Kansas. Success here would provide a tangible example that the move across Missouri had a positive outcome.[37] Thus, Price moved west, hand-railing the Missouri River en route to Kansas.

As the Army of Missouri moved west, Price launched some secondary raids along the route to "liberate" towns and capture Union garrisons and storehouses. Accordingly, on 13 October Price detached Shelby's division and Clark's brigade of Marmaduke's division to capture the town of Glasgow on the north side of the Missouri. The Union garrison there was reputed to have some 5,000 small arms. Capturing this point would provide weapons for all of Price's unarmed soldiers and give the Army of Missouri an instant boost in combat power. Shelby was assigned the mission to secure the south bank and, with his artillery, suppress the Union garrison. Clark would cross the river and surround the town, demanding the surrender of the Union force. This incursion north of the Missouri was the only time any of Price's men operated on that side of the river. The garrison normally amounted to about 200 militia, but on this day a steamboat arrived carrying six companies of the 43rd Missouri Infantry under the command of Colonel Chester Harding, Jr. This gave the Union post a total strength of about 550 men.[38] The stage was set for an embarrassing failure of Union arms.

On 14 October, the Confederate forces got into position, cutting off all approaches to the town and readying for an assault the next morning. Though the Confederates outnumbered the Federals under Harding by more than two to one, the Union men had established a stout defense on high ground outside Glasgow. Shelby had his artillery in position before dawn and began shelling the town at first light. Clark was not quite ready to move when the gray light began to peel away the darkness of night. Upon learning this information, Shelby halted the bombardment to allow Clark to get into his attack positions. Finally, at 7:00 a.m. Clark launched his assault. Shelby's artillery disabled the steamboat in the channel and damaged several buildings while Clark pressed forward. Clark found the going tough, but by 1:00 p.m. things were looking grim for the Union forces. As Clark arrayed his brigade for the final attack, he received a message from Harding asking for terms of surrender. After receiving assurances from Clark of good treatment for his men, Harding capitulated at 1:30 p.m. For minimal loss, the Rebels captured about 1,200 rifles and a large store of much needed winter coats. Though this was far less than the 5,000 small arms expected, it was still a nice haul for the Rebels. The Union leaders were much chagrined by the surrender. Unlike Ewing, who put up a ferocious resistance against much longer odds at Pilot Knob, Harding "did not seem anxious to do more than make a show of resistance," according to one witness.[39] Rosecrans and others felt they had Price where they wanted him and the surrender of Glasgow was an unwarranted loss. Nevertheless, Price was in a tight spot.

As Shelby and Clark were reducing Glasgow, the rest of the army moved westward, arriving in Waverly on 17 October. Along the way, M. Jeff Thompson reduced a Federal garrison at Sedalia, bagging more prisoners and precious supplies. Price and the army once again received a warm welcome at Waverly, but this was the last time the Rebels were feted. Price and the army had rested and refitted for a little over a week. This provided the enemy with the opportunity to perfect their organization for pursuit and to close the distance between Price and Union forces. Thus, on 18 October, when Price pulled out of Waverly, the "picnic period" was over and everyone seemed to believe that the trek west would get tougher. Dr. McPheeters ominously recorded on the 18th that "we must have hard fighting—God defend us." The Army of Missouri was now 26 miles from Lexington, where the advance of the Army of the Border under Blunt was located. Behind Price, Pleasonton and A.J. Smith were pushing their men to make contact with the Confederate rear. From this point forward, the 12,000 Confederates were in constant contact with elements of the Departments of Missouri and Kansas numbering around 37,000 men.[40] Over the course of the next three weeks, Price's army was relentlessly harried by the various Union commands. The result of this running fight would break the collective hearts of the Rebels in the Army of Missouri.

The stage was now set for the culminating battles of the Great Raid. Price's dallying had again provided the Federals with opportunity. While the Union army had issues early on providing for a coherent response to the invasion, they were rapidly improving. Now, if the Federal leaders could coordinate their movements between the two departments, they would make Price pay for his lack of drive. As Price approached the border with Kansas, the Federals now had a chance to utterly destroy the Army of Missouri. Whether or not this would happen depended upon the ability of the Federals to overcome their fragmented command structure. Regardless of these uncertainties, the armies were on a collision course for the little river town of Westport, where they would fight the largest battle of the war west of the Mississippi.

9

Westport

When Sterling Price moved west from Waverly on 19 October, it represented the beginning of the end of the Great Raid. Westport was an epic battle for the Trans-Mississippi in terms of size and consequences. The engagement was the largest fought west of the river, and the result was decisive in that it broke the offensive striking power of the Confederate Trans-Mississippi Department. Westport nearly destroyed the Army of Missouri, but the army survived because of the fragmented command structure of the Union army. Price provided the Federals with an enormous opportunity to destroy his army. His slow pace, combined with his determination to protect the huge wagon train he had accumulated, placed his army in a nearly impossible position. He owed his survival to poor intelligence and disunity of command on the Federal side. Even though the Army of Missouri escaped, the Rebels would suffer much as they retreated south. From 19 October to 2 November 1864, the Federals maintained constant and relentless pressure on the Confederates. This caused a continuous attrition of the Army of Missouri in terms of men and resources. Thus, by the time Price and the army reached safety south of the Arkansas River, they had lost nearly half the force, all the train and artillery, and most of the recruits. Price would have a hard time justifying the expenditure of resources during the campaign, and the bleeding began at Westport.

From the time Price launched the Great Raid until the "picnic period" he had retained all of the initiative and dictated the unfolding of events. When he left Waverly, the initiative passed to the Federals who were now actively plotting his demise. The Federal plan—though poorly coordinated as it turned out—was actually quite sound if the various commands could work together. Curtis could see that Rosecrans' forces and the Missouri River had formed three sides of a box, and as Curtis developed his plan, he determined to use the momentum already gathering to close a trap. To the west, he established his defensive position on the rolling hills overlooking the Big Blue River south of Westport, which is today a suburb of Kansas City. He pushed Blunt's wing forward to delay the Confederates and determine the intent and direction of Price, while he emplaced Deitzler's wing with the Kansas State Militia (KSM) in the static defense on the river. To the east, Pleasonton's provisional cavalry division from the Department of Missouri was closing fast on Price's rear. A.J. Smith's XVI Corps was paralleling Price to the south to block the Army of Missouri's avenues of escape. To the north lay the unfordable Missouri River, a formidable obstacle that would prevent Price from slipping off in that direction.[1] Therefore, the combined Federal forces would trap Price on three sides, while the Missouri River to the north completed the fourth side of a tight box.

While this was a sound plan, there were two significant issues that would undo the preparations. First, there was no overall commander on the scene to synchronize the movement of all the Union forces. Major General E.R.S. Canby was the ostensible Federal commander over all departments west of the Mississippi, but his headquarters was far to the south at New Orleans. Therefore, Canby could exert little influence over events on the ground. This forced Curtis and Rosecrans to work together to coordinate their maneuvers as a cooperative effort. Compounding the problem of command arrangements was the issue of communications. Throughout the campaign, communication between Rosecrans and Curtis was spotty at best. This is because Price and his army were interposed between the Federal headquarters at St. Louis and Fort Leavenworth. When the Rebels cut the telegraph lines, and they did so frequently,[2] communication went by messenger, which was slow and inefficient. The pace of events simply outstripped the velocity of communication. Thus, formulation of plans and coordination of disposition of forces was quite difficult for the Federals, offering Price a chance to slip through the collective fingers of the Union hand.

Price had originally planned to move on Kansas City and Fort Leavenworth to raid the rich storehouses of the Department of Kansas. As events unfolded in late October, Price decided to modify his objective yet again. As he moved west, he slowly began to realize that taking either Kansas City or Fort Leavenworth was impossible. The Federals had arrayed their forces in such a way that attempting to take these points would probably result in the destruction of his army. Therefore, Price eventually decided to push west to the Kansas border and then turn south on the military road to Fort Scott. If he could take this key post and bring out his huge wagon train, he could lay some claim to success in the campaign turned raid.[3] Yet the train would prove an impediment to this change of plan and was the primary reason for Price's difficulties in the coming days.

Price first realized the gravity of his predicament on 19 October as he approached Lexington. While he had not yet issued orders to move south, Price was becoming concerned that he was in trouble. In his interim report of 2 November on the campaign, Price wrote:

> Here [at Lexington], from intercepted dispatches and other sources, I learned that a heavy force under Generals A.J. Smith, McNeil, Sanborn, and others were establishing their lines about thirty miles south and parallel to my line of march and the Missouri River, while General Rosecrans with a heavy column of infantry—in all about 30,000 strong—were following as fast as the impaired state of the roads would admit, and I was obliged, after forcing the enemy into Westport, to fall back southward.

The reason Price hesitated to redirect the army south was probably a lingering belief that he could still take Kansas City or Fort Leavenworth, and the best routes south were closer to the Kansas-Missouri border. As one author points out, Price was very reluctant to abandon his plan because it "was not his *style*."[4] The roads were critical for the safety of the train. As mentioned, Price was dragging 500 loaded wagons and a herd of cattle along with his column. If he was to remove them south, he had to have a supporting road network to move in that direction. The best roads for this purpose were closest to the border. Thus, the impediment of the train was a major reason for Price's undoing. It slowed his movements and dictated the route, making the army vulnerable to Federal counteraction.

Shelby's biographer would later bitterly denounce Price for clinging to the train and thus jeopardizing the army and the lives of the men. "General Price ... traveled it [the road] too slowly, not seeming to think that all the brave fellows falling around Shelby were so many useless human sacrifices," he recorded. Nevertheless, the retention of the train also dictated Price's plan for this stage of the raid. As Price left Waverly, he moved west with the basic organization he would use for the coming engagements of the next two weeks. Shelby, his fireman, would lead the advance and push the Federals westward, in effect opening the passage south. Marmaduke would command the rear guard, holding Pleasonton at bay. Fagan held the center and simultaneously protected the train, ushering it safely to the roads leading south.[5] This order of march and battle was excellent for its intended purpose. However, speed was of the essence and the leisurely pace set by Price throughout the campaign would hold true to the end.

Shelby reluctantly left his hometown of Waverly on the morning of 19 October in the van of the army. His visit was somewhat spoiled by the fact that Waverly, once a prosperous river town, had fallen on hard times due to the war. Manufacturing of hemp and other commodities had nearly ceased and the plantations, including Shelby's, were ravaged by three and a half years of war. One witness recounted, "The rude hands of war had stripped from this quiet little town much of her wealth and beauty; many goodly trees were down and comfortable houses destroyed, among which were his [Shelby's], his dwelling" and many other places in town. Nevertheless, it was likely tough for Shelby to say good-bye to family and friends in his adopted hometown. Shelby's division moved forward on the Lexington road, and the town was less than a day's march from Waverly. The advance of the Federal Army of the Border under Blunt was waiting to contest Shelby's progress. The weather was growing colder every day as the calendar approached November and late fall.[6] Into this raw morning, the troopers moved out, assured of the fact that time for rest was now over.

Blunt had moved east toward Lexington at 7:00 p.m. on the evening of 16 October following the unfortunate incident with General Fishback and Colonel Snoddy. This put the energetic Blunt well behind his self-imposed schedule, but he would make up the lost time by marching all night. Along the way, he did take the time to repair damaged telegraph lines so that he would have reliable communications with Curtis at Westport. Thus, Blunt would not arrive at Lexington until the morning of 18 October, one day before Price moved west from Waverly. Blunt brought with him the 1st and 2nd brigades of his division, leaving the 3rd under Blair, just inside the Missouri border near Kansas City. This gave him a total force of about 2,000 men with eight guns. As he moved east, Blunt learned that elements of A.J. Smith's and Pleasonton's commands were in the vicinity of California and Sedalia, respectively. He telegraphed Curtis on the 17th requesting that he forward the 3rd Brigade to him at Lexington. Blunt hoped that with this extra force, he could hold Price long enough to form a junction with Smith and Pleasonton. Then, the combined forces could trap and defeat Price against the Missouri River. A chagrined Curtis had to inform Blunt that it was not possible to forward Blair to his assistance. It seemed that political considerations would again prevent the movement of Blair's brigade—consisting entirely of KSM—further into Missouri. "Governor Carney," Blunt reported, "and others ... were making much trouble with the militia, [and] he [Curtis] could get them no further into Missouri." The *Weston (Missouri) Border Times*, observing the situation, railed against the lack of preparedness on the part of the politicians. The staunchly Union newspaper stated that "months ago we were told that Price, Shelby, and Marmaduke were preparing on an extensive scale to invade our state. The evidence was plentiful, yet no steps were taken to meet the threatened invasion."[7] Blunt readily agreed with this assessment, however there was little he could do now to prod the reluctant politicians to commit to a more forceful course of action. As a result, Blunt's effort would become a purely delaying action to slow Price because his small force could do little more.

Blunt and Shelby clashed by midday on the 19th of October. Blunt had sent out scouting parties on all approaches to Lexington early that morning. The men chosen for this duty were worn out from the previous all-night marches to get to Lexington. Nevertheless, companies from the 11th Kansas Cavalry and one from the 16th Kansas Cavalry pushed out three miles from the town on roads to the east. These bone-tired and hungry men would provide early warning of Price's approach and develop the situation for Blunt to act upon. They deployed quickly, cleared fields of fire, and waited for the Army of Missouri.[8] The Kansans would not have long to wait.

While the scouts moved out from Lexington, Blunt put the rest of the division to work constructing fortifications. Lexington was a town that held unpleasant memories for the Union cause in Missouri. It was here in 1861 that Colonel James Mulligan had surrendered to Price, handing the Confederate commander his greatest triumph in the war. He therefore put his troops to work digging earthworks, felling trees, and fashioning abatis to make the defense a stout one. Blunt even issued a directive to impress the local male population and put them to work on the fortifications. Further, he appointed the mayor as the "commander" of the townsmen to supervise construction.[9] Though Blunt expended much energy in the construction of the defense, he did not intend to become entrapped there as Mulligan had three years earlier. His purpose was to delay the Rebel advance and inflict casualties on Price's army in order to wear him down before reaching the main defensive line closer to Kansas.

Shelby's division set a brisk pace that morning with nothing to impede his march until reaching Lexington. The Confederates were advancing up three routes that morning, including the Dover, Salt Fork, and Warrensburg roads. Blunt's advanced companies from the 11th and 16th Kansas made contact with Shelby's men about three miles from Lexington around two in the afternoon. The first shots echoed in from the Salt Fork Road, and as soon as Blunt heard them he was in the saddle and moving to the sound of the guns. The advanced companies skirmished for about an hour, holding Shelby at bay, but as Shelby was able to move more men forward, he overwhelmed Blunt's pickets. One witness recalled, "[T]he force in my front increased so fast that we had to fall back or be captured." Captain Henry E. Palmer's Company A, from the 11th Kansas fought Shelby's column on the Dover Road to a standstill. "We were able to drive them back to the timber three times," Palmer reported. In fact, Palmer fought so hard that he lost contact with the other companies on his flank. When he realized what had happened, his company was isolated and cut off when Shelby overlapped his little force. After receiving no word from Blunt for some time, Palmer then had to extract his men from their predicament. Palmer and what was left of his company would move through the cover of darkness to rejoin Blunt on the 20th near the Little Blue River.[10] Palmer's heroic stand allowed Blunt to move back in good order.

The rest of Blunt's division also had a difficult day at Lexington. The other companies on the picket line along the Salt Fork and Warrensburg roads were overwhelmed fairly quickly after a stout fight because Shelby was able to bring the preponderance of his division against them first. Shelby pressed his advantage, pushing Blunt's advance guard back to the Lexington fairgrounds, where a sharp fight ensued. As previously mentioned, Blunt had wanted to make a stand at Lexington in an attempt to give Pleasonton and Smith time to close on Price's rear. But Curtis was unable to send reinforcements due to the Kansas' militia reluctance to move deep into Missouri. "The only thing I could now hope to accomplish," Blunt recorded, "was to develop the enemy's strength and intentions. For this purpose we resisted his [Price's] advance until his whole force was brought into position." Blunt did exactly this, contesting Price's army until Blunt and his heavily outnumbered force could stand no longer. Once he had determined Price's intent, he issued orders for a withdrawal along the Independence Road to the west. *Harper's Weekly* erroneously noted the engagement at Lexington as "a Federal victory," but even so, Blunt was accomplishing his assigned mission.[11]

Blunt assigned Colonel Thomas Moonlight the mission of covering the retreat with his 11th Kansas. Moonlight was an outstanding leader and Kansan transplanted from Scotland. The coming fight was the first in a string of engagements in which Moonlight would distinguish himself during the campaign. In the face of overwhelming force, Moonlight and his 500 men and four howitzers deployed into line of battle four times to halt Shelby's pursuing division. Darkness finally broke off the engagement and Blunt's column once again moved throughout the night to reach the next defensive position.

Blunt halted for what remained of the night at 2:00 a.m. on the morning of the 20th along the banks of the Little Blue River. The men of his division were so exhausted they simply fell down to sleep where they stopped. Daylight revealed another cold, raw morning, but Blunt liked what he saw as he observed his environs. The Little Blue was "admirably [suited] for defense against the advance of Price's column." Blunt therefore concluded that this was the place to make a determined stand against the Army of Missouri. He immediately dispatched a staff officer to Curtis to plead with him to bring the Army of the Border forward to the Little Blue. Curtis responded by ordering him to fall back to Independence, leaving "two or three squadrons at the Little Blue."[12] A frustrated Blunt partially complied.

Colonel Thomas Moonlight, Commander, 2nd Brigade, Provisional Cavalry Division, Army of the Border (Library of Congress).

While he did pull most of his division back, Blunt left the entire 11th Kansas

Cavalry Regiment under Moonlight on the Little Blue "to make as stubborn resistance as he could." Moonlight took to the mission with energetic determination. He arrayed his 400 men and cannon—Moonlight had lost around 100 men during the previous day's fighting—at the most likely crossing points to make the Confederates' attempt to ford the Little Blue a costly affair. There was a bridge over the stream on the Independence Road that Moonlight covered with half his force and the four howitzers under Major Martin Anderson. He ordered Anderson to defend the structure as long as he could and then burn it when it appeared the Rebels would capture it. Moonlight sent another company under Captain James Greer two miles south of the bridge to defend a ford site, and his last company under Captain Joel Huntoon four miles north to guard another. Moonlight was ready to receive an attack by mid-morning, but the rest of the day passed without contact with the Rebels. Thus, he used the balance of the day to improve the position. One eyewitness would later say that the Little Blue was "covered by obstacles of formidable dimension."[13]

The Confederates passed the 20th of October reorganizing at Lexington to continue the advance westward. The citizens of Lexington were happy to see Blunt leave and the Army of Missouri arrive. Captain Palmer noted as he left Lexington that on the evening of the 19th, with the Rebels on his heels, some of the townswomen came out to taunt them as they retreated. "That's right, you old Lincolnites, come in and surrender," they shouted. Close behind came Shelby's men, who occupied Lexington and took the opportunity of a respite from their 26-mile march and hours of fighting. The Rebels spent the 20th resting, enjoying the welcome of Lexington's citizens and changing the march order. While a change in the order of movement was probably necessary and, as one Rebel participant noted, "we also did some heavy fighting near Lexington," the time Price took to reorganize was inordinate. This respite gave Pleasonton time to close the gap between his horsemen and Price. Shelby's men were clearly spent from the previous day's march and fighting, but they could have continued west the next day. Therefore, Price pushed Marmaduke to the front and placed Shelby second in the line of march, while leaving Fagan in the rear with the train.[14] Thus, when the movement recommenced, fresh units would clash with Moonlight's tired troopers at the Little Blue.

Marmaduke's division stepped off early on the cold morning of 21 October, bound for Independence. Moonlight's men awaited them, and an impatient Blunt wanted to strike back at the Rebels hard on the banks of the Little Blue. In Blunt's opinion, if the Rebels got past the Little Blue in good order, they could break into open country and create havoc for Curtis. Blunt made a visit to Curtis' headquarters to lobby with him to bring forward the rest of the Army of the Border to the Little Blue. Upon arrival, Blunt found Curtis in conference with Governor Carney. Blunt was shocked to learn that the Kansas governor intended to recall the militia and disband them at this hour of peril. Carney accused Blunt of lying about his engagement at Lexington and that "he [Carney] knew Price was south of the Arkansas river." Blunt, now agitated by Carney's accusations, pressed his views with Curtis and won permission to return with his division to the Little Blue. While forming his division in the streets of Independence for the movement, Blunt received a telegram from Moonlight stating that he was engaged in a desperate fight. "I now pushed forward at a rapid speed, hoping that Col. Moonlight would be able to hold them in check," Blunt recounted.[15] Fortunately, Moonlight was the right man for the mission.

Marmaduke's division was in the saddle just after dawn on Friday, 21 October, moving west on the Independence Road. In advance of the division was Company D, 5th Missouri Cavalry, commanded by Captain D.R. Stallard. Within a couple of hours, Stallard's company was approaching the bridge over the Little Blue. The captain became suspicious that he might be walking into a trap near the river. He therefore dismounted his company and gingerly moved forward. Then, when in range, Moonlight's men opened up with a sheet of flame, dropping one-third of Stallard's company at the first contact. In spite of the heavy fire, Stallard pressed on, scattering Moonlight's skirmish line on the east side of the Little Blue. Marmaduke, hearing the rising volume of fire, threw two regiments forward to support Stallard and capture the bridge.[16]

Captain Palmer was resting with his men following his harrowing escape from Lexington when the fighting started near the bridge. He had just sat down to repair a hole in his pants when the call came for him to move forward to support the defense. His pants would have to stay ripped for at least another day. The defense at the bridge was going against Major Anderson, as the Confederates were able to bring up more forces. By mid-morning, Clark's entire brigade of Marmaduke's division was up and about to cross the planking. At this point, Anderson called forward a wagon loaded with hay and some daring troopers to ignite it on the bridge. The boys in blue were successful in setting the bridge afire, but a crisis was brewing above and below the bridge site. Moonlight's small companies defending the fords were overmatched, as Clark was able to get the 4th and 14th Missouri Regiments over the fords curling around Moonlight's flanks. The threat of a double envelopment caused Moonlight to detach part of Anderson's men at the bridge to the flanks. As the Union lines thinned, the volume of fire at the bridge slackened. Stallard noticed this and reacted quickly by rushing the bridge with some artillery just before the structure fell into the river. With all of the crossing sites breached, Moonlight began to pull back to a ridge several hundred yards from the Little Blue. As he began the retrograde around 9:00 a.m. the van of Blunt's division was arriving on the field.[17] Marmaduke was about to get a warm reception from the reinforced Federal line.

Blunt pushed his men to the limit to reach Moonlight before the Rebels overwhelmed him, and Blunt arrived just in time. He had three brigades with him, including a fourth brigade that Curtis agreed to release to Blunt to stiffen his resistance. This unit consisted of two regiments, the 2nd Colorado and 16th Kansas, and Captain W.D. McClain's Independent Colorado Battery. As one Rebel witness noted, "it seemed that the Yankees were going to give us a hard fight," and Blunt did not fail to fulfill this prediction.[18]

At the moment Marmaduke believed he had the Federals on the run, he ran into a wall of resistance as Moonlight, now reinforced by the rest of Blunt's division, stopped Marmaduke in his tracks. "[F]rom behind rock walls, trees, and hilltops," one observer noted, "the Federals poured in tremendous volleys" with their repeating rifles, halting the Rebel advance. Marmaduke no longer had a numerical advantage either, and the Union men, armed with repeaters, had immense firepower superiority. Marmaduke bravely attempted to drive the Federals off the ridge and was in the thick of the fight.

The Confederate commander had three horses shot under him and his attacking regiments began to suffer under the pressure. When he saw that he could not push the Federals off the ridge, Marmaduke sent for help from his friend, Jo Shelby. While Shelby made his way to the front, Marmaduke stubbornly held his lodgment on the west side of the Little Blue River.[19]

The fighting now took on the characteristics of a slugfest. Blunt, "posted behind rock fences," and Marmaduke stood toe to toe while maintaining a destructive fire. Each opponent had about the same number of men, but Marmaduke had his back against a stream, in low ground, with single-shot rifles. Blunt now had fifteen cannon anchoring his line of about 3,000 men. If he could coordinate an attack, Blunt might possibly defeat Marmaduke in detail. Shelby could not arrive too soon. When his division arrived at the Little Blue, Shelby had the men dismount and wade the stream on foot so that they were ready to fight upon arriving on the far bank. Shelby pushed his division to the right of Marmaduke, forming a coherent line, at about 10:00 a.m. Then, in conjunction with Marmaduke, the two prepared to launch an attack up the ridge on the stubborn Federals.[20]

With Shelby in line reinforced with Cabell's brigade, the Confederates now had a two to one advantage in men, and Shelby's division overlapped the Federal left flank consisting of Moonlight's 11th Kansas Regiment and his four howitzers. But, before they had moved far, Blunt dismounted his men and launched his own attack. This preemptive assault caught the Rebels off guard and pushed them back a half mile toward the Little Blue. The advantage was short lived, as the Confederates soon recovered and halted Blunt's advance. The Rebel numbers were beginning to tell and the length of the Federal line created a vulnerability that the Confederates could exploit. Blunt realized this and quickly ordered his men back to the crest of the ridge to prepare for the inevitable counterattack.[21]

As Blunt's division regained the ridge, General Curtis arrived on the field with his staff. The commanding general had become curious about the situation at the front and moved forward to find out how Blunt's defense was progressing. When he got to the ridge, Curtis began shifting the artillery around without notifying Blunt. This action caused confusion on the Union line, creating another vulnerability, for it exposed the cannoneers to Confederate sharpshooters. Further, the left flank of Blunt's line was left with no fire support. When Blunt discovered what his unwelcome visitor had done, he became incensed. Yet he had no time to confront Curtis because Blunt had to correct the disposition of his line before the Rebels collapsed his left. To Blunt's relief, Curtis soon left the field, but not before he caused another headache for Blunt. As Curtis rode back to Independence, he encountered Blunt's ammunition train. Curtis found the commander of the train and ordered him to take it back to Independence, contrary to Blunt's orders to come forward. Blunt nearly ran out of ammunition during his retreat back to Independence as a result of Curtis' latest interference.[22]

As Curtis departed, Shelby was massing his division to attack Blunt's left flank. Blunt's chief of artillery observed the Rebels assembling for the assault and sought help to protect the guns of McClain's Independent Colorado Battery in that direction. He found Moonlight, who ordered the ubiquitous Captain Palmer to the front to save the cannons. "He ordered me to charge the enemy with my eighty-eight men," Palmer remembered. Palmer complied, temporarily driving back Shelby's advance. This gave Captain McClain time to limber up and retreat, thus beginning a retrograde from the Little Blue. Blunt assigned the intrepid Moonlight, reinforced by the 2nd Colorado Cavalry, to cover the retreat to Independence. With Shelby closing on the Federal line and guns, Moonlight and Major Nelson Smith, commanding the 2nd Colorado, countercharged. The two lines converged and Smith was quickly shot dead from his horse. The daring charged worked, as it threw Shelby's division into confusion, allowing the rest of Blunt's division to escape in good order. This occurred in the nick of time since Blunt's units were now critically short of ammunition.[23]

Blunt began retreating at about 4:00 in the afternoon and continued until 9:00 p.m. when he closed on Independence. Blunt re-formed his lines twice along the road, daring Shelby to attack his position, but Shelby, again leading the Army of Missouri, would not take the bait. Therefore, Blunt continued to retreat through Independence. Though Shelby did not attack, he stayed close on the heels of the Federals. He pursued the Union cavalry right into the streets of the town, where Moonlight's rear guard precipitated a short firefight in the eerie darkness. The night was punctuated with the flashes of rifles, the clatter of horse hooves, and the crash of shots hitting windows and buildings, while the citizens hid in the cellars. The engagement ended when the last of Moonlight's men exited town into the dark fields west of Independence. Blunt, under orders from Curtis, marched through another night to reach the "fortified position on the Big Blue" where the rest of the Army of the Border was in defensive lines.

One interesting incident occurred in the midst of the night fighting in Independence. Captain George Todd, the famous bushwhacker and companion of Bill Anderson, had attached his band of guerrillas to Cabell's brigade. In the eerie twilight, Todd received a mortal wound through the neck, ending his career as a bushwhacker. Thus, like Anderson, Todd's demise would come during Price's invasion of their beloved Missouri.[24] Blunt had once again demonstrated his enviable qualities as a commander. He led from the front and motivated the men with his presence. According to one witness, "he was the animating spirit of the battle."[25] Blunt would have a chance to show his mettle on many more occasions in the next two weeks.

While Blunt was fighting it out with the Rebels at Lexington and the Little Blue, the rest of Curtis' army was busy forming a defense on the Big Blue. The Kansas militia had finally assembled at Shawneetown by the 16th of October, and Curtis began issuing orders for Deitzler's wing of the army to move up to the Big Blue. That day he informed Blunt, "I have directed General Deitzler to send a large force of cavalry and artillery to Independence today," to begin defensive preparations. The next day, Deitzler reported to Curtis that the militia refused to cross the state line until "after I made them a speech," and then they demanded that Deitzler "not order [them] too far into the state [Missouri]." Of course, this was the major reason why the Army of the Border established its defense on the Big Blue, which is less than five miles from the Kansas state line.[26] The militia regiments would begin moving over to the line of the Big Blue over the next three days.

Private Reader of the 2nd Kansas State Militia moved into Missouri on 21 October 1864. His regiment received the order from Deitzler on the 20th. Up to that point, Reader, as the company quartermaster, had spent the previous days "receiving and distributing shelter tents and camp equipage."[27] Since the Kansas militia was almost wholly without equipment, Curtis had to take several days after their arrival to issue needed supplies. Without simple things like blankets, cooking utensils, and tents, they could not take the field. Thus, the time taken to prepare the militia for combat took away from the time needed to improve the defensive position on the Big Blue.

In spite of this, Curtis was still able to emplace obstacles that would stiffen the position. Since the KSM were mostly green, they would need every advantage they could obtain to help them contend with Price's veterans. The banks of the river were very steep in several places, such as Byram's Ford on the Independence Road. Also, much of the length of the stream contained heavy timber and thick brush to impede movement by the enemy. To reinforce these natural features, Curtis had the men fell trees at the fords and fashion abatis, which would force the Rebels to reduce the obstacles to cross the river. In addition, dams were erected downstream to raise the level of the Big Blue at the fords.[28] Curtis hoped that these improvements would allow the raw militia to hold their positions in the face of hardened units like Shelby's division. He soon learned whether his effort would pay off.

While Curtis had made some improvements to the line, there was much left undone. For example, his line was too long for him to secure with the troops he had available. With some 10,000 troops, Curtis chose to defend a position encompassing

Byram's Ford, site of heavy fighting on 22 and 23 October 1864. This site was alternately defended by Curtis and Price. The photograph depicts the Big Blue River at Byram's Ford looking east. On both days the attackers, Confederate and Federal, made their assaults from the east side to force a crossing (photograph by the author).

The old roadbed of the Independence Road leading to Byram's Ford, site of heavy fighting on 22 and 23 October 1864. This path connected the frontier towns of Independence and Westport and was a well-used route of both armies. This point is on the west side of the Little Blue River in the vicinity of the defenses overlooking Byram's Ford (photograph by the author).

fifteen miles of frontage. This means that there were less than 750 men per mile to secure the line. Thus, the Confederates could mass at any point to punch a hole through the line. Finally, many militia regiments had done nothing to prepare their positions to receive the Rebels. Private Reader's 2nd KSM occupied the Mockabee farm to the rear of Byram's Ford and failed to erect one obstacle. Reader stated that his regiment simply crossed the river and "went into camp among the jack-oak trees." In bivouac, Reader noted, "We had a jolly good time.... It was by far the nicest camp-ground during our trip."[29] The inattention to the taking of defensive improvements would come back to haunt Reader and his comrades the next day.

Alfred Pleasonton's division and the XVI Corps were marching as fast as they could to catch up to Price's rear while Blunt was fighting the delaying action and Curtis was laying out the line on the Big Blue. Pleasonton got the division fully organized for pursuit on the 14th of October and began moving on the 15th. Price was a few days' march ahead of Pleasonton, but the slow pace he kept, combined with Blunt's superb effort to delay the Army of Missouri, allowed Pleasonton to catch up within a week. To his division was added a fourth brigade, commanded by Colonel Edward Winslow, detached from the XVI Corps. Winslow was ordered to join Pleasonton on the 11th of October, but they were posted at St. Louis when they received the order. Thus,

Winslow's brigade had to move over halfway across Missouri just to join the division. This began an odyssey covering 922 miles for the men of the brigade.[30]

William F. Scott was a member of the 4th Iowa Cavalry in Winslow's brigade and he recorded the history of his regiment. "On the 11th the cavalry left Benton Barracks [in St. Louis] and marched westward by Washington, toward Jefferson City," wrote Scott. Though the brigade was cavalry, Colonel Winslow had the men walk every day to prevent breaking down the animals. "The men were dismounted and led their animals from one-eighth to one-fourth of each day's march," Winslow reported. Further, he ensured "every effort was made by steady moving, frequent rests, and regular and abundant feeding, when practicable, to keep the command in an effective condition."[31] As a result of this attention to detail, Winslow's brigade arrived at Independence eleven days later, on Saturday, 22 October, ready for combat, having marched 300 miles all the way across the state to catch up with Pleasonton's division.[32] The march was an impressive feat on the part of a seasoned brigade of veteran soldiers.

Pleasonton struck the Little Blue on the 22nd, the day after Blunt's fight with Price at the stream. "I have just arrived at this point and find the bridge over the creek destroyed," Pleasonton reported to Rosecrans. "I am building a temporary bridge over the creek," he continued. Most important, Pleasonton told his commander that he was skirmishing slightly with the rear guard of the enemy." He concluded, emphatically stating, "I shall press forward as rapidly as possible."[33] Pleasonton meant what he said, because by midday his main body struck Price at Independence, precipitating the second engagement there in as many days.

The short fight through the streets of Independence portended bad tidings for Price since he had to contend with Curtis in front and Pleasonton to the rear. While the people of Independence sought shelter in their cellars, the Rebel rear guard struggled to hold off Pleasonton's troopers so that the cumbersome train could clear the town. The pressure from the rear seemed unusually heavy on this day, and one of the reasons for this was that Pleasonton had finally made contact with Curtis' army. This development seemed to fill Dr. McPheeters with feelings of foreboding, as he wrote in his diary that the enemy "came up on our rear and attacked Gen. Marmaduke."[34] On the Federal side this was a positive development, as heretofore they had brought pressure to bear on the Confederates from only one direction. Yet issues would remain for the Union command, as interdepartmental communication between elements of Curtis and Rosecrans' forces were sporadic at best. This would make it difficult to trap Price as he continued the raid. But with positive contact between Curtis and Pleasonton finally established, the odds of Price's escaping were considerably reduced.

The manner by which Curtis opened the line of communication with Pleasonton is an amazing chronicle of daring and danger. General Deitzler suggested to Curtis that he could send a messenger through Rebel lines to inform Pleasonton of the situation on the Big Blue. Deitzler sought volunteers for the mission, and a man named Daniel W. Boutwell stepped forward to deliver Curtis' message. Boutwell was a soldier in the 2nd KSM who had previously served in the 6th Kansas Cavalry, a veteran regiment with a great deal of service, and he was well suited to take on the task. He had joined the 2nd KSM when Price's army approached Kansas, fortunately for the Army of the Border.[35]

Curtis accepted Deitzler's offer to get a message through the lines, and Deitzler gave Boutwell his instructions on Friday night, 21 October. Boutwell left headquarters at 7:00 p.m. bound for Pleasonton's lines somewhere to the east. He started on his journey riding a horse but then decided to secure a skiff on the Missouri to pass eastward. This worked for a while until he stuck hard on a sandbar in the river. It was still the middle of the night. Boutwell made his way to the shore wet and muddy, and now he was cold as well. Nevertheless, he kept going, taking to the woods to avoid detection by the Rebels. Because it was dark, he became disoriented and accidentally ran into Rebel lines. Nervous pickets fired on Boutwell in the night, but he managed to escape. He again headed into thick woods and gradually worked his way north around Independence, finally reaching Federal lines around mid-morning.[36]

The Union men he encountered were separated from the commands during Blunt's fight on the Little Blue. They were unsure of what to make of Boutwell's disheveled form. It was common for guerrillas to wear Federal uniforms to slip through picket lines, and the guards at first believed that Boutwell could be a Rebel. Once Boutwell convinced them of his identity, they conducted him to Pleasonton's division headquarters. Here, Boutwell was taken to Pleasonton, who received him cordially, though he was suspicious of Boutwell's identity. However, once Pleasonton heard Boutwell's message and questioned him thoroughly, he was "fully satisfied of the correctness of his 'statements.'" The new information gave Pleasonton greater impetus to press forward to gain contact with Price and push him onto the defenses of Curtis on the Big Blue. Pleasonton immediately issued orders to close on Price.[37]

While Pleasonton was aggressively moving against Price, he made a huge blunder that would allow the Army of Missouri to escape the trap the Federals had worked so hard to set. A.J. Smith's corps arrived in Lexington late on 21 October. The XVI Corps of infantry had achieved an amazing feat of marching across two-thirds of Missouri to arrive only one day's march time behind Price's cavalry. At Lexington, Smith received orders from Rosecrans to divert southward to Lone Jack via Chapel Hill to close the trap on the Army of Missouri. The very next day, though, Pleasonton asked Rosecrans to modify the order. After his engagement with Price's rear guard at Independence, Pleasonton became concerned that Curtis was not ready to block Price and the Army of Missouri. He believed that if Price turned his entire force upon his division, Price could defeat Pleasonton's smaller force in a head-to-head fight. Therefore, he requested that Smith come to his support with his infantry to give him the muscle to overpower Price. "If Smith can come up," Pleasonton wrote, "in case we get in a fight it will be well." Rosecrans would later regret acceding to this request, stating in his after action report, "[H]ad he [Smith] been ordered and marched for that point [Lone Jack] instead of Independence the day before General Smith would have arrived in time to strike the enemy's compact column and train.... But it was too late."[38]

Smith's luckless infantry would march across the entire state of Missouri and never participate in an engagement as a result of Pleasonton's ill-timed decision to change Smith's route. This misjudgment by Pleasonton placed Smith out of position to close the box on Price, and it was the direct result of poor coordination between the converging forces and the lack of an overall commander of the two departments. Thus, Price was given a gift when the Federal forces were not in position to block his army when he turned south to escape. Price was able to avoid complete disaster, despite his own mismanagement, because of poor situational awareness and decision-making on the part of the Union commanders. Yet he would not avoid a stinging defeat as the Federals closed in around his army.

On the Confederate side of the line, Price was daily becoming more concerned for the safety of the immense train, though not necessarily his army. As it was more and more beginning to appear that he would not take or achieve any of his major objectives, he now sought to protect the train at all costs. At this point of the Great Raid, Price had come up empty-handed except for the plunder amassed along the way. Since it was becoming more obvious that he would have to turn south to avoid destruction, Price was determined the he must carry the train home with him in order to have some tangible evidence of success.[39] Therefore, as his plans for the rest of the raid evolved, the focus of the operation would center on protection of the train.

As the Army of Missouri approached Westport on the 22nd, Price had determined his next move. The Army of the Border was to the front in defensive position along the Big Blue to block the Army of Missouri. To the rear, Pleasonton was at Independence pushing Price toward Curtis, and Smith was to the south headed toward Hickman Mills, soon to be diverted to support Pleasonton. For Price to make a successful turn to the south, he would have to push back one of the three Federal units bearing down on him in order to open a "door." To push the door open, Price turned to Shelby. Price would focus on the weakest link of the three Federal units to open the path, and this was Curtis' army composed mostly of Kansas militia. He would throw Shelby against the Big Blue to force Curtis back to gain access to the roads leading south. Once Shelby had opened the way, Price would reinforce him with two brigades from Fagan's division and depend on him to hold the door open while the train turned south. Marmaduke would take the rear guard to hold Pleasonton back, while Fagan's third brigade, under Cabell, shepherded the train along the road.[40] The plan was a sound one provided all players did their job.

The battle of Westport was in essence two engagements fought over two days. Day one—22 October 1864—involved Price, with Shelby's spearhead attacking Curtis on the Big Blue and then pivoting to the right to allow the train to turn south. Once Shelby accomplished this, he took up defensive positions along Brush Creek on the south side of Westport to block the Army of the Border from interdicting the train. Marmaduke would move up, face about, and occupy the former Union defensive positions on the Big Blue, blocking Pleasonton. Thus, the two sides virtually exchanged their positions for the fight on the second day. On the 23rd, Curtis would attack Shelby from north of Brush Creek, while simultaneously Pleasonton would assault Marmaduke's positions along the Big Blue. Cabell would push the train south through Little Santa Fe. The 22nd and 23rd of October would represent the largest battle fought west of the Mississippi and have decisive, far-reaching results, essentially that of ending the war west of the Mississippi and sealing the Confederacy's fate east of the river.

Shelby began moving toward the Big Blue on 22 October, a cold, gray Saturday morning. To open the door on the Big Blue, Shelby would have to penetrate the Federal defenses at one of the ford sites and then push the division rapidly across to widen the breach. Once this was accomplished, he would then have to push Curtis to the north

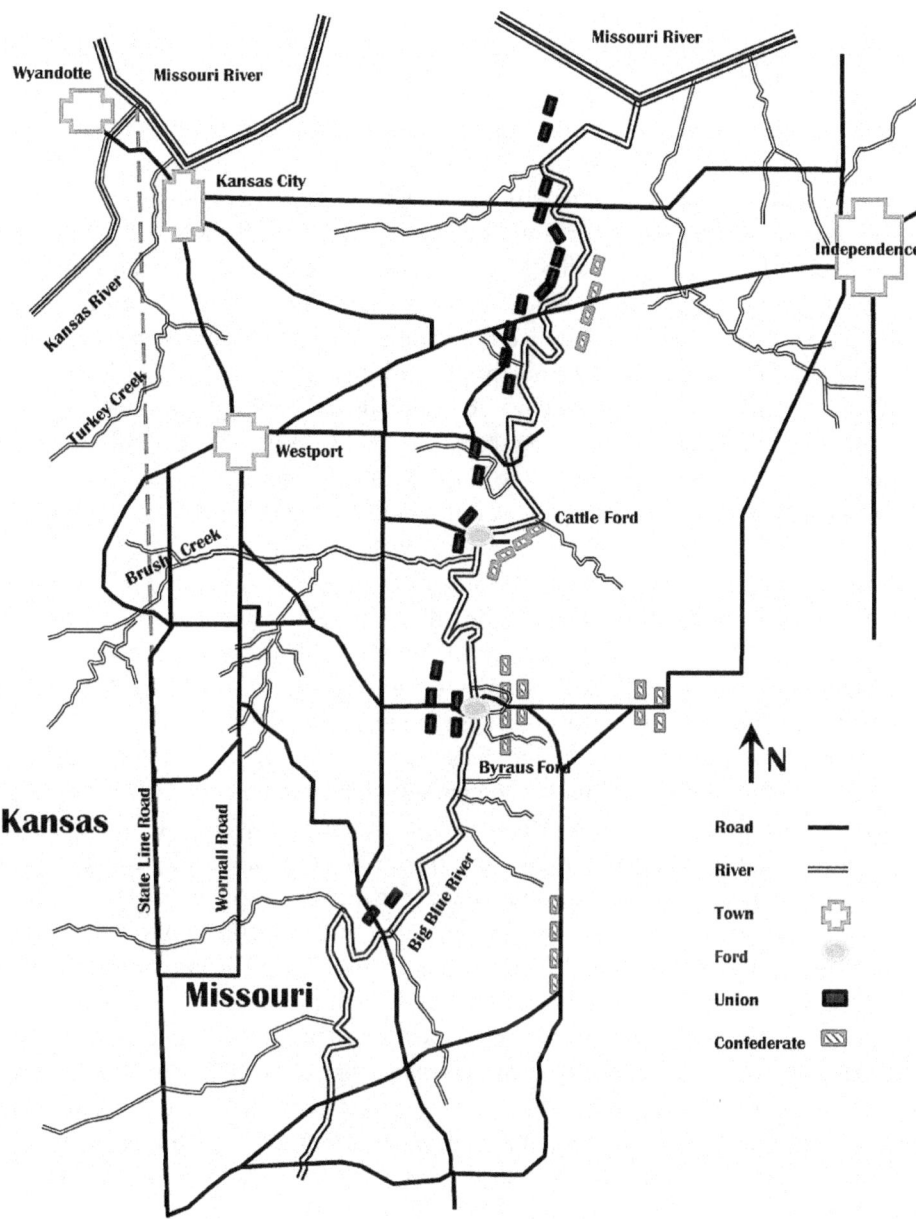

Map 3. Battle of the Big Blue on 22 October 1864 in which Price "opens the door" south to allow the Army of Missouri to escape the closing trap laid by Curtis and Pleasonton (map by Captain Robin Glebes).

to hold the passageway open for the rest of the army to escape. Shelby began to probe on a wide front along the stream at around 9:00 a.m. He sent Sidney Jackman's brigade to fix the Federal left under Deitzler on the north end of the Federal line guarding the main ford along the Kansas City–Independence road, while M. Jeff Thompson with the Iron Brigade began demonstrating around Byram's Ford—guarded by Blunt—looking for an opening. The Federal defense was well situated, taking advantage of the high ground overlooking the Big Blue. Shelby's biographer noted that the attack was "to be made under many disadvantages and in the face of terrific fire from the rock fences." The skirmishing continued for about two hours as, simultaneously, Fagan's division ushered the train southward toward Little Santa Fe. As the hours ticked off without Shelby's forcing a crossing, the train became vulnerable to an attack by Curtis, as it skirted the flank of the Union line.[41] It was now incumbent upon Shelby to get across the Big Blue and push Curtis north to protect the flank on the train.

To force the crossing, Shelby looked to his old Iron Brigade, commanded by Thompson. To add weight to the effort, Shelby shifted Jackman's brigade toward Byram's Ford. Together, these two brigades would dismount and push across the ford, feeling for the Union right to turn it to the north. The terrain at Byram's Ford was highly favorable to the defense. Heavy timber covered each bank of the Big Blue and the Federals had obstructed the approach by felling trees. The banks were elevated above the stream, creating a cauldron through which the Confederates would have to cross under fire. On the west bank—the side occupied by the Federals—the climb out of the stream was up a long slope that rose to 100 feet above the valley. The slope extended for almost a mile, culminating in a plateau where a number of farms were situated.[42] While the Federals had the advantage of terrain, Shelby's division held the edge in experience. The line opposite Shelby was held by green KSM, but the attackers were hardened veterans commanded by the best division commander in the Army of Missouri. The Federals would have their work cut out to stop these tough soldiers.

The attack at Byram's Ford commenced just after 11:00 a.m. In spite of their lack of experience, the Federals stubbornly defended the ford, pouring a galling mix of rifle and cannon fire in on the Rebels. After a couple of hours, a frustrated Shelby decided to change his plan. He sent two regiments, one north and one south of Byram's Ford, under Colonels Frank Gordon and Alonzo Slayback, to find a gap in the line. Both succeeded in finding unguarded fords. Slayback hit an unsuspecting Colonel Jennison in his left flank, while Gordon curled around the Federal right. Shelby quickly exploited the advantage, running guns across the stream to support the attack. The sight of screaming Rebels on their flanks unhinged the Kansas militiamen. In a matter of minutes, Jennison's line collapsed in spite of the Jayhawker's effort to hold the line, carrying with him Moonlight's brigade, which had attempted to shift to the left to support Jennison. One by one, the Federal brigades peeled away from the line while Shelby pivoted right, pushing the bluecoats north toward Westport.[43] At last, Price had the breathing space he needed to slip the train out of the trap.

Curtis disposed of his forces in a fairly coherent manner to meet Price, but his line was too long, making gaps or weak points inevitable. Blunt's division held the right of the line from Brush Creek south to Russell's Ford opposite Hickman Mills. Deitzler's division was arrayed from Brush Creek north to the Missouri River blocking the main ford at the Kansas City-Independence road. Curtis had a high degree of confidence that he could defeat Price along the Big Blue. In a dispatch to Rosecrans written the evening of the 21st Curtis said, "I am confident I can stop Price at this crossing, and hope you will come up in his rear and left." Shelby intended to shatter Curtis' confidence. He made his feint against Deitzler's left wing, intending to cross the Big Blue at some vulnerable point in Blunt's front. At first, all went well for the Federals, but as the hours wore on, tension began to rise among the Federal soldiers. Samuel Reader had heard the distant rumble of the fight at Independence on 21 October with apprehension since he, and most of the men in his regiment, had never seen combat. One messmate of Reader's named David Vaughan confided to him that he believed he would die in the next day's battle. Although Reader tried to reassure Vaughan, he himself was unsure as to what battle would bring.[44]

"The memorable 22nd dawned clear, still and frosty," recorded Reader. Soon the boom of cannon caused the men considerable excitement as their nerves began to tighten. Reader's regiment was posted to the rear between Byram's and Russell's fords on the Mockabee family farm. The mission of the 2nd KSM was to guard against a Rebel crossing of Russell's Ford. Reader realized that his unit was in a vulnerable position, for if the fords to the north were penetrated, the 2nd KSM could become isolated from the rest of the army. Nevertheless, Reader recalled, "I trusted and believed our leaders were in every way competent, and would not fail to give the rebels a rough handling."[45] Reader was to learn that he was wrong.

As the battle was unfolding around the fords, Reader and the 2nd KSM marched to and fro between Byram's and Russell's fords looking for a fight with the Rebels. Finally, near Russell's Ford, a messenger reported to Colonel George Veale—Reader's commander—that the Confederates were firing just beyond the next hill. Pushing forward, the 2nd KSM soon found the enemy, who had affected a crossing of the Big Blue. The 2nd KSM, supported by a brass 24-pounder howitzer, was soon engaged in attempting to stem the tide of Shelby's advancing troopers. Some of the men in line doubted that the men they were encountering were the enemy until Colonel Veale asked rhetorically, "Don't you see the rebel flag?"[46] Within minutes, there was no more doubt about what the men of the 2nd were up against.

The 2nd began exchanging fire with Shelby's men as the two lines closed on each other. The howitzer, commanded by Captain Ross Burns, began throwing grapeshot at the oncoming Rebels. While this cheered the troopers of the 2nd KSM, the cannon fire drew special attention from enemy sharpshooters, who began picking off the cannoneers. The sight of other men wearing blue dropping around them unnerved many in the 2nd. The Confederates got their own battery—the one Shelby sent forward shortly after Gordon and Slayback crossed the stream—into action, and the fire of these guns added weight to Shelby's attack. With rifle shots and shells whistling all around, the 2nd began to waver. Colonel Veale desperately tried to keep the regiment in line, but as the Rebels brought up more men, the pressure became too much for the Kansans. At last, the Rebels charged with their trademark yell, buckling the Federal line. Reader got swept away in a headlong flight to the rear when suddenly two Confederates ordered him to halt. Face to face with a man pointing a double-barreled shotgun at him, Reader dropped his carbine, answering the Rebel's request to give up: "Yes, I surrender." Capitulating with Reader was the fearful David Vaughan, who had the premonition of death the night before. Though the battle was over for both, they had survived, but an ordeal of a different kind awaited them in the days ahead. The fighting near Mockabee farm cost the 2nd KSM over 100 prisoners, along with 50 wounded and an unlucky 30 who were killed.[47] Shelby had crumpled the entire Union right, which was now streaming north toward Westport as the sun began to set in the late afternoon.

The Confederate had accomplished his mission of opening the door to allow the train to pass southward.

While Shelby was driving the bluecoats along the Big Blue, Marmaduke and part of Fagan's division were struggling to hold back the hard-driving Pleasonton and his horsemen. William Scott's 4th Iowa Cavalry had just arrived at Independence after the epic march across Missouri. Pleasonton was already driving Marmaduke through the streets of town when Colonel Winslow reported for duty. In spite of their long, arduous march, Pleasonton immediately threw Winslow's brigade with the 4th Iowa forward into the fight supporting Egbert Brown's brigade. Pleasonton reportedly was excited at the arrival of Winslow because this gave him access to a veteran cavalry brigade experienced in the type of warfare Pleasonton intended to engage in for the coming fighting.[48] Pleasonton's other brigades had cut their teeth fighting guerrillas and so were not well suited for mobile warfare against a conventional enemy.

The newly minted 4th Brigade of Pleasonton's Provisional Cavalry Division went charging through the streets of Independence to relieve McNeil's units, which were running low on ammunition. The 10th Missouri, commanded by Lieutenant Colonel Frederick Benteen, led the charge. As they shot out of the western side of town, Benteen angled his regiment to the left in order to hit Marmaduke's line on the right flank. Benteen—who would become famous, or infamous, at Little Big Horn, depending on one's perspective—was a hard-fighting and energetic commander. No other Union cavalry officer had more combat experience than the almost feminine looking Benteen. "Very quickly the ball opened," Scott recorded, as Benteen signaled his 10th Missouri to charge. His attack found the mark, outflanking Clark's brigade of Marmaduke's division, precipitating a near rout while scooping up dozens of prisoners and capturing a battery from Cabell's brigade. Winslow's brigade now went over from the attack to a pursuit, driving Marmaduke ten miles to the vicinity of Byram's Ford as darkness began to settle over the field at Westport.[49] Pleasonton was now well positioned to deliver a stinging defeat to Marmaduke while jeopardizing the safety of Price's train and army.

In order to increase coordination between his force and the Army of the Border, Pleasonton sent a note to Curtis informing him of his arrival on the Big Blue near Byram's Ford. This and another piece of news cheered the hard-pressed Curtis. Earlier in the day Curtis learned of the death of the bushwhacker Todd, who had participated in the Baxter Springs massacre that claimed the life of his son. In a letter to his wife, Curtis wrote, "It is certain that among the rebels killed yesterday the notorious Todd, one of the murderers of our son, was among the many who were killed [at Independence]." To this was added the welcome news that Pleasonton had arrived and was ready to fight in concert with Curtis. He had spent the late afternoon working to pivot his line back on Westport to reestablish a defensive line while protecting Kansas. Curtis had for the most part accomplished this when darkness suspended the fighting.[50] For the rest of the night on the 22nd and early morning of the 23rd, Curtis would debate the location to make his defense with an aggressive James Blunt. The winner of the argument would drive the action of the second day at Westport.

When the fight of the 22nd went against Curtis, he considered reestablishing his defense far to the rear of Westport near Kansas City. For the time being, the Army of the Border was arrayed now facing south behind Brush Creek. Deitzler was initially aligned along the Big Blue holding the left flank, but on Curtis' order, he would withdraw to Kansas City after Blunt's position was turned to constitute a reserve. Blunt's division held the new line south of Westport along Brush Creek to the Kansas state line. At this point, Thomas Moonlight's brigade turned at a right angle oriented east, protecting the state of Kansas from penetration by the Rebels.[51] Though Curtis seemed well positioned, along with Pleasonton bearing down on Price's rear, to smash the Army of Missouri on the 23rd, he started to have doubts.

During the night, Curtis issued orders removing the army to a position near Kansas City. Blunt was incensed at such a proposition and on his own responsibility countermanded Curtis, leaving his division in place. Then, he galloped off to Curtis' headquarters at the Gillis House in Kansas City. There, Curtis held a council of war to hear the opinions of his subordinates. Curtis favored pulling back, while "every officer present at the council ... felt absolutely certain that even without Pleasonton's division, we had men enough to meet Price." After hearing the opinions of the assembled leaders, Curtis acceded to the will of the group. Blunt then made arrangements to move food and ammunition forward before returning to the front at Westport around 3:00 AM.[52] With new determination, Blunt and his division were ready to meet Shelby and turn the tables in their favor on 23 October.

Crowding Price from the east was Pleasonton, who was busy that night hatching his own plans for Sunday morning. Pleasonton and Curtis had exchanged messages that evening, and upon learning Curtis' intent, Pleasonton planned to push his division to the limit to support him. Pleasonton fought Price all the way from Independence, pressing against his rear guard. The newly arrived Winslow and his brigade led the way, stopping in front of the Big Blue as the day gave way to darkness. That evening Pleasonton sent instructions to his commanders for renewing the fight. First, he ordered Egbert Brown to pass through Winslow's exhausted brigade to the front to lead an assault across Byram's Ford at daylight on the 23rd. Winslow was to support the attack, while Sanborn would follow and exploit success by the leading brigades. Pleasonton's fourth brigade, under McNeil, was sent southward "to Little Santa Fe and from there to the Fort Scott military road, to intercept them [the Confederates], if possible."[53] The plan was sound, and if executed in conjunction with Curtis' attack the next morning, Pleasonton could make the situation uncomfortable for Price. However, had it not been for the misdirection of Smith earlier in the day, the combined Federal forces would have had Price in a trap he could not have escaped from.

On the Confederate side, the leaders were also readying for another hard day's work. However, there was among the Rebels no debate about what to do. Price knew exactly what to do in order to save the train and extract his army from the closing grip of the Union forces. He had to block Curtis in the north and Pleasonton to the east, while ushering the train southward out of harm's way. To accomplish these tasks, Price would ask a great deal of his division commanders. First, Shelby would hold the front door open to all the train to stream south. Shelby was now facing north toward Brush Creek and Blunt's division. He would launch a preemptive assault on this part of the field against Blunt before he could launch his own in the morning. Shelby's men would sleep on their arms this evening as cold air enveloped their lines. Part of Fagan's division moved in beside and behind Shelby to reinforce his defensive position. McCray's brigade of Fagan's division moved in beside Shelby, reforming his line and forming a right angle on Shelby's right flank to prevent Blunt from turning Shelby out of his position. Dobbin's and Slemmon's brigades moved in behind Shelby to support him and close any gaps in an emergency. Marmaduke's division received the difficult task of holding the backdoor and blocking the hard-driving Pleasonton from making a breakthrough at Byram's Ford. Marmaduke had occupied the old positions of the Army of the Border, and he hoped to have better luck holding the Federals back than Curtis had on the 22nd. Finally, Price detached Cabell's brigade from Fagan's division and gave him the task of defending the train while pushing it south.[54]

"The 23rd of October dawned upon us clear, cold, and full of promise," reported Shelby. That promise would turn to desperation by nightfall. Shelby's division initiated the action by moving from its position around the Wornall family home at about 8:00 a.m. to throw Blunt off balance and disrupt an expected attack by the aggressive Union commander. At first, Shelby drove the Federals, who had not expected the Confederates to strike before them. The Rebels "very soon became fiercely engaged," as the Union men stubbornly resisted, giving ground slowly. Nevertheless, the Rebels pushed Blunt's division to the southern outskirts of Westport. The impetus of the attack naturally resulted in disorganization of the line as the Confederates pushed forward and suffered casualties. Thus, Shelby was forced to halt the advance to dress his lines.[55] When he did this, Shelby provided just the reprieve Blunt needed to regroup and prepare his counterattack.

The Confederates would advance no more for the rest of the day. For a time, the regiments exchanged rifle fire, but the real story was the artillery fighting that morning. Both sides brought in battery after battery, massing fire on each other and increasing the din and pageantry of the fighting. Over forty guns were dueling each other, but the Union gunners had the advantage in numbers. "Opposing batteries draped the scene in clouds of dense and sable smoke," Shelby reported. Captain Richard Collins' four-gun Rebel battery maintained a steady fire in the face of several Federal batteries until one of the guns burst. With three guns left in action, Collins valiantly kept up a high volume of fire.[56] However, he was losing cannoneers and the Federals now launched a counterattack.

When Shelby hit Blunt around eight o'clock that morning, Blunt immediately sent Curtis a dispatch requesting that Curtis send Deitzler and all the militia forward. Curtis complied, moving forward himself to observe the action from a rooftop in Westport. Now heavily reinforced, Blunt launched two attacks that buckled, but did not break, Shelby's lines. Shelby fed Slayback's brigade into the fight, stabilizing the defense until about noon. Then, with over 30 cannon massed against Collins and Blocher's batteries, Blunt launched a third attack that pushed Shelby back. The Rebel probably could have held, but to his surprise, Federals were in his rear. Dobbin's brigade now moved up to assist, and a desperate fight ensued over possession of McClain's Colorado Battery. Coming down Wornall's Lane at a full gallop, it appeared Dobbin would take the battery and throw Blunt's assault back. Charles Jennison, the feared Jayhawker, saw the move and threw Company E, 15th Kansas Cavalry, into the breach. The company commander charged directly into Colonel James McGhee's Arkansas Cavalry Regiment. Although heavily outnumbered, Captain Curtis Johnson stopped the attack, and when the young

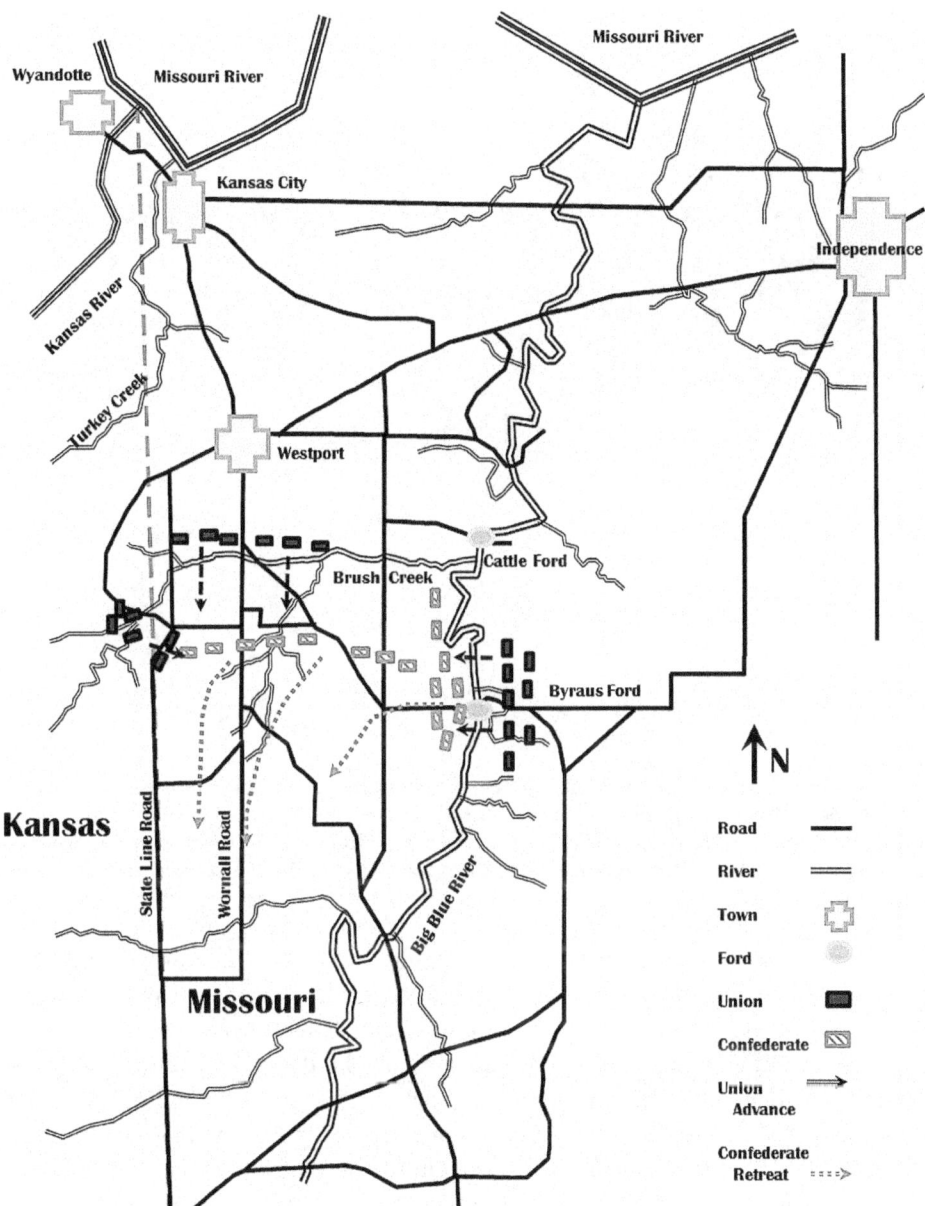

Map 4. Battle of Westport on 23 October 1864. Price narrowly escapes after Pleasonton forces a crossing of the Big Blue threatening to cut him off from roads leading south (map by Captain Robin Glebes).

captain personally killed McGhee, the Arkansans drew back. From this point onward, all of Shelby's efforts would focus on delaying the oncoming Federals and staving off disaster for the rest of Price's army. Shelby later declared that the raid, which had been a "walkover," at that point became a matter of survival.[57]

The Union soldiers prowling behind Shelby's lines were Pleasonton's troopers, who had eviscerated Marmaduke's lines on Byram's Ford. Pleasonton had planned on attack-

This site was occupied by the Confederates, who massed artillery looking north toward Brush Creek. It was used on 23 October 1864, first by the Army of Missouri and then by the Army of the Border after the Federals had driven Shelby south by afternoon. Today this position is in the city of Westport, a suburb of Kansas City, in Loose Park (photograph by the author).

ing at daylight, with Brown's brigade leading the assault. Brown, however, did little to prepare his brigade to execute the order. First, he was supposed to pass through Winslow's brigade, which had the lead on the 22nd. Then, Brown would have to put his brigade in line of battle to advance on the ford. By dawn, he had not even passed through Winslow's lines, thus he was in no position to attack. Pleasonton became concerned about what was happening at the front that morning when he heard no firing after daylight. He immediately rode to the front to see what was holding up the assault. "Not finding any attack being made I went to the front," related Pleasonton. "I found Brown's brigade on the road so disordered as to be in no condition for fighting, and General Brown himself had made no preparations to carry out my order." The cavalry commander now exploded and placed Brown under arrest, along with a Missouri militia colonel "whose regiment was struggling all over the country." Pleasonton then placed Colonel John F. Philips of the 7th Missouri State Militia Cavalry in command of Brown's brigade, with orders to prepare for the assault. He turned to Winslow, who had Pleasonton's confidence, and instructed him to lead the assault with Philips in line beside him and Sanborn in support.[58] Winslow went to work and soon had both brigades moving forward, relieving Pleasonton of his earlier headache.

Colonel Winslow pushed his brigade down the hill toward the Big Blue under fire from Marmaduke's men overlooking the ford from the rise above. Covering the attack was a battery from the 2nd Missouri Light Artillery. Colonel Philips dismounted his brigade on the left of Winslow. Using the cover of the timber, he was able to move up to the steep bank of the river. However, as the bluecoats began to scamper across the ford, Marmaduke's men shot them down when they were exposed in the stream. With the Rebel position some fifteen feet above the stream's west bank, hitting the Federals was like the proverbial shooting fish in a barrel. "The bullets were incessantly pattering," against the rocks on the bank, one witness remembered. With the assault stalled, Pleasonton pushed Sanborn forward to reinforce the attack. Philips remounted his brigade and attempted to gallop across the ford. This failed, with many casualties in the Union brigade, as the horses could not exit the ford on the slick mud and rocks. Then, Colonel Winslow was severely wounded and the attack continued to stall, with the clock now approaching 11:00 a.m.[59]

Lieutenant Colonel Frederick Benteen, the ranking officer in Winslow's brigade, now took command of the unit, and under his leadership the bluecoats finally established a lodgment. The 3rd Battalion, 4th Iowa, and the 7th MSM Cavalry made a mad dash across the Big Blue and got to the other side by using the timber and rocks as cover. Benteen then reinforced this success and the added strength finally cracked Marmaduke's line. Now that the ford was free of fire, the mounted men pressed forward and up the sharp slope of the hills just beyond the stream. Benteen massed the brigade at the top and then moved out onto the open prairie just beyond the Harrisonville Road. Sanborn joined them on the prairie above, and now all three brigades pushed forward in a coordinated attack. Though Marmaduke's men had fought well, they were now flanked on their right and outnumbered. Marmaduke's division broke when Benteen launched a heavy and impetuous attack on the exposed flank. With panic spreading, Marmaduke pulled back, finding a route south to stay between the Federals and the train.[60] It was about this time that Blunt's attack began to push Shelby back, and the redoubtable Rebel noticed the bluecoats in his rear. The crisis of the day had arrived for Price.

While the Union soldiers of Blunt were elated that "Pleasonton has come," the Rebels were fighting for their survival. Curtis, now in general command, launched an assault along the entire Federal line south of Brush Creek. Shelby knew that to prevent a rout he needed to pull back from his forward position facing Brush Creek to one rearward. Regrouping here, he could begin a rearguard action to allow his friend Marmaduke to make it off the field in good order, along with the train further south. Thus, Shelby withdrew under pressure to a line just south of the Wornall house, straddling the lane of the same name. Marmaduke's men were streaming southward with little organization while the division commander was feverishly working to gain control of the mob. Cabell reported that "stragglers and unarmed men were coming in" from Westport, nearly disrupting his defense of the train. To prevent the stragglers from causing confusion, Cabell "made every man fall into line as fast as they came up."[61] While Cabell was catching stragglers, Shelby was desperately trying to hold back the Federals now massed on his front and flanks.

The attack of Pleasonton's lead brigades had caused a great deal of disorder in Benteen and Philips' units, so Pleasonton pushed Sanborn to the front while they regrouped.

The front of the Wornall House in present-day Westport. In 1864 the Wornall family owned a 640-acre farm south of the town. The farm was the scene of heavy fighting on 23 October 1864 as Shelby pulled back from his Brush Creek defensive line. The house was also used as a Confederate hospital during and after the battle. Today it is a museum and when this photograph was taken in late November 2013, it was undergoing refurbishment (photograph by the author).

Sanborn hit the remnants of Marmaduke's division with great force, causing confusion in what remained of the unit. Fagan, on Shelby's right, opened ranks to let the stragglers from Marmaduke pass through and then he staggered Sanborn with a withering fire. Meanwhile, Shelby had re-formed and was holding valiantly to the final line of defense. This line was characterized by rows of stone fences and scattered growths of timber. Shelby had now thrown in all of his men and had no reserve left when Curtis drove home another assault.[62]

It was now around 1:00 p.m. in the afternoon and the culminating moment of the battle was at hand. Colonel Samuel Crawford—soon to be the governor of Kansas—recorded that while he was acting as an aide to Blunt during the fight the general told him to take charge of the 16th Kansas and 2nd Colorado. Blunt wanted him to form these units into a wing and lead it in an assault while Blunt personally led the rest of the line. "When I came up," Crawford said, "both lines were using their carbines in a random sort of way, but [they] were so far apart that neither could hurt the other." Therefore, Crawford sought to close the range with the enemy so the fire from the Union lines could take effect. He ordered the regimental commanders to sling their carbines and draw pistols. Moments later Crawford gave the command to charge. Then, "in less than three minutes the Rebels were flying at full speed over the prairie." Though Shelby was finally forced to retreat and cut his way past Pleasonton's hard-riding horsemen, he had held long enough for Cabell to put distance between the Federals and the train.[63]

As Shelby and Marmaduke desperately attempted to fend off the converging forces of Curtis and Pleasonton, Cabell had his hands full with the train and McNeil's Federal brigade. Most of Fagan's division had been providing security for the train during the march from Independence on the 22nd. But, with pressure building in several different directions, Price had reinforced Shelby with two of Fagan's brigades in anticipation of a tough fight on the 23rd. This left only Cabell's brigade to secure the train, and move it south through Little Santa Fe. This mission would stress Cabell to the limit, but it is interesting to consider what might have happened had Pleasonton not diverted A.J. Smith's XVI Corps to Independence. If Smith had continued to Hickman Mills, it is quite likely that he would have defeated Cabell, destroyed the train, and sealed a trap for Price. However, this did not happen because of an error resulting from poor situational awareness on the part of Pleasonton.

McNeil received his orders on the evening of the 22nd, and just like the hapless Brown, he was tardy in execution. McNeil had to move his brigade several miles south in order to get into position to carry out his attack. Starting around midnight, McNeil marched all night, reaching Hickman Mills at daybreak. Then, inexplicably, McNeil turned his men out of march order to feed the horses rather than starting his assault. All the while, Cabell was forcing the train along the road to get it clear of the fighting. Thus, McNeil was allowing opportunity to slip away due to poor decision making and disobedience to orders. Pleasonton, after his earlier irritation with Brown, again lost his temper. He bluntly noted in his after action report that "McNeil failed to obey this order ... and instead of vigorously attacking the enemy's wagon train ... he contented himself with some skirmishing and cannonading, and the train escaped." Pleasonton concluded his remarks by recommending that Rosecrans reprimand McNeil for his conduct at Westport.[64]

Cabell competently fended off McNeil once the latter finally put his brigade in line of battle to attack using a combination of fighting skill and deception. In addition to the 500 wagons constituting Price's train there were over 5,000 head of cattle and an estimated 1,500 unarmed recruits. Cabell had worked all night on 22–23 October pushing the train and its impediments southward. The length of the procession stretched for miles, with the herd at Little Santa Fe at daybreak while the wagons were moving through Hickman Mills. The recruits were brigaded together under the command of Colonel Charles Tyler from Shelby's division. Price had intended to place this brigade with Cabell's to form a division under overall command of Cabell. Some texts from the period even refer to the conglomeration of the recruits and Cabell's men as "Cabell's Division." However, the disastrous outcome of the campaign prevented the actual formation of this division.[65] Nevertheless, Cabell intended to use these men to help him protect the train, if he could control them.

When the din of firing around Byram's Ford reached the ears of McNeil, he finally pulled his brigade together and formed for an attack on the rear of the train. Initially, McNeil thought the train was lightly guarded. Then, Cabell, alerted to the danger, adroitly maneuvered his brigade to protect it. He did this with such skill that McNeil later reported he "found [himself] in contact with the entire force of the enemy." McNeil felt threatened enough that he brought up his artillery battery of three 3-inch ordnance rifles from Battery L, 2nd Missouri Light Artillery, to drive back the aggressive Cabell. In turn, Cabell put in his own battery, Captain William Hughey's Arkansas.[66] The combined fire of Cabell's artillery and his cavalrymen, halted McNeil temporarily.

As morning turned to afternoon, McNeil prepared to make another attempt to break through to the train. He ordered the 17th Illinois Cavalry under Colonel John L. Beveridge—the man who relieved Ewing at Harrison—to lead the assault. Beveridge, who would soon become the governor of Illinois, began forming as Cabell was working to get the last of the wagons out of Hickman Mills and across the Big Blue. As Cabell observed the scene, he noted the activity to his rear as the enemy massed for another assault. To fend off this attempt, Cabell came up with a novel idea. He had Colonel Tyler form the unarmed recruits into a battle line as if they would defend the train. At this development, McNeil hesitated and recalled Beveridge.[67] There was no assault at this moment and Cabell successfully put the river between the train and the Federals.

One of the most interesting aspects of the fighting at Westport is the conspicuous absence of Price. Though he was on the field, he was almost invisible until the end of the fight. The direction of the fighting fell to the excellent division commanders in the army, most notably the leadership provided by Jo Shelby. By mid-afternoon, as the situation began to unravel along Shelby's front, Price received a message from Cabell describing the action around Hickman Mills and the train. Price, to the rear of Shelby's lines, immediately moved to Cabell's position while simultaneously issuing orders for Shelby and Fagan to fall back, closing on the train. By the time they received the order, events had already forced this upon Shelby and Fagan, as Marmaduke was falling back from Byram's Ford. Price, meanwhile, moved to the head of the column and led it on the retreat south.[68]

Shelby, Marmaduke, and Fagan made a fighting retreat back to the train winding its way past Little Santa Fe onto the Fort Scott military road. As they did so, Cabell again demonstrated how indispensable he was to the army by covering the retreat and the train. As stragglers came in from the divisions, he noted that the prairie grass was very high and dry due to the fall season. He struck upon the idea to set the grass on fire to cover the retreat. The order was given and the prairie grass was soon ablaze. Cabell kept a heavy skirmish line behind the flames and the combination of smoke, flames, and rifle fire drove McNeil and the pursuers from other commands back, allowing the train and the rest of the army to escape the cauldron at Westport.[69] The battle was over and it was the first event of a disastrous series to take place over the next 48 hours.

With Confederates retreating on all fronts, the converging Union forces finally came together along Indian Creek as the clock neared 2:30 p.m. according to Samuel R. Curtis. The leading Union generals met at a nearby farmhouse to discuss future operations. In attendance were Curtis, Pleasonton, Deitzler, Blunt, and Sanborn, along with Governor Carney of Kansas. Deitzler and Carney proposed that the KSM receive an immediate release from further obligation since they believed the militia had done their whole duty. Obviously, Carney was still concerned that the Kansas men would not make it home in time to participate in the election, and an immediate release would afford them the opportunity to vote. Pleasonton countered that his command was exhausted and that his Missouri men deserved the same opportunity to vote as the Kansans. Therefore, Pleasonton wanted to head for Harrisonville in Missouri rather than making a direct pursuit. Curtis, mediating the session, developed a solution that would satisfy all parties. First, he concluded that the KSM had done their duty, but a threat still existed to southern Kansas. Therefore, he decided to lift martial law in north Kansas and release the militia from that region. The militia from southern Kansas would continue in service until the danger to that area was relieved. Second, all regular and volunteer units would commence a direct pursuit of Price, under the overall direction of Curtis, to give the operation unity of command. This last provision was subject to the approval of General Rosecrans, the Department of Missouri, making the entire arrangement more of a gentlemen's agreement. The troops then turned into the neighboring fields for a highly deserved meal, forage for the horses, and rest.[70] Curtis issued the necessary orders for the pursuit that would commence the next morning.

The weary Confederates continued the march south to put some distance between themselves and their pursuers. In spite of the urgent need for a forced march, Price still failed to provide the required discipline to extract the army from danger. Marmaduke noted the slow pace in a meeting with Price and "urged upon General Price the necessity of ... pressing forward vigorously" after a short rest. But, another witness noted that in spite of "the hazard to their [the soldiers] lives" in guarding the train, "the column was moving leisurely and at a speed that would not have been rapid for infantry."[71] Thus, Price, ensconced in his ambulance, was content to amble slowly away from Westport with his loot rather than pushing the limit to gain speed. The result of this would bring on near disaster at Mine Creek.

The Rebels slowly moved south the rest of the 23rd and into the early morning hours of the 24th. Dr. McPheeters noted that he "had nothing to eat all day until night." So, the half-starved Rebels took just enough time at the middle fork of the Grand River

The Battle of Westport painted by N.C. Wyeth. This painting was completed circa 1921 and is a mural in the Missouri State Capitol in Jefferson City on the east end mezzanine.

to snatch a short nap and "cook a hasty meal" before pressing onward. Price now placed Shelby's division in the lead, with Marmaduke resuming rear guard duties. Fagan had the center in the line of march, responsible for protection of the train. For miles along the route, the Rebels shed gear that was now an impediment. One Federal observed that "the road was more thickly strewed with the *debris* of a retreating foe" the farther south they pursued. Broken down wagons, caissons, loose cattle, accouterments, and sick men littered the route. Nevertheless, the sad procession pressed south. Price now set the objective as Fort Scott. Rich with valuable stores, this was the last place that, if taken, could give Price some claim to success. Additionally, Price wanted Kansas to feel the hard hand of war, and so part of his orders were to destroy everything of value along their path.[72] Because of the already loose discipline in the Rebel army, this order seemed an invitation to wanton destruction. Yet the Rebels would soon experience suffering of their own.

The battle of Westport was a decisive victory for the Federal army, albeit one that could have had even greater results than those achieved. Among the many positive outcomes was the fact that the combined Union forces defeated Price in battle, frustrating him yet again. Next, the Army of Missouri suffered significant losses seriously affecting the fighting edge of the Confederates, with the exception of Shelby's division. Although statistics are incomplete at best for the Confederates, it appears Price lost over 200 killed, almost 900 wounded, and over 400 missing and captured for a total of around 1,500 out of an army estimated at 12,000—3–4,000 of whom were unarmed.[73] In addition, the Rebels lost several guns in the running fight from Independence to the Big Blue. This was a 12.5 percent loss, which in modern terms represents neutralization of the force, requiring reorganization before another engagement. Morale in the Army of Missouri took a corresponding plunge as a result of these losses. Most important, Westport forever put an end to the dream to wrest Missouri from the Union orbit. The Federal government, because of this battle, had an iron grip on the state, and it would never relinquish it. Finally, bushwhacker influence was also broken for good. Thus, Westport dashed all of Price's dreams for his home state, but the worst was yet to come.

For the Federals, the outcome was almost all positive. The only criticism from the Union perspective was the failure to capture Price's host due to the poor command arrangements. In victory, the Federals lost many men, though their losses were not grievous. Curtis estimated his loss in killed, wounded, and missing at about 500, while Pleasonton's division suffered 362 casualties between Lexington and Westport for a total of around 862.[74] This is a little over half the number of casualties suffered by the Rebels. Since the Union army was much larger, at an estimated 22–23,000 men engaged, the Federal loss was less than 5 percent. Thus, the Federal army was still capable of conducting follow-on operations, while the Confederates needed time to regroup. Price would not have the luxury of time because the Federals relentlessly pressured the Army of Missouri in pursuing them south.

The largest battle ever fought west of the Mississippi lived up to its billing. The results were decisive in that they ended Confederate hopes for Missouri and forever broke the offensive striking power of the Rebel Trans-Mississippi Department. The Federals consolidated their hold on Missouri and ended the nasty border war that began in 1854, a full seven years before the Civil War started. The battle could have had an even more decisive outcome, but the fractured command structure and some poor decisions made due to incomplete awareness of the situation ensured this would not happen. Nevertheless, the Rebels were not out of the woods. Another decisive battle was in the offing. Mine Creek, the largest battle ever fought in Kansas, would have correspondingly significant results. This mean little fight would nearly destroy the Army of Missouri and its remaining offensive power and effectively ended the war in the Trans-Mississippi.

10

"This has been a disastrous day!"

As Monday morning, 24 October, dawned, the Rebels were in the saddle after snatching a few short hours of sleep and a hasty breakfast. Price had managed to put a few miles between his retreating, ragged army and the victorious Federals. The pace of the march was far too slow and the head start he managed to achieve would soon vanish. The reason for Price's continued plodding was his determination to cling to the ponderous train, which represented the physical evidence of any success of the Great Raid. The train was like an albatross around Price's neck, and his failure to jettison the impediment nearly led to complete disaster. Ironically, it was ongoing friction caused by the fractured Union command structure that would deliver salvation to the Army of Missouri. Although Curtis attempted to establish unity of command by taking charge of the combined forces from his own Department of Kansas and the troops from Missouri, his best effort was not enough to bring them together. Yet, even with all the squabbling among the Federals, Price almost found a way to lose everything. It was the stinging defeat at Mine Creek that finally convinced him to get rid of the cumbersome train to save the army.

Governor Reynolds of Missouri was still traveling with the Army of Missouri and was present at the battle of Westport. What the governor witnessed at Westport and in the days ahead thoroughly disgusted him, and he committed his frustrations to writing. Reynolds believed that the reason for the ugly defeat at Westport was the massive train Price was dragging with the army. He wrote:

> Under his unmilitary management, numerous wagons which the soldiers believed to contain untold wealth of plunder by staff officers and dead-heads, had dangerously augmented his train, so that it numbered over five hundred vehicles, and shockingly controlled and conducted, often stretched out eight or ten miles in length. Marched in the center of the army, flanked, preceded, or followed by a rabble of dead-heads, stragglers and stolen negroes on stolen horses, leading broken down chargers, it gave to the army the appearance of a Calmuck horde. The real fighting soldiers, badly fed, badly marched, and getting little rest in a noisy disorderly camp where their horses, blankets, pistols and even the spurs on their boots were often stolen from them in their sleep, scarcely disguised their apprehension that the odious train would occasion disaster to the army, and they were plainly reluctant to shed their blood to save the plunder it conveyed.[1]

This missive conveyed a great deal about the state of the Army of Missouri as it retreated from Westport prior to Mine Creek. First, it provided a window into the thoughts of the soldiers and their belief that the train contained plunder for the officers. Such a belief was bound to have an effect on morale and the fighting edge of the army. If the soldiers thought they were suffering for the loot of unscrupulous leaders, the men would probably not fight hard in the event the enemy pressed an attack on the retreat. Second, it appeared the army contained a large number of malcontents who were little better than vermin. Feeding such hangers-on took away from the subsistence available for the true soldiers in the organization like Shelby's men. Finally, indiscipline—a trademark of Price's leadership—was destroying the army internally. Marmaduke and Fagan's divisions were already fraying, and if this disease spread any farther, the army was vulnerable in a standup fight with the pursuing Federals.

Even Shelby's division was showing some disturbing signs of indiscipline. As the retreat began on the morning of 24 October, the route carried them through the border counties of Missouri that G.O. #11 had depopulated. Only the chimneys of burned houses, called "Jennison's Tombstones," remained, and the sight of them raised the ire of Shelby's men. About midday the Rebels were crossing the border into Kansas and this brought out an unmitigated vengeance from the Rebels. The military road meandered to the southwest a few miles from Grand River. Therefore, the Confederates were now in the hated home of abolition. When they realized this, the troopers began to exact revenge upon the people of Kansas. "Shelby moved this day with his division in advance, making desolate a broad track through the fertile fields of Kansas, and leaving behind him long trails of fire and smouldering [sic] ruins," one witness recorded. Another noted that "in Linn County, every house was plundered of all kinds of provisions ... that could be carried off."[2] The men were taking out their anger at Kansas for what they believed Kansans like Jennison had perpetrated in Missouri. Unfortunately, the slow pace resulting from dragging along the train and satisfying the lust for destruction meant that the Rebels made only 33 miles this day.[3] The Federals, moving unhindered, were soon in striking distance of the Army of Missouri.

An interesting perspective of the Rebel retreat was provided by Private Reader. Captured at Westport, he was now plodding along cold and hungry with a group of other Union prisoners from Kansas. Though their Confederate captors were suffering too, they were able to appropriate for their needs by taking it from the Federal prisoners and populace. Soon after his capture, a young Rebel soldier forced Reader to give up his overcoat, leaving him vulnerable to "the keen frosty nights." This only compounded the hunger that would dog him for the next several days. When one of the prisoners asked for a drink of water, one of the Rebel guards told the man there was none. Reader realized from this exchange that "it was evident that our personal comfort would not be considered." As the Rebels pushed the prisoners southward there was no food distributed among the Federals. So, for the next several days, Reader and his captured comrades of the 2nd K.S.M. would suffer cold, forced marches, privation, and insults, all with no food as the ragtag Rebels attempted to escape the hard-pressing Union divisions.[4] Eventually, the burden of dragging prisoners along would win the Union prisoners an early parole from their erstwhile captors. For the retreating Rebels, the suffering was only beginning.

As the Confederates moved south, the Federals planned their demise. As mentioned, the principle Union commanders met to plan their next move as the rout was ongoing at Westport. Curtis, in titular command of the combined forces, ordered Blunt's division to take the lead of the pursuing force, followed by Pleasonton's division. To protect the interior of Kansas, Curtis detached Thomas Moonlight from Blunt and pushed his brigade inland parallel to Price's line of retreat. Should Price veer west into Kansas, Moonlight was to block the movement until the rest of the army could close on Price's rear. To chief of staff Halleck, Curtis wrote that while Price was rapidly retreating, "dead horses and debris show his demoralized and destitute condition and my probable success in over-hauling him."[5] Thus, on the morning of the 24th, Curtis felt confident that he could inflict a mortal blow on Price in the next couple of days. Though Curtis was buoyant at the prospect of finishing Price off, the fractured Federal command would not allow him to keep this arrangement together for more than two days.

Price's dispositions were designed to keep the train together and escape south with his spoils intact as a token of success in Missouri. For the retreat south, Price placed Jo Shelby in the lead. Shelby had held the door open at Westport so that the rest of the Army of Missouri could escape the trap the Federals attempted to set for the Confederates. Now, Price asked to make good on their getaway. Also, he wanted to gobble up the Union depot at Fort Scott with its rich storehouse of military supplies. The defeat at Westport forced him to change his objective yet another time. Before Westport, Price was headed for Kansas City and Fort Leavenworth. Taking these was not possible as a result of Westport, so he assigned the new objective of Fort Scott to his fireman. Behind Shelby was Fagan's division, which had the train in tow. Finally, Marmaduke was in charge of the rear guard, tasked with protecting the army from the determined Federal army.[6] Though this was Price's latest plan, the Federals were not about to allow him to get near Fort Scott.

Both sides moved all day on the 24th, with sporadic contact between Blunt's advance guard and Marmaduke's rear guard. The Rebels had a good head start that morning, as they began movement hours before the Federals. The Confederates broke camp on the middle fork of the Grand River just before dawn, achieving a good eight-mile jump ahead of their pursuers. By contrast, the Federals under Blunt did not get moving until 8:00 a.m. while Pleasonton's division was delayed until after 10:00 AM.[7] If Price held to a disciplined march pace, he could very well elude his pursuers. But Price knew no part of discipline in the way he conducted operations. The Federals were determined to catch the foe and Price provided them the opportunity. Two factors enabled the Federals to catch up. First, the train was a tremendous stumbling block to rapid progress. Second, the plundering of the Rebels caused march discipline to break down. The constant breaking of ranks by Shelby's men and others slowed the movement of the column, as they were forced to reassemble frequently before continuing south.

As the column approached the town of Trading Post on the Marais des Cygnes River, the Confederates had moved 33 miles. The prominent terrain feature here was two mounds that overlooked the river and through which the military road passed toward Fort Scott. But the eight-mile head start the Rebels had that morning evaporated during the course of the day. Only two miles away, the lead elements of the Army of the Border were arriving to establish contact with the Rebels. As Blunt pulled up with darkness falling, Curtis ordered Pleasonton to pass through Blunt's lines and take the lead for the following day's pursuit. This did not sit well with Blunt, who wanted to stay in the lead, but Curtis intended to alternate divisions to keep them as fresh as possible to bring Price to bay.[8] Pleasonton was now in very close proximity to Price's rear, and

10. "This has been a disastrous day!"

the next morning the cavalry leader would precipitate a running engagement that would come close to destroying the Army of Missouri.

The Rebels that halted at the Marais des Cygnes were absolutely exhausted following several days in the saddle and almost constant contact with Federal forces. Adding to the discomfort was the weather—cold in late autumn and the "clouds grew darker and a heavy mist began to fall." As a result, the ragged Confederates would get little rest to rejuvenate them for further fighting. Across the lines, the Federals were also dog tired, and the elements compounded the suffering. However, there was a big difference in morale between the two sides this night. The Federals arrived in front of the Marais des Cygnes as victors and in pursuit of wounded prey. This factor gave them great motivation as they took a crude meal of "beef, roasted on sticks ... without salt or bread." The Rebels were running and had taken a beating throughout the Great Raid. They had lost severely at Pilot Knob, been turned away from Jefferson City, and were crushed at Westport. Many at all levels of the army believed they were throwing their lives away for spoils contained within the massive train.[9] These facts were bound to produce a force that was focused on survival rather than hard fighting.

As dawn approached on Tuesday, 25 October, the clouds had diminished somewhat, giving way to a drier day, though it was still gray with a heavy frost. During the night Pleasonton had managed to push his division forward through Blunt's division, taking the lead for the movement on the 25th. Pleasonton placed Sanborn in the lead, followed by Benteen—formerly Winslow's brigade, until the colonel was wounded at Westport—and Philips' brigades. Sanborn initiated the advance south toward the Marais des Cygnes at around four in the morning. As Sanborn pushed through a stand of woods, his brigade ran into Rebel pickets posted forward to provide the Confederates early warning of a Federal attack. Sanborn flushed the pickets, forcing them on the main body camped on the prairie. The Rebels were busy preparing breakfast when Sanborn burst from the timber and they had little time to form a line; but they did and temporarily halted Sanborn's advance. However, Curtis sent Pleasonton some artillery, and he in turn reinforced Sanborn with a six-gun battery. When the unit went into action, the "double-shotted canister soon caused them [the Confederates] to halt and finally beat a hasty retreat." Sanborn secured both mounds, giving him a dominating position overlooking the river and the Rebel camp, which helped speed the Confederates along in their retreat. In their haste to get away, the Rebels left their half-cooked breakfast, equipment, and two artillery pieces scattered about for the Union soldiers to capture.[10] This small engagement on the Marais des Cygnes was just the beginning of a bad day for the Army of Missouri.

The Rebels cleared the area around the mounds north of the stream just after dawn with Sanborn in pursuit. After pressing forward for a mile, Sanborn halted to have breakfast while Pleasonton pushed Benteen and Philips through Sanborn's brigade to the front. As Pleasonton was rearranging his march order, Curtis caught up with him, and the two refined their plans for the day. Curtis decided to move forward with both divisions moving parallel to each other. Blunt's division of Kansas troops would take the left of the Fort Scott Road, while Pleasonton took the right. Further west, Moonlight's brigade was at Mound City moving alongside Price's army to prevent an incursion into the Kansas interior. Once the new dispositions were complete, both divisions began to move south just after 8:00 that morning.[11]

The affair at Marais des Cygnes was an ominous development for the Army of Missouri. Though small, it forced the Confederates to continue their retreat before they were ready. As Marmaduke pulled back, he found his division halted a few miles south in front of a small meandering tributary called Mine Creek. Here, Fagan was struggling to push the train across the steep-sided creek, a process made more difficult by the previous night's rain. The train was tangled up at the narrow crossing, and over 100 of the wagons were on the north side waiting to ford the stream. Fagan's men were fanned out in a hasty defensive position only about two to four hundred yards in front of the jumble of wagons when Marmaduke arrived. This forced Marmaduke to turn about to form a hasty defense in conjunction with Fagan. Close on Marmaduke's heels were the brigades of Benteen and Philips pressing the pursuit after the affair at Marais des Cygnes.[12] As Marmaduke surveyed the landscape, his trained military eye could see that this was not a good position.

Mine Creek, although a minor stream, presented a serious obstacle to movement of a large force with accompanying vehicles. The military road gradually sloped down across an open prairie to a ford with steep sides that were slick on this day due to the previous day's rain. The enormous wagon train of 500 vehicles had churned the area and the steep sides into quagmire, thus the reason for the jumble in front of the ford. As Marmaduke gazed back toward the oncoming Federals, he was looking upslope at the enemy. The Confederates were in low ground, with an obstacle to their back, and only a few hundred yards between the front line and the obstacle. This meant that Marmaduke and Fagan would have no space to maneuver, forcing them into a fixed defense

The battlefield at Mine Creek. This point is facing south from the Federal lines looking toward the Confederate position. The treeline in the distance is the approximate course of Mine Creek. The Confederates formed their defensive line about 300 yards north of the treeline (photograph by the author).

to defend the train. Ideally, Marmaduke would have established a defense south of Mine Creek to use the obstacle to advantage, but now the stream presented a serious disadvantage.[13] With all this weighing heavily on Marmaduke's mind, he began making dispositions to meet the enemy.

Marmaduke did have one advantage on this day and it lay in the number of men he had available for combat. Between his own division and Fagan's, the Confederates brought almost 8,000 men to the field. Moving south with Benteen and Philips were some 2,700 men and now, at 11:00 a.m. the Union brigades were less than 1,000 yards away from their prey. Using the road as a guide, Marmaduke began placing units. In the center, oriented on the road northward, he placed the artillery and the 3rd Missouri Cavalry to support the guns. To the right, he shook out his division into line of battle. Fagan linked in on Marmaduke's left and fanned his division out to the left. Inexplicably, Marmaduke did not designate a reserve should some part of the line become threatened. Even worse, he made the fatal decision to fight mounted. This placed the Rebel caval-

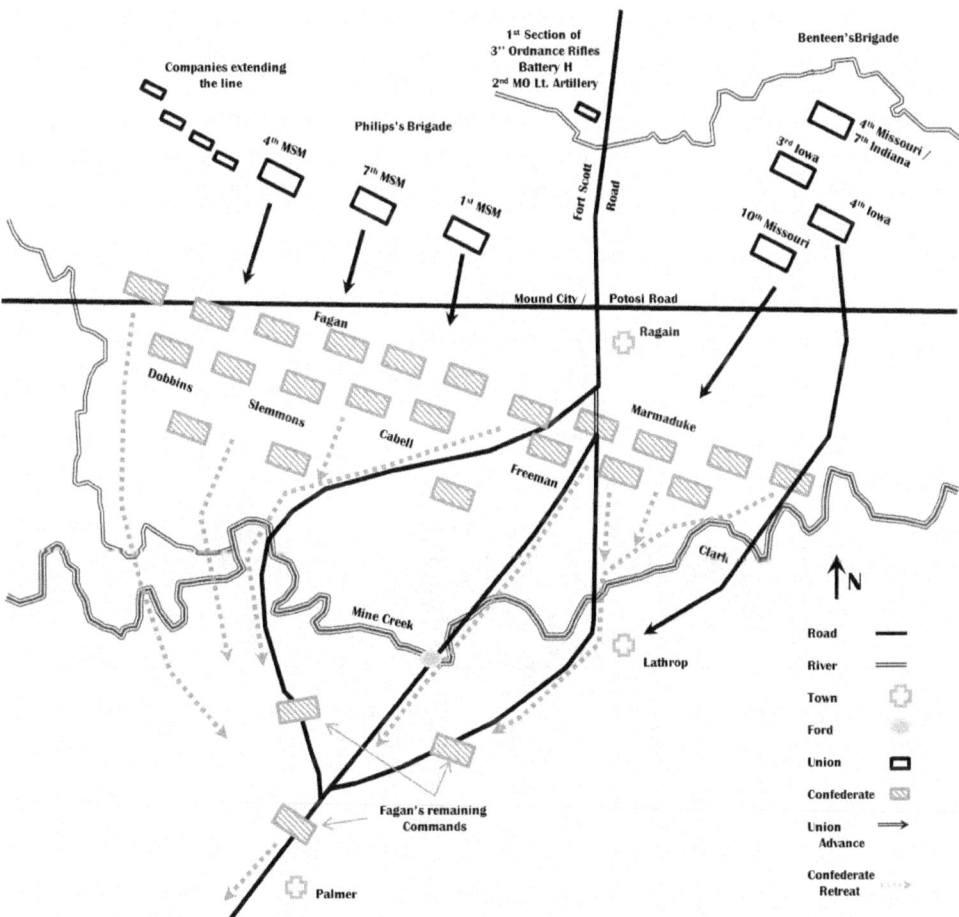

Map 5. Battle of Mine Creek on 25 October 1864. Price's rear guard is crushed here, as the enormous train is unable to negotiate the crossing in good order (map by Captain Robin Glebes).

rymen at an enormous disadvantage because they were armed with single shot, muzzle-loading rifles. Cabell would remark in his report that "the enemy, armed with Henry rifles ... far exceeded any firing we could do from my muzzle-loading Enfields." In essence, this meant the Confederates could fire only one shot because it was nearly impossible to reload such a weapon while mounted.[14] The Confederate divisions were already in trouble because of the nature of the circumstances that forced them to fight. But, these two decisions made by the normally competent Marmaduke made little sense. The only possible explanation for his loss of tactical sense is that the lack of sleep and exertion of the past week might have affected his decision making.

Marmaduke did have the wherewithal to notify Price of the tenuous situation at Mine Creek. Price, riding in his ambulance with Shelby's division, was far ahead of the rear guard that morning. As the situation was unfolding on Mine Creek, Price was already nearing the Little Osage River, with Shelby was some eight miles to the south, far from the action. Marmaduke composed a quick note informing Price that things were becoming uncomfortably dangerous for the rear. He told Price that he might need assistance from Shelby if the train could not make a clean crossing.[15] This message would prove prophetic and, unfortunately for Marmaduke, it would take too long to reach Price due to the separation between commander and subordinate.

The Union brigades sensed an opportunity as they rode into the prairie overlooking Mine Creek and the chaos transpiring along its banks. From the Federal perspective the "open prairie, sweeping away, afforded the grandest possible field for cavalry move-

The approximate location of the Confederate defensive line at Mine Creek looking north toward the Federal attack position. The Federal assault formed up just beyond the current location of the battlefield visitor center seen in the distance (photograph by the author).

ments." When Frederick Benteen moved up in late morning on the left side of Philip's brigade and surveyed the situation, he immediately concluded that he would seize the initiative:

> I at once determined to form on the left of this brigade [Philips'], especially as a few more paces brought us in view of the line of rebels; seeing the position in which he had his artillery, I immediately surmised that the rebel commander [Marmaduke] had committed a fatal blunder, and resolved to capture it. I sent an officer to the commanding officer of the brigade on my right with the information that I was going to charge, and a request for him to charge with me, for God's sake, and at the same time formed my command in to a column of regiments....

The Union brigades under Philips and Benteen were oriented on the military road, using it as a boundary between them and as an axis of advance. Benteen was on the left and Philips on the right. To make the charge, Benteen had each regiment form in a line with one behind the other, forming four successive regimental-sized lines—thus, a column of regiments. Benteen would orient on the Confederate battery in making the charge, splitting the Rebel line and then wheeling to roll the defending regiments up. Philips would support with dismounts, using his repeating rifles to suppress the Confederates. The combination of the strengths of the two brigades would facilitate the success of the charge.[16] Benteen began making the appropriate dispositions for the action.

Marmaduke might have prevented what was coming by seizing the initiative himself. As the Federals began preparing for the assault, they had to form into lines and columns to achieve the preferred method of attack as noted by Benteen in his after action report. This inevitably took time and was the point at which the Union brigades were most vulnerable, because they were not ready to receive an attack. Here again, Marmaduke seems to have lost his military judgment. A spoiling attack is a basic maneuver to buy time by throwing the enemy off balance, which Marmaduke, as a professionally trained officer, would have known.[17] But Marmaduke was in a fog on this day and simply did nothing. The result of this idleness was, in essence, an invitation to the Federals to attack at their leisure. The Union cavalry would do this in short order.

It was about 11:00 a.m. when Benteen and Philips were ready to make the attack. "The skies now cleared, and the sun smiled out upon the scene as if foretelling the glorious day that awaited us," wrote Benteen. Once everything was in order, he notified Philips of his intent to move forward. Then he gave the command to his bugler "and immediately sounded the charge." One witness recorded that "Colonel Benteen's order to charge was instantly obeyed ... [and they] started forward with their 'yell' and their bugles sounding." With Philips providing covering fire, Benteen's brigade charged and within minutes were halfway across the field. Then, unexplainably, Benteen's entire brigade halted and no one was ever able to ascertain why. Benteen's own 10th Missouri was in the lead and stopped cold, much to the chagrin of their commander. Benteen immediately moved to the front urging them to begin moving again, but his entreaties seemed to fall on deaf ears.[18] There are times on the battlefield when an invisible inertia grips a group of men who will act in concert from fear, panic, or anxiety of the unknown. The case of Benteen's brigade halting in the middle of a charge for seemingly no reason could be attributable to one of these reasons. Regardless of what caused it, this incident was the crisis moment of the day, for the Union forces had provided the Rebels with another opportunity to counterattack, upsetting the plan of the Federals. But, the Confederates remained frozen in place.

Benteen continued to plead with his men to resume the charge and "they made spasmodic efforts to brace up, but failed." Benteen was now alarmed, but the boldness of one of his regimental commanders was about to save the day. Major Abial Pierce was the commander of the 4th Iowa Cavalry, which was in column behind the 10th Missouri. When the 10th halted, stopping the rest of the brigade, Pierce had an idea to redeem the situation for Benteen. Pierce rode to the left of the line and ordered the two flank companies, A and K, to extend to the left beyond the 10th's line. Once they cleared the flank of the 10th, Pierce ordered them to charge. "The other companies had to force their way between the men of the Tenth Missouri," wrote a member of the 4th Iowa. Observing their sister regiment forcing their way forward, the 10th Missouri took heart and "joined in the charge."[19]

A much relieved Benteen drove forward, headed for the right flank of Marmaduke's division. Benteen's brigade "struck the enemy's line like a thunderbolt," wrote trooper William Scott of the 4th Iowa. The leading companies hit Marmaduke on a narrow front, followed by the rest of the brigade. The full force of Benteen's unit hit at an angle successively "from left to right, and it [the Rebel line] fell away like a row of bricks." Panic among the Rebels spread like a wildfire, and one of the reasons for their poor showing was their muzzle-loading rifles. Most were able to get one shot off and then had to struggle to reload on horseback. The time it took to perform this maneuver was too much when a cavalry charge was bearing down on them. The Rebel troopers were unable to reload, and the lack of fire during this interval allowed the Federals to close in on the line without taking casualties.[20] Thus, Benteen was able to bring the full force of his brigade to bear at the selected decisive point.

While Benteen was charging across the prairie, Philips' brigade was pouring a devastating fire from their repeating rifles and two cannon that went into action in the Federal center. When the Rebel right began disintegrating, Philips made his charge on the enemy center and left, where the green, untried brigade of Thomas Freeman was posted. The battery at the Rebel center was captured after all the gunners were shot down. Fagan's division in turn threw down the weapons and turned headlong in retreat. The rout was now complete, and for the Confederates it was every man for himself struggling to put Mine Creek between them and the Federals. One Rebel remembered having "great difficulty in crossing the creek with the crossings all blocked. The stream was everywhere full of men and horses, the Confederates trying to make their escape." For the victorious bluecoats the attack had transitioned to a full pursuit. One witness would later write, "[T]hese scenes take longer to describe than to enact." The whole engagement took no longer than thirty minutes.[21]

The hammer blow fell on the Confederate 4th Missouri Cavalry on Marmaduke's extreme right. Next, Clark's reliable brigade was hit in the flank as the men of the 4th Missouri streamed through the brigade. They held for a short time, but the flank assault was too much for them, too. As they began to pull back, Freeman's brigade was exposed to the coming storm. Philips sliced through the center, capturing the guns and turning Cabell's flank. Fagan's line melted away. The Rebel generals were scrambling around in a struggle to get their men back into line, to no avail. "Every effort was made by appeals and threats to retrieve the rout," reported Clark, "but it swept in an irresistible mass." The enemy was now gathering large numbers of prisoners from among the disordered Confederate units as their leaders were unable to get them reorganized.[22] Among the prisoners scooped up were two generals—Marmaduke and Cabell.

The story of the generals is quite intriguing. General Marmaduke was back near a bend in Mine Creek working to rally his men when the 3rd Iowa Cavalry came thundering down on them. Initially, Marmaduke believed they were more of his own men and he did not act to escape the area. Before he realized his mistake, Private James Dunlavy of the 3rd had ridden up to the general. The surprised private ordered Marmaduke from his horse as his prisoner. The young soldier then marched Marmaduke to the rear where he found Colonel Charles W. Blair. The colonel was impressed with Dunlavy's catch and guided him to General Curtis, who was quite pleased with the private's work. Dunlavy was rewarded with the Congressional Medal of Honor for his actions in the capture of Marmaduke.[23] The unfortunate general would spend the rest of the war as a prisoner, never to fight again. In the 1880s, Marmaduke would become the governor of Missouri, one of several who served on both sides during the Great Raid to hold the office.

Another soldier from the 3rd Iowa was credited with the capture of General Cabell. Like Marmaduke, Cabell was feverishly working to re-form his brigade. He became isolated and had to attempt to break out of a pocket. "I then told these thirty men to follow me," Cabell recalled. He added that "we charged through the enemy's lines and then scattered." With only three men left with him Cabell still had to jump the creek to make good his escape. His horse failed to negotiate the jump and fell on Cabell. The general was now on foot, and a party including a Federal lieutenant and three men rode up and "demanded my surrender." Cabell complied and they ordered him to the rear without an escort. The general took advantage of the lax security and made his way back to a knot of his own men. He procured a horse and again attempted to elude capture. His group, however, "rode into a company of the Third Iowa Cavalry." A running gun battle took place during which Cabell was unhorsed and captured again. As before, the captors ordered him to the rear. The wily general again looked for a way to escape, acquiring yet another horse, but his luck was about to run out.[24]

Cabell fell in with a few men from Colonel Anderson Gordon's Arkansas regiment, but as they worked to skirt the ubiquitous Federal forces, they ran into another patrol from the 3rd Iowa. Cabell had his latest horse shot from under him and was on foot when Sergeant C.M. Young cornered him demanding his surrender. Cabell complied, but this time the captor escorted him to the rear. Along the way, a Rebel deserter who had joined a Federal regiment ambled up and threatened to kill his former Confederate commander. Young jumped between the two men and drove away the erstwhile Yankee with his pistol. "I have always had a great feeling of admiration and friendship for that dashing Federal sergeant," Cabell recalled with clear feeling of respect for his captor. Sergeant Young would likewise receive the Congressional Medal Honor for his actions.[25]

As the disaster was unfolding around Mine Creek, Jo Shelby was riding hard to the rear to save the day. When Price received the dispatch from Marmaduke, he was already eight miles away, halted at the Little Osage River. The disaster on Mine Creek had already turned into a rout by the time the dispatch found him. Now alarmed, Price "immediately ordered Brigadier-General Shelby to take his old brigade … and return to the rear as rapidly as possible to support Major-Generals Fagan and Marmaduke." When Price's messenger found Shelby, he delivered the order to turn about with a verbal flourish, stating, "You alone can save the army." Shelby's biographer added affirmatively that "Shelby *did* it." Price also decided that it was time for him to pay a personal visit to the scene of the fighting. "I immediately mounted my horse and rode back at a gallop," Price reported. Shelby was ahead of him pushing his men forward to stem the tide. Price had not gone far when he met the remnants of Fagan and Marmaduke's divisions streaming to the rear. Price described this mass as retreating in "utter and indescribable confusion many of them having thrown away their arms."[26] It would take all of Shelby's skill as a leader to stop the hemorrhaging.

Only a short distance from the Little Osage, Shelby ran into the stragglers. He began working to re-form them to no avail, as "they were deaf to all entreaties and commands." Close on the heels of the fugitives was "the advancing Federals, flushed with success and clamorous for more victims." Unable to rally the panic-stricken Rebels, Shelby turned his attention to the Union brigades thundering southward. Shelby, after observing the depressing scene, "knew from the beginning that I could do nothing but resist their advance, delay them as much as possible, and depend on energy and night for the rest." Therefore, Shelby deployed his division to first slow the Union momentum, and then stop them to allow the rest of the army and trains to escape to safety. He halted a mile north of the Little Osage at a place called Charlot's Farm and "worsted" the enemy. As the Federals halted to regroup, Shelby moved rearward and redeployed for another fight on the bank of the Little Osage, where he again bloodied the nose of the bluecoats. He then crossed the river and occupied a hill overlooking the south bank. After an hour, he fell back again, but by this time darkness was setting in, putting an end to the horrible day.[27] For the rest of the night the disorganized Army of Missouri would continue south to attempt to put some distance between them and the Federals.

The entry in Dr. McPheeters' diary on this day exclaimed, "This has been a disastrous day!" The surgeon was shocked by the scene, remarking that it "beggars description and I shall not attempt it." The scene was indeed one of destruction. The Confederates had suffered a devastating loss and had come within a hair's breadth of total destruction, Shelby finally arresting the disaster. Nevertheless, the loss was extensive. For example, the divisions of Fagan and Marmaduke were rendered combat ineffective as a result of the battle of Mine Creek. Between their divisions, they lost around 900–1,000 men, including 300–400 killed and wounded, and 500 prisoners. Further, Benteen and Philips captured eight guns, quantities of horses, ammunition, arms, and a large number of wagons that were trapped on the north side of Mine Creek. They also lost several key leaders, like Cabell and Marmaduke, Colonel Slemmon, three more colonels, and a host of field grade officers. Thus, the fighting power of the Rebels was significantly reduced, exposing them to the possibility of eventual destruction unless they could escape the grip of the relentless Army of the Border. By contrast, the Federals lost only eight killed and sixty wounded, and the victory gave them a sense of euphoria combined with the feeling that the Rebels were on the ropes.[28] If the Federals could keep up the pressure, the end of the Army of Missouri was at hand.

Unfortunately, the combined Union army was about to come apart due to the ad hoc command arrangements, resulting in a loss of pressure on their prey. As the battle at the Little Osage was winding down, Alfred Pleasonton was already making arrangements to break off the action. His division was admittedly exhausted and hungry, both men and horses. In light of this, he decided to divert his command from pursuit of Price to Fort Scott, where rest and rations awaited.[29] Of course, Fort Scott was southwest of the main road and Price was now headed southeast, in the opposite direction. The relaxation of pressure would likely allow Price to escape rather than the Union finishing off the Army of Missouri. Letting Price off the hook was not what Curtis had in mind.

General Curtis was attempting to push more troops to the front during the pursuit when he heard of Pleasonton's intent to move to Fort Scott. Curtis immediately went there to discuss the situation with Pleasonton, as he was "anxious to procure cordial cooperation between our forces." As the two were conferring Pleasonton told Curtis of his intent to refit his command and added that "his health would not admit his further continuance in the field." There is some evidence that Pleasonton may have had some physical issues by this point in the campaign. Pleasonton seems to have suffered a fall from his horse in the days leading up to Mine Creek. Thus, it is quite possible that the physical exertion of the campaign, combined with the fall, could have incapacitated him.[30] Regardless of the issue, it was clear that Pleasonton was not motivated to continue with his role in the operation. Curtis' entreaties fell on deaf ears and his anger at the situation rose in proportion.

Another development this evening would deepen Curtis' anger and make it more likely that Price's army would make its escape. James Blunt stewed all day at having a supporting position in the pursuit of Price. His division had seen no action all day, but Curtis had intended to alternate his divisions at the front to keep them fresh, which meant that Blunt would move forward the next day. However, Blunt upset this plan when he too decided—without authorization—to divert his division to Fort Scott. He reported, "I learned that General Pleasonton, with the remainder of his command, had marched to Fort Scott. My command needing subsistence and forage, I made a detour to the right, passing through Fort Scott for the purpose of supplying them and be in readiness to follow the pursuit the next morning."[31] In truth, this move would not place Blunt in readiness to pursue the next morning because he was so far out of position. With Price moving southeast and most of Curtis' army at Fort Scott to the southwest, Price could move away unmolested.

Curtis had planned to resupply his troops in the field so they could remain forward and in contact with Price. Earlier that day, Curtis sent a staff officer to Fort Scott to coordinate the assembly of a train with rations and forage for the divisions. The train actually formed and marched out to meet the divisions in the field. However, the commander of the train encountered Pleasonton's and Blunt's divisions moving toward Fort Scott and he turned it around, heading back to the fort. Unfortunately, two brigades were not with the divisions, and as a result of miscommunication, Benteen and McNeil's units spent the night in the field with nothing to eat.[32] Meanwhile, Price was making rapid progress in moving away from the discordant Union army.

The Army of Missouri arrived at the Marmiton River very late on the 25th of October. Here, Price reluctantly made the decision to abandon the objective of taking Fort

Scott, and, much to his chagrin, to destroy the precious train. The Marmiton is about ten miles south of Mine Creek and upon arrival, Price's staff began writing the order that would tell the men to destroy the train—the only evidence of any positive result from the invasion. G.O. #22 designated the starting time for the march as 2:00 a.m. on the 26th of October. It changed the order of march, designating Shelby's division as the rear guard and pushing the remnants of Fagan and Marmaduke's divisions to the front with what was left of the train between their units. Paragraph II of the order stated, "The army train, with the following exceptions, will be parked under directions of division commanders and burnt before leaving camp." There were not many exceptions, but it did allow each division and brigade headquarters one wagon, another to each division and brigade for supplies, and an ambulance. The ordnance wagons were reduced to what was "absolutely required." Finally, all remaining ambulances were consolidated under the control of the army surgeon.[33] It must have pained Price greatly to issue this order. Price's surgeon, Dr. McPheeters, was busy all night executing his part of G.O. #22. He recorded: "It was ordered to destroy part of the train. [I] arranged and consolidated my baggage and medicines and gave up one wagon. We were to start at 2 a.m. and it was 1 a.m. before I completed my arrangements. [I] destroyed a great many valuables and personal effects. We had a bon fire of wagons and other things. The command moved at 2 [A.M.] but we did not get off until ½ past 3 [A.M.] so I got no sleep."

Lack of sleep was a common occurrence on this night, for every Rebel was engaged in executing the order. Shelby's chief of staff wrote that "all night, with the exception of an hour's halt, the march went on." At the Marmiton "nearly all the wagons were burned, vast quantities of ammunition destroyed ... in one mass smoking smouldering [sic] ruin.[34] Price should have destroyed the train weeks earlier in order to obtain speed in consonance with a raid once the invasion changed from a campaign to hold land. Price's stubbornness would not allow him to do this and thus he created a vulnerability that the converging Federal forces were able to exploit. Retaining the train nearly destroyed the army and many men were lost in defending it. The irony of the raid is that the only positive result—and the train was a questionable positive—was destroyed at the hands of Price's own men. Jettisoning the train finally allowed Price to make some real distance, covering almost sixty miles in the next 24 hours.[35]

As the Confederates were casting off all their impediments, the Union prisoners captured at Westport were still in tow. Private Reader had marched over sixty miles from Westport to Mine Creek in less than 48 hours. All along, Reader and his comrades were subjected to verbal abuse at the hands of the captors, hunger, and exposure. One guard took Reader's overcoat, and another traded his own ragged butternut jacket for the Kansan's vest. Reader now looked more like the enemy than like his own army, and he would soon use this to his advantage.[36]

Reader remembered that as he was tramping along on 25 October, he "drank [water] from horse tracks" because of his thirst. Nevertheless, the Rebels were about to lose interest in their prisoners due to the unfolding fight. "About noon we crossed a creek," he recalled, while many squads of Rebels were headed in the opposite direction to join the fighting. "We heard firing off and on, for several hours afterwards," recorded Reader. This hard, running fight caused the guards to let their vigilance down. In so doing, Reader saw an opportunity to escape. When the column stopped on the Marmiton, darkness began to set in. The prisoners were moved into a stand of timber that accentuated the black of night. With no guards in sight, Reader slipped away down to the stream. A Confederate trooper, believing that the butternut-clad Reader was a Rebel, befriended him. Reader kept up the ruse by taking on the identity of a Confederate. Then, he slipped away again, making his way north using the stars as his guide.[37]

The next morning, Reader ran into a farmer in the farmer's field and the scared private inquired of him, "[A]re you a Union man?" The man replied that he was, to which Reader exclaimed, "Then I am all right!" The farmer was not so sure since Reader looked like a Confederate. But, since Reader was "going the wrong way for a rebel," the man was willing to give him the benefit of the doubt. He agreed to take Reader to Fort Scott to sort things out and they proceeded there, after "an epicurean feast of biscuit, fresh pork, and sweet potatoes." When they reached Barnesville near Fort Scott, the farmer turned him over to a detachment of the 15th Kansas Cavalry. After some questioning about Reader's hometown of Topeka, the sergeant in charge accepted his story. The private was released to return home the next day. He arrived back in Topeka on the 30th of October, where he reported to his commander, Colonel Veale, and received his discharge.[38] For Reader, the war was over and he had done his service.

While Price was lightening the army's load, the Federal army was imploding because of poor command relationships. William S. Rosecrans was losing interest in pursuing Price. Since the Army of Missouri had crossed into Kansas, Rosecrans viewed the Confederate invasion as a problem for Curtis and his department. Therefore, Rosecrans issued orders to his units to return to their bases on the 27th of October. This would remove almost 8,000 veteran troops from the pursuit and this prospect was unsettling to Curtis. On the 25th, immediately after the victory at Mine Creek, Curtis had issued G.O. #57 rescinding martial law and sending the rest of the Kansas State Militia home. The next day, U.S. Grant issued an order to Rosecrans through Halleck telling him to send Smith's troops back to George Thomas at Nashville. Thus, information received on the 27th from Pleasonton that Rosecrans had ordered him back to Missouri did not sit well. The combination of these losses pulled over 20,000 troops from the operation, leaving Curtis with less than 4,000 men for the pursuit. Of these, Blunt had less than 2,000 readily available, and they were at Fort Scott.[39] The lack of unity of command had once again intervened to prevent the Federal forces from achieving a more decisive outcome from the campaign.

Curtis sent off a flurry of dispatches to try to reverse the drain of his available forces. In a dispatch to Halleck, Curtis informed him of Rosecrans' orders in a veiled appeal for Halleck or Grant to countermand the orders from Rosecrans. Grant obliged his request by ordering that all available troops from both departments continue the pursuit of Price to the Arkansas River. Curtis received this dispatch around 1:00 a.m. on 30 October 1864 and within minutes informed Rosecrans and all his subordinates of Grant's order.[40] Curtis now believed he could maintain the pressure on Price with a credible force, but his confidence was misplaced.

Rosecrans did nothing to comply with either Grant's order or Curtis' request. Further, only Benteen of all Rosecrans' subordinates obeyed the order received from Curtis, and he was not able to move into position in time to affect the remainder of the pursuit. Thus, Curtis was able to keep only Blunt, with less than 2,000 men, in the field. Curtis reported this to Halleck, who was livid at Rosecrans' failure to obey. Rosecrans' intransigence would cost him his job. On 9 December 1864, Rosecrans acknowledged receipt of G.O. #294 from the War Department relieving him of command. Major General Grenville Dodge assumed command and so ended Rosecrans' service in the Civil War.[41] The fractured Union command structure had prevented the destruction of Price, in spite of the Confederate commander's many mistakes. Had Rosecrans at least attempted to establish a more cooperative relationship with Curtis, it is quite possible Price would not have left Missouri with his army intact, but such a relationship did not happen. Ultimately, if Grant and Halleck wanted Price destroyed, they should have promulgated an order assigning one of the two to command or brought in another general to command both departments as a theater of operations. The failure to adhere to this basic principle of war cost the Federals a great opportunity.

While Price may have received a reprieve from the Federal armies, the forces of nature would provide no relief. "Never did men suffer greater hardships than did Gen. Sterling Price's troops after this defeat [at Mine Creek]," one Rebel recounted. There were several reasons for this. First, there was no time for foraging because the army had to keep moving and stay together to maintain the march pace. The Rebels had to put distance between themselves and the Federals, leaving no time to search for food. One Union commander presciently noted that "Price will be pursued by General Starvation across the river [the Arkansas]—a most formidable enemy to him." Second, the areas they were now moving through were denuded of forage. After four years of war, there was little left for man or beast. Third, the weather was becoming harsh, as winter was not far off. Finally, disease would become an issue as the lack of nutrition and unsanitary conditions would make the men susceptible to contracting virulent infections.[42] It would take several weeks and hundreds of miles of marching to return the Army of Missouri's starting point.

The Battle of Mine Creek was the largest engagement ever fought on Kansas soil and the only fight between conventional forces during the Civil War. But, more important, it was a decisive battle that effectively destroyed the remaining offensive combat power of the Army of Missouri. Aside from a couple of minor actions during the final stages of the retreat, the Trans-Mississippi Confederates would never again fight a battle of any consequence. The Rebel forces west of the river were essentially out of the war. Price finally had to abandon his precious train and he came away from the invasion-turned-raid with nothing to show for his effort or the sacrifices of the men. He accomplished none of his objectives and had to abandon his last point of interest, Fort Scott. The defeat at Mine Creek sealed the fate of Missouri and the upcoming elections. Missouri was solidly in the Union camp and would turn out decisively for Lincoln in two weeks. Thus, Mine Creek was the emphatic exclamation point on the entire disastrous campaign.

The northern press locally and nationally extolled the victory at Mine Creek. An article in the *Weston Border Times* a few days after the fight described the disaster at Mine Creek with a mix of exaggeration and accuracy: "The rebel army [is] steadily driven southward, retreating near the Kansas line. About 5,000 prisoners have been captured, among them Generals Marmaduke and Cabell, much of Price's plunder retaken, and the balance destroyed by himself to prevent it from falling into our hands."

The article concluded by noting that "Gen. Curtis is in hot pursuit." The threat to western Missouri and eastern Kansas had now abated and the people could rest easy. *Harper's Weekly* told its readers that "Price is retreating toward Cassville [Missouri], and will be vigorously pursued." The paper went on to state, "Price has been utterly defeated in his Missouri campaign, and chiefly by the cooperation of Kansas troops and by Pleasanton's [sic] prompt movements." In the writer's enthusiasm, he added an interrogative to conclude the article: "Will Rosecrans give us a second Pea Ridge?"[43] The answer to this question was an emphatic no.

The fragmented command situation in the Federal western departments guaranteed Price's safety. When he issued orders to move his forces back to their posts in Missouri, Rosecrans tacitly accepted that the Army of Missouri would survive. The pursuit would continue under Curtis, who would do his best to keep up the pressure, but he simply did not have the force left to pin Price down. Aside from a couple of minor engagements, the campaign was over except for the long retreat. Though the Rebels had accomplished little and were destined to suffer, they would at least escape, much to the chagrin of Curtis, Grant, and President Lincoln.

11

"This unfortunate campaign"

The Army of Missouri arrived at Carthage on the night of 26 October 1864 after crossing the state border on the previous evening. The Rebels had marched over 56 miles and only stopped long enough to burn their wagons in the aftermath of Mine Creek. Thus, they had marched for almost twenty-four hours without rest. The long retreat would now begin in earnest. While the situation was already in dire straits, things were about to get much worse for the Rebels. Morale was low in the ranks and after destroying the train the Rebels were left with no evidence that they had accomplished anything during the march through Missouri. Now, Price had to focus on extending his army back to Arkansas safely to prevent the Federals from achieving destruction of it. While Price would make his escape, the army would continue to lose men at an alarming rate to various causes, including desertion, disease, and indefinite furloughs. His escape was made possible in part because of the fizzling Federal pursuit. In spite of a valiant effort on Curtis' part, his attempt to corner Price failed because he could not bring enough troops together to hurt the retreating Confederates. Nevertheless, the invasion-turned-raid was a disaster for the Trans-Mississippi Confederacy and the recriminations would begin almost immediately.

The Confederates had a dreary march on 26 March since "it was very dark and inclined to rain." Yet the army continued southward in the effort to make a clean break from their Federal tormentors. "No stops could be made for rest," remembered one participant. There was no food to eat because the troopers could not halt to forage. The Army of Missouri pulled into Carthage—a town thoroughly ravaged by the war—around 9:00 p.m. after an epic march. Within a couple of hours, the Rebels finally had a meal and then lay down to rest. Price's surgeon remembered finally getting to bed around 1:00 a.m. on 27 October and that he "slept soundly once I got at it."[1] In spite of the hard marching of the previous day, Price's lax discipline allowed the men to sleep in on the 27th far longer than prudence dictated.

The army did not get started on Thursday, 27 October, until 11:00 a.m. Considering the pressing need to increase the gap between the Army of Missouri and Curtis' forces, it seems incredible that the Rebels failed to move sooner. Price reported that he issued the orders to move after 9:00 a.m. but it took a couple of hours before the rear was finally moving. Part of the reason for the late start was that Price decided to lighten his load even further. Though Private Reader had made his escape from the Rebels, Price's men were still dragging along several hundred prisoners from Westport. These men were on foot and had already marched well over 100 miles in the four days since their capture. Price noted that they "became so much exhausted by fatigue that out of humanity I paroled them." Casting off the prisoners should have facilitated the coverage of distance and speed by the Confederates, but this did not happen. Though they marched all day, when the Rebels came to a halt at Shoal Creek around dusk, they had marched only about 22 miles.[2] Price had seemingly resumed the precedent for marching he had kept the whole campaign. Such a slow pace again allowed the pursuing Federals to catch up.

The Confederates could have continued moving after the onset of darkness on the evening of the 27th. However, Price opted for more rest and feeding the troops. Plus, some incidents of the day's march worked against progress on the 27th. The Rebels were unexpectedly held up by a small stream that they struggled to ford. Shelby was livid with his division when he found them milling around what he considered nothing more than a creek. One observer noted that Shelby yelled and "cursed himself hoarse" encouraging his old brigade across the stream. This allowed the pesky Federals to eliminate the lead Price had gained on the 26th. Yet the men must have become reenergized on the 27th. Reports from that day note that morale improved considerably, primarily because the Army of Missouri made no contact with the enemy and the weather improved. Though this was positive, there were other signs that morale remained frayed. In Price's report, he noted that "a number of desertions took place among the Arkansas troops and new recruits."[3] The dichotomy between these two observations reveals that the overall morale of the army was still poor and improvement would depend on making a clean escape and the ability to meet the physical needs of the troops. Only time would tell if Price could achieve these conditions.

The Rebels took up the line of march on the morning of the 28th somewhat refreshed after a full night's rest. Again, the march took on the characteristics of a leisurely stroll through the country as the army set a slow pace. The Rebels marched for only half a day on the 28th for two reasons. First, Price learned that a small Federal outpost was located at Newtonia and he intended to eliminate it. Second, Newtonia contained a flour mill and stopping there would provide the opportunity to supply the army with bread. The Confederates quickly accomplished the task of scattering the small Union post at Newtonia and then Price stopped to camp, in spite of the fact that it was only noon. The Confederates had moved a mere seventeen miles on this day when they needed to push harder to keep ahead of their pursuers.[4] Despite the tenuous situation of the Army of Missouri, Price had inexplicably slowed the pace back to the average he had maintained throughout the raid. As a result, the Federals were able to catch up to the slow moving Confederates.

The Army of the Border had not been idle since the night of the 25th. Though internal divisions had caused myriad issues, Curtis and Blunt were determined to bring Price and his army to bay. In order to do so, the Union army would need a man of energy, drive, and boldness to corner the Rebels. Curtis had just this sort of man in James Blunt, and the latter was certainly eager to come to grips with the enemy. Blunt lobbied hard on the night of the 25th at Fort Scott to hit the road early the next morning in order to "place ourselves on the enemy's flank." Curtis agreed, and since Pleasonton was now out of the picture, he placed Blunt in the advance with orders to "move early on the 26th." Due to issues of supply and command arrangements, Blunt did not get started until noon on the 26th.[5] Though he got a late start, he drove his men relentlessly.

Blunt was able to close the gap between himself and the enemy largely because of the fact that Price slowed the pace of his march on the 27th.

Blunt was pleased to lead the pursuit out of Fort Scott. He moved due east with a little over a thousand men in his small division, followed by Sanborn and Moonlight's brigades—altogether slightly over 2,000 men. Blunt pushed his men hard to catch up with Price and late on the 26th he "struck the enemy's trail near Shanghai [in Barton County, Missouri] and pressed forward as rapidly as the condition of our stock would permit." Blunt drove on through the 27th, bivouacking near Carthage late that evening. All around he found evidence of the retreating Rebels, who had spent the previous evening at Carthage. Here, Blunt's division discovered abandoned sick and wounded Rebels, the paroled prisoners, and debris commonly associated with a retreating army. Blunt determined to move "at daylight" in order to gain contact with Price on the 28th. Before he did so, Blunt sent messages to McNeil and Pleasonton to request support, as he surmised that he was close to Price. Blunt pushed out on the morning of the 28th, arriving at Granby around noon, only five miles north of Newtonia. His scouts found the Confederates, camped on the prairie just south and west of Newtonia, that afternoon and Blunt determined to bring on an engagement that day.[6] The last battle of the Great Raid was about to begin.

Price was in camp on the prairie near Newtonia at mid-afternoon on the 28th. His men were busily making use of the flour mill in Newtonia grinding grain to feed the troops. This delay—whether necessary or not—allowed Blunt, with the advance of the Army of the Border, to catch up on 28 October. Another probable reason for the Confederate stopover at Newtonia was the mistaken belief that the Federal army had stopped pursuing the Army of Missouri.[7] This seems incredible, but Price's previous pattern of behavior and lack of discipline lend credence to this argument.

The 28th was a Friday and the weather was fair as the Federals under Blunt debouched onto the prairie north of Newtonia. As Blunt observed the assembled Rebels around Newtonia, he immediately decided to attack the much larger Army of Missouri. "General Blunt determined to push forward with the small force at his disposal," one participant noted, "trusting to the arrival of other troops to complete the rout which he predetermined upon." This was boldness bordering on rashness on Blunt's part. He arrived at Newtonia with, by his own account, a force "not to exceed one thousand men."[8] Yet he was charging headlong into battle against a force that still numbered at least 7–8,000 men. Further, the commander of the Rebel rear guard was Jo Shelby with 2,000 men in his division. He was Price's best commander and probably the best combat general in the entire Trans-Mississippi. Such facts never seemed to stop Blunt and he charged into a battle that came very close to becoming a stinging defeat for his force.

The battle began about 2:00 p.m. when the main body of Blunt's small division arrived on an eminence overlooking Newtonia. Blunt immediately shook his division out into two brigade lines from march column, posting the 1st Colorado Battery on the rise overlooking the plain. Then he ordered a charge under the covering fire from the artillery, with Colonel James Ford's 4th Brigade in the lead. The 16th Kansas of the 4th Brigade was on the left and the 2nd Colorado on the right. Behind these regiments was a second line consisting of the 14th and 15th Kansas cavalries, with two mountain howitzers, all commanded by the Jayhawker Colonel Charles Jennison. Blunt personally led the charge of the first line and "they swept across the plain at a gallop until within musket range of the enemy's line." Since Blunt was "convinced of their intention to avoid a fight" he was surprised when he met stiff resistance just north of a line of timber bordering Newtonia.[9] Blunt's rashness placed these two small brigades in a very difficult position, and he realized it as soon as Shelby's men opened fire.

Jo Shelby knew what was happening as soon as he heard the report of the 1st Colorado's cannons. He immediately formed his division for battle: "[D]ismounting every man of my division, I formed my line of battle just in time to meet the onset." The Confederates emerged from the timber in a solid line consisting of Thompson's brigade on the left and Jackman's on the right. Since the Rebels were dismounted, they could quickly reload their muskets to pour a high volume of fire into the oncoming Federal brigades. Shelby added the weight of his artillery under Captain Richard Collins, and soon both sides were face-to-face trading shots.[10] As Shelby brought more troops and firepower into the fight it was soon evident that Blunt was in deep trouble.

Thompson saw that the Confederates had the advantage and he ordered a countercharge. Moving forward "with a loud and ringing cheer," Thompson, with Shelby's old Iron Brigade, was soon driving the Federal line back on its supports. Though the Confederates were dismounted, they had the advantage of overlapping the Union flanks, in addition to having numerical superiority. Therefore, Blunt's men were forced to fall back. The sight of Ford's brigade falling back nearly caused a panic in Jennison's brigade and a stampede almost unfolded. However, Blunt and several other officers managed to stabilize the line. The Colorado took the dismounted Confederates under fire and the countercharge halted. In one funny incident, a participant recalled that some apples he was carrying were "made pomace," ruining his lunch when a Federal cannonball took the tail of his coat off. Though the Rebel's lunch was gone, he survived the fight with nothing worse than embarrassment. Meanwhile, Blunt's decision to attack the superior Confederates was beginning to haunt him since the counted-upon reinforcements were much farther from the battlefield than he expected. In addition, he was running short of ammunition because, during the toe-to-toe fighting, copious amounts were expended. Compounding this problem was the fact Blunt had outrun his supply train, which contained the ordnance.[11] If help did not arrive soon he was in real danger of capture or annihilation.

Blunt fully realized the gravity of the situation and "sent back messengers repeatedly to hurry forward the other troops," but none were forthcoming. Dusk was nearing and Shelby was preparing to open a flank attack on Blunt's exposed left. Blunt was about to send orders for a general retreat when "the brigade of Gen'l Sanborn came in sight." He reversed his decision and "immediately ordered him [Sanborn] forward to form on my left." This extended the Federal line so that the Rebels no longer overlapped Blunt's line. This fact, combined with the onset of darkness, convinced Shelby of the need to withdraw and the Confederates took up their retrograde movement. Price had already sent the small train and the remnants of Marmaduke and Fagan's divisions south out of danger. Now, Shelby pulled back and resumed his position as the army's rear guard.[12] The battle of Newtonia was concluded and both sides continued south in its aftermath.

Newtonia was a minor engagement in terms of the larger campaign, but it demonstrated the fact that the pursuit was not over. Price, before Newtonia, seems to have believed that the Federals had stopped pursuing his army. The encounter at Newtonia disabused him of this notion and he was soon on the road south, albeit at a moderate pace. Only the continued turmoil in the Union high command provided Price with the respite he needed to make a clean escape. The battle of Newtonia involved 4–5,000 troops engaged on both sides. Blunt reported that he lost 18 killed, 95 wounded, and one missing for a total of 114 casualties. No Confederate leader made a report of Rebel casualties, but based on anecdotal evidence we can make a reasonable estimate. Price's chief surgeon reported treating some 25 soldiers, while Federal commanders reported total casualties ranging from 175 to 500.[13] These, as in most cases in the Civil War, are almost certainly overestimates. It is safe to estimate that Rebel casualties were probably roughly equal to or less than the Federal losses. Therefore, it is reasonable to suppose that Price's army lost somewhere between 100 and 125 total casualties.

Newtonia was the last significant engagement of the Civil War in Missouri. After ten years of guerrilla and open warfare, the ensuing quiet was welcome to those who remained in the border region. Both sides claimed Newtonia as a victory. It is true that Shelby checked Blunt's advance with a stinging defeat, but Price had to abandon the field, leaving his sick and wounded. Thus, from an operational perspective, nothing had changed and the Rebels were still reeling. Newtonia simply informed Price that he was still in trouble and needed to continue moving south, preferably at an accelerated pace. He would press the retreat, but at the same plodding rate of march for the next ten days. The chaos in the Federal command allowed Price to get away in spite of the slow rate of movement the Rebels continued to set. One Rebel noted, "After our rout at Marais des Cygne [sic] there was not a day but what the Federals could have bagged Price's demoralized and cut-to-pieces army had they pressed it with vigor and military skill."[14] This is certainly true, but "vigor and military skill" was lacking because of the nagging issue of a fragmented command structure.

Curtis made herculean efforts in the aftermath of Newtonia to remedy the command situation, but with even less success than earlier in the campaign. In the wake of Newtonia, Curtis wrote to Halleck to inform him of the "victory" there and his next steps, including continuing the pursuit of Price. But he also penned a complaint about Rosecrans' efforts to pull his troops back to their respective districts. "Orders from General Rosecrans," he recounted, "were received, taking General McNeil to Rolla and General Sanborn to Springfield.... I am left with only the fragment of my own regular volunteers, not exceeding 1,000 fit for duty." Halleck reiterated in his reply that Grant wanted Price pursued to the line of the Arkansas River. Curtis, in turn, sent a series of dispatches in an attempt to reassemble a credible force to pressure the Army of Missouri.[15] Yet Rosecrans and his subordinates demurred, and every minute the various Federal commands wasted while dispersed in several directions gave Price the respite he needed to make his way south of the Arkansas.

One incident in relation to the sparring between Curtis and Rosecrans is instructive of the lack of teamwork and cooperation by units in Rosecrans' Department of Missouri. Sanborn, like the other brigade commanders, received the order from Curtis to rejoin the pursuit on 30 October. However, rather than comply, Sanborn appealed to Rosecrans for relief from obeying the order by claiming that it was not "legitimate under the circumstances." Rosecrans knew of Halleck and Grant's desire to continue the pursuit, but instead of ordering Sanborn to abide by Curtis' instruction, he simply told Sanborn to make "judicious dispositions." What did this mean? Sanborn took more than 48 hours in requesting clarification before doing nothing.[16] Thus, Sanborn hid behind Rosecrans—his commander—to find a way to contravene the order. The result was that Curtis did not have adequate forces to mount a credible pursuit.

On the evening of 30 October, Curtis wrote a long report to Halleck again pressing the chief of staff to order Rosecrans to his support. He wrote:

> He [Price] has destroyed most of his train and is very destitute, but all of his men being mounted he continues to make rapid progress, which can only be overcome by extraordinary efforts on the part of our troops. The delay occasioned by General Rosecrans' orders will be equivalent to thirty-six hours, but it is partially compensated by a little rest which we were enabled to procure in this vicinity.... I do not mean to deprecate others, of whom I shall speak in my proper report, and who have not only been gallant on many fields, but are constantly willing to aid me to the utmost of human endurance to carry out what I consider a complete result of this campaign.[17]

The last sentence was a veiled slap at Rosecrans for not providing the support Curtis believed would enable him to destroy Price. Though he was polite in his report, Curtis was seething with anger at Rosecrans' behavior. Unfortunately, nothing that Curtis wrote would convince Rosecrans to change course and, as a result, Price would make it nearly unscathed to the Arkansas River. Blunt would later lament the loss of time in trying to cajole Rosecrans into supporting Curtis. "We had now lost two days' time," he wrote, "which rendered it very improbable that we could again overtake the enemy."[18] He was correct in this assessment.

Price moved south from Newtonia in the aftermath of the battle, making several miles before stopping just short of the Arkansas state line. In his report, Price noted that he was under no pressure from the Federals, stating there was "nothing known of any advance on the part of the enemy." Curtis' worst fear had already come to fruition, as Price made his way south with no contact from his pursuers. Thus, on the 29th the Army of Missouri reentered Arkansas, marching 26 miles and moving at their leisure. Over the next couple of days, Price put another 43 miles behind him, stopping near Boonsborough on the border of the Indian Territory. The weather had turned sharply colder and disease was already beginning to strike the weakened Confederate troops. Nevertheless, Price momentarily saw an opportunity to make an attack at a Federal garrison that might add laurels to this disappointing campaign.[19]

On 1 November 1864, Price received a message through Fagan from Colonel William H. Brooks, commanding the 34th Arkansas north of the Arkansas River. Colonel Brooks had invested the Federal garrison at Fayetteville, and with Price and his army passing by, Brooks requested assistance in capturing the place. Brooks sent the message to Fagan, who endorsed it with a request for permission to assist Brooks' men. "As this was a place of considerable importance," reported Price "its capture would be of great advantage to the cause.... I ordered a detail of 500 men and two guns to be made for that purpose."[20] Clearly, Price was grasping for one last chance to justify the great expenditure of resources during the Great Raid.

The detail sent to Fayetteville came from Shelby's division, although Fagan assumed command of the effort. This is indicative of the state of morale and discipline within

Fagan's division. His Arkansas troops were roughly handled at Mine Creek, and a week later they were still suffering the ill effects of the battle. Price knew this and decided to have Shelby's men shoulder the load in taking Fayetteville since this division was the only effective fighting force he had available. Yet, even Shelby's division had no enthusiasm for the task. Fagan diverted east from the line of march, moving on Fayetteville on 2 November. The force arrived after a 20-mile march, joining Brooks' Arkansas troops in the investment of Fayetteville. Upon conferring with Brooks, Fagan decided to attack the Federal garrison of 1,100 Arkansas Unionists in an attempt to capture it immediately rather than continuing the siege. However, Fagan could not convince his forces to close with the enemy, as not even Shelby's men had the stomach to risk their lives in this venture. Further, horrible weather in the form of a fall snowstorm inhibited the desire to make an assault. Thus, Price would not take his latest objective, maintaining the pattern of failure he had set since the start of the campaign. Fagan pulled back from Fayetteville in the wake of the abortive assault and again joined the procession southward to avoid pursuing Federal forces.[21]

The Army of Missouri arrived at Cane Hill on 1 November with the weather turning even colder, but with no sign of the enemy in the rear. Price had hugged the border with Indian Territory as he moved through Arkansas, and at one point the army temporarily crossed into the future state of Oklahoma. After the failed stab at Fayetteville, Price's goal was focused on placing the army safely south of the Arkansas River and beyond reach of its Union pursuers. The weather was making this difficult, as on 2 November a deluge of rain soaked the army. Then, on 3 November, the Army of Missouri remained in camp due to snow. The ragged condition of the army combined with the lack of food and the poor weather was giving rise to a new danger, disease. Dr. McPheeters noted in his diary that the weather was "horrible" on 2 November and "miserable, cold, snowy, muddy disagreeable" on the 3rd. Eleven days later he recorded an outbreak of smallpox in the ranks.[22] All of this was depressing morale, which was already poor as the calendar turned the page to November. The combination of a series of defeats, poor discipline, hunger, and the deteriorating weather would wear down the army to the point that it would lose combat effectiveness. This would happen free of molestation from the Federal forces.

Try as he might, Samuel R. Curtis could not muster a worthwhile pursuit in the first week of November. In spite of Grant's orders, all of Rosecrans' units failed to report to Curtis, with the exception of Benteen's brigade. This left Curtis with Blunt's tiny division, Benteen's brigade, and the small garrison at Fayetteville, which Curtis ordered to join the pursuit after Fagan broke off the engagement there. This was a total of about 3,000 troops available to continue the pursuit. Curtis had these men assembled near Fayetteville on 4 November, and he started south from that point, camping on the old Prairie Grove battlefield in the evening. As Blunt later observed, "We were twenty-four hours behind them [the Rebels]," making it difficult to catch up with Price in the poor weather conditions. Price had left Cane Hill that very morning, angling west along the border of the Indian Territory. The army marched about fourteen miles on the 4th, keeping a full day ahead of the Federals.[23]

Curtis remained at Prairie Grove on the 5th to gather forage for the horses, which were now depleted from days of pursuing the Confederates. Price took advantage of

Curtis' lethargy by marching another 18 miles on 5 November to the Sallisaw River in Indian Territory, placing him within a day's march of the Arkansas River and safety. Curtis finally moved on 6 November at daylight, and as he arrived at Cane Hill, the army took "a large number of sick and broken-down rebel prisoners." Obviously, Price was abandoning any impediments to his movement south. Also, he had begun furloughing some of his Arkansas troops. Morale was extremely low in Fagan's division and desertions had already started. Price decided to provide furloughs to these men with the expectation that they would rejoin the army in the spring. John Darr recounted that he and about thirty men left the army following the attack at Fayetteville. They made their way to Clarksville, Arkansas, nearly running afoul of Federals who "infested" the country. From there, they scattered to their homes, but Darr was captured shortly after arriving home and he would spend the rest of the war in a Federal prison.[24] Though Price's army was growing smaller, casting off the impediments was helping it stay ahead of its pursuers.

The 6th of November was a Sunday and Dr. McPheeters was unhappy that the army was moving on the Sabbath. For once, Price had made the right decision and pushed his army another twenty miles to the north bank of the Arkansas. Upon arrival there Price made preparations for a crossing the next morning at a place called Pheasant Ford in the Indian Territory, halfway between Fort Smith and Fort Gibson. Meanwhile, Curtis was moving south attempting to intercept Price before he could make a crossing. He placed Benteen in the lead, followed by Blunt's division and Colonel Marcus LaRue Harrison commanding the troops from the Fayetteville garrison. Benteen reached the Sallisaw that evening, which was the site of Price's camp on the previous night.[25] It now seemed very unlikely that the Union army would overtake Price.

The Army of Missouri moved to the ford on Monday morning, 7 November, and began the crossing. Before they could cross, the Rebels had to cut a road two miles long through a thicket to the bank. The troopers were then able to get over the river to safety. The army was over the Arkansas by 1:00 p.m. except for the train and a small rear guard. The Army of Missouri had crossed to the north side of the Arkansas exactly two months earlier on their way to Missouri, full of hope that they would liberate the state. Now they were returning defeated, dejected and having accomplished nothing of significance. Behind them the Federals were driving toward the Arkansas in a vain attempt to stop Price one last time. Curtis had shuffled the order of march, placing Colonel Harrison in the lead. Curtis' advance would not reach Pheasant Ford until early morning on the 8th, and by that time the only thing left of Price's army was a few stragglers from the rear guard. Harrison's men scooped up the fugitives and placed a battery in position to send a few parting shots at the Army of Missouri. Curtis reported that "a shout went up from the Army of the Border" when they realized the campaign was over.[26] Indeed, for the Union army, the Great Missouri Raid had concluded.

In a twist of irony, Halleck wrote an order dated 7 November 1864—the day Price recrossed the Arkansas River—placing all troops from the Department of Missouri "now serving on the west border of that State" under Curtis' direct command. One writer speculates that had Halleck or Grant issued such an order earlier in the campaign, such as the first week of October, the Army of Missouri "might well have been captured or destroyed." This would have provided unity of command sooner and facilitated cooperation between the departments by virtue of having one commanding officer.[27] This is certainly a logical and feasible assertion. However, we will never know what Curtis—or Rosecrans—could have accomplished, since this order came down far too late to have any effect on the campaign.

On the afternoon of 8 November—the day after Price crossed the Arkansas—Curtis issued a general order announcing the end of the campaign:

> The object of this organization and campaign is accomplished. The rebel army under General Sterling Price has been confronted, beaten in several conflicts, pursued and driven over 350 miles, from the Missouri to the Arkansas. This has been the work of fourteen days. Your marches have been incessant, sometimes for days and nights, in rain and snow, and generally on short rations, gathered from the herds lost by the enemy. Your privations, toil, and gallantry deserve the highest commendation, and the success of the campaign in which you have so gloriously participated, most of you from the beginning to the end, must entitle you to the thanks of your Government and the gratitude of the loyal people of our country.

Curtis went on to give instructions on the disbanding of the Army of the Border, to commend several key leaders, and to order the submission of final reports.[28] While much of Curtis' general order sounds flowery and exaggerated, it is quite remarkable what the Army of the Border accomplished. This ad hoc organization assembled in less than two weeks, then fought and defeated Price in two major engagements at Westport and Mine Creek. The army nearly destroyed the Army of Missouri and prevented Price from achieving any major objective. Further, Curtis and company forced the Rebels to abandon all of their spoils so that Price would have no tangible evidence of success. The Army of the Border did this in difficult conditions, marching hundreds of miles, and with intermittent logistical support. Perhaps the most remarkable aspect of the success of the Army of the Border was the fact that Curtis did all this without unity of command. If he had been able to pull together all units under his command, the Army of the Border might have destroyed the Army of Missouri. However, this did not happen because of the fragmentation of the Union commands west of the Mississippi and difficult personalities of men like William S. Rosecrans.

Though the campaign was officially over for the Federals, the Confederates had many hardships ahead. For Price and his army the fighting was over, but the elements would now take their toll on the ragged Rebels. The Army of Missouri was still hundreds of miles from their southern Arkansas starting point at Camden and the route of retreat extended the already daunting task. Price and his men were in the Choctaw country of Indian Territory, and they would have to traverse the length of the territory into Texas before turning east back into Arkansas. This area was inhospitable, as many of the tribes friendly to the Confederacy were displaced by the war. They had not planted crops and had taken their animals with them. Therefore, there was little sustenance for the men or animals along the way. When this was added to the increasingly miserable weather, the Rebels were in for an arduous march.

Once south of the Arkansas, Price continued his previous policy of furloughing entire units from the army. This would serve to lower the number of mouths to feed and perhaps raise the morale of the troops by allowing a visit home. He also sent local units such as those of Freeman and Dobbin home to Arkansas border areas to gather up absentees. These units would then return with absentees in December, bringing an accession of strength while unburdening the main army from feeding these men.²⁹ The risk in this was that the units might never return, but Price was willing to accept this in order to extract his army from further danger. The net result was that, as Price moved south, he lost a great deal more combat power so that by the time he reached safety he would have less than half of his strength left.

Between 7 November and 18 November, Price's army suffered horribly in the desolate country of the eastern Indian Territory. Animals were breaking down, men were hungry, and smallpox began to spread. Dr. McPheeters and Shelby's biographer both chronicle the sufferings of the men during this time. Price's chief surgeon made arrangements to evacuate those stricken with the disease to prevent its spread throughout the rest of the army. By 16 November conditions finally improved somewhat when the army reached Boggy Depot. Here, along the banks of the Boggy River in Indian Territory, the soldiers got their first decent meal in a week and a half. Forage and cattle were abundant and the small Confederate depot provided flour for bread. Shelby's division, the only one fit for duty, fanned out along the valley to bring in forage for men and animals.³⁰ This improved morale enough to enable the army to push on to the Red River bordering Texas.

For the next week, Price pressed southward in a rather uneventful march. His after action report simply notes the various camps and miles traveled by the army before they reached Bonham, Texas, on 23 November. Here the army rested before turning east toward Arkansas on the final leg of the journey. To people along the route, the procession must have been startling. The Rebel soldiers who marched along were in rags, on gaunt horses and no doubt filthy from weeks in the saddle. Further, there is evidence that citizens did not welcome the passing army because the soldiers tended to steal from the people. Also, the citizens were reluctant to sell anything to the Rebels, and when they did, it was at exorbitant prices. Price's indiscipline had made his own army unwelcome in the heart of the South. Dr. McPheeters recorded a striking example of indiscipline when he wrote about a group of Price's own staff officers who got drunk and engaged in "a disgraceful fight."³¹ Wearing out their welcome, the Army of Missouri plodded on until reaching Laynesport, Arkansas, on 2 December 1864. Here, Price decided to make winter camp, ending a sad chapter in the history of the Confederate army in the Trans-Mississippi.

What had started with such hope and promise for the Confederates ended in an unmitigated disaster, regardless of the spin Price put on it in his official report. Price and the high command of the Trans-Mississippi Department established several lofty goals, many of which were actually within reach of the department and its available resources. However, Kirby Smith and Price were not in agreement on what these were, as Smith focused his objectives on tactical concerns, while Price tended to emphasize strategic goals linked to political considerations. This cognitive disagreement between the two men meant that Smith—as department commander—failed to provide the proper resources to achieve anything. Thus, the linkage between ends, ways, and means was disconnected. Whereas Price commanded a cavalry force, the objectives assigned by Smith, and that Price sought to achieve, demanded a task organization with infantry. Since Smith did not provide this asset, the operation should have been a raid from the start. Ultimately, this poor planning on the part of the department's senior leaders ensured failure before the force even stepped off.

In terms of real losses, the Army of Missouri lost over two-thirds of its strength during the course of the operation, arriving at Laynesport with only 3,500 troops fit for duty. Price won only minor engagements at Glasgow and Newtonia—and in the latter the Confederates relinquished the field in order to continue retreating. The army lost every major engagement, including the disasters at Pilot Knob, Westport, and Mine Creek. Price failed to take St. Louis or Jefferson City, as well as his subsequent key points at Kansas City, Fort Leavenworth, and Fort Scott. Further, he was forced to destroy the enormous train in the wake of Mine Creek, ensuring he would have no physical evidence of any success.[32] The result of all this at the strategic level was nothing, as the Great Raid had almost no effect on operations in the east, failed to challenge Union control of Missouri, and did not sway the national election. While the Union high command did postpone the Mobile campaign and divert A.J. Smith's XVI Corps, this only delayed the inevitable outcome of the war by a few short weeks.

Price's inattention to discipline and his tactical incompetence also contributed significantly to the outcome of the campaign. From start to finish, he failed to impose rudimentary disciplinary measures. The men foraged freely without respect to the local populace and regardless of sympathies. The march was of a character that would not do justice to good infantry troops. Tactically, Price made repeated mistakes, starting at Pilot Knob and going through Mine Creek. Further, he failed to display any battlefield presence as his personal leadership—a hallmark of his early career—was absent at decisive points in the campaign. He rode in an ambulance due to poor health and obesity, the latter a condition which seems curious considering the deprivations the South was suffering by late 1864.[33] Thus, Price's significant character flaws were a major factor in the failure of the entire operation.

None of this was lost on observers of the Great Raid, and the recriminations began within days of the army's arrival at Laynesport, Louisiana. Among the shrillest of the accusers was the exiled governor of Missouri, Thomas C. Reynolds. As already noted, Reynolds wrote a long opinion paper he titled a "Memoir" for the pages of the *Marshall (Texas) Republican*. But, before Reynolds submitted it for publication, he wrote a letter to Price to make him an offer. In the letter, Reynolds told Price about the article and offered to prevent its publication if Price would agree to resign his commission. The article, Reynolds told Price, promised to "place the lat Missouri campaign in a proper light." Price did not respond to the letter, snubbing Reynolds, so the latter went forward with publication.[34] This would spark controversy and a demand for justice by Price.

The article by Reynolds characterized the campaign as a failure due to "distressing mental and physical military incapacity of Major General Sterling Price." As expected, this publication infuriated the general, and he demanded a court of inquiry to clear his name from what he considered a smear. It is incredible to think that at this point in the war, with the Confederacy literally crumbling all around, the high command would countenance such petty squabbling, but this is exactly what happened. Kirby Smith granted Price's request and appointed a court of senior officers and military lawyers on 8 March 1865 to hear the case. The court began proceedings on 21 April 1865, a full twelve days after the surrender of Robert E. Lee's army in Virginia and only five days before Joseph E. Johnston capitulated in North Carolina.[35] Thus, the whole proceeding seemed superfluous in light of the imminent collapse of the Confederacy. Nevertheless, the court convened and began hearing the case, continuing until the Trans-Mississippi Department fell to Union forces.

The proceeding began at Shreveport, Louisiana, with a chronological recounting of the campaign by Price's chief engineer, Captain Thomas J. Mackey. Then the court began inquiring about the events at Pilot Knob. The line of questioning attempted to hone in on the reasons why Ewing and his garrison were able to escape and how the assaults on Fort Davidson failed. However, the court was unable to obtain any definitive answers on these events because Captain Mackey claimed no personal knowledge of how Price arrayed his surveillance or dispositions made for the assault.[36] This seems incredible since, as chief engineer, Mackey made personal recommendations to Price with reference to Fort Davidson and the assault. This established a pattern for the whole proceeding, in that nothing of substance would emerge from the questioning despite ten days of examination.

From the 25th of April until the 2nd of May, the testimony ranged from the events occurring at the momentous battles to the most mundane instances of military operations. The members of the court examined several witnesses, and Sterling Price personally conducted the cross-examination. The witnesses included the aforementioned Captain Mackey, Price's chief of staff, Lieutenant Colonel Lauchlan MacLean, and his assistant adjutant general, Major James Shaler. The court attempted to call Governor Reynolds to the witness stand to discuss the contents of his op-ed, but he declined because of the "delicacy" of the case. Price then requested that the court compel Reynolds to testify. The members went into recess to consider the request, but rejected it because the court members believed that they had no authority to do so, since Reynolds was not in the army.[37] This motion occurred on the sixth day of testimony, and the proceeding continued for another three days with nothing of substance forthcoming.

The court was forced to suspend the proceeding on 3 May 1865, as Union forces were closing in on Shreveport. The court agreed to reconvene at the first opportunity when it was safe to do so in another location, stated as Washington, Arkansas.[38] However, it was never able to come to order again and the matter ended with no decision. In fact, many of the senior leaders of the Trans-Mississippi command made their way to Mexico rather than accept surrender to the hated Federals. Among those who escaped were Price, Shelby, and Smith. Since the court never again met, there was no deliberation or determination of whether or not Price was culpable for the failure of the campaign. Thus, it was left to the historians to make a determination about the campaign and to assess the relative competence of Sterling Price. Based on the available evidence—and there is ample documentation—it is clear that when Price brought the Army of Missouri in to Laynesport the Great Raid had been an utter failure. Perhaps the best assessment of the campaign is supplied by two of the participants. Shelby's biographer stated that "the great expedition to Missouri, begun in joy and high expectation, terminated in this little Texas [Arkansas] village, in doubt, misery, and despair." Private Darr, a common soldier, described the affair as "this unfortunate campaign," which is an apt interpretation.[39]

The dismal retreat is indicative of the entire operation. The ragged force returned from the expedition lacking even the most basic needs, having accomplished nothing of significance. The losses in battle were compounded in the retreat, rendering the striking power of the Trans-Mississippi Confederacy completely ineffective. All of this is attributable to the commander, who is responsible for everything that happens or fails to happen in his formation. Therefore, Sterling Price, as the commander of the operation, was culpable for the outcome. This was in many ways due to his incompetence as a military leader.

12

Epilogue

Price's Great Missouri Raid was an effort to capitalize on the advantages the Trans-Mississippi Confederacy had accrued from the successful defense of the Red River Valley and in Arkansas during the spring of 1864. The Trans-Mississippi Department, a sprawling backwater in the minds of policymakers North and South, was ironically the Confederacy's strongest in terms of relative combat power. The Rebels in the west had thrown back the two invasion thrusts, and afterward, the Federals transferred many of their troops from the trans–Mississippi to bolster armies in the East. Kirby Smith then had the advantage in terms of initiative and freedom of maneuver. The Federals west of the Mississippi held Missouri, but they were forced into enclaves at other points, such as Little Rock and New Orleans. Therefore, with Confederate armies in Virginia and Georgia outnumbered and pinned down, the Trans-Mississippi Department was the field of action with a good window of opportunity. Yet the leaders of the western Confederacy would fumble the chance to upset Federal plans in the East due to a combination of factors such as indecision, poor planning, dallying, and incompetence.

At this point in the war, it is questionable whether the Confederates west of the Mississippi could have affected the war in the East. Whatever chance they had would require immediate action by the Confederates to capitalize on their successes from the spring. The Federal forces withdrew from the Red River Valley and went back to Little Rock by mid–May 1864. The Union armies east of the Mississippi, though making progress in their campaigns, were suffering heavy casualties, while the Confederates in the field were still potent. However, by mid-summer both Lee and Johnston would find themselves cornered at Richmond and Atlanta. Therefore, if the Rebels in the west had any chance to succor their comrades, they had to strike in June and no later than July. This would not happen because of a combination of reasons, which all arose from an embarrassing ineptness in the Confederate high command.

The senior leaders of the Confederacy did not even begin considering courses of action until 9 July when Braxton Bragg sent his dispatch ordering a transfer of troops from the Trans-Mississippi to the East. His order was not routed properly, instead going through Lieutenant General Stephen D. Lee to Richard Taylor. To marshal the required forces, the order should have gone to Kirby Smith. This note started the whole quixotic attempt to cross the river with reinforcements for the East. The venture would drag on for almost six weeks before Smith finally abandoned the effort upon Taylor's recommendation. By August the Rebels began to consider other courses that could assist their comrades to the east. By this time it was already too late for the Trans-Mississippi Department to make a meaningful contribution to halt the slide to inexorable defeat that would soon engulf the Confederacy. Nevertheless, the Rebels began planning for what would become the Great Missouri Raid, with the hope that an invasion of the state would divert Federal attention from the east in their direction.

The invasion of Missouri was a natural sequel to follow the defeat of Banks and Steele in May, and the Rebels could have launched it in June. Instead, the real planning effort did not begin until the 4 August conference at Shreveport with Smith, Price, and other leaders from the Trans-Mississippi. Now a flawed planning process would enter the mix to ensure that little, if any, substantial results would accrue from a campaign in Missouri. Smith, as the department commander, failed in many respects to set the conditions for success during the session. First, he selected Price to command the expedition, in spite of his own misgivings about his leadership ability. Second, the objectives Smith established for the expedition were decidedly tactical in nature, where he, as a theater commander, should have set objectives at the operational and strategic levels. Establishing tactical objectives ensured from the start that the operation could not have appreciable effects east of the river. Next, though Price acknowledged the mission Smith gave him, he proceeded to designate his own operational and strategic objectives. It is ironic that Price was thinking at the higher level, while his commander, the professional West Point-trained Smith, was thinking about more mundane objectives. As a result, there was a lack of agreement on just what the invasion was supposed to accomplish.

Smith told Price in his directive to launch the campaign that he wanted Price to take St. Louis, gather supplies, and recruit. Of these objectives, only the capture of St. Louis was a potential operational objective. On the other hand, Price intended to take Jefferson City and St. Louis, install a Confederate government, and attempt to foster a large uprising among the copperhead groups with a view toward swaying the Federal election in November. To accomplish Price's objective required a force consisting of infantry and cavalry to hold Missouri so that he could install a Confederate regime. To take St. Louis would also require a significant body of infantry to storm and hold the place, though the other objectives Smith designated were suited to cavalry. This illustrates the last failure on Smith's part, which was the designation of a flawed task organization.

Smith had sufficient infantry in the department to provide Price with a strong contingent to accomplish the mission. However, Smith provided Price only with cavalry, which is best suited for raiding, not storming or holding ground. Thus, Smith did not link ends, ways, and means to achieve the objectives, because the means provided were ill-suited to the stated ends. Price fully intended to pursue his own goals, and as an experienced commander he should have requested infantry to accompany the expedition. As we have seen, his experience did not translate into competence, and he overlooked the requirement for infantry. This meant that the invasion of Missouri went forward with an improper mix of forces that were better suited for a large-scale raid. Price went forward intent on conducting a campaign to take and hold ground, but the whole enterprise would devolve into a raid as the flaws in planning forced this upon him.

For all the problems in planning, the issues arising from the preparation and execution would doom the whole operation. Though Smith issued orders for the invasion on 11 August, Price did not begin movement until the 30th from Camden and only reached the Arkansas River on 6 September. The reason for this was the need to make logistic arrangements for the campaign. The rickety supply network made the gathering of transport and ammunition difficult. Plus, the Rebel units were dispersed, after the Camden Expedition and Red River Campaign, widely across Arkansas to provide subsistence and forage for the men and animals. Before Price could start, he had to concentrate the scattered elements of his command and then organize the army. This took more time, so that the Army of Missouri did not cross the Missouri state line until 19 September. By this time, Atlanta had fallen, Lee was immobilized at Richmond and Petersburg, and Sheridan that very day heavily defeated Early at Winchester in the Shenandoah Valley. In sum, the Confederates were reeling everywhere and the incursion into Missouri was simply too little and far too late.

While the planning and preparation efforts were lacking in clarity and timeliness, solid leadership could have salvaged something of substance from the expedition. Leadership however, was incredibly weak with Price at the helm, as he bungled the operation from start to finish. The first days of the campaign set the tone for the entire endeavor. Despite having a force composed entirely of cavalry, Price's rate of march averaged between fifteen and sixteen miles a day.[1] As previously noted, such a pace did not do justice to infantry in a mobile campaign. Speed was critical to the success of the expedition, regardless of the objectives to keep the enemy off balance and retain the initiative. Yet Price established a rate of movement that allowed the Federals to react, make arrangements for counterblows, and thwart all of the Confederate's plans. The slow pace is indicative of Price's inability to impose any sort of discipline, which all armies need to achieve their stated mission.

This lack of discipline also came to the fore in the manner by which the Rebels conducted themselves in Missouri with the populace. Throughout the Great Raid, the Rebels made little distinction between Union and Confederate sympathizers. They stole from both equally to sustain the operation and also took things they did not need. The net effect of this behavior was to drive away the very people the Confederates were supposed to be liberating. While Price issued orders during the expedition to control troop behavior, he failed to enforce his directive. Therefore, the soldiers did what they wanted, to the detriment of their own cause.

Another glaring example of the indiscipline of the army was the handling of prisoners. Major James Wilson and several of his comrades were murdered in cold blood after their capture at Pilot Knob. Wilson's "crime" deserving of execution was his effectiveness in combating guerrillas. He had a reputation for ruthlessness that had enabled his unit—the 3rd Missouri State Militia Cavalry—to secure the Arcadia Valley for the Union. Wilson was well known for his ability among Southern leaders, and when it was known that he was captured, the Confederates took revenge. The valiant Union major was ignominiously executed in some woods along the Confederate route of advance. Such behavior would convince the Union soldiers to fight harder to avoid capture, making the Confederate operation a more difficult proposition from a fighting standpoint.

The conduct of the battle was arguably Price's weakest attribute during the Great Raid. The first blunder came at Pilot Knob. The very decision to attack the place was a mistake because it diverted the Rebels from their primary objective during this phase of the campaign, St. Louis. This small Union garrison was no threat to the Army of Missouri and the Confederates could have easily bypassed Fort Davidson. Price could have then advanced rapidly toward St. Louis and perhaps taken it because, at this point, Rosecrans did not have Smith's XVI Corps in place to defend it. Instead, Price moved on Pilot Knob to reduce the fort, wasting valuable time that Rosecrans used to frantically prepare the defenses of St. Louis. By the time Price was able to extract his wounded army from Pilot Knob, Rosecrans was ready to receive him and the opportunity to take the city had passed.

During the battle, Price made two egregious blunders that resulted in a lengthy casualty list and the escape of Thomas Ewing with the Union garrison. First, Price opted to make a frontal assault on Fort Davidson rather than to invest the earthwork. Then he failed to use his artillery to advantage in support of the assault from the surrounding hills. He therefore nullified all of the advantages of terrain that the Arcadia Valley provided the Rebels. After the failed attacks on the afternoon of 27 September, Price next failed to post adequate pickets and guards. Though he controlled all of the approaches to Pilot Knob, the lack of discipline in the brigades allowed the entire garrison to escape in the middle of the night on the road to Potosi right under the noses of the Rebels. Compounding the negligence of poor posting of the units was the lack of action following the explosion of the magazine. Rather than investigating why the bunker had exploded, Price went back to sleep while Ewing escaped with all of the Federal soldiers. This first engagement was but the first disaster in a string of defeats that would plague the Rebels throughout the Great Raid.

Price then moved toward St. Louis before turning toward Jefferson City when he decided that there was no way he could take St. Louis. Thus, the first objective of the campaign—one that Smith assigned—was lost. The next target, chosen by Price, was the Missouri capital. Price wanted to take it and install a Confederate government in order to demonstrate to the North that the Federal hold on Missouri had never been better than tenuous. Taking Jefferson City, combined with an uprising by the O.A.K., could upset Lincoln's reelection prospects, in Price's estimation. To have a chance to take the Missouri capital, Price would have to move quickly, but he did not. Instead, he maintained his slow rate of march, allowing the Federals to pull together a patchwork defense of Jefferson City. When Price arrived there on 7 October and surveyed the ground and defenses of the capital, he decided he could not take it. He turned west toward Boonville, beginning the "picnic period" in the middle of the expedition.

With the second major objective now unfulfilled, the campaign, whose poorly articulated purpose was to take and hold key ground, evolved into a raid to upset Federal plans and destroy property. Yet, even as the nature of the expedition had changed to a raid, implying the need for speed, Price actually slowed the pace. When he arrived at Boonville, he was feted by a raucous Southern crowd. Price was very happy to find comfortable surroundings among friends, so he stayed at Boonville for three days, immobile—not exactly the expectation of troops involved in a raid. This period of rest allowed the hard-driving Alfred Pleasonton to organize a pursuit force. To the west, Price's dallying allowed Samuel R. Curtis to organize his forces to defend Kansas. Had Price kept moving, he could have outrun Pleasonton and plowed into Kansas before Curtis was ready. Again his lack of discipline and poor decision making provided the fragmented Federal command time to recover from its own haphazard performance.

When Price finally moved on from Boonville ending the "picnic period," the situation for the Army of Missouri was rapidly deteriorating. The Union commanders in Missouri and Kansas had not worked well together since they first heard rumblings that Price was moving on Missouri. Now, things were beginning to come together for the Union leaders to the detriment of Price. Through a combination of planning, luck, and timing, the Federals had managed to devise a trap for Price. The Confederate actually noticed the sides of the box closing in on him, but he stubbornly wanted to continue the raid when it was no longer feasible. Only when the situation forced his hand did Price finally decide to turn south to escape the closing trap.

At Westport, and later at Mine Creek, Price was mostly absent, providing little in the way of battlefield leadership. For this, he was dependent upon his subordinates, in particular Jo Shelby. The main reason for Price's conspicuous absence on the field was his poor health. As we have seen, he had a number of ailments and was extremely overweight to the point that he traveled in the back of an ambulance. At Westport, when Price's lines were breaking, Shelby was the man who saved the day. While the Rebels were meeting disaster at Mine Creek, Price was well to the rear with the precious train. The one area in which he had actually demonstrated some competence in past battles such as Wilson's Creek was front-line leadership, but even this was lacking during the Great Raid. Thus, he did not inspire the troops or provide sound direction to guide the course of the operation. An example of his poor judgment is the stubborn manner by which Price clung to the cumbersome train. This was a direct cause of the defeat at Westport and the disaster at Mine Creek and indicative of the level of incompetence displayed by him during the Great Raid.

Price filed his report of the expedition on 28 December 1864, and in the document he engaged in an exercise in artful exaggeration:

> [I]n my opinion the results flowing from my operations in Missouri are of the most gratifying character. I marched 1,434 miles; fought forty-three battles and skirmishes; captured and paroled over 3,000 Federal officers and men; captured 18 pieces of artillery, 3,000 stand of small arms, 16 stand of colors that were brought out by me (besides many others that were captured and afterward destroyed by our own troops who took them), at least 3,000 overcoats, large quantities of blankets, shoes, and ready-made clothing for soldiers, a great many wagons and teams, large numbers of horses, great quantities of subsistence and ordnance stores. I destroyed miles upon miles of railroad, burning the depots and bridges; and taking this into calculation, I do not think I go beyond the truth when I state that I destroyed in the late expedition to Missouri, property to the amount of $10,000,000 in value. On the other hand, I lost 10 pieces of artillery, 2 stand of colors, 1,000 small arms, while I do not think I lost 1,000 prisoners, including my wounded left in their hands and other recruits on their way to join me.

In addition, he said,

> I brought with me at least 5,000 new recruits, and they are still arriving in large numbers daily within our lines, who bring cheering intelligence that there are more on their way to the army.... I am satisfied that could I have remained in Missouri this winter the army would have been increased 50,000 men.[2]

Upon closer examination, Price's assertions of his success are magnified, while the acknowledged losses in the operation are minimized to put the best face on an operation that achieved none of its goals.

As the Confederates continued south on the retreat, it was already evident that the whole endeavor was a complete failure on all levels. Price burned the train in the aftermath of Mine Creek, and as he moved southward the Army of Missouri began to hemorrhage men at an alarming rate to various causes. With the loss of the train and most of the recruits he had picked up along the way, Price had absolutely nothing to show for the expenditure of resources. The losses suffered at the tactical, operational, and strategic level during the Great Raid sealed the fate of the Confederate cause regionally and nationally. The immediate physical losses of the expedition paint an ugly picture for the Confederates in spite of the spin in Price's report. Price entered Missouri with an estimated 12,000 men, with fourteen guns, organized in three divisions. When Price arrived at Laynesport, John Magruder estimated that the Army of Missouri had only 3,500 effectives left in the formation. All of Price's artillery was lost except four guns in Collins' battery of Shelby's division. And, for all practical purposes, the divisions of Marmaduke and Fagan were destroyed by losses on the battlefield, desertion, and furloughs.[3] Thus, at the tactical, operational, and strategic level in the Trans-Mississippi, the force was rendered ineffective and the effort had done nothing to wrest Missouri from the Federal grip. On the national stage, the loss was even more telling.

Price's objectives for the invasion of Missouri were linked to events that could have influenced the trajectory of the war. Two of his objectives in particular were directly focused on strategic-level ends. First, taking Jefferson City and installing a Confederate government would cleave Missouri from the Union orbit, placing the state in the Rebel camp. Price believed that wresting control of the state from the Federals before the national election could affect its outcome to the South's advantage. Second, he hoped to foster an uprising in Missouri and across the old northwest. If he could generate unrest among the O.A.K. members, perhaps the people of Illinois, Iowa, and other northwestern states would reconsider their selection for president. The first of these two objectives was somewhat realistic if Price could move quickly, but he did not, and the Rebels missed the slim opportunity they had. The second objective to foster an uprising was a pipe dream. The copperhead organizations in the northwest were never as formidable as many people had hoped. When the chance came for them to leverage the organizations before the election, they fizzled ingloriously. The best example of this is the failed uprising at the Democratic convention in August 1864. Therefore, Price and many other Confederate leaders should have known from this event that the influence of the copperheads was overblown. However, leading Confederates continued to overestimate the copperheads in their hopes that such organizations could deliver a victory for them off the battlefield.[4] Such thinking was grandiose, indeed. When the national election occurred, Lincoln won every state in the old northwest handily, dashing all Rebel hopes for survival.

One other end the Confederates hoped to accomplish was the diversion of Federal troops from the East to contend with Price across the Mississippi. As noted, Confederate armies east of the Mississippi were struggling against much stronger Union forces in Virginia and Georgia. The genesis of the expedition originated from a desire by the authorities in Richmond to aid the hard-pressed Armies of Tennessee and Northern Virginia. The idea proposed by Bragg was to shift troops from the Trans-Mississippi to the east side of the river. When this proved infeasible, Kirby Smith offered that a move west of the river could siphon off Union forces in the East, forcing them to deal with rampaging Rebels in Missouri. As Price moved into the state, Rosecrans petitioned Halleck to allow him to commandeer the XVI Corps, which was headed east to Sherman's army following the failed Red River Campaign. Halleck agreed to the request, providing Rosecrans with a veteran infantry corps to contest Price on better terms. The diversion of Smith and his corps subtracted about 10,000 troops from campaigns in the East. Therefore, the Confederates actually accomplished this end. Smith was finally released from the Department of Missouri in late October when he was ordered to report to George Thomas at Nashville.[5] Though the Rebels enjoyed success here, it made little difference in the long run. Thomas probably could have defeated Hood without Smith in December at Nashville. At best the diversion of force may have delayed the eventual Confederate defeat by a month.

For the Federals, the Great Missouri Raid amounted to little more than an irritant to their cause. Though Lincoln, Grant, and Halleck were genuinely concerned about what Price was doing in Missouri, their focus remained east of the Mississippi. The real source of their frustration was centered on William S. Rosecrans, who seemed to either drag his feet or purposely thwart the wishes of his superiors at every turn. Nevertheless, the Union army in Missouri and Kansas won a great victory against Price that accomplished much for the Union cause. Total losses for the Union armies during the campaign totaled about 2,000 to 2,500 men,[6] along with much booty captured by the Confederates. The Union armies recaptured a good deal of the lost equipment, or the Rebels destroyed it in order to make good their escape south. For this cost, the Federals successfully defended Missouri and Kansas, ensuring that the Federals would retain control of Missouri and prevent Price from devastating Kansas. The two largest battles ever fought in both states resulted in Union victories. These came only weeks before the all important Federal election and they helped convince voters in the northwest that the cause was worth their sacrifices.

To summarize, the Union army defeated the Army of Missouri tactically, and this forced the Confederates from Missouri operationally for the duration of the war. Also, the defeats failed to provide any relief to the Confederate armies in the East. At the strategic level, Missouri was solidly in the Union camp and would remain so. Further, and most important, Lincoln was reelected, guaranteeing that current Federal policy to reunite the country with the complete defeat of the rebellion would remain in place until the Confederates capitulated. Of all the Federal campaigns conducted throughout the Civil War, few obtained such decisive results for Union arms as this one did.

The chain of events after December 1864 was anticlimactic for both sides in the Trans-Mississippi. The Confederate armies west of the river did next to nothing following the Great Raid. Likewise, the Federals did little, as they seemed more content to consolidate their hold on Missouri while keeping a wary eye on the idle Confederates everywhere else. Meanwhile, to the east, the Federal armies were on the move cutting swaths of destruction through Georgia and the Carolinas, strangling the capital at Richmond, and closing the remaining ports still open to the Confederacy. The Southern government was dying to the east of the river while the Rebels to the west could only watch helplessly. It seemed that the Trans-Mississippi region was now truly the backwater that many had always considered it.

As the Confederate armies to the east were suffering through their death throes, the leaders in the Trans-Mississippi Department were wasting their time squabbling. As we have seen, Kirby Smith agreed to convene a court of inquiry in March 1865 to examine the events in Missouri and determine culpability for any failures. This came about by request of Price to defend his reputation that Governor Reynolds disparaged in his op-ed to the *Marshall Republican* newspaper. The entire endeavor determined nothing, and before it could close out the proceedings, the court adjourned when the enemy forced it to disband. The leaders involved in the whole fiasco and inquiry then escaped south toward Mexico as the Union armies closed in on Shreveport. Kirby Smith abdicated his command of the department in a pathetic display of poor leadership, reminiscent of his hands-off approach during the whole Missouri affair, leaving Simon Bolivar Buckner to surrender the department.

General Buckner had to submit himself to the humiliation of capitulating for a second time in this war. In 1862 at Fort Donelson, John Floyd and Gideon Pillow both passed their responsibility for command to Buckner, leaving him to surrender the garrison to U.S. Grant. Buckner was a man of dignity and honor, and he accepted the responsibility then as he did in 1865. So, on 26 May 1865, Simon Buckner surrendered the Trans-Mississippi Department to Major General E.R.S. Canby, ending the war west of the river. E. Kirby Smith endorsed this action on 2 June 1865 in Galveston as he was en route to Mexico. In reality the war was effectively over in the Trans-Mississippi when Price arrived at Laynesport on 2 December 1864.

Price's Great Missouri Raid is an intriguing story that holds all the irony, stories of sacrifice, funny anecdotes, and tragedy of any campaign fought in Virginia, Georgia, or Tennessee. Though largely unknown, it deserves a place in the pantheon of Civil War historiography beside such pivotal events as the Overland Campaign, the Atlanta Campaign, and all the other more familiar acts of this American tragedy. The Great Missouri Raid is a story of the forlorn hope of a people whose time had passed. There was little chance that the Confederates could have changed the outcome of the Civil War at that point in 1864. Events to the east had outstripped the velocity of the slow-moving Trans-Mississippi Department, and Confederate defeat was a foregone conclusion. If there was any opportunity for the Trans-Mississippi Department to affect the outcome of the war, their leaders should have made a move in the immediate aftermath of the successful Red River Campaign. This did not happen because of the incompetence of Smith and Price, poor planning and decision making, and the utterly inadequate execution of the campaign-turned-raid. This guaranteed failure for the Rebels and gave the inept Federals a victory in spite of their own significant shortcomings in Missouri and Kansas. Ultimately, the weakness of the leaders in both armies had its greatest impact on the lives of the common soldiers in both armies. The soldiers bore every burden in the service of their respective causes, and they did it with dignity and honor worthy of their sacrifices.

Appendix A

Chronology[1]

Date	Event
1864	
3 May	Major General Frederick Steele arrives in Little Rock, Arkansas, concluding the Camden Expedition at the point where his army started.
4	Overland Campaign begins in Virginia as the Army of the Potomac crosses the Rapidan River.
7	Major General William T. Sherman begins march to Atlanta.
21	Major General Nathaniel P. Banks' Army of the Gulf crosses the Atchafalaya River, successfully escaping from the Confederate army commanded by Major General Richard Taylor. This concludes the Red River Campaign.
June	Confederate authorities in the Trans-Mississippi Department and Richmond begin debate as to how to follow up the successful defense of the department. Major General Sterling Price suggests in a letter to General E. Kirby Smith that an invasion of Missouri is the appropriate manner in which to follow up the Camden Expedition and Red River Campaign.
18	The Army of the Potomac invests Petersburg, beginning a long siege in the Virginia theater.
18 July	General Braxton Bragg orders General Smith to begin making preparations to transfer the command of Richard Taylor to the east side of the Mississippi in order to assist in the defense of Mobile. By August Smith determines that any substantial crossing of forces from the Trans-Mississippi to the east is impractical.
4 August	General Smith issues an order to Sterling Price "to make immediate arrangements for a movement into Missouri."
5–8	Federal fleet under Admiral David G. Farragut steams into Mobile Bay, while elements of the army take Forts Gaines and Morgan, effectively closing the port.
29 August	General Price assumes command of the Army of Missouri at Princeton, Arkansas.
2 September	Brigadier Jo Shelby has skirmish with Federal forces at DuVall's Bluff as he moves to link up with Price's main column moving north into Missouri. On the same day, Atlanta falls to Sherman's army.
8	Cabell's brigade engages the Union Third Arkansas and captures several prisoners, whom they execute on the spot.
19	Army of Missouri crosses the state line into Missouri in three widely scattered columns. Shelby skirmishes with elements of Union reconnaissance at Doniphan. The town is destroyed during the course of the action.
20	Two skirmishes occur at Ponder's Mill and Little Black River, Missouri. Also,

(**1864** Sept)	small Missouri Enrolled Militia detachment surrenders to small group of Confederate guerrillas at Keytesville. Treachery is suspected on the part of the militia.
22	Skirmishes occur at several locations across the breadth of Price's columns, including Patterson, Sikeston, and Fredericktown.
23	Guerrilla activity increases across the state, including an affair at Rocheport, where the Third Missouri State Militia reports 11 casualties.
24	Several skirmishes along the line of Price's advance. At Farmington, elements of Shelby's column are turned back by a small detachment of Missouri cavalry defending the town.
25	Shelby again attacks Farmington and this time successfully overcomes the defenders. At Huntsville guerrillas skirmish with elements of Missouri Enrolled Militia.
26	Multiple clashes along Price's front, with the most significant at Ironton, setting the stage for battle of Fort Davidson.
27	Battle of Fort Davidson, resulting in a significant defeat of Price's army following multiple assaults. Confederates suffer several hundred casualties. That night Union forces under Brigadier General Thomas W. Ewing conduct a successful withdrawal and blow up the magazine after they begin the retreat. Also on this date "Bloody Bill" Anderson attacks Centralia and murders a group of soldiers on furlough at the railroad depot along with other veterans and civilians. He later ambushes pursuing forces from the 39th Enrolled Missouri Militia, killing nearly 150 soldiers, many after capture.
28	Elements of Shelby's and Marmaduke's divisions clash with Union forces retreating from Fort Davidson at Caledonia and Princeton. Another clash occurs at Centralia between Anderson and the 9th Missouri State Militia Cavalry.
29	More clashes between Ewing's retreating force and Price's columns at Leasburg, Cuba, and vicinity. Price begins movement toward St. Louis with Fagan's division.
30	Ewing again makes contact with Confederate pursuers, but Shelby's division breaks contact and turns northeast advancing up the Pacific Railroad line toward St. Louis.
1 October	Multiple skirmishes, including Franklin, where Shelby and Fagan unite for push on St. Louis. At Lake Springs, some Missouri militia clashes with straggling elements of Confederate army following Fort Davidson.
2	Elements of Marmaduke's division occupy Washington just outside St. Louis, where the depot is burned and Confederates fire on steamboats on the river. Price decides to bypass St. Louis and begins turning army west toward Jefferson City.
3	Clark's brigade of Marmaduke's division capture trains and stores at Miller's Station west of Washington. Skirmish occurs at Hermann as Missouri militia retreat toward Jefferson City.
4	Skirmish at rear Confederate column as clash occurs at Richwoods.
5	Skirmishing begins at multiple points along Osage River as Confederate lead elements probe for crossing site as Union cavalry defends on the far side.
6	Continued skirmishing as Confederates successfully force a crossing at Castle Rock.
7	As Union forces collapse on the defenses of Jefferson City, elements of Fagan's division press the retreating Federals along Moreau Creek.

8	Confederates arrayed at Jefferson City find defenses too strong to assault. Price decides to break contact and bypass Missouri capital. Army heads west with Fagan acting as rear guard.
9	Several skirmishes with Union cavalry as Price continues march westward. Shelby's division destroys Pacific Railroad near California.
10	Engagement at Boonville. Shelby's division captures town and several hundred Federal defenders. Citizens reportedly turn out to welcome Price's men as liberators.
11	Fagan's division attacked by Federals beyond Boonville. Army turns out to meet assault and repulses the attack. The first states hold their elections in Pennsylvania, Ohio, and Indiana, delivering Lincoln and the Republicans a decisive victory and foretelling of administration dominance in November when the rest of the North will go to the polls. This will lead to a continuation of Lincoln policies for winning the war.
12	March continues west as Price leaves Boonville.
14	Engagement at Glasgow, which Shelby captures after extended fight with elements of several regiments under command of Colonel Chester Harding, Jr., of the 43rd Missouri Infantry. Price makes impromptu plea to citizens to rise up to liberate the state. Simultaneously M. Jeff Thompson moves toward Sedalia.
15	Confederates capture Sedalia after local home guard abandon positions. The regular Union troops put up tough fight before surrendering the town.
16	Skirmishing on road between Georgetown and Lexington.
17	Federals occupy Lexington preparing to defend town from approaching Confederates. Federals at rear of Confederate column begin to place heavy pressure on Price, hastening his movements. Smithville burned by Confederates as they move.
18	Price continues moving toward Lexington. Federals closing in from rear as Blunt holds Lexington.
19	Heavy fighting around Lexington as Brigadier General Blunt defends town. Price, in fear that Blunt's forces from Department of Kansas could unite with Major General A.J. Smith's from XVI Corps and Brigadier General McNeil's, moving from Jefferson City, presses Blunt hard, outflanking him to clear the way forward. Blunt, heavily outnumbered, pulls back toward Independence, establishing defense on Little Blue River crossings. In Virginia, Jubal Early is decisively defeated at Cedar Creek by an army under Major General Phillip Sheridan. This seals the fate of Lee's army at Richmond and Petersburg.
20	Blunt's force sets the defense at Little Blue River. Price's scouts report movements of Federal forces and dispositions. Confederates begin movement west toward Little Blue River crossings, with Smith and Pleasonton closing in on his force from the rear. Price in danger of encirclement deep in enemy territory.
21	Battle of the Little Blue. Marmaduke attacks the crossing to fix Blunt while Shelby moves to the left to outflank the Union positions forcing Blunt to evacuate and move out through Independence. Price's army pivots south to attempt maneuvering out of the tightening trap of the converging Federal forces.
22	Heavy fighting around the Big Blue River as Price sends his train south to

(**1864** Oct)	protect it from the approaching Federal forces. Shelby and Fagan attack in front upon Major General Samuel R. Curtis' Army of the Border while Marmaduke defends the rear from Pleasonton's cavalry.
23	Battle of Westport, the largest battle in the history of Missouri. Confederates attack with intent to defeat Curtis' Army of the Border in front and then turn on Pleasonton in his rear. After initial success the Federals were able to turn the Confederate left while Pleasonton attacked in the rear. Only hard fighting by Shelby's division saves the Confederates from destruction. Price abandons the field hard pressed by pursuing Federals.
24	After some delay, the united forces of Curtis and Pleasonton begin pursuit of Price's army. Price inexplicably does not press the retreat, instead attempting to protect his long, plunder-filled train.
25	Pursuing Federals catch Price's army at Mine Creek and in a pitched battle break up his army, partially destroy his train, and capture Generals Marmaduke and Cabell. Price, in need for haste, is forced to burn the remainder of the train.
26	Skirmishing continues as Price continues to retreat south toward Arkansas border. Pleasonton breaks off the pursuit by diverting to Fort Scott, Kansas. He and Curtis get into a heated debate over the decision and command prerogatives. Curtis continues the pursuit, but with the lessened pressure Price is able to pull away. Simultaneously, "Bloody Bill" Anderson is killed in an ambush by Federal forces.
27	Retreat continues with no contact between Curtis and Price. However, desertions among Arkansas troops increase.
28	Battle of Newtonia. Curtis' pursuing Army of the Border regains contact and forces under Blunt launch an ill-coordinated attack. Shelby repulses the attack. Meanwhile, Curtis has more command issues, as elements from the Department of Missouri are ordered back to their garrisons. Curtis protests to no avail. Grant demands that Curtis continue the pursuit. The squabble again allows Price to escape.
29	Skirmish at Upshaw's farm in Barry County marks end of Federal pursuit as Price continues south toward the Arkansas state line.
31	Price camps on the Illinois River on the Arkansas line near Indian Territory intent on moving toward Fayetteville.
1 November	Elements of Price's army under Fagan move toward Fayetteville, which is garrisoned by Federal troops. Price's log kept by Lieutenant Colonel Lauchlan A. Maclean states that it rained all day during the march. XVI Army Corps commanded by Major General A.J. Smith, which was detained in Missouri due to Price's expedition, finally begins movement to rejoin Major General George Thomas' Army of the Cumberland at Nashville.
2	Fagan surrounds Fayetteville, completing the investment as the rain continues. In the East Major General William T. Sherman cuts loose from his base in Atlanta to embark on his march to the sea. His march cuts a 60-mile wide swath through central Georgia, destroying everything in the army's path.
3	Detachment from the Army of Missouri camped at Fayetteville as weather worsens with rain and snow. Fagan decides not to make an assault due to the weather and low morale among the troops, who do not relish attacking entrenched Federal troops.
4–5	Price begins moving again as weather clears.

6	Skirmish near Cane Hill, Arkansas, as army moves toward Indian Territory.
7	Price crosses the Arkansas River, and the Army of the Border under Curtis ends its pursuit, effectively ending the campaign for the Federal army.
8	Rain begins again, lowering the morale of Price's troops as they move south. Lincoln officially reelected as president, guaranteeing that his policy for complete defeat of the Confederacy will continue.
	A.J. Smith's XVI Corps departs St. Louis bound for Nashville to join the Army of the Cumberland in the defense of Tennessee.
2 December	Major General Price with the remnants of the Army of Missouri arrives in Laynesport, Louisiana, concluding the Great Missouri Raid and the last major Confederate operation west of the Mississippi.
15–16	General Hood's Army of Tennessee is destroyed in the Battle of Nashville by Major General George Thomas' Army of the Cumberland, with the XVI Corps playing a prominent role.
20	Major General William T. Sherman takes Savannah, concluding his famous march to the sea through Georgia.
27	Publication of Governor Thomas Reynolds' scathing evaluation of Price's conduct during the invasion of Missouri, in the *Marshall Texas Republican*.

1865

15 January	Fort Fisher falls to Union forces, sealing the Confederacy's last open port of Wilmington to the outside world.
21	General Sherman commences his Carolinas Campaign moving, north to join forces with General Grant at Richmond and Petersburg.
9 April	General Robert E. Lee surrenders the Army of Northern Virginia to Lieutenant General Ulysses S. Grant at Appomattox Court House, Virginia.
25	Court of Inquiry begins in Shreveport to review the events surrounding the outcome of the Great Raid and Sterling Price's conduct in particular. Price requested the inquiry in order to defend his honor against accusations of misconduct levied by Carney and others.
26	General Joseph E. Johnston surrenders the remnants of the Army of Tennessee to Major General William T. Sherman at Bennett's House near Durham Station, North Carolina.
	General E. Kirby Smith evacuates Shreveport with his staff, bound for Texas and effectively abdicating his command.
26	May Lieutenant General Simon B. Buckner surrenders all remaining Confederate forces west of the Mississippi.
Mid–June	Shelby and remnants of the Iron Brigade cross the Rio Grande into Mexico to avoid surrendering to Federal authorities. Sterling Price and other notables of the Trans-Mississippi army will join that procession because they refuse the terms offered by the Federal government.

Appendix B

Order of Battle[1]

Confederate Forces in the Missouri Raid of 1864

Army of Missouri
Major General Sterling Price

FAGAN'S DIVISION
Major General James F. Fagan

CABELL'S BRIGADE
Brigadier William L. Cabell (captured at Mine Creek), Lieutenant Colonel A.V. Reiff
Gordon's Arkansas Cavalry, Colonel Anderson Gordon
Gunter's Arkansas Cavalry Battalion, Lieutenant Colonel Thomas M. Gunter
Harrell's Arkansas Cavalry Battalion, Lieutenant Colonel John M. Harrell
Hill's Arkansas Cavalry, Colonel John F. Hill
Monroe's Arkansas Cavalry, Colonel James C. Monroe
Morgan's Arkansas Cavalry, Colonel Thomas J. Morgan
Witherspoon's Arkansas Cavalry Battalion, Major J.L. Witherspoon
Hughey's Arkansas Battery (2 guns), Captain William M. Hughey

DOBBIN'S BRIGADE
Colonel Archibald S. Dobbin
Dobbin's Arkansas Cavalry, Colonel Archibald S. Dobbin
McGhee's Arkansas Cavalry, Colonel James J. McGhee (wounded at Westport—23 October 1864)
Witt's Arkansas Cavalry, Colonel A.R. Witt
Blocher's Arkansas Battery (2 guns), Lieutenant J.V. Zimmerman

SLEMONS' BRIGADE
Colonel William F. Slemons, Colonel William A. Crawford
2nd Arkansas Cavalry, Colonel William F. Slemons
Carlton's Arkansas Cavalry, Colonel Charles H. Carlton
Crawford's Arkansas Cavalry, Colonel William A. Crawford
Wright's Arkansas Cavalry, Colonel John C. Wright

McCRAY'S BRIGADE
Colonel Thomas H. McCray
15th Missouri Cavalry, Colonel Timothy Reeves

45th Arkansas Infantry (mounted), Colonel Milton D. Baber
47th Arkansas Infantry (mounted), Colonel Lee Crandall

UNATTACHED
Anderson's Arkansas Cavalry, Captain William L. Anderson
Lyle's Arkansas Cavalry, Colonel Oliver P. Lyle
Rogan's Arkansas Cavalry, Colonel James W. Rogan

MARMADUKE'S DIVISION
Major General John S. Marmaduke (captured at Mine Creek)
Brigadier General John B. Clark, Jr.
Escort. Company D, Fifth Missouri Cavalry, Captain D.E. Stallard

MARMADUKE'S BRIGADE
Brigadier General John B. Clark, Jr., Colonel Colton Greene
3rd Missouri Cavalry, Colonel Colton Greene
4th Missouri Cavalry, Colonel John Q. Burbridge
7th Missouri Cavalry, Colonel Solomon G. Kitchen
8th Missouri Cavalry, Colonel William L. Jeffers
10th Missouri Cavalry, Colonel Robert R. Lawther
14th Missouri Cavalry Battalion, Lieutenant Colonel Robert C. Wood
Davies' Missouri Battalion Cavalry, Lieutenant Colonel J.F. Davies
Harris' Missouri Battery, Captain S.S. Harris
Hynson's Texas Battery, Captain Henry C. Hynson
Hogane's Engineer Company, Captain James T. Hogane

FREEMAN'S BRIGADE
Colonel Thomas R. Freeman
Freeman's Missouri Cavalry, Lieutenant Colonel Joseph R. Love
Fristoe's Missouri Cavalry, Colonel Edward T. Fristoe
Ford's Arkansas Cavalry, Lieutenant Barney Ford

SHELBY'S DIVISION
Brigadier General Joseph O. Shelby

SHELBY'S BRIGADE
Colonel David Shanks, Colonel Moses W. Smith, Brigadier General M. Jeff Thompson
5th Missouri Cavalry, Colonel Frank B. Gordon
11th Missouri Cavalry, Colonel Moses Smith
12th Missouri Cavalry, Lieutenant Colonel William H. Erwin
Crisp's Cavalry Battalion, Lieutenant Colonel John T. Crisp
Elliot's Missouri Cavalry, Colonel Benjamin F. Elliot
Johnson's Cavalry Battalion, Major Rector Johnson
Slayback's Missouri Cavalry Battalion, Lieutenant Colonel Alonzo Slayback
Collins' Missouri Battery (2 guns), Lieutenant Richard A. Collins
1st Cavalry Battalion or 1st Indian Brigade, Major Thomas R. Livingston (included recruits from the Indian Territory, Arkansas, and Missouri)

JACKMAN'S BRIGADE
Colonel Sidney D. Jackman
Hunter's Missouri Cavalry, Colonel DeWitt C. Hunter
Jackman's Missouri Cavalry, Lieutenant Colonel C.H. Nichols
Schnable's Missouri Cavalry Battalion, Lieutenant Colonel John A. Schnable
Williams' Missouri Cavalry Battalion, Lieutenant Colonel D.A. Williams
Collins' Missouri Battery (2 guns), Lieutenant Jacob D. Conner

TYLER'S BRIGADE
Colonel Charles H. Tyler
Coffee's Missouri Cavalry, Colonel John T. Coffee
Perkins' Missouri Cavalry, Colonel Caleb Perkins
Searcey's Missouri Cavalry, Colonel James T. Searcey
Unorganized Missouri Conscripts or Recruits

UNATTACHED
46th Arkansas Infantry (Mounted), Colonel W.O. Coleman

Union Forces
(Those available from beginning of invasion through defense of Jefferson City)

Department of the Missouri
Major General William S. Rosecrans

AT FORT DAVIDSON
Brigadier General Thomas Ewing
Major James Wilson

GARRISON
2nd Missouri State Militia Cavalry (1 company)
3rd Missouri State Militia Cavalry (6 companies)
1st Missouri State Militia Infantry (1 company)

REINFORCEMENTS BROUGHT BY BRIGADIER GENERAL EWING
47th Missouri Infantry (6 companies)
50th Missouri Infantry
14th Iowa Infantry (5 companies)
2nd Missouri Light Artillery
Company H (2 guns)
Company L

Also, various unorganized civilians and
African Americans aided in the defense of fort.

Troops Involved in the Defense of St. Louis

XVI Army Corps
Major General Andrew J. Smith

FIRST DIVISION
Brigadier General Joseph Mower (absent in Arkansas)
Colonel Joseph J. Woods

FIRST BRIGADE
Colonel William L. McMillen
114th Illinois, Major Joseph M. McLane
93rd Indiana, Captain Charles A. Hubbard
10th Minnesota, Lieutenant Colonel Samuel P. Jennison
72nd Ohio, Lieutenant Colonel Charles G. Eaton
95th Ohio, Lieutenant Colonel Jefferson Brumback
1st Illinois Light Artillery, Battery E, Captain John A. Fitch

SECOND BRIGADE
Colonel Lucius F. Hubbard
47th Illinois (detachment), Lieutenant Edward Bonham
5th Minnesota, Lieutenant Colonel William B. Gere
9th Minnesota, Major Horace B. Strait
11th Missouri, Major Eli Bowyer
8th Wisconsin, Lieutenant Colonel William B. Britton
Iowa Light Artillery, 2nd Battery, Lieutenant John W. Coons

THIRD BRIGADE
Colonel Sylvester G. Hill
12th Iowa, Lieutenant Colonel John H. Stibbs
35th Iowa, Captain Abraham N. Snyder
7th Minnesota, Colonel William R. Marshall
33rd Missouri, Lieutenant Colonel William H. Heath

THIRD DIVISION
Colonel David Moore

FIRST BRIGADE
Colonel Thomas J. Kenney
58th Illinois, Major Robert W. Healy
119th Illinois, Lieutenant Colonel Samuel E. Taylor
89th Indiana, Lieutenant Colonel Hervey Craven
21st Missouri, Lieutenant Colonel Edwin Moore

SECOND BRIGADE
Colonel James I. Gilbert
122nd Illinois, Colonel James F. Drish
27th Iowa, Major George W. Howard
32nd Iowa, Lieutenant Colonel Gustavus A. Eberhart

THIRD BRIGADE
Colonel Edward H. Wolfe
49th Illinois, Colonel Phineas Pease
117th Illinois, Colonel Risdon M. Moore

52nd Indiana, Captain Eli Mattocks
178th New York, Captain John B. Gandolfo

ARTILLERY
2nd Illinois Light, Battery G, Captain John W. Lowell
Indiana Light, 3rd Battery, Lieutenant Thomas J. Ginn
Indiana Light, 9th Battery, Lieutenant Samuel G. Calfee

Troops Assigned to the Various Districts

District of St. Louis
Brigadier General Thomas Ewing, Jr.

BENTON BARRACKS
Colonel Pitcairn Morrison
1st Missouri State Militia (two companies), Captain John Rupp
40th Missouri (recruits), Major George Hoffmann
41st Missouri (recruits), Major Henry F. Dietz
18th U.S. Colored Troops (two companies), Lieutenant Colonel John J. Sears
17th Illinois Cavalry (four companies), Colonel John L. Beveridge
2nd Wisconsin Cavalry (four companies), Major Nicholas H. Dale
Paroled men, Lieutenant Samuel O. Smith

BLOOMFIELD
2nd Missouri State Militia Cavalry (two companies), Captain Lewis Sells

CENTREVILLE
3rd Missouri State Militia Cavalry (one company), Captain John W. Hendrick

CHARLESTON
2nd Missouri State Militia Cavalry (one company), Captain James A. Ewing

DE SOTO
2nd Missouri State Militia Cavalry (one company), Captain Amos P. Wright

CAPE GIRARDEAU
1st Missouri State Militia (one company), Lieutenant Oliver P. Johnson
2nd Missouri State Militia (two companies), Major Josephus Robbins
2nd Missouri Artillery (section two guns), Lieutenant William Rinne
Tacke's Company (six months volunteers), Captain Adolph Tacke

HERMANN
3rd Missouri State Militia Cavalry (one company), Captain William T. Hunter

IRON BRIDGE
135th Illinois (one company), Captain Benjamin Burt

NEW MADRID
1st Missouri State Militia (one company), Captain Henry Kelling
2nd Missouri State Militia Cavalry (two companies), Captain James W. Edwards

PATTERSON
3rd Missouri State Militia Cavalry (two companies), Captain Robert McElroy

PILOT KNOB
1st Missouri State Militia (one company), Lieutenant John Fessler
2nd Missouri State Militia Cavalry (three companies), Captain Frederick R. Vincent
3rd Missouri State Militia Cavalry (three companies), Captain Hiram A. Rice
2nd Missouri Artillery (2 guns), Lieutenant Isaac H. Ferguson

SULPHUR SPRINGS
135th Illinois (detachment), Lieutenant Peter Jones

SAINTE GENEVIEVE
3rd Missouri State Militia Cavalry (one company), Captain Henry B. Milks

SAINT LOUIS
135th Illinois (five companies), Captain Samuel G. McAdams
145th Illinois (two companies), Captain Tamerlane Chapman
10th Kansas (four companies), Lieutenant Frederick A. Smalley
1st Missouri State Militia (one company), Lieutenant Colonel John N. Herder
40th Missouri (one company) Captain Adam Bax
6th Missouri Cavalry (four companies), Major Samuel Montgomery
2nd Missouri State Militia Cavalry (one company), Captain Luzern Bulkley
13th Missouri Cavalry (detachment), Captain William Flentz

Troops in Physical Defense of Jefferson City

Brigadier General Egbert B. Brown, Brigadier General Clinton B. Fisk

District of Central Missouri
Brigadier General Egbert B. Brown
45th Missouri Infantry (two companies), Colonel T.A. Switzler
3rd Missouri State Cavalry Militia (detachment), Lieutenant Colonel Henry A. Matthews
1st Missouri State Militia Cavalry (detachment), Colonel James McFerran
4th Missouri State Militia Cavalry (detachment), Major George W. Kelly
7th Missouri State Militia Cavalry (detachment), Colonel John F. Phillips, Lieutenant Colonel Thomas T. Crittenden
28th Enrolled Missouri Militia (Osage County), Colonel Lebbeus Zevely
34th Enrolled Missouri Militia (Gasconade County), Colonel Rudolph Poser
43rd Enrolled Missouri Militia (Coles County), Colonel A.J. Hart

District of Northern Missouri
Brigadier General Clinton B. Fisk
1st Iowa Cavalry (detachment), Major John McDermott
17th Illinois Cavalry (detachment)
39th Missouri (detachment)

43rd Missouri (detachment)
49th Missouri (detachment)
2nd Missouri Light Artillery, Company C (two howitzers)

District of Rolla
Brigadier General John McNeil
17th Illinois Cavalry (detachment)
5th Missouri State Militia Cavalry, Lieutenant Colonel Joseph Eppstein
9th Missouri State Militia Cavalry (detachment)
2nd Missouri Light Artillery, Company B (two guns) Lieutenant John J. Sutter

District of Southwest Missouri
Brigadier General John B. Sanborn
2nd Arkansas Cavalry (detachment), Colonel John E. Phelps
6th Missouri State Militia Cavalry (detachment), Major William Plumb
8th Missouri State Militia Cavalry (detachment), Colonel Joseph J. Gravely
6th Enrolled Missouri Militia Provisional Battalion later reorganized as a federalized volunteer regiment—16th Missouri Cavalry (detachment), Lieutenant Colonel John F. McMahan
7th Enrolled Missouri Militia Provisional Battalion reorganized as 15th Missouri Cavalry (detachment) Major William B. Mitchell

District of St. Louis
troops that Brigadier General Ewing brought from St. Louis for defense of Fort Davidson and later made their way to Jefferson City under McNeil and Sanborn
3rd Missouri State Militia Cavalry (detachment), Lieutenant Colonel Henry M. Matthews
2nd Missouri Light Artillery, Company L (four guns), Captain Charles H. Thurber

Enrolled Missouri Militia Units
54th and 55th Enrolled Missouri Militia (Franklin County) Colonel Daniel Q. Gale
10th Provisional Enrolled Missouri Militia
40th Enrolled Missouri Militia (Johnson County)
42nd Enrolled Missouri Militia
35th Enrolled Missouri Militia
33rd Enrolled Missouri Militia (St. Joseph)
51st Provisional Enrolled Missouri Militia (Carroll and Ray Counties)
65th Enrolled Missouri Militia (Carroll County)
70th Enrolled Missouri Militia (Howard and Monroe Counties)
63rd Enrolled Missouri Militia (Crawford County), Colonel Isaac C. Warmouth

Order of Battle for Westport

Army of the Border
Department of Kansas, Major General Samuel R. Curtis

Escort: Company G, 11th Kansas Cavalry with two guns attached, Lieutenant Edward Gill
Chief of Artillery, Major Robert H. Hunt

Provisional Cavalry Division
Major General James G. Blunt

First Brigade
Colonel Charles R. Jennison
3rd Wisconsin Cavalry (detachment), Captain Robert Carpenter
15th Kansas Cavalry, Lieutenant Colonel George H. Hoyt
Foster's Missouri Cavalry Battalion, Captain George S. Grover
Battery of five guns manned by men of 15th Kansas Cavalry, Lieutenant Henry L. Barker

Second Brigade
Colonel Thomas Moonlight
5th Kansas Cavalry (Companies L and M), Captain James H. Young
11th Kansas Cavalry, Lieutenant Colonel Preston B. Plumb
16th Kansas Cavalry (Companies A and D), Lieutenant Colonel Samuel Walker
Battery of four guns manned by men of Company E, 11th Kansas Cavalry

Third Brigade
Colonel Charles W. Blair
4th Kansas Militia, Colonel W. D. McCain
5th Kansas Militia, Colonel G. A. Colton
6th Kansas Militia, Colonel James D. Snoddy (arrested 16 October), Colonel James Montgomery
10th Kansas Militia, Colonel William Pennock
14th Kansas Cavalry, (Company E), Lieutenant William B. Clark
19th Kansas Militia, Colonel A. C. Hogan
24th Kansas Militia Battalion, Lieutenant Colonel George Eaves
2nd Kansas State Artillery (2 guns), Lieutenant Daniel C. Knowles
9th Wisconsin Battery, Captain James H. Dodge

Fourth Brigade
Colonel James H. Ford
2nd Colorado Cavalry, Major J. Nelson Smith (killed 21 October), Major J. H. Pritchard
16th Kansas Cavalry (detachment), Major James Ketner
McLain's Independent Colorado Battery, Captain W. D. McLain

Kansas State Militia Division
Major General George W. Deitzler
Brigadier Generals M.S. Grant and William H.M. Fishback

Units
(none were organized above regimental level)
1st Kansa Militia, Colonel Charles H. Robinson
2nd Kansas Militia, Colonel George W. Veale
2nd Kansas Colored Militia, Captain James L. Rafferty, Captain Richard J. Hinton
7th Kansas Militia, Colonel Peter McFarland

9th Kansas Militia, Colonel Frank M. Tracy
12th Kansas Militia, Colonel L.S. Treat
13th Kansas Militia, Colonel Alexander S. Johnson
14th Kansas Militia, Colonel William Gordon
18th Kansas Militia, Colonel Matthew Quigg
20th Kansas Militia, Colonel J.B. Hubbell
21st Kansas Militia, Colonel Sandy Lowe
22nd Kansas Militia, Colonel William Weer
Kansas City Home Guards, Colonel Kersey Coates

ARTILLERY
Independent Colored Battery, Captain H. Ford Douglas
Zesch's Battery, Kansas Militia Light Artillery (2 guns), Captain Gustavus Zesch
Topeka Battery of 2nd Kansas Militia (1 gun), Captain Ross Burnes

Troops from the Department of Missouri at Westport and the Pursuit from That Town

Major General William S. Rosecrans

Provisional Cavalry Division
Major General Alfred S. Pleasonton

FIRST BRIGADE
Brigadier General Egbert B. Brown (arrested 23 October), Colonel John F. Philips
1st Iowa Cavalry (detachment), Major John McDermott
1st Missouri Militia Cavalry, Colonel James McFerran (arrested 23 October), Lieutenant Colonel Bazel Lazear
4th Missouri Militia Cavalry, Major George W. Kelly
7th Missouri Militia Cavalry, Colonel John F. Philips, Lieutenant Colonel Thomas T. Crittenden

SECOND BRIGADE
Brigadier General John McNeil
2nd Missouri Cavalry (detachment), Captain George M. Houston
3rd Missouri Militia Cavalry (detachment), Lieutenant Colonel Henry M. Matthews
5th Missouri Militia Cavalry, Lieutenant Colonel Joseph Eppstein
7th Kansas Cavalry, Major Francis Malone
9th Missouri Militia Cavalry (detachment), Lieutenant Colonel Daniel M. Draper
13th Missouri Cavalry, Colonel Edwin C. Catherwood
17th Illinois Cavalry, Colonel John L. Beveridge

THIRD BRIGADE
Brigadier General John B. Sanborn
2nd Arkansas Cavalry, Colonel John E. Phelps
6th Missouri Militia Cavalry (detachment), Major William Plumb

6th Enrolled Missouri Militia Cavalry (detachment), Lieutenant Colonel John F. McMahan
7th Enrolled Missouri Militia Cavalry (detachment), Major W. B. Mitchell
8th Missouri Militia Cavalry, Colonel Joseph J. Gravely

FOURTH BRIGADE
Colonel Edward F. Winslow (wounded 23 October) Lieutenant Colonel Frederick W. Benteen
3rd Iowa Cavalry, Major Benjamin S. Jones
4th Iowa Cavalry, Major Abial R. Pierce
4th Missouri Cavalry (detachment), Captain George D. Knispel
7th Indiana Cavalry (detachment), Major S.W. Simonson
10th Missouri Cavalry, Lieutenant Colonel Frederick W. Benteen, Major William H. Lusk

ARTILLERY
Colonel Nelson Cole
Company H, 2nd Missouri Light Artillery (2 guns), Captain C.F. Montgomery
Section, Company H, 2nd Missouri Light Artillery (detached), Lieutenant Philip Smiley
Company L, 2nd Missouri Light Artillery (4 guns), Captain Charles H. Thurber
2 guns from the 5th Missouri Militia Cavalry, Lieutenant Adam Hillerich

UNASSIGNED
2nd New Jersey Cavalry (detachment), Captain Michael Gallagher
19th Pennsylvania Cavalry (one company)

Detachment from two Divisions of XVI Army Corps
Major General A.J. Smith

FIRST DIVISION
Colonel Joseph J. Woods

SECOND BRIGADE
Colonel Lucius F. Hubbard
5th Minnesota Infantry
7th Minnesota Infantry
8th Wisconsin Infantry
9th Minnesota Infantry
10th Minnesota Infantry
12th Iowa Infantry
47th Illinois Infantry
Battery G, 2nd Illinois Light Artillery

THIRD BRIGADE
Colonel Sylvester G. Hill
33rd Missouri Infantry
35th Iowa Infantry

THIRD DIVISION
Colonel David Moore

First Brigade
Colonel T.J. Kinney
58th Illinois Infantry
89th Illinois Infantry
119th Illinois Infantry

Second Brigade
Colonel James I. Gilbert
14th Iowa Infantry
24th Missouri Infantry
27th Iowa Infantry
32nd Iowa Infantry

Third Brigade
Colonel Edward H. Wolfe
49th Illinois Infantry
52nd Indiana Infantry
117th Illinois Infantry
178th New York Infantry
3rd Indiana Battery
9th Indiana Battery

Order of Battle for Mine Creek

Department of Missouri Provisional Cavalry Division
Major General Alfred S. Pleasonton

First Brigade
Colonel John F. Philips
1st Iowa Cavalry (detachment), Major John McDermott
1st Missouri Militia Cavalry, Lieutenant Colonel Bazel Lazear
4th Missouri Militia Cavalry, Major George W. Kelly
7th Missouri Militia Cavalry, Colonel John F. Philips, Lieutenant Colonel Thomas T. Crittenden

Fourth Brigade
Lieutenant Colonel Frederick W. Benteen
3rd Iowa Cavalry, Major Benjamin S. Jones
4th Iowa Cavalry, Major Abial R. Pierce
4th Missouri Cavalry (detachment), Captain George D. Knispel
7th Indiana Cavalry (detachment), Major S.W. Simonson
10th Missouri Cavalry, Major William H. Lusk

Artillery
Company H, 2nd Missouri Light Artillery (2 guns), Captain C.F. Montgomery

Chapter Notes

Preface

1. Michael J. Forsyth, *The Red River Campaign of 1864 and the Loss by the Confederacy of the Civil War* (Jefferson, NC: McFarland, 2002); *The Camden Expedition of 1864* (Jefferson, NC: McFarland, 2003).
2. United States War Department, *War of the Rebellion: A Compilation of the Official Records of the Union and Confederate Armies*, Series 1, Vol. 41, Part 1 (Washington, D.C.: United States Government Printing Office, 1885), 90 (hereafter cited as *OR*); Richard J. Hinton, *The Rebel Invasion of Missouri and Kansas* (Chicago: Church & Goodman, 1865), v, republished by Kansas Heritage Press, Ottawa, Kansas, 1994.

Introduction

1. United States War Department, *War of the Rebellion: A Compilation of the Official Records of the Union and Confederate Armies*, Series 1, Vol. 41, Part 1 (Washington, D.C.: United States Government Printing Office, 1885), 90.
2. Ibid., 116, 122.
3. The term Copperhead was used to describe "Peace" Democrats. They got this label because of their habit of wearing a copperhead penny on their lapels to identify each other.
4. Hinton, *The Rebel Invasion of Missouri and Kansas*, v-viii; Mark A. Lause, *Price's Lost Campaign: The 1864 Invasion of Missouri* (Columbia: University of Missouri Press, 2011), 2–3.
5. Robert Garlick Hill Kean, *Inside the Confederate Government: The Diary of Robert Garlick Hill Kean*, ed. Edward Younger (New York: Oxford University Press, 1957), 153.
6. Ibid.
7. Jack D. Welsh, *Medical Histories of Confederate Generals* (Kent, OH: Kent State University Press, 1995), 177.
8. U.S. Grant, *Personal Memoirs of U.S. Grant*, vol. 2, 350; William T. Sherman, *Memoirs of General Sherman*, vol. 2, 162.

Chapter 1

1. Louis S. Gerteis, *The Civil War in Missouri: A Military History* (Columbia: University of Missouri Press, 2012), 1.
2. James M. McPherson, *Battle Cry of Freedom* (London: Oxford University Press, 1985), 7–9.
3. Albert Castel, *General Sterling Price and the Civil War in the West* (Baton Rouge: Louisiana State University Press, 1968).
4. Library of Congress, "Missouri Compromise," in *A Century of Lawmaking for a New Nation*, 16th Congress, 1st Session, 548, http://memory.loc.gov/cgi-bin/ampage?collId=llsl&fileName=003/llsl003.db&recNum=587 .
5. McPherson, *Battle Cry of Freedom*, 7–9.
6. Library of Congress, "Kansas-Nebraska Act of 1854," in *A Century of Lawmaking for a New Nation*, 33rd Congress, 1st Session, 283, http://memory.loc.gov/cgi-bin/ampage?collId=llsl&fileName=010/llsl010.db&recNum=304.
7. Jay Monaghan, *Civil War on the Western Border, 1854–1865* (Boston: Little, Brown, 1955), 3.
8. Ibid., 7–8.
9. Ibid., 4.
10. Ibid., 6–15; Eli Thayer, *The History of the Kansas Crusade: Its Friends and Its Foes* (New York: Harper and Brothers, 1889), 23–30; John C. Moore, "Missouri," *Confederate Military History*, vol. 9, Clement A. Evans, ed. (Atlanta: Confederate, 1899), 5–6.
11. Monaghan, *Civil War on the Western Border*, 16–17; U.S. Congress, *Report No. 200*, Sub-Committee of the Committee on Elections, 34th Congress (Washington, D.C.: U.S. Government Printing Office, 1856), 72–100, from the Kansas Census section of the report (hereafter cited as *Report No. 200*).
12. Monaghan, *Civil War on the Western Border*, 18–19; U.S. Congress, *Report No. 200*, 3–4, 81–82; August Bondi Papers, Autobiography, 125, http://www2.ku.edu/~maxkade/bondi_and_index.pdf (accessed 13 February 2013).
13. Monaghan, *Civil War on the Western Border*, 20.
14. Ibid., 27.
15. Ibid., 29–35; Moore, "Missouri," 6.
16. Monaghan, *Civil War on the Western Border*, 23, 35–39.
17. Ibid., 54–59; August Bondi Papers, Autobiography, 128.
18. August Bondi Papers, Autobiography, 129.
19. Yankl Stillman, "August Bondi and the Abolitionist Movement," *Jewish Currents* (March 2004), http://jewishcurrents.org/2004-mar-stillman.htm (accessed 4 February 2013).
20. Ibid.; Bondi Papers, Autobiography, 129–134; Monaghan, *Civil War on the Western Border*, 62–63.

21. Ibid., 65–68.
22. Ibid., 24; Joseph C.G. Kennedy, *Population of the United States in 1860: Compiled from the Original Returns of the Eighth Census* (Washington, D.C.: U.S. Government Printing Office, 1864), iv, http://www2.census.gov/prod2/decennial/documents/1860-01.pdf.
23. Monaghan, *Civil War on the Western Border*, 96–99.
24. Ibid., 103–105.
25. Louis G. Gerteis, *The Civil War in Missouri: A Military History*, 8–9.
26. Moore, "Missouri," 20–21.
27. Kennedy, *Population of the United States*, iv, xvii; Robert L. Kerby, *Kirby Smith's Confederacy: The Trans-Mississippi South, 1863–1865* (Tuscaloosa: University of Alabama Press, 1972), 9–10; Gerteis, *The Civil War in Missouri*, 5.
28. Gerteis, *The Civil War in Missouri*, 516–17.
29. Thomas L. Snead, *The Fight for Missouri from the Election of Lincoln to the Death of Lyon* (New York: Scribner's, 1886), 22–23; Thomas L. Snead, "The First Year of the War in Missouri," in *Battles and Leaders of the Civil War* (hereinafter *B&L*), vol. 1, 264; Wiley Britton, *The Civil War on the Border;1861–1862*, vol. 1 (New York: G.P. Putnam's Sons, 1890), 2, reprinted by Kansas Heritage Press, Ottawa, 1994.
30. Monaghan, *Civil War on the Western Border*, 25–27; Gerteis, *The Civil War in Missouri*, 14–15.
31. Gerteis, *The Civil War in Missouri*, 22–25; *OR*, Vol. I, Part 3, 6–7; Moore, "Missouri," 31–33; Thomas L. Snead, "The First Year of the War in Missouri," 262–263, 265; Britton, *The Civil War on the Border*, vol. 1, 3–4, 7–9.
32. Gerteis, *The Civil War in Missouri*, 25–26; John McElroy, *The Struggle for Missouri* (Washington, D.C.: National Tribune, 1913), 78–79; Moore, "Missouri," *Confederate Military History*, vol. 9, 35–36.
33. Moore, "Missouri," *Confederate Military History*, vol. 9, 38; McElroy, *The Struggle for Missouri*, 80–81 (quoted from this source; the full text of the Price-Harney agreement is found therein); *OR*, Vol. I, Part 3, 374–375; Thomas C. Reynolds, *General Sterling Price and the Confederacy*, edited by Robert G. Schultz (St. Louis: Missouri History Museum, 2009), 32–35, 221–222.
34. Britton, *The Civil War on the Border*, vol. 1, 16–17.
35. Moore, "Missouri," *Confederate Military History*, vol. 9, 38–39; Abraham Lincoln, *Abraham Lincoln's Complete Works: Comprising His Speeches, Letters, State Papers, and Miscellaneous Writings*, ed. John G. Nicolay and John Hay (New York: Century, 1894), vol. 6, 307–308, from President Lincoln's 4 July 1861 Message to Congress in Special Session.
36. Quote from McElroy, *The Struggle for Missouri*, 96–97; Moore, "Missouri," *Confederate Military History*, vol. 9, 40–41; Snead, *The Fight for Missouri*, 200.
37. Snead, *The Fight for Missouri*, 229–230; Gerteis, *The Civil War in Missouri*, 36; Donald Stoker, *The Grand Design: Strategy in the U.S. Civil War* (London: Oxford University Press, 2010), 117; Edwin C. Bearss, *The Battle of Wilson's Creek* (Cassville, MO: Litho, 1992), 19–20.

38. Bearss, *The Battle of Wilson's Creek*, 41–44; William H. Wherry, "Wilson's Creek and the Death of Lyon," in *B&L*, vol. 1, 289; *OR*, Series 1, Vol. 3, 59; Britton, *The Civil War on the Border*, vol. 1, 84–85.
39. Bearss, *The Battle of Wilson's Creek*, 161–164.
40. Ibid, 49; Wherry, "Wilson's Creek and the Death of Lyon," in *B&L*, vol. 1, 291; Britton, *The Civil War on the Border*, vol. 1, 86–87.
41. Wherry, "Wilson's Creek and the Death of Lyon," in *B&L*, vol. 1, 292; Bearss, *The Battle of Wilson's Creek*, 134, 162.
42. *OR*, Series 1, Vol. 3, 672.
43. Anne J. Bailey, "The Abandoned Western Theater: Confederate National Policy Toward the Trans-Mississippi Region," *Journal of Confederate History* 5 (1990), 35–54; Stoker, *The Grand Design*, 46–47, 232–233; Dale Davis, "Guerrilla Operations in the Civil War: Assessing Compound Warfare During Price's Raid," master's thesis, Command and General Staff College Fort Leavenworth, Kansas, 2004, 3–5. On a personal note, Dale Davis is an old friend from our days at Murray State University ROTC, from which we were commissioned as officers many years ago. His assessment of Price's raid from the perspective of the interaction of guerrilla and conventional operations is worth examining and provides an excellent perspective of the lack of coordination between the South's regular and irregular forces.
44. Snead, "The First Year of the War in Missouri," in *B&L*, vol. 1, 273; Gerteis, *The Civil War in Missouri*, 99–101.
45. Gerteis, *The Civil War in Missouri*, 100–101.
46. Colonel James A. Mulligan, "The Siege of Lexington," in *B&L*, vol. 1, 307–313; Britton, *The Civil War on the Border*, vol. 1, 140, 142.
47. Britton, *The Civil War on the Border*, vol. 1, 140–142; Mulligan, "The Siege of Lexington," in *B&L*, vol. 1, 307–313.
48. Kerby, *Kirby Smith's Confederacy*, 31.
49. Major General John C. Fremont, "In Command in Missouri," in *B&L*, vol. 1, 279.
50. Gerteis, *The Civil War in Missouri*, 156–157.
51. Andy Turner, "On This Day: The Battle That Saved Missouri for the Union," *Gatehouse Press* (March 2013), http:www.gatehousepress.com/?p=3377 (accessed 7 March 2013); Stoker, *The Grand Design*, 117–118.
52. Gerteis, *The Civil War in Missouri*, 137–141.
53. Bailey, "The Abandoned Western Theater," *Journal of Confederate History* 5, 35–37; Kerby, *Kirby Smith's Confederacy*, 146–147; Forsyth, *The Camden Expedition of 1864*, 58–59.
54. Davis, "Guerrilla Operations in the Civil War: Assessing Compound Warfare During Price's Raid," 1–4.
55. Forsyth, *The Red River Campaign of 1864*, 119–127; Stoker, *The Grand Design*, 362, 364, 374–376.
56. *OR*, Series 1, Vol. 41, Part 1, 89; Stoker, *The Grand Design*, 361; Kerby, *Kirby Smith's Confederacy*, 323–324.
57. Kerby, *Kirby Smith's Confederacy*, 333–335; *OR*, Series 1, Vol. 41, 117.

Chapter 2

1. Robert E. Shalhope, *Sterling Price: Portrait of a Southerner* (Columbia: University of Missouri Press, 1971), 1–4.
2. Ibid., 5–11.
3. Ibid., 6–10.
4. Ibid., 12–13.
5. Ibid., 15–16; Albert Castel, *General Sterling Price and the Civil War in the West* (Baton Rouge: Louisiana State University Press, 1968), 3.
6. Castel, *General Sterling Price and the Civil War in the West*, 3; Shalhope, *Sterling Price*, 30.
7. Castel, *General Sterling Price*, 4.
8. Shalhope, *Sterling Price*, 56–58.
9. Ralph R. Rea, *Sterling Price: The Lee of the West* (Pioneer, 1959), 1–3, 7, 199–200; Castel, *General Sterling Price*, 3.
10. Jack D. Welsh, M.D., *Medical Histories of Confederate Generals* (Kent, OH: Kent State University Press, 1995), 177; Castel, *General Sterling Price*, 5.
11. Castel, *General Sterling Price*, 5; Shalhope, *Sterling Price*, 73–75; Ralph Emerson Twitchell, *The History of the Military Occupation of the Territory of New Mexico from 1846 to 1851* (Denver, CO: Smith-Brooks, 1909), 86–87, 96, 122–133.
12. Twitchell, *The History of the Military Occupation*, 116–117; Castel, *General Sterling Price*, 6.
13. Castel, *General Sterling Price*, 6; Shalhope, *Sterling Price*, 116–117.
14. Castel, *General Sterling Price*, 7.
15. Snead, *The Fight for Missouri*, 78–81, 86–87.
16. Bearss, *The Battle of Wilson's Creek*, 62–63, 78–79; Snead, "The First Year of the War in Missouri," 262–277.
17. Snead, "The First Year of the War in Missouri," 273; Castel, *General Sterling Price*, 48–49; *OR*, Vol. 3, 747; Sterling Price Papers, Missouri Digital Heritage Collections, Jefferson City, Missouri, http://cdm.sos.mo.gov/; Letter from W.R. Bradfute, McCulloch's adjutant to Sterling Price, dated 23 August 1861.
18. Castel, *General Sterling Price*, 64–65; Shalhope, *Sterling Price*, 184–188; Snead, "The First Year of the War in Missouri," 274–275.
19. Castel, *General Sterling Price*, 68; William L. Shea and Earl J. Hess, *Pea Ridge: Civil War Campaign in the West* (Chapel Hill: University of North Carolina Press, 1992), 22, 56–57.
20. Major General Franz Sigel, "The Pea Ridge Campaign," in *B&L*, vol. 1, 321, 324; Shea and Hess, *Pea Ridge*, 78–87; Welsh, *Medical Histories of Confederate Generals*, 177.
21. Ibid., 284–289; "The Trans-Mississippi Department of the Confederacy," in *Writers of History*, http://writersofhistory.com/?p=200 (accessed 28 March 2013); Castel, *General Sterling Price*, 82–83. At this point in the war the Trans-Mississippi was not a full-fledged department in the Confederate command structure. It still held only district status, but this would soon change.
22. Snead, "The First Year of the War in Missouri," 84.
23. *OR*, Series 1, Vol. 13, 838.
24. Thomas L. Snead, "With Price East of the Mississippi," *B&L*, vol. 2, 724 (emphasis in original).
25. Ibid., 726; Thomas C. Reynolds, *General Sterling Price and the Confederacy*, ed. Robert G. Schultz (St. Louis: Missouri History Museum, 2009), 45–49, 53.
26. Ibid., 46.
27. Snead, "With Price East of the Mississippi," *B&L*, vol. 2, 725–726; *OR*, Series 1, Vol. 17, Part 2, 656.
28. *OR*, Series 1, Vol. 17, Part 2, 705–706; C.S. Hamilton, "The Battle of Iuka," *B&L*, vol. 2, 734–736; Peter Cozzens, *The Darkest Days of the War: The Battles of Iuka and Corinth* (Chapel Hill: University of North Carolina Press, 1997), 139–140, 126–128.
29. Reynolds, *Price and the Confederacy*, 51–59.
30. Castel, *General Sterling Price*, 165–171; Thomas L. Snead, "The Conquest of Arkansas," in *B&L*, vol. 3, 455–459.
31. Reynolds, *Price and the Confederacy*, 99–109, 247. This text contains the copy of G.O. #6 by which Price assumed command from Holmes due to his illness; Joseph H. Parks, *General Edmund Kirby Smith, C.S.A.* (Baton Rouge: Louisiana State University Press, 1954), 368–369.
32. *OR*, Series 1, Vol. 34, Part 2, 1028–1029.
33. Ibid.; Shalhope, *Sterling Price*, 256–257; Castel, *General Sterling Price*, 171–175; Reynolds, *General Sterling Price and the Confederacy*, 129. Governor Reynolds notes in his account that General Smith was one of the few superiors Price approached with deference rather than agitation.
34. *OR*, Series 1, Vol. 34, Part 1, 481–482, 486, 531–532; Part 2, 1145–1146; Forsyth, *The Camden Expedition of 1864*, 66, 184.
35. Daniel O'Flaherty, *General Jo Shelby: Undefeated Rebel* (Chapel Hill: University of North Carolina Press, 2000), 9–10.
36. Ibid., 10–11.
37. Ibid., 11–12.
38. Ibid., 13.
39. Ibid., 13–18.
40. Ibid., 19–21.
41. Ibid., 21–23.
42. Ibid.; Thayer, *Kansas Crusade*, 98–99.
43. U.S. Congress, *Report No. 200*, 3–4, 81–82; Flaherty, *General Jo Shelby*, 33–35.
44. Flaherty, *General Jo Shelby*, 42–43.
45. Ibid., 52–59; Edwards, *Shelby and His Men*, 22–24. As long as the Federal government made no overt moved against Missouri, Shelby was at least tentatively loyal; but any Federal action, however slight, would push him straight into secessionist hands.
46. O'Flaherty, *General Jo Shelby*, 65–67.
47. Ibid., 28, 69–71; Britton, *The Civil War on the Border*, vol. 1, 55.
48. Ibid., 80–81; Bearss, *The Battle of Wilson's Creek*, 56–59; Edwards, *Shelby and His Men*, 34–36; O'Flaherty, *General Jo Shelby*, 84–85.
49. Ibid.; Britton, *The Civil War on the Border*, vol. 1, 89–90, 100–108.
50. *OR*, Series 1, Vol. 8, 328.
51. O'Flaherty, *General Jo Shelby*, 103–105; Edwards, *Shelby and His Men*, 56–57.

52. Ibid., 115; *OR*, Series 1, Vol. 8, 97.
53. O'Flaherty, *General Jo Shelby*, 129–130.
54. Ibid., 134–142; Stephen B. Oates, *Confederate Cavalry West of the River* (Austin: University of Texas Press, 1961), 91–95; Edwards, *Shelby and His Men*, 99–101; Samuel Jones, "The Battle of Prairie Grove: December 7, 1862," *Southern Bivouac* (1885), 203–211. Samuel Jones, who was a major general in the Confederate Army, misspells Shelby's name, referenced as Shelley in the text, throughout his account of the battles of Cane Hill and Prairie Grove.
55. Jones, "The Battle of Prairie Grove," 210–211; O'Flaherty, *General Jo Shelby*, 156–162.
56. O'Flaherty, *General Jo Shelby*, 162–171; Oates, *Confederate Cavalry West of the River*, 115, 123.
57. O'Flaherty, *General Jo Shelby*, 171–172.
58. Ibid., 163–174.
59. Ibid., 177–178; Snead, "The Conquest of Arkansas," in *B&L*, vol. 3, 454–456.
60. Ibid., 456; O'Flaherty, *General Jo Shelby*, 184–186; Edwards, *Shelby and His Men*, 167–168; Jack Welsh, *Medical Histories of Confederate Commanders* (Kent, OH: Kent State University Press, 1995), 195.
61. O'Flaherty, *General Jo Shelby*, 188; Edwards, *Shelby and His Men*, 197.
62. O'Flaherty, *General Jo Shelby*, 206–207; Edwards, *Shelby and His Men*, 198–211; Oates, *Confederate Cavalry West of the River*, 138–140.
63. O'Flaherty, *General Jo Shelby*, 207–213; Forsyth, *The Camden Expedition of 1864*, 130–133.
64. Evans, *Confederate Military History*, vol. 9, 215; Gerteis, *The Civil War in Missouri*, 30.
65. Evans, *Confederate Military History*, vol. 9, 215.
66. *Official Register of the Officers and Cadets of the U.S. Military Academy* (West Point, NY, 1857), 7; William E. Parrish, Perry McCandless, and William E. Foley, *A History of Missouri* (Columbia: University of Missouri Press, 1971), 16–17.
67. Foley, *A History of Missouri*, 16–17.
68. U.S. Congress, *The Utah Expedition*, Executive Doc. No. 71, 35th Congress, 1st Session (Washington, D.C.: U.S. Government Printing Office, 1858), 4–5, 7–9, 21–23, 92–99.
69. Ibid., 1–4, 92–99.
70. Gerteis, *The Civil War in Missouri*, 30.
71. Ibid., 37–38.
72. Evans, *Confederate Military History*, vol. 9, 215.
73. John H. Eicher and David J. Eicher, *Civil War High Commands* (Stanford: Stanford University Press, 2001), 23, 66–70; Evans, *Confederate Military History*, vol. 9, 215.
74. William Preston Johnston, "Albert Sidney Johnston at Shiloh," in *B&L*, vol. 1, 557.
75. Evans, *Confederate Military History*, vol. 9, 215; Larry J. Daniel, *Shiloh: The Battle That Changed the Civil War* (New York: Simon & Schuster, 1997), 209–214; *OR*, Series I, Vol. 10, Part I, 574.
76. Evans, *Confederate Military History*, vol. 9, 215; Welsh, *Medical Histories of Confederate Generals*, 154.
77. O'Flaherty, *General Jo Shelby*, 140–141; Oates, *Confederate Cavalry West of the River*, 91–95; Thomas L. Snead, "The Conquest of Arkansas," in *B&L*, vol. 3, 446–449.
78. Thomas L. Snead, "The Conquest of Arkansas," in *B&L*, vol. 3, 450; Oates, *Confederate Cavalry West of the River*, 102–109; Jones, "The Battle of Prairie Grove," *Southern Bivouac* (1885), 203–211; Evans, *Confederate Military History*, vol. 9, 216.
79. Oates, *Confederate Cavalry West of the River*, 112.
80. Gerteis, *The Civil War in Missouri*, 149; O'Flaherty, *General Jo Shelby*, 162; Oates, *Confederate Cavalry West of the River*, 115.
81. Gerteis, *The Civil War in Missouri*, 150–152.
82. Ibid., 152; O'Flaherty, *General Jo Shelby*, 160–161.
83. O'Flaherty, *General Jo Shelby*, 171–173; Gerteis, *The Civil War in Missouri*, 154–156; Oates, *Confederate Cavalry West of the River*, 130.
84. Snead, "The Conquest of Arkansas," in *B&L*, vol. 3, 456; O'Flaherty, *General Jo Shelby*, 180–181; *OR*, Series 1, Vol. 22, Part 1, 437; Leo E. Huff, "The Last Duel in Arkansas: The Marmaduke-Walker Duel," *Arkansas Historical Quarterly* 23, no. 1 (Spring 1964), 36.
85. Huff, "The Last Duel," 37–45.
86. Forsyth, *The Camden Expedition*, 111–116.
87. Warner, *Generals in Gray*, 85.
88. Evans, *Confederate Military History*, vol. 10, 399.
89. Ibid.; "Arkansas in the Mexican War," *Encyclopedia of Arkansas History and Culture*, http://www.encyclopediaofarkansas.net/encyclopedia/entry-detail.aspx?entryID=4206 (accessed 15 May 2013).
90. "Arkansas in the Mexican War," (accessed 15 May 2013).
91. Michael J. Forsyth, "Effective Termination of Conflict: Perspectives from 1847 and 2003," Strategy Research Project (Carlisle, PA: U.S. Army War College, 2012), 14–15. *Ranchero* was a derisive label given to Mexican guerrillas by the American troops in the Mexican War. It implied that men fighting as guerrillas were nothing more than bandits and thus outside the law, which would make poor treatment by American captors acceptable.
92. Ibid.
93. Evans, *Confederate Military History*, vol. 10, 399.
94. Ibid.
95. Johnston, "Albert Sidney Johnston at Shiloh," in *Battles & Leaders*, vol. 1, 557 (italics in original).
96. Daniel, *Shiloh*, 210.
97. Ibid., 211–212.
98. Evans, *Confederate Military History*, vol. 10, 399–400.
99. Jones, "The Battle of Prairie Grove," *Southern Bivouac*, 203–211; Britton, *Civil War on the Border*, vol. 1, 422–423; Oates, "The Prairie Grove Campaign," 130–131; Oates, *Confederate Cavalry West of the River*, 105–106, 109.
100. Reynolds, *General Sterling Price and the Confederacy*, 245.
101. Snead, "The Conquest of Arkansas," in *B&L*, vol. 3, 455–457.

102. Forsyth, *The Camden Expedition*, 106.
103. Ibid., 127–134.

Chapter 3

1. William M. Lamers, *The Edge of Glory: A Biography of General William S. Rosecrans, U.S.A.* (New York: Harcourt, Brace & World, 1961), 450, 8–9.
2. Ibid., 9–10.
3. *Official Register of the Officers and Cadets of the U.S. Military Academy for 1842*, 7; Lamars, *The Edge of Glory*, 11–12.
4. Lamars, *The Edge of Glory*, 13–15.
5. Ibid., 14–16.
6. Ibid., 17–18; Jack D. Welsh, *Medical Histories of Union Generals* (Kent, OH: Kent State University Press, 1996), 283.
7. Lamers, *The Edge of Glory*, 17.
8. Ibid., 20–27. The area described is now in West Virginia; the mountain counties seceded from Virginia to form the new state in 1863.
9. Jacob D. Cox, "McClellan in West Virginia," in *B&L*, vol. 1, 131; Jacob D. Cox, *Military Reminiscences of the Civil War, April 1861–November 1863*, vol. 1 (New York: Scribner's, 1900), 51.
10. Cox, "McClellan in West Virginia," in *B&L*, vol. 1, 131–133; Andy Turner, "On this Day: The Battle of Rich Mountain," *Gatehouse Press Online* (July 2013), http://www.gatehouse-press.com/?p=4211 (accessed 11 July 2013).
11. Ibid.; Cox, "McClellan in West Virginia," in *B&L*, vol. 1, 132–133.
12. Lamers, *The Edge of Glory*, 33; Andy Turner, "On this Day: The Battle of Rich Mountain," http://www.gatehouse-press.com/?p=4211 (accessed 11 July 2013).
13. Cox, *Military Reminiscences*, 74.
14. Lamars, *The Edge of Glory*, 44–52; Cox, "McClellan in West Virginia," in *B&L*, 142–148; Cox, *Military Reminiscences*, 97–104.
15. Lamers, *The Edge of Glory*, 85–87; Peter Cozzens, *The Darkest Days of the War: The Battles of Iuka and Corinth* (Chapel Hill: University of North Carolina Press, 1997), 23, 26–32.
16. Cozzens, *The Darkest Days*, 50–52.
17. Ibid., 63–65; Lamars, *The Edge of Glory*, 108–116.
18. Lamers, *The Edge of Glory*, 117–130.
19. William S. Rosecrans, "The Battle of Corinth," in *B&L*, vol. 2, 740–741.
20. Ibid., 744–753; Lamers, *The Edge of Glory*, 148–153, 170–180.
21. Lamers, *The Edge of Glory*, 191–195.
22. Philip Sheridan, *Civil War Memoirs* (New York: Bantam Books, 1991), 66–67, 75–76; Peter Cozzens, *No Better Place to Die: The Battle of Stones River* (Champaign: University of Illinois Press, 1990), 166.
23. Sheridan, *Civil War Memoirs*, 77–78; Lamars, *The Edge of Glory*, 245, 272–273.
24. Sheridan, *Civil War Memoirs*, 85–86, 89–90.
25. Ibid., 90–93; Lamars, *The Edge of Glory*, 275–277; Gilbert C. Kniffen, "Maneuvering Bragg Out of Tennessee," in *B&L*, vol. 3, 635–637.
26. Lamers, *The Edge of Glory*, 307–314; Sheridan, *Civil War Memoirs*, 99–100.
27. Daniel Harvey Hill, "Chickamauga: The Great Battle of the West," in *B&L*, vol. 3, 640–641.
28. Peter Cozzens, *This Terrible Sound: The Battle of Chickamauga* (Champaign: University of Illinois Press, 1992), 365–367, 374–375; Hill, "Chickamauga," in *B&L*, vol. 3, 657; Lamers, *The Edge of Glory*, 342–346.
29. Lamers, *The Edge of Glory*, 360–361, 379–380, 406; Lincoln, *The Collected Works of Abraham Lincoln*, ed. Roy Basler, vol. 6, 472, 498; James M. McPherson, *Tried By Fire: Lincoln as Commander-in-Chief* (New York: Penguin, 2008), 196.
30. McPherson, *Tried by Fire*, 196–197; Lamers, *The Edge of Glory*, 406–408; U.S. Grant, "Chattanooga," in *B&L*, vol. 3, 680–682.
31. Sheridan, *Civil War Memoirs*, 115.
32. Lamers, *The Edge of Glory*, 415–416; McPherson, *Tried By Fire*, 197.
33. Warner, *Generals in Blue*, 147; Ronald D. Smith, *Thomas Ewing, Jr.: Frontier Lawyer and Civil War General* (Columbia: University of Missouri Press), 3–4.
34. Smith, *Thomas Ewing, Jr.*, 4–5.
35. Ibid., 6–11, 14–15.
36. Ibid., 21, 27–29; Whitelaw Reid, *Ohio in the War: Her Statemen, Her Generals, and Soldiers* (New York: Moore, Wilstach & Baldwin, 1868), 834.
37. Smith, *Thomas Ewing Jr.*, 27–29.
38. Ibid., 29–33.
39. Ibid., 34–38.
40. Ibid., 49.
41. Ibid., 58–65.
42. Ibid., 93–95, 125.
43. Ibid., 146–152.
44. Ibid., 152, 166.
45. Ibid., 164–167; Harrison Hannahs, "General Thomas Ewing, Jr.," *Collections of the Kansas State Historical Society* 12 (1912), 276.
46. Albert Castel, *A Frontier State at War: Kansas, 1861–1865* (Ithaca, New York: Cornell University Press, 1958), 89; Smith, *Thomas Ewing Jr.*, 176–177.
47. Smith, *Thomas Ewing Jr.*, 177–178; Crawford, *Kansas in the Sixties*, 57–58; Welsh, *Medical Histories of Union Generals*, 111–112; Britton, *Civil War on the Western Border*, vol. 1, 368–374; *OR*, Series 1, Vol. 13, 760–761.
48. Smith, *Thomas Ewing, Jr.*, 179–180; Britton, *Civil War on the Western Border*, vol. 1, 390–391, 394; *OR*, Series 1, Vol. 22, Part 1, 52–54.
49. Smith, *Thomas Ewing, Jr.*, 181–183; Britton, *Civil War on the Western Border*, vol. 1, 421–425; Kim Allen Scott, "The Preacher, the Lawyer, and the Spoils of War," *Kansas History* 13 (1991), 212–214.
50. Smith, *Thomas Ewing, Jr.*, 187; Castel, *A Frontier State at War*, 111.
51. Castel, *A Frontier State at War.*, 103–105, 112.
52. Smith, *Thomas Ewing Jr.*, 193; O.S. Barton, *Three Years with Quantrill: A True Story Told by His Scout John McCorkle* (Norman: University of Oklahoma Press, 1992), 123.
53. Castel, *A Frontier State at War*, 126–128; Smith, *Thomas Ewing, Jr.*, 195–196; Barton, *Three Years with*

Quantrill, 124; George Miller, *Missouri's Memorable Decade, 1860–1870: An Historical Sketch* (Columbia, MO: E.W. Stephens, 1898), 98.

54. Barton, *Three Years with Quantrill*, 125–126; Miller, *Missouri's Memorable Decade*, 99; John B. Jones, *A Rebel War Clerk's Diary*, ed. Earl Schenck Miers (New York: A.S. Barnes, 1958), 265; Castel, *A Frontier State at War*, 128–135.

55. Smith, *Thomas Ewing, Jr.*, 199–201; Castel, *A Frontier State at War*, 142–144.

56. Text of the order extracted from Barton, *Three Years with Quantrill*, 132–133.

57. Castel, *A Frontier State at War*, 152–153; Smith, *Thomas Ewing, Jr.*, 207–210; Miller, *Missouri's Memorable Decade*, 102–103. George Bingham's famous painting, called, appropriately enough, *G.O. #11*, is at the State Historical Society of Missouri.

58. Smith, *Thomas Ewing, Jr.*, 210–211; Schofield, *Forty-Six Years in the Army*, 108–110.

59. *Official Register of the Officers and Cadets of the U.S. Military Academy for 1844*, 7; Warner, *Generals in Blue*, 377; Edward G. Longacre, "Alfred Pleasonton: 'Knight of Romance,'" *Civil War Times Illustrated*, no. 13 (December 1974), 13.

60. *Civil War Times Illustrated*, no. 13, 13; Warner, *Lives of Union Generals*, 377.

61. Warner, *Lives of Union Generals*, 377; Longacre, "Alfred Pleasonton: 'Knight of Romance,'" 13.

62. Longacre, "Alfred Pleasonton: 'Knight of Romance,'" 13.

63. Ibid.

64. Ibid.

65. Stephen Z. Starr, *The Union Cavalry in the Civil War*, vol. 1 (Baton Rouge: Louisiana State University Press, 1979), 314.

66. Longacre, "Alfred Pleasonton," 14–15; Starr, *The Union Cavalry in the Civil War*, vol. 1, 313–316.

67. *OR*, Series 1, Vol. 21, 815.

68. Alfred Pleasonton, "The Successes and Failures of Chancellorsville," in *B&L*, vol. 3, 177–181; Eric J. Wittenberg, *The Union Cavalry Comes of Age: Hartwood Church to Brandy Station, 1863* (Washington, D.C.: Brasseys, 2003), 162–168; Longacre, "Alfred Pleasonton," 16–17.

69. Ibid., 17–18; Robert L. Murphy, "'I Have No Faith in Foreigners': Pleasonton Clears the Way for His Boy Generals," *Gettysburg*, issue 45 (Summer 2013), 3–10.

70. Longacre, "Alfred Pleasonton," 18; Bill Hyde, *The Union Generals Speak: The Meade Hearings on the Battle of Gettysburg* (Baton Rouge: Louisiana State University Press, 2003), 135.

71. Ibid.; Longacre, "Alfred Pleasonton," 18.

72. Hyde, *The Union Generals Speak*, 136–143.

73. Longacre, "Alfred Pleasonton," 19–20.

74. Warner, *Generals in Blue*, 107–108; Ruth A. Gallagher, "Samuel Ryan Curtis," *Iowa Journal of History and Politics* 35, no. 3 (July 1927), 331.

75. Gallagher, "Samuel Ryan Curtis."

76. Ibid.; Warner, *Generals in Blue*, 107–108.

77. Warner, *Generals in Blue*, 107–108; Gallagher, "Samuel Ryan Curtis," 331; Hawkins, "General Curtis," *Iowa Historical Record* 3, 562; *Official Register of the Officers and Cadets of the United States Military Academy, Class of 1831*, 7.

78. Hawkins, "General Curtis," 562; Gallagher, "Samuel Ryan Curtis," 332.

79. Gallagher, "Samuel Ryan Curtis," 332.; Taylor, "General Curtis," 562.

80. Gallagher, "Samuel Ryan Curtis," 332–333.

81. Ibid.

82. Ibid., 334–335.

83. Ibid., 336–337; Taylor, "General Curtis," 563–565.

84. Taylor, "General Curtis," 565; Gallagher, "Samuel Ryan Curtis," 337–338.

85. Gallagher, "Samuel Ryan Curtis," 337–338; Taylor, "General Curtis," 561.

86. Gallagher, "Samuel Ryan Curtis," 340; William L. Shea and Earl J. Hess, *Pea Ridge: Civil War Campaign in the West* (Chapel Hill: University of North Carolina Press, 1992), 5.

87. Gallagher, "Samuel Ryan Curtis," 340–341; David L. Holst, "General Samuel Curtis and the Civil War in the West," master's thesis, Illinois State University, 1974, 22.

88. Holst, "General Samuel Curtis and the Civil War in the West," 341.

89. *OR*, Series 1, Vol. 3, 540–541; Franz Sigel, "The Pea Ridge Campaign," in *B&L*, vol. 1, 314–316.

90. Gallagher, "Samuel Ryan Curtis," 342–343; Sheridan, *Civil War Memoirs*, 6.

91. Sheridan, *Civil War Memoirs*, 6; Sigel, "The Pea Ridge Campaign," 316.

92. Sigel, "The Pea Ridge Campaign," 318–319.

93. Britton, *The Civil War on the Border*, vol. 1, 215–216.

94. Ibid., 225–231; Sigel, "The Pea Ridge Campaign," 321.

95. Ibid., 326–329; Britton, *The Civil War on the Border*, vol. 1, 265–270; Shea and Hess, *Pea Ridge*, 59, 86–87, 235–236, 248–250.

96. Gallagher, "Samuel Ryan Curtis," 344–345; Holst, "General Samuel Curtis," 37; Sheridan, *Civil War Memoirs*, 9.

97. Gallagher, "Samuel Ryan Curtis," 346; Sigel, "The Pea Ridge Campaign," 331, 334.

98. Holst, "General Samuel Curtis," 41–42.

99. Sigel, "The Pea Ridge Campaign," 349.

100. Gerteis, *The Civil War in Missouri*, 147, 149, 152; Gallagher, "Samuel Ryan Curtis," 350–352; Holst, "General Samuel Curtis," 46, 51–52, 60–62, 88; *OR*, Series 1, Vol. 22, Part 2, 290–293.

101. Gallagher, "Samuel Ryan Curtis," 352; Robert Collins, *General James G. Blunt: Tarnished Glory* (Gretna, LA: Pelican, 2005), 153–157; Barton, *Three Years with Quantrill*, 136–137; Monaghan, *Civil War on the Western Border*, 293–295.

102. Gallagher, "Samuel Ryan Curtis," 352–353.

103. Josephy, *The Civil War in the American West*, 351.

104. Collins, *General James G. Blunt*, 15–16.

105. Ibid., 17; James G. Blunt, "General Blunt's Account of His Civil War Experiences," *Kansas Historical Society* 1, no. 3 (May 1932), 214.

106. Collins, *General James G. Blunt*, 18–20.

107. Ibid., 25–31; Blunt, "General Blunt's Account," 211.
108. Blunt, "General Blunt's Account," 213–214; Collins, *General James G. Blunt*, 35–36.
109. Blunt, "General Blunt's Account," 213–214.
110. Ibid., 214.
111. Ibid., 218.
112. Stephen B. Oates, "The Prairie Grove Campaign, 1862," *Arkansas Historical Quarterly* 19, no. 2 (Summer 1960), 119–122; Alvin M. Josephy, Jr., *The Civil War in the American West* (New York: Alfred A. Knopf, 1991), 363; Blunt, "General Blunt's Account," 222, 229–230.
113. Blunt, "General Blunt's Account," 230–231; Collins, *General James G. Blunt*, 92–93; Oates, "The Prairie Grove Campaign," 123–127; Wiley Britton, *The Civil War on the Border*, vol. 1, 385–395.
114. Oates, "The Prairie Grove Campaign," 130–131; Britton, *The Civil War on the Border*, vol. 1, 408; Blunt, "General Blunt's Account," 232–233; Josephy, *The Civil War in the American West*, 364–365.
115. Oates, "The Prairie Grove Campaign," 140–141; Britton, *The Civil War on the Border*, vol. 1, 426–429; Josephy, *The Civil War in the American West*, 366; *OR*, Series 1, Vol. 22, Part I, 143–144; Collins, *General James G. Blunt*, 99–103, 110.
116. Collins, *General James G. Blunt*, 111–114, 121; Blunt, "General Blunt's Account," 235, 242; James M. Schofield, *Forty-Six Years in the Army* (New York: Century, 1897), 64.
117. Britton, *The Civil War on the Border*, vol. 1, 436–441; Collins, *General James G. Blunt*, 106–108; Blunt, "General Blunt's Account," 236–237.
118. Collins, *General James G. Blunt*, 137–142.
119. Ibid., 142–144; Josephy, *The Civil War in the American West*, 370–371; Blunt, "General Blunt's Account," 244–246.
120. Welsh, *Medical Histories of Union Generals*, 32; Blunt, "General Blunt's Account," 244–247; Collins, *General James G. Blunt*, 150–151.
121. Collins, *General James G. Blunt*, 153–162; O.S. Barton, *Three Years With Quantrill: A True Story Told by His Scout John McCorkle* (Norman: University of Oklahoma Press, 1992), 136–137; Blunt, "General Blunt's Account," 247–248.
122. Blunt, "General Blunt's Account," 248; Lincoln, *The Collected Works of Abraham Lincoln*, vol. 6, 495; Collins, *General James G. Blunt*, 167–175.
123. Collins, *General James G. Blunt*, 182–184, 188–189; Blunt, "General Blunt's Account," 250–252.

Chapter 4

1. *OR*, Series 1, Vol. 34, Part 3, 828–829; Vol. 39, 1011, 1052.
2. Ibid., Vol. 53, 998–999; Reynolds, *Sterling Price and the Confederacy*, 250–252; Shalhope, *Sterling Price*, 256–257; Jeffery S. Prushankin, *A Crisis in Command: Edmund Kirby Smith, Richard Taylor, and the Army of the Trans-Mississippi* (Baton Rouge: Louisiana State University Press, 2002), 190.
3. *OR*, Series 1, Vol. 41, Part 2, 1011; Reynolds, *Sterling Price and the Confederacy*, 79–80, 252–254; Reynolds Papers, Library of Congress, letter to Kirby Smith dated 25 July 1864 delivered to Smith by Simon Bolivar Buckner.
4. *OR*, Series1, Vol. 41, Part 1, 89–90, Lee to Smith, 9 July 1864, Lee to Smith, 23 July 1864, Boggs to Taylor, 28 July 1864; Kean, *Inside the Confederate Government*, 167.
5. Reynolds, *General Sterling Price and the Confederacy*, 123; *OR*, Series 1, Vol. 41, Part 1, 91, 99–100.
6. *OR*, Series l, Vol. 41, Part 1, 96–97, Douglas to Taylor, 4 August 1864.
7. Ibid., 97–98.
8. Ibid.
9. *OR*, Series 1, Vol. 41, Part 1, 98, Douglas to J.G. Meem of the Engineer Department of the Trans-Mississippi army, 4 August 1864.
10. Ibid., 110–112, three letters from Richard Taylor to E.K. Smith, two dated 18 August 1864 and one dated 19 August; United States Navy Department, *Official Records of the Union and Confederate Navies in the War of the Rebellion* (Washington, D.C.: U.S. Government Printing Office, 1914), 513 (hereinafter cited as *ORN*).
11. *OR*, Series 1, Vol. 41, Part 1, 110–112, 117; *ORN*, Series 1, Vol. 26, 517, 522, 534; Richard Taylor, *Destruction and Reconstruction*, ed. Paul Hutton (New York: Bantam Books, 1992), 233. Pagination is different from the original text published in 1879 by D. Appleton.
12. *OR*, Series 1, Vol. 41, Part 1, 109–110, 123: 15 August 1864 note from Smith to Taylor and a letter from Jefferson Davis to Smith dated 24 December 1864.
13. Jeffery S. Prushankin, *A Crisis in Confederate Command: Edmund Kirby Smith, Richard Taylor, and the Army of the Trans-Mississippi* (Baton Rouge: Louisiana State University Press, 2002), 160–161; T. Michael Parrish, *Richard Taylor: Soldier Prince of Dixie* (Chapel Hill: University of North Carolina Press, 1992), 394–395; Parks, *General Edmund Kirby Smith*, 420–430; *OR*, Series 1, Vol. 41, Part 1, 93–94.
14. *OR*, Series 1, Vol. 41, Part 2, 1040.
15. Reynolds, *Sterling Price and the Confederacy*, 124 (emphasis in original).
16. Ibid., 125; *OR*, Series 1, Vol. 41, Part 1, 104.
17. Reynolds, *Sterling Price and the Confederacy*, 121–122.
18. *OR*, Series 1, Vol. 41, Part 1, 639.
19. Reynolds, *Sterling Price and the Confederacy*, 122–124.
20. Ibid., 123–124; Reynolds Papers, Library of Congress, letters from Reynolds to Smith dated 25 July 1864 and Reynolds to Senator Waldo Johnson dated 14 July 1864; Edwards, *Shelby and His Men*, 378; Castel, *General Sterling Price*, 201; Norman Potter Morrow, "Price's Missouri Expedition, 1864," master's thesis, University of Texas, 1949, 30–31. Morrow's thesis has an excellent discussion of the command issue.
21. Reynolds, *Sterling Price and the Confederacy*, 127–131.
22. Ibid.; Reynolds Papers, Library of Congress, letter from Reynolds to E.C. Cabell dated 22 July 1864.

23. Reynolds, *Sterling Price and the Confederacy*, 124, 126; Reynolds Papers, Library of Congress, letter from Reynolds adjutant general Lieutenant Colonel Henry Bragg to Price's adjutant general Colonel L.C. Bohannon dated 11 August 1864.

24. "Price's Missouri Expedition," 23–26; Cyrus A. Peterson and Joseph Mills Hanson, *Pilot Knob: The Thermopylae of the West* (New York: Neale, 1914), 22–23. This book contains interviews of over forty Union participants of the battle of Pilot Knob and is an excellent source of primary material on the fighting there.

25. Ibid., 29–30; Morrow, "Price's Missouri Expedition," 23–26; Kean, *Inside the Confederate Government*, 170; *OR*, Series 1, Vol. 34, Part 2, 1029; Vol. 41, 1011–1012, 1020, 1029, 1040–41, series of letters between Reynolds and Price dated 18 July 1864, 22 July 1864; Bragg's aide Thomas Butler to Smith dated 29 July 1864; Smith to Price 4 August 1864.

26. Morrow, "Price's Missouri Expedition," 54–55; Shalhope, *Sterling Price*, 267; Nelson, *Bullets, Ballots, and Rhetoric*, 97, 147; Reynolds, *Sterling Price and the Confederacy*, 54; *OR*, Series 1, Vol. 41, Part 3, 975.

27. Edwards, *Shelby and His Men*, 379.

28. *OR*, Series 1, Vol. 41, Part 2, 1040–1041.

29. Morrow, "Price's Missouri Expedition," 57–58.

30. *OR*, Series 1, Vol. 41, Part 4, 1068–1069, report of Smith to President Davis dated 21 November 1864; Castel, *General Sterling Price*, 200–201, 253–255; Morrow, "Price's Missouri Expedition," 56–58.

31. Morrow, "Price's Missouri Expedition," 56–58.; Lause, *Price's Lost Campaign*, 14–15.

32. *OR*, Series 1, Vol. 41, Part 1, 116; Castel, *General Sterling Price*, 200–201, 253–255; Morrow, "Price's Missouri Expedition," 56–58; Kerby, *Kirby Smith's Confederacy*, 335–336.

33. *OR*, Series 1, Vol. 41, Part 1, 92–93.

34. Ibid., 92–93, 103, 111; Morrow, "Price's Missouri Expedition," 7–8.

35. John N. Edwards, *Shelby's Expedition to Mexico: An Unwritten Leaf of the War*, ed. Conger Beasley, Jr. (Fayetteville: University of Arkansas Press, 2002), 4.

Chapter 5

1. *OR*, Series 1, Vol. 41, Part 1, 625.

2. Reynolds Papers, Library of Congress, two letters to the Trans-Mississippi quartermaster at Marshal, Texas, and Brigadier General James Rains dated 17 August 1864; *OR*, Series 1, Vol. 41, Part 1, 626; Part 2, 1052–1053, 10 August 1864 report from Major C.D. Hill to Lieutenant Colonel A.H. Cole, inspector general for transportation, C.S.A. War Department.

3. *OR*, Series 1, Vol. 41, Part 1, 625–626, 642–643, 649, 671, 678–679, 687, information assembled from reports of Price and his division and brigade commanders; William L. Cabell, "Report of Gen. W.L. Cabell in Price's Raid in Missouri and Kansas in 1864," *Confederate Veteran* (1900), 1–2.

4. *OR*, Series 1, Vol. 41, Part 3, 527, from the returns of the Division of West Mississippi for September 1864.

5. Ibid., Part 1, 625, from Price's report; Scott A. Porter, "Thunder Across the Arkansas Prairie: Shelby's Opening Salvo in the 1864 Invasion of Missouri," *Arkansas Historical Quarterly* 66, no. 1 (Spring, 2007), 46.

6. *OR*, Series 1, Vol. 41, Part 1, 287–288, 30 August report of Jo Shelby; Part 3, report of C.C. Washburn to E.R.S. Canby dated 2 September 1864; Porter, "Thunder Across the Arkansas Prairie," 49–55.

7. Porter, "Thunder Across the Arkansas Prairie," 56; *OR*, Series 1, Vol. 41, Part 1, 280, report of Frederick Steele to E.R.S. Canby dated 26 August 1864; Peterson and Hanson, *Pilot Knob*, 39–40.

8. *OR*, Series 1, Vol. 41, Part 1, 626–627; Morrow, "Price's Missouri Expedition," 64; Cabell, "Report of Gen. W.L. Cabell," 3; John C. Darr, "Price's Raid into Missouri," *Confederate Veteran* 9 (1903), 359.

9. Welsh, *Medical Histories of Confederate Generals*, 177.

10. William M. McPheeters, *I Acted from Principle: The Civil War Diary of Dr. William M. McPheeters, Confederate Surgeon in the Trans-Mississippi*, ed. Cynthia DeHaven Pitcock and Bill J. Gurley (Fayetteville: University of Arkansas Press, 2002), 216; *OR*, Series 1, Vol. 41, Part 1, 627, 643. MacLean's itinerary was kept meticulously by him as the army marched north during the course of the expedition. Due to the detailed nature of the itinerary, it is reasonable to believe that this is more accurate then the dates Price gives in his report written in December 1864.

11. *OR*, Series 1, Vol. 41, Part 1, 623, 641–642, from a 19 September 1864 report in which Price states that he had 4,000 unarmed men with him when he crossed the Missouri border; Part 3, 940, 943; Morrow, "Price's Missouri Expedition," 66–71; Darr, "Price's Raid into Missouri," 359.

12. Warner, *Generals in Gray*, 41–42.

13. Darr, "Price's Raid into Missouri," 359; Morrow, "Price's Missouri Expedition," 66–71; *OR*, Series 1, Vol. 41, Part 1, 641–642.

14. *OR*, Series 1, Vol. 41, Part 3, 943; McPheeters, *I Acted from Principle*, 221; Peterson and Hanson, *Pilot Knob*, 37–38; Darr, "Price's Raid into Missouri," 359.

15. *OR*, Series 1, Vol. 41, Part 1, 623, 643; McPheeters, *I Acted from Principle*, 221 (emphasis in original); Peterson and Hanson, *Pilot Knob*, 35.

16. *OR*, Series 1, Vol. 41, Part 2, 940–941; *St. Louis Daily Missouri Republican*, "An Intercepted Rebel Letter," 28 September 1864.

17. *OR*, Series 1, Vol. 41, Part 3, 25–27.

18. Ibid., 39.

19. Ibid., Part 2, 967; Davis, "Guerrilla Operations in the Civil War," 19; Lause, *Price's Lost Campaign*, 21–22; Morrow, "Price's Missouri Expedition," 60–61.

20. Lause, *Price's Lost Campaign*, 21–23; *OR*, Series 1, Vol. 41, Part IV, 360.

21. *OR*, Series 1, Vol. 41, Part IV, 360.

22. Lause, *Price's Lost Campaign*, 23; Davis, "Guerrilla Operations in the Civil War," 34; *OR*, Series 1, Vol. 41, Part 3, 155–156.

23. Morrow, "Price's Missouri Expedition," 55–57; *St. Louis Daily Missouri Republican*, "Six Months

Men," 26 September 1864; Davis, "Guerrilla Operations in the Civil War," 43; *OR*, Series 1, Vol. 41, Part 1, 307, Report of Rosecrans dated 7 December 1864; *OR*, Series 1, Vol. 41, Part 3, 168, 175–179, series of orders to Rosecrans' district commanders dated 12 and 13 September 1864.
  24. *OR*, Series 1, Vol. 41, Part 3, 26–27.
  25. Ibid., 69–70.
  26. Ibid., 88, 95, 105, 141.
  27. Ibid., Part 3, 164–165.
  28. Ibid., 176–179; Lause, *Price's Lost Campaign*, 45; Peterson and Hanson, *Pilot Knob*, 42–43.
  29. *OR*, Series 1, Vol. 41, Part 2, 180, 214–215, 231.
  30. Ibid., 269–270; Part 1, 308, 445, containing Rosecrans and Ewing's after action reports; Smith, *Thomas Ewing, Jr.*, 232–236; Peterson and Hanson, *Pilot Knob*, 42–43.
  31. *OR*, Series 1, Vol. 41, Part 1, 308, Part 3, 302; *St. Louis Daily Missouri Republican*, "General Orders," 29 September 1864; Smith, *Thomas Ewing, Jr.*, 235; Gerteis, *The Civil War in Missouri*, 182–183.
  32. *OR*, Series 1, Vol. 41, Part 3, 180, 234, 279, 351, series of messages from Rosecrans to Curtis.
  33. *St. Louis Daily Missouri Republican*, "The Rebel Raid," 26 September 1864.

Chapter 6

  1. Walter E. Busch, *Fort Davidson and the Battle of Pilot Knob: Missouri's Alamo* (Charleston, South Carolina: History, 2010), 19; Richard S. Brownlee, "The Battle of Pilot Knob: Iron County, Missouri, September 27, 1864," *Missouri Historical Review* 59, no. 1 (October 1964), 16.
  2. Busch, *Fort Davidson*, 15–19.
  3. Ibid., 21–23.
  4. Ibid., 24.
  5. Ibid., 24–26.
  6. *OR*, Series 1, Vol. 41, Part 2, 975, Part 1, 446–447; Lause, *Price's Lost Campaign*, 42; Busch, *Fort Davidson*, 24–25; Peterson and Hanson, *Pilot Knob*, 101–102, 122–123, from Ewing's after action report.
  7. *OR*, Series 1, Vol. 41, Part 1, 446–447, from Ewing's after action report.
  8. Peterson and Hanson, *Pilot Knob*, 135, testimony of Captain W.V. Lucas; Brownlee, "The Battle of Pilot Knob," 16–17.
  9. Morrow, "Price's Missouri Expedition," 76.
  10. Peterson and Hanson, *Pilot Knob*, 82, testimony of Sergeant J.C. Steakley; *OR*, Series 1, Vol. 41, Part 3, 948, report of Jo Shelby dated 21 September 1864.
  11. *OR*, Series 1, Vol. 41, Part 3, 84–85. These men were executed in a well-known incident involving the murder of Major James Wilson, the commander at Pilot Knob before Ewing's arrival at the garrison.
  12. Ibid., 93–96; *OR*, Series 1, Vol. 41, Part 3, 951–952, reports of Marmaduke and Shelby dated 22 September 1864.
  13. *OR*, Series 1, Vol. 41, Part 3, 322, 342–345, reports from Wilson, Rosecrans, A.J. Smith, Ewing; Part 1, 308, 445–446, after action reports of Rosecrans and Ewing.
  14. *OR*, Series 1, Vol. 41, Part 1, 652, after action review of Shelby; Peterson and Hanson, *Pilot Knob*, 99–101, letter from Shelby to Major C.C. Rainwater dated 5 January 1888; Shalhope, *Sterling Price*, 264–265; Castel, *General Sterling Price*, 208–210; Brownlee, "The Battle of Pilot Knob," 18; *OR*, Series 1, Vol. 41, Part 3, 954, report of Shelby dated 24 September 1864.
  15. Peterson and Hanson, *Pilot Knob*, 100–101, from Shelby letter to Rainwater.
  16. Ibid.; *OR*, Series 1, Vol. 41, Part 1, 628, 652, after action reports of Price and Shelby; Part 3, 959–960, Price's orders to the divisions.
  17. Peterson and Hanson, *Pilot Knob*, 103–105, testimony of Ewing and Fletcher.
  18. Ibid., 104–105, 111, 122–123, testimony of Fletcher, Lieutenant W.C. Shattuck, and Lieutenant T.M. Montgomery; Brownlee, "The Battle of Pilot Knob," 16.
  19. Peterson and Hanson, *Pilot Knob*, 107–110, testimony of Sergeant Azariah Martin; William L. Cabell, "Report of Gen. W.L. Cabell's Brigade in Price's Raid in Missouri and Kansas in 1864," *Confederate Veteran* (January 1900), 5.
  20. Ewing's estimate of the situation is very good, but he had it slightly wrong. Price's main body was coming through Arcadia Valley, while a detachment—Shelby's—had bypassed to the north to cut the railroad (*OR*, Series 1, Vol. 41, Part 3, 384, Ewing to Rosecrans dated 26 September 1864 at 3:30 P.M.).
  21. *OR*, Series 1, Vol. 41, Part 3, 384, Ewing to Rosecrans dated 26 September 1864 at 3:30 p.m.
  22. Peterson and Hanson, *Pilot Knob*, 111–113, testimony of Lieutenant W.C. Shattuck.
  23. Ibid., 113–115; Cyrus A. Peterson, "Narrative of the Capture and Murder of Major James Wilson," *Missouri Historical Review* (January 1906), 10; *OR*, Series 1, Vol. 41, Part 1, 447, from Ewing's after action report.
  24. *OR*, Series 1, Vol. 41, Part 1, 447.
  25. Ibid., 385, Ewing to Rosecrans dated 26 September 1864.
  26. Ibid., 628–629, Price's after action report.
  27. Ibid., 713–714, testimony from Price's chief engineer Captain T.J. Mackey during court of inquiry 25 April 1865.
  28. McPheeters, *I Acted from Principle*, 224; Cabell, "Report of Gen. Cabell's Brigade," 5; Peterson and Hanson, *Pilot Knob*, 125–129, testimony of Captain William J. Campbell.
  29. Peterson and Hanson, *Pilot Knob*, 125–129, 138–139, 142–143, testimony of Sergeant Major Lewis W. Sutton and First Lieutenant W. H. Smith.
  30. Peterson and Hanson, *Pilot Knob*, 125–129, 155–156, testimony of First Lieutenant David Fletcher; Brownlee, "The Battle of Pilot Knob," 22; *OR*, Series 1, Vol. 41, Part 1, 447.
  31. *OR*, Series 1, Vol. 41, Part 1, 447; Peterson and Hanson, *Pilot Knob*, 158–159, 164, testimony of Captain William J. Campbell, Lieutenant Smith Thompson, and Private Azariah Martin; Brownlee, "The Battle of Pilot Knob," 21; Peterson, "Capture and Murder of Major James Wilson," 10–11.

32. Castel, *General Sterling Price*, 213; Peterson and Hanson, *Pilot Knob*, 165, testimony of Private Azariah Martin.

33. Castel, *General Sterling Price*, 214–215; Peterson and Hanson, *Pilot Knob*, 181, testimony of Sergeant Major John H. Delano; Darr, "Price's Raid into Missouri," 360.

34. *OR*, Series 1, Vol. 41, Part 1, 629, Price's after action report; Cabell, "Report of Gen. W.L. Cabell's Brigade," 5.

35. *OR*, Series 1, Vol. 41, Part 1, 713–714, testimony of Captain T.J. Mackey during the court of inquiry 25 April 1865; Cabell, "Report of Gen. W.L. Cabell," 5–6; Darr, "Price's Raid into Missouri," 360; McPheeters, *I Acted from Principle*, 224; Peterson and Hanson, *Pilot Knob*, 169–170, testimony of First Lieutenant Murphy.

36. Cabell, "Report of Gen. W.L. Cabell," 6; Darr, "Price's Raid into Missouri," 360.

37. Peterson and Hanson, *Pilot Knob*, 175–176, testimony of Captain William J. Campbell (emphasis in original); Brownlee, "The Battle of Pilot Knob," 26; *OR*, Series 1, Vol. 41, Part 1, 709, testimony from the court of inquiry 24 April 1865.

38. Darr, "Price's Raid into Missouri," 360; Brownlee, "The Battle of Pilot Knob," 27; Peterson and Hanson, *Pilot Knob*, 169–174, 176–177, testimony of Captain William J. Campbell, Lieutenant David Murphy, and Lieutenant Smith Thompson; Busch, *Fort Davidson*, 31.

39. Peterson and Hanson, *Pilot Knob*, 176, testimony of Captain William J. Campbell.

40. *OR*, Series 1, Vol. 41, Part 1, 448, 709, 715, Ewing's after action report and testimony from the court of inquiry 24 and 26 April 1865; Brownlee, "The Battle of Pilot Knob," 28; Peterson and Hanson, *Pilot Knob*, 180, testimony of Captain Campbell.

41. Busch, *Fort Davidson*, 31.

42. Ibid.; Peterson and Hanson, *Pilot Knob*, 218, testimony of Colonel Thomas Fletcher.

43. Peterson and Hanson, *Pilot Knob*, 217–225, testimony of the following: Colonel Thomas Fletcher, Peter Shrum, Sergeant Major Lewis W. Sutton, and Captain H.B. Milks; *OR*, Series 1, Vol. 41, Part 1, 448–449, Ewing after action report.

44. Peterson and Hanson, *Pilot Knob*, 224, testimony of Captain H.B. Milks; Busch, *Fort Davidson*, 31.

45. *OR*, Series 1, Vol. 41, Part 1, 449, Ewing after action report; Brownlee, "The Battle of Pilot Knob," 28; Peterson and Hanson, *Pilot Knob*, 224, testimony of Captain H.B. Milks.

46. *OR*, Series 1, Vol. 41, Part 1, 709, testimony from the court of inquiry 24 April 1865; Busch, *Fort Davidson*, 34–35.

47. Peterson and Hanson, *Pilot Knob*, 217–227, testimony of Colonel Fletcher, Peter Shrum, Sergeant Major Sutton, and Captain H.B. Milks; Brownlee, "The Battle of Pilot Knob," 29; *OR*, Series 1, Vol. 41, Part 1, 326, 448–449, after action reviews of Captain William J. Campbell and Ewing.

48. *OR*, Series 1, Vol. 41, Part 1, 449; Peterson and Hanson, *Pilot Knob*, 217–227; Cole, "The Battle of Pilot Knob," 417.

49. Peterson and Hanson, *Pilot Knob*, 217–227; Castel, *General Sterling Price*, 217; *OR*, Series 1, Vol. 41, Part 1, 449, 629, 710, after action reports of Ewing and Price and the court of inquiry 24 April 1865; McPheeters, *I Acted from Principle*, 225.

50. *OR*, Series 1, Vol. 41, Part 1, 449–450; Peterson and Hanson, *Pilot Knob*, 252–254, testimony of Captain William J. Campbell.

51. Peterson and Hanson, *Pilot Knob*, 220, testimony of Colonel Fletcher; *OR*, Series 1, Vol. 41, Part 1, 629–630, 710, Price's after action report and court of inquiry 24 April 1865; Castel, *General Sterling Price*, 217.

52. Morrow, "Price's Missouri Expedition, 1864," 85–86; Moore, "Missouri," *Confederate Military History*, vol. 9, part 2, 181; *OR*, Series 1, Vol. 41, Part 1, 449–450, Ewing's after action report.

53. Ibid. For consistency's sake I have chosen to refer to the village of Harrison by its name at the time of the battle. Some accounts written long after the battle refer to the town by its modern name of Leasburg, but I preferred to keep the name used during the period.

54. Ibid.; 653, Shelby's after action report.

55. Ibid.; Peterson and Hanson, *Pilot Knob*, 251, 256, report of Ewing and testimony of Sergeant Major Lewis W. Sutton.

56. Ibid., 258–275, testimony of Peter Shrum, Captain H.B. Milks, and Sergeant J.C. Steakley. These accounts, recorded long after the battle, refer to Harrison as Leasburg, as it had assumed that name by then.

57. *OR*, Series 1, Vol. 41, Part 1, 450, Ewing's after action report; Peterson and Hanson, *Pilot Knob*, 283, testimony of Captain W.V. Lucas.

58. Peterson and Hanson, *Pilot Knob*, 283–284.

59. Ibid., 285–287.

60. *OR*, Series 1, Vol. 41, Part 1, 653; Peterson and Hanson, *Pilot Knob*, 287, 293, testimony of Captain Lucas and Quartermaster Sergeant Sam B. Rowe.

61. *OR*, Series 1, Vol. 41, Part 1, 450–451, Ewing after action report; Peterson and Hanson, *Pilot Knob*, 287–288, testimony of Captain Lucas.

62. *OR*, Series 1, Vol. 41, Part 1, 451, 630, after action reports of Ewing and Price; McPheeters, *I Acted from Principle*, 224; Morrow, "Price's Missouri Expedition," 83.

63. Peterson and Hanson, *Pilot Knob*, 100–101; *St. Louis Daily Missouri Republican*, "Gen. Orders No. 176," 27 September 1864, and "General Orders," 29 September 1864.

64. Castel, *General Sterling Price*, 218–219; *Harper's Weekly*, "Invasion of Missouri," 15 October 1864.

65. *OR*, Series 1, Vol. 41, Part 1, 451, Ewing's after action report.

66. Peterson, "Capture and Murder of Major James Wilson," 11; McPheeters, *I Acted from Principle*, 225. Dr. McPheeters reported meeting with Dr. Carpenter that day and they "exchanged civilities" before continuing with their respective duties.

67. Peterson, "Capture and Murder of Major James Wilson," 12–13.

Chapter 7

1. Three authors suggest that Price had already decided before Pilot Knob that taking St. Louis was impossible and to divert to Jefferson City. I believe he certainly was concerned that his task was more difficult, but Price still hoped to make the attempt. The evidence for this is in his after action report, in which he positively states that he made the decision to go to Jefferson City after Pilot Knob. These authors include Brownlee, "The Battle of Pilot Knob," 14; Castel, *General Sterling Price*, 210; Morrow, "Price's Missouri Expedition," 76.
2. *OR*, Series 1, Vol. 41, Part 1, 628, Price's after action report.
3. Ibid., 630.
4. Reynolds, *General Sterling Price*, 136–137.
5. Reynolds Papers, Library of Congress, letter from Reynolds to Price dated 2 October 1864.
6. Davis, "Guerrilla Operations in the Civil War," 39; Monaghan, *Civil War on the Western Border*, 316–317; Gerteis, *The Civil War in Missouri*, 189.
7. Thomas M. Huber, ed., "Compound Warfare: A Conceptual Framework," in *Compound Warfare: That Fatal Knot* (Fort Leavenworth, Kansas: Command and General Staff College Press, 2002), 1–2.
8. Davis, "Guerrilla Operations in the Civil War," 85–86.
9. Lause, *Price's Lost Campaign*, 60; *OR*, Series 1, Vol. 41, Part 1, 415, Fisk to Rosecrans, 27 September 1864.
10. *OR*, Series 1, Vol. 41, Part 2, 976; Part 1, 416; Lause, *Price's Lost Campaign*, 60.
11. Monaghan, *Civil War on the Western Border*, 280.
12. Andy Turner, "On This Day: The Centralia Massacre," *Civil War Online* (2012), http://gatehouse-press.com/?p=2305; Monaghan, *Civil War on the Western Border*, 317; *St. Louis Missouri Daily Republican*, "Guerrilla Attack on North Mo. Railroad," "Further Particulars from Centralia," 30 September 1864.
13. *St. Louis Missouri Daily Republican*, "Guerrilla Attack on North Mo. Railroad"; Monaghan, *Civil War on the Western Border*, 318; Turner, "The Centralia Massacre," http://gatehouse-press.com/?p=2305.
14. *St. Louis Missouri Daily Republican*, "Guerrilla Attack on North Mo. Railroad"; Monaghan, *Civil War on the Western Border*, 317–319; *St. Louis Daily Missouri Republican*, "Guerrilla Attack on North Mo. Railroad," "Further Particulars From Centralia," 30 September 1864; *OR*, Series 1, Vol. 41, Part 1, 418, Fisk's after action report; Part 3, 488, Fisk to Rosecrans dated 29 September 1864.
15. Cabell, "Report of Gen. Cabell's Brigade," 6; Lause, *Price's Lost Campaign*, 112–113; Morrow, "Price's Missouri Expedition," 91; *OR*, Series 1, Vol. 41, Part 1, 644; Reynolds Papers, Library of Congress, Letter to Price dated 2 October 1864.
16. Darr, "Price's Raid into Missouri," 360. Instead of calling it Union City Private Darr called the town Union (Cabell, "Report of Gen. W.L. Cabell's Brigade," 6–7).
17. *OR*, Series 1, Vol. 41, Part 1, 645; Morrow, "Price's Missouri Expedition," 91–92; Lause, *Price's Lost Campaign*, 112–119.
18. Morrow, "Price's Missouri Expedition," 92; Lause, *Price's Lost Campaign*, 97–102; *St. Louis Daily Missouri Republican*, series of articles and notices to the public printed between 26 September and 30 September 1864.
19. Warner, *Generals in Blue*, 306; Hinton, *Rebel Invasion of Missouri and Kansas*, 345–347.
20. Hinton, *Rebel Invasion of Missouri and Kansas*, 47–48.
21. Hinton, *Rebel Invasion of Missouri and Kansas*, 418–419.
22. *OR*, Series 1, Vol. 41, Part 3, 558, 581–582, messages from Merrill to Rosecrans dated 2 and 3 October 1864, message from A.J. Smith to Rosecrans dated 3 October 1864.
23. *OR*, Series 1, Vol. 41, Part 3, pp., 448, 488–489, 521, 546, 591, 646, 666, orders from Rosecrans to McNeil, Fisk, Sanborn; George S. Grover, "The Price Campaign of 1864," *Missouri Historical Review* 6, no. 4 (July 1912), 168.
24. *OR*, Series 1, Vol. 41, Part 3, 564–565, 569–571, Curtis to Rosecrans dated 4 October; Part 1, 464–467, Curtis's after action report.
25. Ibid., Part 3, 448, 484, messages from McNeil to Colonel J.V. Dubois (Rosecrans' chief of staff) and Rosecrans to McNeil dated 28 and 29 September 1864; Lause, *Price's Lost Campaign*, 145–146.
26. Lause, *Price's Lost Campaign*, 149; *OR*, Series 1, Vol. 41, Part 1, 366–368, after action reports of Captains Eitzen and Onken.
27. Ibid.
28. *OR*, Series 1, Vol. 41, Part 3, 579, General Order #185; McPheeters, *I Acted from Principle*, 227.
29. *OR*, Series 1, Vol. 41, Part 1, 418–419; Part 3, 591, Fisk's after action report and message to Rosecrans informing him of his arrival at Jefferson City 3 October 1864, Fisk's commission to brigadier general of volunteers dated 24 November 1862. Both Brown and McNeil's commissions were on 29 November 1862 and Sanborn's date of rank was 8 August 1863, according to Warner, *Generals in Blue*, 47–48, 154–155, 306, 418–419.
30. *OR*, Series 1, Vol. 41, Part 3, 515, 591, reports of Brown and Fisk to Dubois and Rosecrans dated 30 September and 3 October 1864; Part 1, 345–346, Brown's after action report; Lause, *Price's Lost Campaign*, 152–153, 160–163; Morrow, "Price's Missouri Expedition," 93–94.
31. *OR*, Series 1, Vol. 41, Part 1, 345, 358, 654, 665, after action reports of Brown, Colonel James McFerran, Colonel Rudolph Poser, and Shelby; Part 3, 647, Fisk to Rosecrans dated 5 October; Lause, *Price's Lost Campaign*, 164.
32. *OR*, Series 1, Vol. 41, Part 1, 654, Shelby's after action report; Lause, *Price's Lost Campaign*, 166–167.
33. Lause, *Price's Lost Campaign*, 168–170; *OR*, Series 1, Vol. 41, Part 1, 419, Fisk's after action report; Part 3, 647, 667, Fisk to Rosecrans dated 5 and 6 October 1864; *Weston (MO) Border Times*, "By Telegraph," dated 7 October 1864 from published reports from Fisk to Curtis, messages dated 5–6 October 1864.

34. Darr, "Price's Raid into Missouri," 360; Cabell, "Report of Gen. W.L. Cabell's Brigade," 7; Lause, *Price's Lost Campaign*, 169–170.

35. *OR*, Series 1, Vol. 41, Part 3, 689; Edwards, *Shelby and His Men*, 393–394; McPheeters, *I Acted from Principle*, 227; Morrow, "Price's Missouri Expedition," 95–96.

36. Cabell, "Report of Gen. W.L. Cabell's Brigade," 7; *OR*, Series 1, Vol. 41, Part 1, 419, Fisk's after action report.

37. *OR*, Series 1, Vol. 41, Part 1, pp., 376, 633, 655, McNeil, Price, and Shelby's after action reports; McPheeters, *I Acted from Principle*, 228–229.

38. *OR*, Series 1, Vol. 41, Part 1, 376, 419, McNeil and Fisk's after action reports; Cabell, "Report of Gen. W.L. Cabell's Brigade," 7; Darr, "Price's Raid Into Missouri," 360; *Harper's Weekly*, "The Invasion of Missouri," 22 October 1864.

39. Lause, *Price's Lost Campaign*, 174–175. The conversion of the operation into a raid is the central thesis of Mark A. Lause's excellent book, which I agree with.

40. Edwards, *Shelby and His Men*, 396.

41. Ibid.

42. Lause, *Price's Lost Campaign*, 178–181; Morrow, "Price's Missouri Expedition," 102; *OR*, Series 1, Vol. 41, Part 1, 631, Price's after action report.

43. Reynolds, *General Sterling Price*, 137–139; Josephy, *The Civil War in the American West*, 380.

44. Longacre, "Alfred Pleasonton," 19–20; Morrow, "Price's Missouri Expedition," 98–99.

45. *OR*, Series 1, Vol. 41, Part 3, 302, Rosecrans to Pleasonton, 22 September 1864.

46. Morrow, "Price's Missouri Expedition," 99–100; *OR*, Series 1, Vol. 41, Part 1, 311, 385, Rosecrans and Sanborn's after action reports; Part 3, 708–709.

47. *OR*, Series 1, Vol. 41, Part 1, 464–467, Curtis's after action report; Part 2, 980, strength returns for the Department of Kansas. The text of Curtis's after action report in the *OR* is also encompassed in his "Campaign Book of the Army of the Border: October and November 1864," microfilm roll #303, Kansas State Historical Society.

48. *OR*, Series 1, Vol. 41, Part 3, 650, Curtis to Governor Carney dated 5 October 1864.

49. Castel, *A Frontier State at War*, 186–187; Albert Castel, "War and Politics: The Price Raid of 1864," *Kansas Historical Quarterly* 24, no. 2 (Summer, 1968), 132; Josephy, *The Civil War in the American West*, 380–381; Howard N. Monnett, *Action Before Westport, 1864*, rev. ed. (Boulder: University of Colorado Press, 1995), 36–37.

50. Monnett, *Action Before Westport*, 37; *OR*, Series 1, Vol. 41, Part 2, 465, 471, Curtis's after action report; Castel, "War and Politics," 132–133; Crawford, *Kansas in the Sixties*, 143–144; Castel, *A Frontier State at War*, 187.

51. Blunt, "Blunt's Account," 251–252; Castel, "War and Politics," 133; *OR*, Series 1, Vol. 41, Part 1, 468, governor's proclamation; Part 3, 724, correspondence of Governor Carney and Rosecrans dated 9 October 1864.

52. *OR*, Series 1, Vol. 41, Part 1, 469, 471, 614, Curtis and Deitzler's after action reports; Monnett, *Action Before Westport*, 38–47; Hinton, *Rebel Invasion of Missouri and Kansas*, 46.

Chapter 8

1. *OR*, Series 1, Vol. 41, Part 1, 385–386, 631, 645, 681, from after action reports of Sanborn, Price, and Clark; Moore, "Missouri," *Confederate Military History*, vol. 9, p. 2, 182; Morrow, "Price's Missouri Expedition," 106. Morrow coins the term "picnic period" in his excellent thesis.

2. *OR*, Series 1, Vol. 41, Part 1, 388, 631, 655, 681, from after action reports of Sanborn, Price, Shelby, and Clark; Morrow, "Price's Missouri Expedition," 101–102.

3. *OR*, Series 1, Vol. 41, Part 3, 388, from after action report of Sanborn.

4. Hinton, *Rebel Invasion of Missouri and Kansas*, 113.

5. *OR*, Series 1, Vol. 41, Part 1, 631, from Price's after action review; McPheeters, *I Acted from Principle*, 229; Cabell, "Report of Gen. W.L. Cabell's Brigade," 8; Darr, "Price's Raid Into Missouri," 360.

6. Reynolds Papers, Library of Congress, Reynolds to Price dated 10 October 1864 at Boonville, Missouri.

7. Castel, *General Sterling Price*, 223–227; Shalhope, *Sterling Price*, 268; Edwards, *Shelby and His Men*, 471; *OR*, Series 1, Vol. 41, Part 1, 663, from Thompson's after action review.

8. *OR*, Series 1, Vol. 41, Part 1, 632, 663, from Price and Thompson's after action reviews and McPheeters, *I Acted from Principle*, 232.

9. William T. Dameron Papers, Missouri Secretary of State, Missouri Digital Heritage Collection, Prisoner Examination of William T. Dameron dated 8 February 1865.

10. Ibid., a letter from citizens of Randolph County vouching for the veracity of Dameron's story and his loyalty, dated 6 January 1865.

11. *OR*, Series 1, Vol. 41, Part 1, 640, from Price's after action review; Kerby, *Kirby Smith's Confederacy*, 359–360; Morrow, "Price's Missouri Expedition," 20; Lause, *Price's Lost Campaign*, 182–183.

12. Davis, "Guerrilla Operations in the Civil War," 54; Castel, *General Sterling Price*, 226–227; Monaghan, *Civil War on the Western Border*, 322.

13. Davis, "Guerrilla Warfare in the Civil War," 54–55; Castel, *General Sterling Price*, 226–227; *OR*, Series 1, Vol. 41, 632, from Price's after action report.

14. Davis, "Guerrilla Warfare in the Civil War," 55.

15. Ibid.; Castel, *General Sterling Price*, 226–227; *OR*, Series 1, Vol. 41, Part 1, 317, General Order #216 from General Rosecrans dated 2 December 1864.

16. Nelson, *Bullets, Ballots, and Rhetoric*, 97, 147; Morrow, "Price's Missouri Expedition," 54–55 (Cabell is quoted in this text); *OR*, Series 1, Vol. 41, Part 2, 1085.

17. Reynolds, *General Sterling Price and the Confederacy*, 117–119; Castel, *General Sterling Price*, 92–96; Shalhope, *Sterling Price*, 267.

18. *OR*, Series 1, Vol. 41, Part 3, 975–976, Taylor's proclamation to OAK membership dated 1 October 1864.

19. Edwards, *Shelby and His Men*, 379; Morrow, "Price's Missouri Expedition," 54–55.

20. Morrow, "Price's Missouri Expedition," 101; *OR*, Series 1, Vol. 41, Part 1, 311, from Rosecrans' after action review.

21. *OR*, Series 1, Vol. 41, Part 1, 310–311, from Rosecrans' after action review.

22. Ibid.; Lause, *Price's Lost Campaign*, 156–157.

23. *OR*, Series 1, Vol. 41, Part 3, 763–764, series of messages between Curtis, Sykes, and Blunt on 10 October 1864; Blunt, "Blunt's Account," 252–253; Morrow, "Price's Missouri Expedition," 110–111; Hinton, *Rebel Invasion of Missouri and Kansas*, 63–64.

24. *OR*, Series 1, Vol. 41, Part 1, 469–473, from Curtis's after action report; Hinton, *Rebel Invasion of Missouri and Kansas*, 62; Samuel J. Reader, "Autobiography," Kansas State Historical Society Digital Collection, Topeka, Kansas, http//:www.kansasmemory.org/item/206900 (accessed 19 November 2013).

25. Jeffrey D. Stalnaker, *The Battle of Mine Creek: The Crushing End to the Missouri Campaign* (Charleston, SC: History, 2011), 43; *OR*, Series 1, Vol. 41, Part 3, 845, correspondence between Curtis and Blunt dated 13 October 1864; Hinton, *Rebel Invasion of Missouri and Kansas*, 60, 62; Reader, "Autobiography," 13.

26. Westport Historical Society, *The Battle of Westport* (Kansas City: Westport Historical Society, 1976), 21–22: Kansas State Militia order of battle.

27. Stalnaker, *The Battle of Mine Creek*, 43; Hinton, *Rebel Invasion of Missouri and Kansas*, 43–44.

28. *OR*, Series 1, Vol. 41, Part 1, 472, from Curtis's after action report; Part 3, 869–870, Curtis to Blunt dated 14 October 1864; Hinton, *Rebel Invasion of Missouri and Kansas*, 56–60.

29. Morrow, "Price's Missouri Expedition," 105–106; Hinton, *Rebel Invasion of Missouri and Kansas*, 60, 80–81; *OR*, Series 1, Vol. 41, Part 3, 869–870, correspondence between Curtis and Blunt; Reader, "Autobiography," 17.

30. Hinton, *Rebel Invasion of Missouri and Kansas*, 62–63.

31. *OR*, Series 1, Vol. 41, Part 1, p. 572, from Blunt's after action report; Part 3, 896–898, correspondence between Blunt and Fishback dated 15 October 1864; Blunt, "Blunt's Account," 253; Hinton, *Rebel Invasion of Missouri and Kansas*, 64.

32. Hinton, *Rebel Invasion of Missouri and Kansas*, 64–65; *OR*, Series 1, Vol. 41, Part 1, 572, from Blunt's after action report; Part 3, 898, Fishback to Blunt dated 15 October 1864; Collins, *General James G. Blunt*, 192; Blunt, "Blunt's Account," 253.

33. *OR*, Series 1, Vol. 41, Part 1, 572 from Blunt's after action review; Morrow, "Price's Missouri Expedition," 112–113; Crawford, *Kansas in the Sixties*, 144–145; Hinton, *Rebel Invasion of Missouri and Kansas*, 65; Blunt, "Blunt's Account," 253.

34. Lincoln, *The Collected Works of Abraham Lincoln*, ed., Roy Basler, vol. 8 (New Brunswick, NJ: Rutgers University Press, 1958), 57.

35. Ibid.; *OR*, Series 1, Vol. 41, Part 4, 157–158, messages to Rosecrans on 21 October 1864 indicating that he was "in the field."

36. *OR*, Series 1, Vol. 41, Part 3, 853–854, correspondence between Stanton, Halleck, and Grant dated 14 October 1864; Part 4, 126, message from Grant to Halleck dated 20 October 1864; Gerteis, *Civil War in Missouri*, 182; U.S. Grant, *Personal Memoirs of U.S. Grant*, vol. 2 (New York: Charles L. Webster, 1886), 593–594.

37. *OR*, Series 1, Vol. 41, Part 1, 631, from Price's after action report; Stalnaker, *The Battle of Mine Creek*, 32.

38. *OR*, Series 1, Vol. 41, Part 1, 311–312, 632, 656, 681, from Rosecrans, Price, Shelby, and Clark's after action reports; Gerteis, *The Civil War in Missouri*, 192–193.

39. *OR*, Series 1, Vol. 41, Part 1, 312, 632, 656–657, 681–682, 686–687, from Rosecrans, Price, Shelby, and Clark's after action reports and a report on the taking and parole of the prisoners; McPheeters, *I Acted from Principle*, 232; Moore, "Missouri," *Confederate Military History*, vol. 9, Part 2, 184–185.

40. *OR*, Series 1, Vol. 41, Part 1, 665, from after action report of M. Jeff Thompson; Part 3, 527–528, returns for the Departments of Missouri and Kansas at the end of September 1864; McPheeters, *I Acted from Principle*, 233; Monnett, *Action Before Westport*, 40.

Chapter 9

1. Moore, "Price's Missouri Expedition," 115–119; *OR*, Series 1, Vol. 41, Part 1, 312–313, 472–475, from the after action reviews of Rosecrans and Curtis.

2. There are numerous reports in the *OR* by Rebel commanders of their troops destroying telegraph nodes. Shelby's account in Vol. 41, Part 1, 653, provides one example.

3. Morrow, "Price's Missouri Expedition," 114, 118–119; Edwards, *Shelby and His Men*, 428–430, 435, 440; Moore, "Missouri," *Confederate Military History*, vol. 9, part 2, 189–191; *OR*, Series 1, Vol. 41, Part 1, 623–624, from Price's 2 November 1864 report.

4. *OR*, Series 1, Vol. 41, Part 1, 624; Edwards, *Shelby and His Men*, 436 (emphasis in original).

5. Edwards, *Shelby and His Men*, 430; *OR*, Series 1, Vol. 41, Part 1, 633–634, 657, 666, 682–684, 690, 700, from the after action reports of Price, Shelby, Thompson, Clark, Greene, and Tyler.

6. Edwards, *Shelby and His Men*, 417; Monnett, *Action Before Westport*, 49–50.

7. Blunt, "Blunt's Account," 253–254; *Weston (MO) Border Times*, "The Price Invasion," dated 21 October 1864; *OR*, Series 1, Vol. 41, Part 1, 573–574, from Blunt's after action report.

8. *OR*, Series 1, Vol. 41, Part 1, 573–574; Blunt, "Blunt's Account," 254–255; Monnett, *Action Before Westport*, 50–51.

9. *OR*, Series 1, Vol. 41, Part 1, 574–575, from Blunt's after action report; Part 4, 118, Field Order #6 dated 19 October 1864; Monnett, *Action Before Westport*, 51; Blunt, "Blunt's Account," 253–255.

10. Monnett, *Action Before Westport*, 50–53; *OR*, Series 1, Vol. 41, Part 1, 591, from Moonlight's after action report; Hinton, *Rebel Invasion of Missouri and Kansas*, 86; Henry A. Palmer, "Eleventh Kansas Reg-

iment in the Price Raid," *Transactions of the Kansas State Historical Society* 9 (1905–06), 435–438.

11. Blunt, "Blunt's Account," 255; *OR*, Series 1, Vol. 41, Part 1, 574–575, from Blunt's after action report; "The Western Campaign," *Harper's Weekly*, 5 November 1864.

12. "The Western Campaign," *Harper's Weekly*; Blunt, "Blunt's Account," 255.

13. Monnett, *Action Before Westport*, 54; Edwards, *Shelby and His Men*, 420.

14. Palmer, "Co. A, 11th Kansas Regiment," 436; *OR*, Series 1, Vol. 41, Part 1, 633, 657, 682, from the after action reports of Price, Shelby, and Clark; Monnett, *Action Before Westport*, 56–57.

15. Blunt, "Blunt's Account," 256; Castel, "War and Politics," 136.

16. *OR*, Series 1, Vol. 41, Part 1, 682, from Clark's after action report; Monnett, *Action Before Westport*, 56–57; Edwards, *Shelby and His Men*, 420.

17. Palmer, "Co. A, 11th Kansas Regiment," 439; *OR*, Series 1, Vol. 41, Part 1, 633, 657, 682–683, from the after action reports of Price, Shelby, and Clark; Hinton, *Rebel Invasion of Missouri and Kansas*, 94–95.

18. Blunt, "Blunt's Account," 256–257; McPheeters, *I Acted from Principle*, 234; Monnett, *Action Before Westport*, 59–60.

19. Edwards, *Shelby and His Men*, 420; Grover, "The Price Campaign of 1864," 174; Cabell, "Report of Gen. W.L. Cabell," 10.

20. Blunt, "Blunt's Account," 256–257; *OR*, Series 1, Vol. 41, Part 1, 575, 657, from the after action reports of Blunt and Shelby; Edwards, *Shelby and His Men*, 435; Grover, "The Price Campaign of 1864," 174; Hinton, *Rebel Invasion of Missouri and Kansas*, 95–97; Monnett, *Action Before Westport*, 59–62.

21. Blunt, "Blunt's Account," 256–257; Hinton, *Rebel Invasion of Missouri and Kansas*, 97; Cabell, "Report of Gen. W.L. Cabell," 10; Monnett, *Action Before Westport*, 62.

22. Blunt, "Blunt's Account," 256–257; Crawford, *Kansas in the Sixties*, 147–148; *OR*, Series 1, Vol. 41, Part 1, 476–477, from Curtis's after action report.

23. Blunt, "Blunt's Account," 256–257; *OR*, Series 1, Vol. 41, Part 1, 575, 592–593, from the after action reports of Blunt and Moonlight; Moore, "Missouri," in *Confederate Military History*, vol., 9, part 2, 186; Palmer, "Co. A, 11th Kansas Regiment," 439–440; Hinton, *Rebel Invasion of Missouri and Kansas*, 97.

24. Blunt, "Blunt's Account," 257; *OR*, Series 1, Vol. 41, Part 1, 575, 592–593, from the after action reports of Blunt and Moonlight; Hinton, *Rebel Invasion of Missouri and Kansas*, 100; Cabell, "Report of Gen. W.L. Cabell," 10; Moore, "Missouri," in *Confederate Military History*, vol. 9, part 2, 186.

25. Hinton, *Rebel Invasion of Missouri and Kansas*, 100.

26. *OR*, Series 1, Vol. 41, Part 1, 474–475, from Curtis's after action report; Part 4, 16, 59, dispatches between Curtis, Deitzler, and Blunt.

27. Hinton, *Rebel Invasion of Missouri and Kansas*, 126; Reader, "Autobiography," 17–18.

28. Monnett, *Action Before Westport*, 69.

29. Hinton, *Rebel Invasion of Missouri and Kansas*, 127; Reader, "Autobiography," 25–26.

30. *OR*, Series 1, Vol. 41, Part 1, 312, 328–329, from the after action reports of Rosecrans and Winslow and William Forse Scott, *Story of a Cavalry Regiment* (New York: G.P. Putnam's Sons, 1893), 316–317.

31. Ibid., 317; *OR*, Series 1, Vol. 41, Part 1, 329, from Winslow's after action report.

32. Scott, *Story of a Cavalry Regiment*, 319.

33. *OR*, Series 1, Vol. 41, Part 4, 182, Pleasonton to Rosecrans dated 22 October 1864.

34. Ibid., 183, Pleasonton to Rosecrans dated 22 October 1864; McPheeters, *I Acted from Principle*, 235.

35. Hinton, *Rebel Invasion of Missouri and Kansas*, 117–118; Monnett, *Action Before Westport*, 73.

36. Monnett, *Action Before Westport*, 73–74; Hinton, *Rebel Invasion of Missouri and Kansas*, 118.

37. Hinton, *Rebel Invasion of Missouri and Kansas*, 118–119; *OR*, Series 1, Vol. 41, Part 1, 340, from Pleasonton's after action report; Part 4, 183, Pleasonton to Rosecrans dated 22 October 1864; Monnett, *Action Before Westport*, 74–75.

38. *OR*, Series 1, Vol. 41, Part 3, 13, from Pleasonton's after action report.

39. Stalnaker, *The Battle of Mine Creek*, 55.

40. Monnett, *Action Before Westport*, 77–78; Moore, "Missouri," *Confederate Military History*, vol. 9, part 2, 189–190; Edwards, *Shelby and His Men*, 430; *OR*, Series 1, Vol. 41, Part 1, 497–484, 634–635, 658, from the after action reports of Curtis, Price, and Shelby.

41. *OR*, Series 1, Vol. 41, Part 1, 658, 666, 675, from the after action reports of Shelby, Thompson, and Jackman; Hinton, *Rebel Invasion of Missouri and Kansas*, 127; Blunt, "Blunt's Account," 258; Edwards, *Shelby and His Men*, 430; Monnett, *Action Before Westport*, 78–79.

42. Monnett, *Action Before Westport*, 78–79; Hinton, *Rebel Invasion of Missouri and Kansas*, 128; *OR*, Series 1, Vol. 41, 479–480, 666, from the after action reports of Curtis and Thompson.

43. *OR*, Series 1, Vol. 41, 480, 658, 667, 675, from the after action reports of Curtis, Shelby, Thompson, and Jackman; Hinton, *Rebel Invasion of Missouri and Kansas*, 129–132.

44. *OR*, Series 1, Vol. 41, Part 1, 479, dispatch enclosed in Curtis's report dated 21 October 1864; Reader, "Autobiography," 30–33.

45. Reader, "Autobiography," 33–34; Hinton, *Rebel Invasion of Missouri and Kansas*, 126, containing the text of Special Order #15 assigning the 2nd KSM their mission.

46. Reader, "Autobiography," 55–72.

47. Ibid., 98–138; Hinton, *Rebel Invasion of Missouri and Kansas*, 133–137, 139–143; Moore, "Missouri," *Confederate Military History*, vol. 9, part 2, 190.

48. Scott, *Story of a Cavalry Regiment*, 319–320; Monnett, *Action Before Westport*, 89.

49. Scott, *Story of a Cavalry Regiment*, 320; Monnett, *Action Before Westport*, 89–90; Darr, "Price's Raid into Missouri," 361; Cabell, "Report of Gen. W.L. Cabell," 10–11.

50. *OR*, Series 1, Vol. 41, Part 4, 189–190, messages from Curtis to Halleck and Mrs. Curtis.

51. Blunt, "Blunt's Account," 258–259; *OR*, Series 1, Vol. 41, Part 1, 484–489, 575, from the after action reviews of Curtis and Blunt; Castel, "War and Politics," 138; Hinton, *Rebel Invasion of Missouri and Kansas*, 143–146.

52. Blunt, "Blunt's Account," 259; Crawford, *Kansas in the Sixties*, 148–150; Hinton, *Rebel Invasion of Missouri and Kansas*, 145–146.

53. *OR*, Series 1, Vol. 41, Part 1, 336–337, 485, from the after action reports of Pleasonton and Curtis; Part 4, 184–185, Pleasonton to Rosecrans dated 22 October 1864 at 8:00 p.m. In this message Pleasonton states that he has heard nothing from Curtis, but Curtis's after action report provides specific instances of communication. Therefore, it is reasonable to conclude that he and Curtis exchanged messages after 8:00 p.m. to coordinate the attack. Also, Blunt notes in his account that he made contact with Pleasonton and he worked for Curtis, thus, communication was positively established; Blunt, "Blunt's Account," 258; Monnett, *Action Before Westport*, 110–111.

54. *OR*, Series 1, Vol. 41, Part 1, 635, 658, 667, 683, from the after action reviews of Price, Shelby, Thompson, and Clark; Cabell, "Report of Gen. W.L. Cabell," 11; Monnett, *Action Before Westport*, 93–94.

55. *OR*, Series 1, Vol. 41, Part 1, 658, from Shelby's after action report; McPheeters, *I Acted from Principle*, 235.

56. McPheeters, *I Acted from Principle*, 235; Monnett, *Action Before Westport*, 100–105.

57. Monnett, *Action Before Westport*, 106–107; Blunt, "Blunt's Account," 259; Hinton, *Rebel Invasion of Missouri and Kansas*, 152–153; Moore, "Missouri," *Confederate Military History*, vol. 9, Part 2, 191; Castel, "War and Politics," 138; *OR*, Series 1, Vol. 41, Part 1, 487–489, 658–659, from the after action reports of Curtis and Shelby.

58. *OR*, Series 1, Vol. 41, Part 1, 337, from Pleasonton's after action report; Scott, *Story of a Cavalry Regiment*, 321; Hinton, *Rebel Invasion of Missouri and Kansas*, 169; Monnett, *Action Before Westport*, 110–111. Brown was later tried by court-martial at St. Louis, where he was acquitted of dereliction of duty.

59. Monnett, *Action Before Westport*, 113–115; Scott, *Story of a Cavalry Regiment*, 322; *OR*, Series 1, Vol. 41, Part 1, 337, from Pleasonton's after action report.

60. Scott, *Story of a Cavalry Regiment*, 322–325; Monnett, *Action Before Westport*, 115–116; *OR*, Series 1, Vol. 41, Part 1, 337, from Pleasonton's after action report; Grover, "The Price Campaign," 176.

61. Grover, "The Price Campaign," 176; Monnett, *Action Before Westport*, 115–116; Cabell, "Report of Gen. W.L. Cabell," 11.

62. *OR*, Series 1, Vol. 41, Part 1, 337, 486, 659, 676, from the after action reports of Pleasonton, Curtis, Shelby, and Jackman; Hinton, *Rebel Invasion of Missouri and Kansas*, 157.

63. Crawford, *Kansas in the Sixties*, 152; Hinton, *Rebel Invasion of Missouri and Kansas*, 157; Blunt, "Blunt's Account," 260; *OR*, Series 1, Vol. 41, Part 1, 659, from Shelby's after action report; McPheeters, *I Acted from Principle*, 236.

64. Monnett, *Action Before Westport*, 117–119; Hinton, *Rebel Invasion of Missouri and Kansas*, 176–177. McNeil, like Brown, was tried by court-martial at St. Louis. However, unlike Brown, McNeil was found guilty and sentenced to suspension of rank and pay for three months. On appeal, the judge advocate general overturned the conviction and restored McNeil to full rank and pay (*OR*, Series 1, Vol. 41, Part 1, 337, 372, from the after action reports of Pleasonton and McNeil).

65. Cabell, "Report of Gen. W.L. Cabell," 11; *OR*, Series 1, Vol. 41, Part 1, 635–636, from Price's after action report; Monnett, *Action Before Westport*, 118–119; Paul B. Jenkins, *The Battle of Westport* (Kansas City: Franklin Hudson, 1906), 165. Jenkins describes the plan to form Cabell's division.

66. *OR*, Series 1, Vol. 41, Part 1, 372, from McNeil's after action review; Cabell, "Report of Gen. W.L. Cabell," 11; Darr, "Price's Raid Into Missouri," 361. It is interesting to note that the text of Cabell's and Darr's accounts are almost exactly alike. Darr's was published after Cabell's; therefore, it is reasonable to conclude that Darr plagiarized Cabell's report almost verbatim (Monnett, *Action Before Westport*, 120–121).

67. Cabell, "Report of Gen. W.L. Cabell," 11; Darr, "Price's Raid Into Missouri," 361; *OR*, Series 1, Vol. 41, Part 1, 372, 379, from the after action reports of McNeil and Beveridge.

68. *OR*, Series 1, Vol. 41, Part 1, 635–636, from Price's after action report.

69. Cabell, "Report of Gen. W.L. Cabell," 11.

70. *OR*, Series 1, Vol. 41, Part 1, 313, 337–340, 491–492, from the after action reports of Rosecrans, Pleasonton, and Curtis; Hinton, *Rebel Invasion of Missouri and Kansas*, 175–177.

71. Edwards, *Shelby and His Men*, 440; Moore, "Missouri," *Confederate Military History*, vol. 9, part 2, 192.

72. Edwards, *Shelby and His Men*, 440; McPheeters, *I Acted from Principle*, 236; Hinton, *Rebel Invasion of Missouri and Kansas*, 185 (emphasis in original).

73. *OR*, Series 1, Vol. 41, Part 1, 670, 686, 692–693, 697–700, from the after action reports of Confederate commanders Thompson, Clark, Davies, Lawther; Tyler and Britton, *Civil War on the Border*, part 2, 504–505.

74. *OR*, Series 1, Vol. 41, Part 1, 344, 393, 491, from casualty returns and reports from the campaign.

Chapter 10

1. Reynolds, *General Sterling Price*, 145, excerpt from a letter to Reynolds written to the *Marshal (TX) Republican*, 23 December 1864.

2. Edwards, *Shelby and His Men*, 440; Hinton, *Rebel Invasion of Missouri and Kansas*, 190–191; Edgar Langsdorf, "Price's Raid and the Battle of Mine Creek," *Kansas Historical Quarterly* 30 (Autumn, 1964), 298.

3. *OR*, Series 1, Vol. 41, Part 1, 646, from Price's after action report.

4. Reader, "Autobiography," 162, 169–170, 205.

5. Langsdorf, "Price's Raid and the Battle of Mine Creek," 293–294; *OR*, Series 1, Vol. 41, Part 1, 337, 492–493, from the after action reports of Pleasonton and Curtis; Hinton, *Rebel Invasion of Missouri and Kansas*, 188–189.

6. Stalnaker, *The Battle of Mine Creek*, 59–60; Edwards, *Shelby and His Men*, 440; *OR*, Series 1, Vol. 41, Part 1, 636–637. Price's after action report explicitly states his intent to capture Fort Scott.

7. Stalnaker, *The Battle of Mine Creek*, 62; Hinton, *Rebel Invasion of Missouri and Kansas*, 183–184; Scott, *Story of a Cavalry Regiment*, 328.

8. Stalnaker, *The Battle of Mine Creek*, 63; *OR*, Series 1, Vol. 41, Part 1, 493, from Curtis's after action report; Hinton, *Rebel Invasion of Missouri and Kansas*, 188–189, 197–198; Langsdorf, "Price's Raid and the Battle of Mine Creek," 294.

9. Hinton, *Rebel Invasion of Missouri and Kansas*, 188; Scott, *Story of a Cavalry Regiment*, 328; Langsdorf, "Price's Raid and the Battle of Mine Creek," 294; Edwards, *Shelby and His Men*, 440–441.

10. *OR*, Series 1, Vol. 41, Part 1, 332, 337, 391, from the after action reviews of Pleasonton, Sanborn, and Benteen; Hinton, *Rebel Invasion of Missouri and Kansas*, 198; Stalnaker, *The Battle of Mine Creek*, 67–68.

11. *OR*, Series 1, Vol. 41, Part 1, 337, 494–495, from the after action reports of Pleasonton and Curtis and Langsdorf, "Price's Raid and the Battle of Mine Creek," 294–295.

12. *OR*, Series 1, Vol. 41, Part 1, 332, 337–338, 352, 684, from the after action reports of Benteen, Pleasonton, Philips, and Clark; Stalnaker, *The Battle of Mine Creek*, 75–79; Cabell, "Report of Gen. W.L. Cabell," 12; Scott, *Story of a Cavalry Regiment*, 331–332; Langsdorf, "Price's Raid and the Battle of Mine Creek," 295.

13. Hinton, *Rebel Invasion of Missouri and Kansas*, 206; Stalnaker, *The Battle of Mine Creek*, 73–76; Langsdorf, "Price's Raid and the Battle of Mine Creek," 295; Scott, *Story of a Cavalry Regiment*, 331–332.

14. Stalnaker, *The Battle of Mine Creek*, 79; Cabell, "Report of Gen. W.L. Cabell," 12.

15. *OR*, Series 1, Vol. 41, Part 1, 637, from Price's after action report; Langsdorf, "Price's Raid and the Battle of Mine Creek," 297–298; McPheeters, *I Acted from Principle*, 236.

16. Hinton, *Rebel Invasion of Missouri and Kansas*, 206; *OR*, Series 1, Vol. 41, Part 1, 332, from Benteen's after action report.

17. *OR*, Series 1, Vol. 41, Part 1, 332; Stalnaker, *The Battle of Mine Creek*, 77.

18. *OR*, Series 1, Vol. 41, Part 1, 332, from Benteen's after action report; Scott, *Story of a Cavalry Regiment*, 333.

19. Scott, *Story of a Cavalry Regiment*, 333–335; *OR*, Series 1, Vol. 41, Part 1, 336, from the after action report of Major Pierce.

20. Scott, *Story of a Cavalry Regiment*, 335.

21. *OR*, Series 1, Vol. 41, Part 1, 352, from Philips' after action report; Darr, "Price's Raid into Missouri," 361; Hinton, *Rebel Invasion of Missouri and Kansas*, 209; Crawford, *Kansas in the Sixties*, 161.

22. *OR*, Series 1, Vol. 41, Part 1, 684, 694, from the after action reviews of Clark and Colonel Burbridge; Cabell, "Report of Gen. W.L. Cabell," 12.

23. *OR*, Series 1, Vol. 41, Part 1, 335, from the after action report of Major Jones, 3rd Iowa Cavalry; Langsdorf, "Price's Raid and the Battle of Mine Creek," 297; Stalnaker, *The Battle of Mine Creek*, 92–93.

24. W.L. Cabell, "Capture of Cabell and Marmaduke," *Confederate Veteran* 8 (1900), 153–154.

25. Ibid.; *OR*, Series 1, Vol. 41, Part 1, 335, from the after action report of Major Jones; Stalnaker, *The Battle of Mine Creek*, 93–94.

26. *OR*, Series 1, Vol. 41, Part 1, 637, from Price's after action report; Edwards, *Shelby and His Men*, 450 (emphasis in original).

27. *OR*, Series 1, Vol. 41, Part 1, 637, 659–660, from the after action reports of Price and Shelby; Edwards, *Shelby and His Men*, 451–454.

28. McPheeters, *I Acted from Principle*, 236–237; *OR*, Series 1, Vol. 41, Part 1, 332, 337–338, 352, from the after action reports of Benteen, Pleasonton, and Philips (the number of losses for the Confederates is an estimate based on their reports, which are wildly underestimated); Part 4, 238, Pleasonton to Rosecrans dated 25 October 1864 at 1:45 p.m. Crawford, *Kansas in the Sixties*, 162. Field grade officers are in the rank of major and above.

29. *OR*, Series 1, Vol. 41, Part 1, 338, 502, from the after action reports of Pleasonton and Curtis.

30. Ibid., 502–503, from Curtis's after action review; "The Western Campaign," *Harper's Weekly*, 12 November 1864. This update on the campaign notes that "Pleasanton [sic], who has been engaged in pursuit, was injured a few days since by a fall from his horse"; Welsh, *Medical Histories of Union Generals*, 260–261.

31. *OR*, Series 1, Vol. 41, Part 1, 576–577, from Blunt's after action report; Blunt, "Blunt's Account," 261.

32. *OR*, Series 1, Vol. 41, Part 1, 503, from Curtis's after action report.

33. Ibid., Part 4, 1013–1014; Crawford, *Kansas in the Sixties*, 168–170; Hinton, *Rebel Invasion of Missouri and Kansas*, 216–217.

34. McPheeters, *I Acted from Principle*, 237; Edwards, *Shelby and His Men*, 455.

35. *OR*, Series 1, Vol. 41, Part 1, 646–647, from Price's after action report.

36. Reader, "Autobiography," 279–280.

37. Ibid., 301, 303, 315–318, 324.

38. Ibid., 352, 354, 356–363.

39. *OR*, Series 1, Vol. 41, Part 1, 504, from Curtis's after action report; Part 4, 246, 263, 277, 287, Grant to Halleck 26 October 1864, 7:00 p.m. and 27 October 1864, 9:00 p.m. Rosecrans to Smith 27 October 1864 and Pleasonton to Curtis 27 October 1864; Hinton, *Rebel Invasion of Missouri and Kansas*, 247–250.

40. *OR*, Series 1, Vol. 41, Part 4, 318, Curtis to Halleck 29 October 1864, 5:00 a.m. 330–333, Curtis to Halleck 30 October 1864, 1:00 a.m. Curtis to Rosecrans, Smith, McNeil, Sanborn, Philips, and Benteen, all dated 30 October 1864, 1:00 a.m.

41. Ibid., 811, Dodge's assumption of command dated 9 December 1864 and Rosecrans' order to the Department of Missouri relinquishing command on the same date; Langsdorf, "Price's Raid and the Battle of Mine Creek," 300–301; Stalnaker, *The Battle of Mine Creek*, 106–107.

42. Darr, "Price's Raid into Missouri," 361; *OR*, Series 1, Vol. 41, Part 4, 334, dispatch from Sanborn to Pleasonton dated 30 December 1864, 9:00 p.m.

43. "The News," *Weston Border Times*, 28 October 1864; "The Western Campaign," *Harper's Weekly*, 19 November 1864.

Chapter 11

1. McPheeters, *I Acted from Principle*, 237–238; Darr, "Price's Raid into Missouri," 361; *OR*, Series 1, Vol. 41, 661, 669, from the after action reports of Shelby and Thompson.

2. McPheeters, *I Acted from Principle*, 238; *OR*, Ser. 1, Vol. 41, Part 1, 637, 647, from Price's after action report.

3. *OR*, Ser. 1, Vol. 41, Part 1, 637, 647, from Price's after action report; 669, from Thompson's after action report; McPheeters, *I Acted from Principle*, 238.

4. *OR*, Series 1, Vol. 41, Part 1, 637, 647, 661, 669, from the after action reports of Price, Shelby, and Thompson; Larry Wood, *The Two Civil War Battles of Newtonia* (Charleston, SC: History, 2010), 114–118.

5. *OR*, Series 1, Vol. 41, Part 1, 505, from Curtis's after action report; Blunt, "Blunt's Account," 261–262. There is a conflict between Curtis's after action report and "Blunt's Account." Blunt claims that Curtis would not allow him to move at daylight on the 26th, while Curtis claims he issued orders to move "early" on the 26th. Curtis alludes to matters of supply and the issue with command and control following Pleasonton's withdrawal from the campaign, which required reorganization in order to begin the pursuit on the 26th. Curtis's account seems more plausible than Blunt's claim that Curtis would not allow him to start when he wanted that morning. Thus, while Blunt was highly motivated to come to grips with the enemy, his willingness to ignore shortfalls in supply and poor organization makes his accusations toward Curtis seem unfair and his actions rash.

6. Blunt, "Blunt's Account," 262; Hinton, *Rebel Invasion of Missouri and Kansas*, 261–262; *OR*, Series 1, Vol. 41, Part 1, 577, from Blunt's after action review.

7. Blunt, "Blunt's Account," 262; Hinton, *Rebel Invasion of Missouri and Kansas*, 264; Wood, *The Two Civil War Battles of Newtonia*, 118–119.

8. Wood, *The Two Civil War Battles of Newtonia*, 118–119; Blunt, "Blunt's Account," 262.

9. Blunt, "Blunt's Account," 262; *OR*, Series 1, Vol. 41, Part 1, 577, from Blunt's after action report; Wood, *The Two Civil War Battles of Newtonia*, 120.

10. *OR*, Series 1, Vol. 41, Part 1, 661, from Shelby's after action report.

11. Ibid., 577, 661, 669, from the after action reports of Blunt, Shelby, and Thompson; Blunt, "Blunt's Account," 263; W.T. Gass, "Two Close Calls," *Confederate Veteran* 9 (1904), 39; Wood, *The Two Civil War Battles of Newtonia*, 122–125.

12. Blunt, "Blunt's Account," 262–263; *OR*, Series 1, Vol. 41, Part 1, 577–578, 637–638, 661, from the after action reports of Blunt, Price, and Shelby.

13. McPheeters, *I Acted from Principle*, 238–239; *OR*, Series 1, Vol. 41, Part 1, 507–509, 578, from the after action reports of Curtis and Blunt; Part 4, 333–334, Sanborn to Rosecrans dated 30 October 1864; Hinton, *Rebel Invasion of Missouri and Kansas*, 277–278; Blunt, "Blunt's Account," 263; Wood, *The Two Civil War Battles of Newtonia*, 130–131.

14. Darr, "Price's Raid into Missouri," 362.

15. *OR*, Series 1, Vol. 41, Part 1, 510–512, from Curtis's after action report.

16. Ibid., Part 4, 333, 350, 403–404, correspondence between Sanborn and Rosecrans dated 30–31 October 1864 and 2 November 1864.

17. Ibid., Part 1, 513, Curtis to Halleck dated 30 October 1864.

18. Blunt, "Blunt's Account," 263.

19. *OR*, Series 1, Vol. 41, Part 1, 638, 647, from Price's after action report.

20. Ibid.; Wood, *The Two Civil War Battles of Newtonia*, 134–135.

21. *OR*, Series 1, Vol. 41, Part 1, 515, 638, from the after action reports of Curtis and Price; Darr, "Price's Raid into Missouri," 362; Wood, *The Two Civil Battles of Newtonia*, 135.

22. *OR*, Series 1, Vol. 41, Part 1, 647, from Price's after action report; McPheeters, *I Acted from Principle*, 240–244.

23. *OR*, Series 1, Vol. 41, Part 1, 516, 647, from the after action reports of Curtis and Price; Blunt, "Blunt's Account," 263.

24. *OR*, Series 1, Vol. 41, Part 1, 516, 647, from the after action reports of Curtis and Price; Darr, "Price's Raid into Missouri," 362.

25. McPheeters, *I Acted from Principle*, 241; *OR*, Series 1, Vol. 41, Part 1, 516, 647, from the after action reports of Curtis and Price.

26. *OR*, Series 1, Vol. 41, Part 1, 516, 647; Blunt, "Blunt's Account," 263–264; McPheeters, *I Acted from Principle*, 241–242.

27. *OR*, Series 1, Vol. 41, Part 1, 519, Halleck to Curtis dated 7 November 1864; Morrow, "Price's Missouri Expedition, 1864," 153.

28. *OR*, Series 1, Vol. 41, Part 1, 517–518, from Curtis's after action report.

29. Morrow, "Price's Missouri Expedition, 1864," 155–156.

30. McPheeters, *I Acted from Principle*, 242–245; Reynolds, *General Sterling Price*, 148; *OR*, Series 1, Vol. 41, Part 1, 647–648; Edwards, *Shelby and His Men*, 463–464.

31. *OR*, Series 1, Vol. 41, Part 1, 647–648, from Price's after action report; Reynolds, *General Sterling Price*, 142–144; McPheeters, *I Acted from Principle*, 247.

32. *OR*, Series 1, Vol. 41, Part 4, 1052, 1078, 1112, 1114, correspondence between Magruder, Smith, and Price; Morrow, "Price's Missouri Expedition, 1864," 164.

33. Welsh, *Medical Histories of Confederate Generals*, 177.
34. Reynolds, *General Sterling Price*, 134–152; *OR*, Series 1, Vol. 41, Part 4, 1123, Reynolds to Price dated 24 December 1864; Morrow, "Price's Missouri Expedition, 1864," 167–168.
35. Reynolds, *General Sterling Price*, 134; *OR*, Series 1, Vol. 41, Part 1, 701–702, Special Order #s 58 and 81 dated 8 March 1865 and 5 April 1865 appointing the court at Price's request, and the first-day record of proceedings dated 21 April 1865.
36. Ibid., 702–710, from the court of inquiry, 22 and 24 April 1865.
37. Ibid., 718, from the day-six proceedings of the court and a letter to the court from Governor Reynolds dated 27 April 1865.
38. Ibid., 726–727, from day-ten proceedings dated 3 May 1865.
39. Edwards, *Shelby and His Men*, 465; Darr, "Price's Raid into Missouri," 362.

Chapter 12

1. The detailed itinerary from Price's after action report in *OR*, Series 1, Vol. 41, Part 1, 642–648, shows the Army of Missouri moved 789 miles between 19 September and 7 November 1864, which was the actual period of the campaign. Price marched 52 of the 57 days, when not in battle or encamped due to poor weather. When taking the total distance divided by the 52 marching days, Price averaged 15.17 miles per day.
2. Ibid., 640, from Price's after action report.
3. Ibid., Part 4, 1077–1079, 1107–1108, 1140, Magruder to Brigadier General William R. Boggs, Smith's chief of staff, 26 November and 12 December 1864, and returns from the Trans-Mississippi Department for December 1864. A footnote in the returns contains an estimate of what was left in the Army of Missouri.
4. Nelson, *Bullets, Ballots, and Rhetoric*, 97–98, 111–113, 147.
5. *OR*, Series 1, Vol. 41, Part 4, 299, 328–329, dispatches from Rosecrans' chief of staff and assistant adjutant general to A.J. Smith dated 28 and 30 October 1864.
6. This total is purely an estimate based on reviewing the various after action reports in the *OR*, Series 1, Vol. 41, Part 1, filed by the Union commanders. Some of these contain only estimates of their losses, which are subject to exaggeration, while other reports, like Blunt's after Newtonia, contains wording such as "near one-eighth of my force engaged were killed and wounded" (Part 1, 578). Since we do not know exactly how many troops Blunt had engaged, such comments make it difficult to ascertain exact figures of losses, and therefore we are left to make an educated guess.

Appendix A

1. *OR.*, Series 1, Vol. 41, Part 1, 303–304, 642–648; E.B. Long, *The Civil War Day by Day*, 562–605; Forsyth, *The Camden Expedition*, 187–191; Lause, *Price's Lost Campaign*, 195–201.

Appendix B

1. *OR*, Series 1, Vol. 41, Part I, 641–42; Part 2, 974–978; Part 4, 360, 367–372, 732, 972, 978–983; Lause, *Price's Lost Campaign*, 203–209; Westport Historical Society, *The Battle of Westport*, 19–24; Davis, "Guerrilla Operations in the Civil War," 103–110.

Bibliography

Unpublished Sources

Blue and Gray Education Society. "Price's 1864 Missouri Raid Preservation Conference Report." Kansas City, University of Missouri, March 1996.

Bondi, August. Papers. Kansas Historical Society, Topeka, Kansas.

Curtis, Samuel R. Papers. Campaign Book, Army of the Border, October–November 1864. Microfilm Call #303, Kansas State Historical Society, Topeka, Kansas.

Dameron, William T. Papers. Missouri Secretary of State, Missouri Digital Heritage Collection, Jefferson City, Missouri. http://cdm.sos.mo.gov.

Davis, Dale E. "Guerrilla Operations in the Civil War: Assessing Compound Warfare During Price's Raid." Master's thesis, United States Army Command and General Staff College, Fort Leavenworth, Kansas, 2004.

Ewing, Thomas, Jr. Papers. Microfilm Call #569 and #570, Kansas State Historical Society. Topeka, Kansas.

Forsyth, Michael J. "Effective Termination of Conflict: Perspectives from 1847 and 2003." Strategy Research Project. Carlisle Barracks, PA: U.S. Army War College, 2012.

Holst, David L. "General Samuel Curtis and the Civil War in the West." Master's thesis, Illinois State University, 1974.

Moonlight, Thomas. Papers, 1861–1871. Kansas State Historical Society, Topeka, Kansas.

Morrow, Norman Potter. "Price's Missouri Expedition, 1864." Master's thesis, University of Texas, 1949.

Price, Sterling. Papers. Missouri Secretary of State, Missouri Digital Heritage Collections. Jefferson City, Missouri. http://cdm.sos.mo.gov.

____. Western Historical Manuscript Collection. State Historical Society of Missouri, Columbia, Missouri.

Reader, Samuel J. Autobiography. Kansas State Historical Society Digital Collection, Topeka, Kansas. http://www.kansasmemory.org/item/206900.

Reynolds, Thomas C. Papers. Microfilm, roll no. 13.777-IP, Library of Congress, Washington, D.C.

"Scouts, Spies, and Detectives." Missouri Secretary of State, Missouri Digital Heritage Collection, Jefferson City, Missouri. http://cdm.sos.mo.gov.

Smith, Edmund Kirby. Papers, #404. Southern Historical Collection, Wilson Library, University of North Carolina at Chapel Hill. http://www2.lib.unc.edu/mss/inv/k/Kirby-Smith,Edmund.html.

Newspapers

Harper's Weekly. New York. http://sonofthesouth.net/leefoundation/civil-war1864/.

St. Louis Daily Missouri Republican. http://statehistoricalsocietyof missouri.org/cdm.

Weston (MO) Border Times. http://statehistoricalsocietyof missouri.org/cdm.

Primary Sources

Barton, O.S. *Three Years with Quantrill: A True Story Told by His Scout John McCorkle*. Norman: University of Oklahoma Press, 1992.

Blunt, James G. "General Blunt's Account of His Civil War Experiences." *Kansas Historical Quarterly* 1, no. 3 (May 1932), 211–265.

Britton, Wiley. *The Civil War on the Border*. 2 Vols. New York and London: Putnam, 1904.

Cabell, William L. "Capture of Cabell and Marmaduke." *Confederate Veteran* 8 (1900), 153–154.

____. "Report of Gen. W.L. Cabell's Brigade in Price's Raid in Missouri and Kansas in 1864." Dallas, Texas: Adjutant General, Confederate Veterans, 1900. http://cdm16084.contentdm.oclc.org/cdm/search/searchterm/Fagan's (accessed 10 November 2013, Fort Worth Library Digital Archives).

Cole, Birdie H. "The Battle of Pilot Knob." *Confederate Veteran* 22 (1914), 417.

Cox, Jacob D. *Military Reminiscences of the Civil*

War, April 1861–November 1863. Vol. 1. New York: Scribner's, 1900.
Crawford, Samuel J. *Kansas in the Sixties.* New York: A.C. McClurg, 1911. Reprint Ottawa, KS: Kansas Heritage Press, 1994.
Darr, John C. "Price's Raid into Missouri." *Confederate Veteran* 11 (1903), 359–362.
Edwards, John N. *Shelby and His Men; or, The Civil War in the West.* Cincinnati: Miami, 1867.
———. *Shelby's Expedition to Mexico: An Unwritten Leaf of the War.* Edited by Conger Beasley, Jr. Fayetteville: University of Arkansas Press, 2002.
Elder, P.P. *Price Raid Commission: Report to Legislature.* Topeka: Kansas State Legislature, Special Session, 1886.
Forse, William Scott. *The Story of a Cavalry Regiment: The Career of the 4th Iowa Veteran Volunteers, from Kansas to Georgia, 1861–1865.* New York: G.P. Putnam's Sons, 1893.
Gass, W.T. "Two 'Close Calls.'" *Confederate Veteran* 12 (1904), 38–39.
Grant, Ulysses S. *Personal Memoirs of U.S. Grant.* 2 Vols. New York: Charles L. Webster, 1886.
Grissom, Daniel M. "Personal Recollections of Distinguished Missourians." *Missouri Historical Review* 20, no. 1 (October 1925), 110–111.
Grover, George S. "The Price Campaign of 1864." *Missouri Historical Review* 6, no. 4 (July 1912), 167–181.
Hannahs, Harrison. "General Thomas Ewing, Jr." *Kansas Historical Collections* 12 (1912), 276–282.
Hinton, Richard J. *Rebel Invasion of Missouri and Kansas and the Campaign of the Army of the Border Against General Sterling Price in October and November 1864.* Chicago: Goodman and Donnelly, 1865. Reprinted, Ottawa, KS: Kansas Heritage Press, 1994.
Johnson, Robert U., and Clarence C. Buell, eds. *Battles and Leaders of the Civil War.* 4 Vols. New York: Century, 1886.
Jones, John B. *A Rebel War Clerk's Diary.* Edited by Earl Schenck Miers. New York: A.S. Barnes, 1961.
Jones, Samuel. "The Battle of Prairie Grove, December 7, 1862." *Southern Bivouac* 1, no. 1 (1885), 203–211.
Kean, Robert Garlick Hill. *Inside the Confederate Government: The Diary of Robert Garlick Hill Kean, Head of the Bureau of War.* Edited by Edward Younger. New York: Oxford University Press, 1957.
Library of Congress. *A Century of Lawmaking for a New Nation: U.S. Congressional Documents and Debates, 1774–1875.* "The Kansas-Nebraska Act." 33rd Congress, 1st Session. Washington, D.C.: U.S. Government Printing Office. http://memory.loc.gov/cgi-bin/ampage?collId=llsl&fileName=010/llsl010.db&recNum=298 (accessed 12 February 2013).
———. *A Century of Lawmaking for a New Nation: U.S. Congressional Documents and Debates, 1774–1875.* "The Missouri Compromise." 16th Congress, 1st Session. Washington, D.C.: U.S. Government Printing Office. http://memory.loc.gov/cgi-bin/ampage?collId=llsl&fileName=003/llsl003.db&recNum=587 (accessed 11 February 2013).
Liddell, St. John R. *Liddell's Record.* Edited by Nathaniel Cheairs Hughes, Jr. Baton Rouge: Louisiana State University Press, 1985.
Lincoln, Abraham. *The Collected Works of Abraham Lincoln.* Edited by Roy P. Basler. Vol. 8. New Brunswick, NJ: Rutgers University Press, 1953.
———. *Complete Works of Abraham Lincoln: Comprising His Speeches, Letters, State Papers, and Miscellaneous Writings.* Edited by John G. Nicolay and John Hay. New York: Century, 1894.
Moore, John C. "Missouri." In *Confederate Military History,* vol. 9. Edited by Clement A. Evans. Atlanta, GA: Confederate, 1899.
Official Register of the Officers and Cadets of the U.S. Military Academy. West Point, NY: U.S. Government Printing Office. Years referenced: 1831, 1842, 1844, 1857.
Palmer, Henry E. "Company A, Eleventh Kansas Regiment, in the Price Raid." *Transactions of the Kansas State Historical Society, 1905–1906,* Vol. 9. Ed. George W. Martin. Topeka: State Printing Office, 1906.
Pitcock, Cynthia DeHaven, and Bill J. Gurley, eds. *I Acted from Principle: The Civil War Diary of Dr. William M. McPheeters, Confederate Surgeon in the Trans-Mississippi.* Fayetteville: University of Arkansas Press, 2002.
Reynolds, Thomas C. *General Sterling Price and the Confederacy.* Edited by Robert G. Schultz. St. Louis: Missouri History Museum, 2009.
Schofield, John M. *Forty-Six Years in the Army.* New York: Century, 1897.
Sheridan, Philip. *Civil War Memoirs.* Edited by Paul A. Hutton. New York: Bantam Domain, 1991. This edition in a single volume does not maintain the original pagination of the *Personal Memoirs of P.H. Sheridan* published in 1888 by Charles L. Webster in two volumes.
Sherman, William T. *Memoirs of William T. Sherman.* New York: D. Appleton, 1875.
Snead, Thomas L. *The Fight for Missouri from the Election of Lincoln to the Death of Lyon.* New York: Scribner's, 1886.
Taylor, Richard. *Destruction and Reconstruction: Personal Experiences of the Late War.* New York: D. Appleton, 1879. Reprint, New York:

Bantam, 1992. This version does not contain the original pagination of the 1879 edition.
Thayer, Eli. *A History of the Kansas Crusade: Its Friends and Its Foes.* New York: Harper and Brothers, 1889.
United States Congress. *Report No. 200 of the Sub-Committee of the Committee on Elections.* 34th Congress, Washington, D.C.: U.S. Government Printing Office, 1856.
———. *The Utah Expedition: Message from the President of the United States, Transmitting Reports from the Secretaries of State, of War, of the Interior, and of the Attorney General, Relative to the Military Expedition Ordered into the Territory of Utah, Executive Document No. 71, 35th Congress, 1st Session, February 26, 1858.* Washington, D.C.: U.S. Government Printing Office, 1858.
United States Department of the Interior. *Population of the United States in 1860: Compiled from the Original Returns of the Eighth Census.* Washington, D.C.: U.S. Government Printing Office, 1864. http://www2.census.gov/prod2/decennial/documents/1860-01.pdf (accessed 6 February 2013).
United States Department of the Navy. *Official Records of the Union and Confederate Navies in the War of the Rebellion.* Series I in 27 Vols. Washington, D.C.: U.S. Government Printing Office, 1894–1922.
United States War Department. *War of the Rebellion: Official Records of the Union and Confederate Armies.* 128 Vols. Washington, D.C.: U.S. Government Printing Office, 1880–1901.

Secondary Sources

"Arkansas in the Mexican War." *Encyclopedia of Arkansas History and Culture* (2012). http://www.encyclopediaofarkansas.net/encyclopedia/entry-detail.aspx?entryID=4206 (accessed 15 May 2013).
"August Bondi." *Jewish Virtual Library.* American-Israeli Cooperative Enterprise 2013. http://www.jewishvirtuallibrary.org/jsource/biography/bondy.html (accessed 4 February 2013).
Bailey, Anne J. "The Abandoned Western Theater: Confederate National Policy Toward the Trans-Mississippi Region." *Journal of Confederate History* 5 (1990), 35–54.
Bailey, Anne J., and Daniel E. Sutherland, eds. *Civil War Arkansas: Beyond Battles and Leaders.* Fayetteville: University of Arkansas Press, 2000.
"Battle of Pilot Knob." Missouri Department of Natural Resources Bulletin, undated. http://freepages.military.rootsweb.ancestry.com/~caulleyfamilyinfo/HISTORY.HTML (accessed 16 January 2013).
Bearss, Edwin C. *The Battle of Wilson's Creek.* Cassville, MO: Litho, 1992.
Birtle, Andrew J. *U.S. Army Counterinsurgency and Contingency Operations Doctrine, 1860–1941.* Washington, D.C.: U.S. Government Printing Office, 1994.
Brownlee, Richard S. "The Battle of Pilot Knob: Iron County, Missouri, September 27, 1864." *Missouri Historical Review* 59, no. 1 (October 1964), 1–30.
Busch, Walter E. *Fort Davidson and the Battle of Pilot Knob.* Charleston, SC: History, 2010.
Castel, Albert. *A Frontier State at War: Kansas, 1861–1865.* Ithaca, NY: Cornell University Press, 1958.
———. *General Sterling Price and the Civil War in the West.* Baton Rouge: Louisiana State University Press, 1968.
———. "War and Politics: The Price Raid of 1864." *Kansas Historical Quarterly* 24, no. 2 (Summer 1958), 129–143.
Catton, Bruce. *Never Call Retreat.* New York: Doubleday, 1965.
———. *The Coming Fury.* New York: Doubleday, 1961.
Collins, Robert. *General James G. Blunt: Tarnished Glory.* Gretna, LA: Pelican, 2005.
Cottrell, Steve. *Civil War in the Indian Territory.* Gretna, LA: Pelican, 1998.
Cozzens, Peter. *The Darkest Days of the War: The Battles of Iuka and Corinth.* Chapel Hill: University of North Carolina Press, 2006.
———. *No Better Place to Die: The Battle of Stones River.* Champaign: University of Illinois Press, 1990.
———. *This Terrible Sound: The Battle of Chickamauga.* Champaign: University of Illinois Press, 1996.
Craven, Avery O. *Civil War in the Making, 1815–1860.* Baton Rouge: Louisiana State University Press, 1959.
Daniel, Larry J. *Shiloh: The Battle that Changed the Civil War.* New York: Simon & Schuster, 1997.
Eicher, John H., and David J. *Civil War High Commands.* Palo Alto, CA: Stanford University Press, 2001.
Fellman, Michael. *Inside War: The Guerrilla Conflict in Missouri During the American Civil War.* New York: Oxford University Press, 1989.
Foote, Shelby. *The Civil War: A Narrative.* 3 Vols. New York: Random House, 1958.
Forsyth, Michael J. *The Camden Expedition of 1864 and the Opportunity Lost by the Confederacy to Change the Civil War.* Jefferson, NC: McFarland, 2003.
———. *The Red River Campaign of 1864 and the Loss by the Confederacy of the Civil War.* Jefferson, NC: McFarland, 2002.

Gallaher, Ruth A. "Samuel Ryan Curtis." *Iowa Journal of History and Politics*. Iowa City: State Historical Society of Iowa (July 1927), 331–358.

Gaylord, Kristina. *Kansas Territory: Timeline*. Topeka: Kansas State Historical Society, 2011. http://www.kshs.org/kansapedia/kansas-territory-timeline-more/14726 (accessed 24 March 2013).

Gerteis, Louis S. *The Civil War in Missouri: A Military History*. Columbia: University of Missouri Press, 2012.

Huff, Leo E. "The Last Duel in Arkansas: The Marmaduke-Walker Duel." *Arkansas Historical Quarterly* 23 (Spring 1964), 36–49.

Hyde, Bill. *The Union Generals Speak: The Meade Hearings on the Battle of Gettysburg*. Baton Rouge: Louisiana State University Press, 2003.

Jenkins, Paul B. *The Battle of Westport*. Kansas City, MO: Franklin Hudson, 1906.

Josephy, Alvin M., Jr. *The Civil War in the American West*. New York: Alfred A. Knopf, 1991.

Kerby, Robert L. *Kirby Smith's Confederacy: The Trans-Mississippi South, 1863–1865*. Tuscaloosa: University of Alabama Press, 1972.

Kirkman, Paul. *The Battle of Westport: Missouri's Great Confederate Raid*. Charleston, SC: History, 2011.

Lamars, William M. *The Edge of Glory: A Biography of General William S. Rosecrans, USA*. Chapel Hill: University of North Carolina Press, 1999.

Langsdorf, Edgar. "Price's Raid and the Battle of Mine Creek." *Kansas Historical Quarterly* 30, no. 3 (Autumn 1964), 281–306.

Lause, Mark A. *Price's Lost Campaign: The 1864 Invasion of Missouri*. Columbia: University of Missouri Press, 2011.

Long, David E. *The Jewel of Liberty: Abraham Lincoln's Re-election and the End of Slavery*. Mechanicsburg, PA: Stackpole Books, 1994.

Long, E.B., and Barbara Long. *The Civil War Day by Day: An Almanac, 1861–1865*. New York: Da Capo, 1971.

_____. "Alfred Pleasonton: Knight of Romance." *Civil War Times Illustrated* 13 (December 1974), 12–23.

Longacre, Edward G. *The Commanders of Chancellorsville*. Nashville, TN: Rutledge Hill, 2005.

McElroy, John. *The Struggle for Missouri*. Washington, D.C.: National Tribune, 1913.

McPherson, James M. *Battle Cry of Freedom*. New York: Oxford University Press, 1988.

_____. *Tried by War: Abraham Lincoln as Commander in Chief*. New York: Penguin, 2008.

Miller, George. *Missouri's Memorable Decade: 1860–1870*. Columbia, MO: E.W. Stephens, 1898.

Monaghan, Jay. *Civil War on the Western Border, 1854–1865*. Boston: Little, Brown, 1955.

Monnett, Howard. *Action Before Westport, 1864*. Kansas City: Westport Historical Society, 1964. Revised edition published in 1994 by University of Colorado Press.

Murphy, Robert L. "'I Have No Faith in Foreigners': Pleasonton Clears the Way for His Boy Generals." *Gettysburg*, no. 45 (Summer 2013), 1–10.

Nelson, Larry E. *Bullets, Ballots, and Rhetoric: Confederate Policy for the United States Presidential Contest of 1864*. Tuscaloosa: University of Alabama Press, 1980.

Nichols, Bruce. *Guerrilla Warfare in Civil War Missouri, 1862*. Jefferson, NC: McFarland, 2004.

O'Flaherty, Daniel O. *General Jo Shelby: Undefeated Rebel*. Chapel Hill: University of North Carolina Press, 1954.

Oates, Stephen B. *Confederate Cavalry West of the River*. Austin: University of Texas Press, 1961.

_____. "The Prairie Grove Campaign, 1862." *Arkansas Historical Quarterly* 19, no. 2 (Summer 1960), 119–141.

Parks, Joseph H. *General Edmund Kirby Smith, C.S.A.* Baton Rouge: Louisiana State University Press, 1982.

Parrish, Michael T. *Richard Taylor: Soldier Prince of Dixie*. Chapel Hill: University of North Carolina Press, 1992.

Parrish, William E., Perry McCandless, and William E. Foley. *A History of Missouri*. Columbia: University of Missouri Press, 1971.

Peterson, Cyrus A. *Narrative of the Capture and Murder of Major James Wilson*. St. Louis: A.R. Fleming, 1906.

Peterson, Cyrus A., and Joseph M. Hanson. *Pilot Knob: The Thermopylae of the West*. Lexington, KY: Forgotten Books, 2012. Reprint of the original text published in 1914 by Neale, New York.

Porter, Scott A. "Thunder Across the Arkansas Prairie: Shelby's Opening Salvo in the 1864 Invasion of Missouri." *Arkansas Historical Quarterly* 66, no. 1 (Spring 2007), 43–56.

Prushankin, Jeffery S. *A Crisis in Command: Edmund Kirby Smith, Richard Taylor, and the Army of the Trans-Mississippi*. Baton Rouge: Louisiana State University Press, 2005.

Rea, Ralph R. *Sterling Price: The Lee of the West*. Little Rock, AK: Pioneer, 1959.

Reid, Whitelaw. "Brevet Major-General Thomas H. Ewing, Jr." In *Ohio in the War: History of Ohio During the War, and the Lives of Her Generals*. Cincinnati: Robert Clarke, 1895.

Scott, Kim Allen. "The Preacher, the Lawyer, and the Spoils of War." *Kansas History: A Journal of the Central Plains* 13 (1991), 206–215.

Shalhope, Robert E. *Sterling Price: Portrait of a Southerner*. Columbia: University of Missouri Press, 1971.

Shea, William L., and Earl J. Hess. *Pea Ridge: Civil War Campaign in the West*. Chapel Hill: University of North Carolina Press, 1992.

Smith, Ronald D. *Thomas Ewing Jr.: Frontier Lawyer and Civil War General*. Columbia: University of Missouri Press, 2008.

Stalnaker, Jeffrey D. *The Battle of Mine Creek: The Crushing End of the Missouri Campaign*. Charleston, SC: History, 2011.

Starr, Stephen Z. *The Union Cavalry in the Civil War*. Vol 1. Baton Rouge: Louisiana State University Press, 1979.

Steele, Phillip W., and Steve Cottrell. *Civil War in the Ozarks*. Gretna, LA: Pelican, 1998.

Stillman, Yankl. "August Bondi and the Abolitionist Movement." *Jewish Currents* (March 2004). http://jewishcurrents.org/2004-mar-stillman.htm (accessed 4 February 2013).

Stoker, Donald. *The Grand Design: Strategy and the U.S. Civil War*. London: Oxford University Press, 2010.

Taylor, Hawkins. "General Curtis." *Iowa Historical Record*, Vol. 3, 561–567. Iowa Historical Society, 1975.

"The Trans-Mississippi Department of the Confederacy." *Writers of History* (August 2012). http://writersofhistory.com/ (accessed 24 March 2013).

"The Trans-Mississippi Department of the Confederacy." *Writers of History* (22 August 2012). http://writersofhistory.com/?p=200 (accessed 30 March 2012).

Turner, Andy. "On This Day: The Battle of Rich Mountain." *Gatehouse Press Online* (July 2013). http://www.gatehouse-press.com/?p=4211 (accessed 11 July 2013).

———. "On This Day: The Battle That Saved Missouri for the Union." *Gatehouse Press Online* (March 2013). http://www.gatehouse-press.com/?p=3377 (accessed 7 March 2013).

———. "On This Day: The Centralia Massacre." *Gatehouse Press Online* (September 2012). http://www.gatehouse-press.com/?p=2305 (accessed 2 December 2013).

Twitchell, Ralph Emerson. *The History of the Military Occupation of the Territory of New Mexico from 1846 to 1851*. Denver, CO: Smith-Brooks, 1909.

Warner, Ezra J. *Generals in Blue: The Lives of Union Commanders*. Baton Rouge: Louisiana State University Press, 1964.

———. *Generals in Gray: The Lives of Confederate Commanders*. Baton Rouge: Louisiana State University Press, 1959.

Waugh, John C. *Reelecting Lincoln: The Battle for the 1864 Presidency*. New York: Crown, 1997.

Welsh, Jack D. *Medical Histories of Confederate Generals*. Kent, OH: Kent State University Press, 1995.

———. *Medical Histories of Union Generals*. Kent, OH: Kent State University Press, 1996.

Westport Historical Society. *The Battle of Westport, October 2–23, 1864*. Kansas City, Missouri: Harris-Kenney House, 1996.

Wittenberg, Eric J. *The Union Cavalry Comes of Age: Hartwood Church to Brandy Station*. Washington, D.C.: Brassey's, 2003.

Wood, Larry. *The Two Civil War Battles of Newtonia*. Charleston, SC: History, 2010.

Woodworth, Steven E. *The Art of Command in the Civil War*. Lincoln: University of Nebraska Press, 1998.

Index

Page numbers in *bold italics* indicate pages with illustrations.

Adams, John Q. 81
Adams, Samuel 53
Alabama Mississippi, and East Louisiana, department of (Confederate) 94
Anderson, "Bloody" Bill 23, 72, 142–144, 148, 161–162, 179, 238; death of 162, 240
Anderson, Martin 176–177
Anthony, Dan 72
Antietam, battle of 77
Arkansas, department of (U.S.) 164
Arkansas, district of (Confederate) 36–37, 44, 103
Atchison, David Rice 13–17, 39

Banks, Nathaniel P. 1, 5–6, 8, 24, 37, 57, 97, 230, 237
Baxter Springs, affair at 81, 86, 91–92, 188
Beauregard, Pierre Gustave Toutant 34–35, 62
Bent, Charles 30
Benteen, Frederick 188, 193, 203–205, 207–208, 210–211, 213, 222, 233, 251–252
Beveridge, John L. 137, 196, 250
Bingham, George 74
Blair, Charles W. 164–165, 173, 209
Blair, Francis P., Jr. 19–20, 38–40
Blair, Francis P., Sr. 20, 38
Blue Lodge Organization 14, 40
Blunt, James G. 42–43, 49–50, 55, 69–71, 86, *88*, 165, 170–171, 181, 249; actions to control militia 166–167; administrative incompetence 89; background 87–92; character 87–89; chronology 239–340; commands Army of the Border cavalry 156, 164; diverts to Fort Scott 211, 213; final pursuit 221–223; at Lexington 173–175; at Little Blue 178–179, 183; at Newtonia, battle of 217–219; pursuit of Price to Mine Creek 201–203; recalled from frontier 155; at Westport, battle of 185–186, 188, 190

Boggs, William R. 94
Bondi, August 15
Boonville, battle of 48
Border, Army of the (U.S.) 156, 164–165, 168, 170, 173, 175–176, 179, 182, 184, 188, 202, 210, 217–218, 224, 240–241, 248–252
Border, district of 72, 74
"Border Ruffians" 14, 16, 31, 39–40, 74, 87, 165
Boutwell, Daniel W. 182–183
Bragg, Braxton 1, 6, 25–26, 35–36, 49, 54–55, 62–65, 94, 97–98, 105, 229, 234, 237
Brooks, William H. 221
Brown, B. Gratz 138, 145
Brown, Egbert 145–147, 149–151, 154–155, 189, 195, 250; arrested 192
Brown, John 15, 68, 87–88
Buchanan, James 16, 47
Buckingham, Belinda (Curtis) 81
Buckner, Simon Bolivar 75, 99–100, 236, 241
Buell, Don Carlos 49, 59, 62–63
Buena Vista, battle of 53–54, 81
Bull, John P. 128
Burns, Ross 187
Byram's Ford *180*–181, 185–189, 191, 195

Cabell, William L. 107, 109–110, *129*, 145, 159, 162; assigned to guard train 184; capture of 209–210, 214; event chronology 237–241; at Jefferson City 151; at Little Blue 178; at Mine Creek, battle of 206, 208–209; at Pilot Knob, battle of 127–131; at Westport, battle of 188, 193, 195–196
Cabin Creek, battle of 91
Camden Expedition 1, 6, 24–25, 37, 45, 52, 56–57, 93, 98, 104, 107, 231, 237
Cameron, Simon 20
Campbell, William J. 127, 130, 133, 136
Canby, Edward R. S. 25, 94, 112, 115, 172, 236
Cane Hill, battle of 43, 50, 55, 71, 90
Carney, Thomas 117, 155–156, 164–166, 173, 176, 196
Carpenter, Seymour D. 139
Carthage, battle of 40–41
Catherwood, Edwin 164, 250
Central Missouri, district of (U.S.) 145–146, 154
Centralia Massacre 143–144, 238
Chamberlain, Joshua L. 87
Chancellorsville, battle of 78
Cheat Mountain 61
Chickamauga, battle of 65–66
Clark, John B. 110, 130, 149, 158, 169–170, 177, 188, 208–209, 238, 243
Clay, Henry 38
Collins, Richard 190, 219, 234, 243
Compound Warfare 142, 162
Conditional Unionists 17
Confederate national policy 22, 102; strategy in Trans-Mississippi 24
Confederate Units: Order of Battle 242–244
1st Arkansas Battalion 48

277

Index

1st Arkansas Infantry Regiment 54–55
3rd Confederate Infantry Regiment 48–49, 55
3rd Missouri Cavalry 205, 243
4th Missouri Cavalry 177, 208, 243
5th Missouri Cavalry 177, 243
14th Missouri Cavalry Battalion 177, 243
34th Arkansas Cavalry 221
Blocher's Arkansas Battery 190, 242
Cabell's Brigade 242
Churchill's Division 103
Collins' Missouri Battery 189–190, 219, 234, 243–244
Fagan's Division 242–243
Hughey's Arkansas Battery 196, 242
Marmaduke's Division 243
McGhee's Arkansas Cavalry Regiment 190–191
Parson's Division 103
Polignac's Division 103
Shelby's Division 243–244
Cooper, Douglas 91, 116
Corinth, battle of 36, 62–63, 66
Cox, S. P. 162
Crawford, Samuel 71, 88, 194
Crittenden, John J. 38
Cumberland, Army of the (U.S.) 58, 63, 65–66, 168, 240–241
Curtis, Henry 81, 86, 91, 188
Curtis, Samuel R. 24, 33–34, 42, 70, 75, 79, *80*, 91–92, 105, 115–116, 150–151, 157, 167–168, 184, 200, 248; background 80–87; capture of Marmaduke 209; character 81–84; command issues 211, 213–215, 220; disbands Army of the Border 224; event chronology 240–241; fears move on Kansas 148, 155; final pursuit 216–217, 222–223; at Little Blue 178; organizes defense 156, 163–166, 172–173, 175–176, 232; plan for Westport 171, 179; preparations 117, 180–183; pursuit of Price 201–203; relations with civil authorities 85–86; at Westport 186–198

Dameron, William T. 160–161
Dana, Charles A. 65
Darr, John 130, 223, 227
Davidson, John W. 120
Davis, Jefferson 6, 35, 94, 97
Dennison, William 60
Dietzler, George 156, 165–167, 171, 179, 182–183, 185–186, 188, 190, 196, 249
Dobbin, Archibald S. 132–134, 190, 224, 242
Dodge, Grenville 214
Douglas, H. T. 95–96
Douglas, Stephen 12–13, 31–32
Drake, Francis M. 57
Dunlavy, James 209

Early, Jubal 231, 239
Edwards, John N. 42, 153, 172, 186, 225
Eitzen, Charles 148–149
Enrolled Missouri Militia (EMM) 112–115, 148, 160, 238
Ewing, Hugh Boyle 68
Ewing, Thomas, Jr. 23, *68*, 116, 121, 144, 154, 156–157, 169, 196, 226, 232, 235, 244, 246, 248; background 66–75; character 69–74; at Pilot Knob 123–139

Fagan, James F. 99, 104, 107, 109–111, 144–145; background 52–57; character 54; event chronology 237–241; at Fayetteville, Arkansas 221–222
Farragut, David G. 237
Fayetteville, Arkansas, affair 221–223, 240
final retreat 212, 219, 223, 234; leadership 56; at Mine Creek 205, 208, 210; in "picnic period" 158; at Pilot Knob 123–131, 137–138; march to Westport 173, 176; plan for Westport 184–186; retreat from Westport 202, 204; at Westport 188, 194–196, 198
Fishback, William H. 167, 173
Fisk, Clinton B. 143–144, 147, 149–152, 155, 247
Fletcher, Thomas C. 124, 132–133
Floyd, John 61, 236
Ford, James 218–219, 249
Forney, John A. 103

Forrest, Nathan Bedford 2, 99, 114
Fort Curtis 118, 120
Fort Davidson 66, 116, 118, 120–121, *122*, 130, *131*, 132–135, 137–138, 141, 143, 226, 232, 236
Fort Donelson 236
Fort Hovey 120
Fort Leavenworth 153, 155, 164, 169, 172, 202
Fort Scott 70, 86–87, 89, 91–92, 153, 172, 198, 202, 211, 213, 214, 218, 240
Freeman, Thomas 208, 224
Frémont, John C. 23, 83, 87, 89
Frontier, district of the (U.S.) 92
Frost, Daniel 19, 40
Fugitive Slave Law 67

Gamble, Hamilton 86
General Order #8 110–111
General Order #11 23, 73, *74*–75, 123, 127, 132, 201
General Order #22 212
General Order #57 213
General Order #107 113
General Order #184 154
General Order #185 149
General Order #294 214
Gettysburg, battle of 78–79
Gibson, Randall K. 54–55
Gilpatrick, Rufus 87
Glasgow, capture of 169–170, 226, 239
Goodman, Thomas 144
Gordon, Anderson 209, 242
Gordon, Thomas 144
Gourley, William W. 140
Grant, Ulysses S. 5, 25, 36, 44, 48–49, 62, 66–67, 114–115, 120, 168, 213–215, 220, 222–223, 235–236, 241
Gratz, Benjamin 38
Gratz, Howard 38–39
Gravely, Joseph, J. 151, 251
Greeley, Horace 14
Greer, James 176
Grotts, William E. 140
Guadalupe Hidalgo, treaty of 31
Gulf, Army of the (U.S.) 1, 5, 8, 24–25, 37, 97, 237

Halleck, Henry W. 25, 34, 62, 64, 92, 114, 123, 168, 202, 213–214, 220–221, 223, 235
Hancock, Winfield Scott 75

Index

Hardee, William 48–49
Hardie, James A. 115
Harding, Chester, Jr. 169, 239
Harney, William S. 19–20, 76
Harney-Price Agreement 19–20, 32
Harrison, Marcus Lane 223
Harrison, William Henry 58, 6
Hayes, Rutherford B. 60
Helena, battle of 36, 44, 51, 56
Herron, Francis J. 42–43, 50, 55–56, 71, 90
Hill, Daniel Harvey 65
Hindman, Thomas C. 42, 48–50, 55–56, 70–71, 89–90
Holabaugh, John 140
Holmes, Theophilus 36, 44, 56
Honey Springs, battle of 91
Hood, John Bell 5, 47, 241
Hooker, Joseph 78
Hughey, William M. 128, 196, 242
Hunter, David 83
Huntoon, Joel 176

Independence, engagement at 179
Island #10 24
Iuka, battle of 36, 62–63, 66

Jackman, Sidney 185–186, 219, 244
Jackson, Claiborne Fox 14, 18–20, 32, 39–40, 46–48
Jackson, Thomas J. "Stonewall" 78
Jayhawkers 142, 164, 186, 190
Jefferson City, defense of 149–150, 238–239
Jennison, Charles 72, 164, 186, 190, 201, 218–219, 249
Johnson, Curtis 190
Johnson, Thomas W. 138
Johnston, A.V.E. 144
Johnston, Albert Sidney 47–48, 54
Johnston, Joseph E. 5, 25, 94, 227, 229, 241
Joint Congressional Committee on the Conduct of the War 79

Kansas, Department of 79, 86, 89–90, 92, 105, 117, 148
Kansas-Nebraska Act 11–13, 23
Kansas State Militia (KSM) 148, 165, 167–168, 171, 173, 180–181, 196–197, 213, 249
Kearney, Stephen W. 29–30

Lamson, Earl J. 136–137
Lane, James 15–16, 68–70, 72–75, 88–89, 91–92, 155
Lawrence, Kansas, Raid 23, 72, 165
Lecompton Constitution 69
Lee, Robert E. 5, 25, 30, 47, 61–62, 78–79, 226, 229, 231, 239, 241
Lee, Stephen D. 94, 229
Lexington, battle of 23, 33, 89
Lincoln, Abraham 1, 7–8, 18, 20, 63, 65, 69–70, 74–75, 78–79, 83, 86, 92, 101, 168–169, 215, 232, 235, 239, 240
Little Blue, battle of 175–178, 239
Longstreet, James 59, 65
Lowell, Charles Russell 77
Lucas, W.V. 136–137
Lyon, Nathaniel 18–21, 32, 40–41, 48, 83, 89

Mackey, Thomas J. 119, 227
Magruder, John B. 35, 99, 234
Marais de Cygnes, engagement of 203–204
Marais de Cygnes Massacre 17
Marks Mill 57
Marmaduke, John S. 24, 42–44, *46*, 55–57, 71, 86, 90, 109, 144–146, 174, 182, 243; background 45–52; capture of 209–210, 214; character 52; division in final retreat 212, 219, 234; leader development 47, 50; at Little Blue, battle of 177–178; march to Jefferson City 149; march to Westport 173; at Mine Creek, battle of 205–210; opinion of Price 98–99; in "picnic period" 158; at Pilot Knob 123–138; plan for Westport 184; retreat from Westport 202–204; at Westport 188–198
Martin, Azariah 125, 128
Massachusetts Emigrant Aid Society 13
Mathews, John 89
Mathews, Stanley 60
Maxey, Samuel B. 52
Meade, George G. 75, 78–79
Merrill, Lewis 147
Milks, H. B. 133
Mine Creek, battle of 79, 110, 161, 197, 199–200, *204*, *205*, *206*, 214, 226, 233, 240, 252

Mississippi, Army of the (CS) 34, 48–49, 54
Mississippi, Military Division (U.S.) 66
Mississippi River Squadron (U.S.) 1, 5, 25, 97, 112
Missouri Compromise 11–13
Missouri, Army of (CS) 27, 38, 45, 57–58, 75, 104–105, 108, 110, 116, 121, 145, 148, 150–151, 153, 155–157, 166–167, 169–171, 174, 175, 179, 183–184, 186, 189, 197–199, 210–211, 213, 218, 220, 223, 235, 240; composition 110, 234; event chronology 237–241; final retreat of 222–224; indiscipline 111, 225, 236; morale of 200–204, 216–217, 222, 227; order of battle 242–244; in "picnic period" 157–170, 232; strength of 110, 234
Missouri, Department of (U.S.) 58, 66, 71, 75, 79, 86, 92, 101, 105, 115, 117, 138, 164; strength of 112
Missouri Raid 7, 75, 230; change to objectives 152–153, 156; conclusion and results 223, 226, 234–235; court of inquiry 226–228; objectives 7–9, 101–102, 230; planning 93–103, 230; reasons for failure 104–105, 230–235; statistics 8, 234–235
Missouri State Militia (MSM) 112
Moonlight, Thomas 164, *175*–179, 186, 189, 202–203, 218, 249
Moore, W.H. 133–134
Morgan, John Hunt 2, 38, 40
Mormon War 47
Mulligan, James 22–23, 33, 174
Murphy, David 124, 129–130

Navoo Legion 47
Newtonia, battle of 218–220, 226, 240
North Missouri, district of (U.S.) 143
Northern Virginia, Army of (CS) 6, 77, 234

Ohio, Army of the (U.S.) 49
Ohio, Department of the (U.S.) 61, 75

Onken, Francis 148–149
Order of American Knights (O.A.K.) 101, 113, 162–163, 232, 234

Palmer, Henry E. 174, 176–179
Palo Alto, battle of 76
Pea Ridge, battle of 24, 33–34, 41–42, 80, 84–85, 87, 157
Pegram, John 60–61
Pemberton, John C. 44
Peninsula Campaign 77
Phelps, S. V. 112
Philips, John F. 192–193, 203–205, 207–208, 210–211, 250, 252
Pierce, Abial 208, 252
Pierce, Franklin 13, 16
Pillow, Gideon 236
Pilot Knob, battle of 66, 75, 116, 118–132, *119*, 154, 169, 226–227, 231–232, 238; results 137–139; retreat from 133–137
Pleasonton, Alfred 66, **76**, 152, 157, 173, 176, 215, 217–218, 232, 240, 250, 252; background 75–79; character 75–77; at Independence 182–183; organizes for pursuit 167–168; organizing skill 78; pursuit from Jefferson City 154–155, 159, 163–164, 170, 173; pursuit to Mine Creek 201–203; return to Missouri 211; at Westport 188–198
Pleasonton, Stephen 75
Poison Spring 52, 57, 132
Polk, James K. 29
Pomeroy, Samuel C. 167
Pope, John 24, 62
Porter, David Dixon 97, 116
Potomac, Army of the (U.S.) 64, 75, 77–79, 164, 237
Prairie D' Ane, battle of 52
Prairie Grove, battle of 42–43, 49, 55–56, 70–71
Prentiss, Benjamin 49, 55
Price, Edwin 101, 162–163
Price, Sterling 2, 5, 7–8, 12, 18–22, 24–26, **28**, 38, 41, 45, 52, 56, 62–63, 66, 79, 84, 87, 89, 99, 105, 115–116, 144, 154, 166–167, 173–174, 176, 183, 212, 235, 242; background 27–37; cedes initiative 171; changes objectives 152–153, 156; character 29–30, 32, 37; clings to train 200–201; cooperation with guerrillas 142, 161–162; cooperation with O.A.K. 102, 162–163, 234; decides to move south 172, 184; destroys train 212–213; engagement at Jefferson City 152; event chronology 237–241; final retreat 214, 216–217, 222–225; Great Raid preparations 93–94, 98, 101–103, 106–109, 111, 230–231; leadership in campaign 226–228, 231–234; march on St. Louis 145; march to Jefferson City 145, 148–151; march to Kansas 156, 182; in Mexican War 29; at Mine Creek 206, 209–210; as Missouri governor 29; at Newtonia 218; physical condition 109, 233; in "picnic period" 158–170; at Pilot Knob 118–140; plan for Westport 184; reassesses objectives 141; retreat from Westport 202–203; at Westport 186–198
Proffet, W.W. 123
Provisional Enrolled Missouri Militia (PEMM) 113

Quantrill, William 17, 23, 72–73, 86, 91–92, 142, 166

Radical Republicans 79
Rains, James S. 40–42
Reader, Samuel J. 165–166, 179–181, 187, 201, 212–213, 216
Red River Campaign 1, 6, 24–26, 37, 52, 56, 93, 95, 114, 231, 235, 239
Redlegs 72, 142
Reeder, Andrew 13–14, 16
Reeves, Timothy 139–140
Resaca de la Palma, battle of 76
Reynolds, Thomas C. 35–36, 44–45, 56, 95, 107, 144, 160; Great Raid planning 94, 98, 101–102; opinion of Price 99–100, 153–154, 163, 200, 226–227, 236, 241; after Pilot Knob 142
Rich Mountain 60
Rosecrans, Crandall 58–59
Rosecrans, William S. 36, **59**, 75, 79, 92, 101, 105, 107, 109, 123, 125–126, 135, 139, 156, 171–172, 182, 186, 195, 197, 200, 221–222, 224, 235, 244, 250; background 58–66; character 59–61, 63–66; defense of Jefferson City 147, 150–151; event chronology 238–240; lack of initiative 168–169; orders Pleasonton forward 154–155; preparation of defense 106, 111–113, 116, 138, 145, 232; pursuit of Price 147–148, 163–164, 183; recalls Missouri troops 244, 250; relationship with U.S. Grant 63, 115, 235; relieved of command 214

St. Louis, District of (U.S.) 66, 75
Sanborn, John B. 111, 116, 146–147, 149, 151, 154, 158–159, 163, 172, 189, 192–194, 196, 203, 218–221, 248, 250
Santa Anna, Antonio Lopez 53–54
Santa Cruz de Rosales, battle of 31
Scaggs, William 140
Schofield, John M. 72, 74–75
Scott, William F. 182, 188, 208
Scott, Winfield 47, 81, 83
Seddon, James 36, 98
Selfridge, Thomas O. 97, 112
Shaler, James 227
Shanks, David 108, 150–151
Shannon, Wilson 16
Shaw, John W. 140
Shelby, Joseph O. "Jo" 15, 17, **39**, 49–50, 55, 57, 99, 107, 110, 145, 180, 243; background 37–45; captures Glasgow 169–170; event chronology 237–241; at Fayetteville, Arkansas 222; final retreat 212, 215–217, 221, 225, 227, 235; fixes Steele 108; at Jefferson City 150; leadership 41, 233; at Little Blue 178–179; march to Westport 173–176; at Mine Creek 206, 209–210; morale of his division 201; at Newtonia 218–220; in "picnic period" 158–159, 169–170; at Pilot Knob 122–125, 134–138; plan for Westport 184; retreat from Westport 202; at Westport 185–198
Sheridan, Philip 64, 66, 78, 84–85, 168, 231, 239

Sherman, William T. 2, 5, 23, 25, 67–68, 94, 109, 180, 237, 240–241
Shiloh, battle of 48–49, 55
Shoup, Francis A. 55–56
Sigel, Franz 21, 40–41, 84, 114
Slayback, Alonzo 132, 186–187, 190, 243
Slemmons, William F. 125, 190, 210, 242
Smith, Andrew J. 9, 109, **114**, 116, 123–124, 133–134, 141, 145, 147, 149, 155, 164, 167, 170–171, 173, 183–184, 189, 195, 213, 226, 232, 235, 239–241, 244, 251
Smith, Edmund Kirby 1, 5–7, 24, **25**, 36–37, 44, 52, 93, 96, 100–102, 225–227, 229, 230, 232, 234, 236; event chronology 241; orders to Price 102, 105; quarrel with Taylor 95, 97–98
Smith, Nelson 179
Snead, Thomas 35
Snoddy, James D. 167, 173, 249
Southwest, Army of the (U.S.) 84–85
Southwest Missouri, District of (U.S.) 111, 146
Special Order #1 (S.O. #1) 154
Stallard, D.R. 177, 243
Stanton, Edwin 79, 114–115, 168
Steakley, J.C. 122–123
Steele, Frederick 1, 5–6, 25, 36–37, 45, 52, 56–57, 93, 98, 106–109, 114, 164, 230
Stones River, battle of 63
Stringfellow, Ben Franklin 13
Stuart, J.E.B. 2, 47, 77–78, 99
Sturgis, Samuel D. 21
Sumner, Edwin V. 16
Sutter, John 151
Sykes, George 164

Taylor, John H. 163
Taylor, Richard 1–2, 5–6, 37, 94–99, 104, 229, 237
Taylor, Zachary 53–54, 67, 76, 81, 95
Tennessee, Army of (CS) 5–6, 25, 35, 63–65, 234, 241
Texas, District of (CS) 99
Thayer, Eli 13
Thomas, George 47, 65–66, 213, 235, 240–241
Thompson, M. Jeff 144, 151, 160, 170, 185–186, 219, 239, 243

Thurber, Charles 151
Todd, George 72, 142–144; death of 179, 188
Townsend, Robert 96
Trans-Mississippi Department (CS) 1–2, 6, 8, 25, 34–37, 44, 93–98, 102–103, 105, 138, 171, 198, 225, 227, 229, 236–237
Tullahoma Campaign 64
Tyler, Charles 195–196
Tyler, John 67

Union Army Units:
 III Corps 78
 V Corps 164
 VII Corps 1, 5, 106–107
 XI Corps 78
 XVI Corps 9, 109, 114–115, 123, 167, 171, 181, 183, 195, 226, 232, 235, 239–241, 244, 251
 Colorado:
  1st Colorado Battery 218–219, 249
  2nd Colorado Cavalry 177, 179, 194, 218, 249
  McClain's Independent Colorado Battery 177–179, 190, 249
 Illinois:
  17th Illinois Cavalry 137, 143, 196, 247–248, 250
  21st Illinois Infantry 120
  33rd Illinois Infantry 120
  54th Illinois Infantry 108
 Iowa:
  1st Iowa Cavalry 143, 250, 252
  2nd Iowa Infantry 83
  3rd Iowa Cavalry 209, 251, 252
  4th Iowa Cavalry 182, 188, 193, 208, 251, 252
  14th Iowa Infantry 121, 124, 126, 128, 132–133, 135–136
 Kansas:
  1st Kansas Infantry (Colored) 52
  2nd Kansas Cavalry 71
  2nd Kansas Infantry 88
  2nd Kansas State Militia (KSM) 165, 79, 181–182, 187, 201, 249
  3rd Kansas Infantry 88–89
  6th Kansas Cavalry 182, 244
  6th Kansas State Militia (KSM) 167, 249

  10th Kansas Infantry 71, 135
  11th Kansas Cavalry 174–176, 178, 249
  11th Kansas Infantry 70–71
  14th Kansas Cavalry 218
  15th Kansas Cavalry 167, 190, 213, 218, 249
  16th Kansas Cavalry 144, 177, 194, 249
 Missouri:
  1st Missouri State Militia (MSM) Infantry 121, 244, 247
  2nd Missouri Cavalry 147
  2nd Missouri Light Artillery 121, 149, 151, 193, 196, 247–248; Batteries—B 151; C 151; H 121, 124, 133, 251–252; L 151, 196, 251
  2nd Missouri State Militia (MSM) Cavalry 121, 244, 247–248
  3rd Missouri State Militia (MSM) Cavalry 116, 121, 125, 128, 132–133, 139–140, 143, 231, 238, 244, 247–248, 250
  4th Missouri Infantry 146
  4th Missouri State Militia (MSM) Cavalry 150, 247, 252
  6th Missouri State Militia (MSM) Cavalry 151
  7th Missouri State Militia (MSM) Cavalry 150, 192–193, 247, 250, 252
  8th Missouri State Militia (MSM) Cavalry 151, 251
  9th Missouri State Militia (MSM) Cavalry 238, 250
  10th Missouri Cavalry 188, 207–208, 251–252
  34th Enrolled Missouri Militia (EMM) 148, 247
  39th Missouri Mounted Infantry 144, 238, 247
  43rd Missouri Infantry 169, 239
  47th Missouri Infantry 121, 124–125, 132–133, 135, 244, 251
  50th Missouri Infantry 121, 244
 Nebraska:
  1st Nebraska Infantry 120

Van Dorn, Earl 24, 33–36, 59, 62–63, 84–85
Vaughan, David 187
Veale, George 187, 213, 249

Wakarusa War 14
Walker, Lucien M. 51–52
Walker, Robert J. 16
Washburn, C.C. 112, 114
Watie, Stand 91, 108
Watson, J.S. 96
West, Army of the (CS) 33–35, 42
West Tennessee, Army of (U.S.) 62
West Tennessee, District of (U.S.) 112
Westport, battle of 43, 79, 161, 170–171, 184–198, *185*, *191*, *197*, 226, 233, 239–240; order of battle 248–250; results 198
Williams, H.H. 135
Wilson, James 116, 122–127, 244; captured 128; murder of 139–140, 231
Wilson's Creek, battle of 21, 32, 41, 89
Winslow, Edward 181–182, 188–189, 192–193, 203, 251
Wise, Henry 61
Wool, John E. 53, 81

Yell, Archibald 53–54
Young, Brigham 47
Young, C.M. 209
Youngblood, A.M. 123
Younger, Cole 23